OXFORD CONSTITUTIONAL

Series Editors:
Martin Loughlin, John P. McCormick, ana ivcii vvaiic..

The Twilight of Constitutionalism?

OXFORD CONSTITUTIONAL THEORY

Series Editors:

Martin Loughlin, John P. McCormick, and Neil Walker

One consequence of the increase in interest in constitutions and constitutional law in recent years is a growing innovative literature in constitutional theory. The aim of *Oxford Constitutional Theory* is to provide a showcase for the best of these theoretical reflections and a forum for further innovation in the field.

The new series will seek to establish itself as the primary point of reference for scholarly work in the subject by commissioning different types of study. The majority of the works published in the series will be monographs that advance new understandings of the subject. Well-conceived edited collections that bring a variety of perspectives and disciplinary approaches to bear on specific themes in constitutional thought will also be included. Further, in recognition of the fact that there is a great deal of pioneering literature originally written in languages other than English and with regard to non-anglophone constitutional traditions, the series will also seek to publish English language translations of leading monographs in constitutional theory.

Also available in this series:

The Constitutional State *by Nick Barber*
Sovereignty's Promise: The State as Fiduciary *by Evan Fox-Decent*
Beyond Constitutionalism: The Pluralist Structure of Postnational Law *by Nico Krisch*

Soon to come in this series:

Constitutional Referendums: A Theory of Republican Deliberation
by Stephen Tierney
Constitutional Fragments: Societal Constitutionalism and Globalization
by Gunther Teubner

The Twilight
of Constitutionalism?

Edited by

Petra Dobner
and Martin Loughlin

OXFORD
UNIVERSITY PRESS

OXFORD
UNIVERSITY PRESS

Great Clarendon Street, Oxford OX2 6DP

Oxford University Press is a department of the University of Oxford.
It furthers the University's objective of excellence in research, scholarship,
and education by publishing worldwide in

Oxford New York

Auckland Cape Town Dar es Salaam Hong Kong Karachi
Kuala Lumpur Madrid Melbourne Mexico City Nairobi
New Delhi Shanghai Taipei Toronto

With offices in

Argentina Austria Brazil Chile Czech Republic France Greece
Guatemala Hungary Italy Japan Poland Portugal Singapore
South Korea Switzerland Thailand Turkey Ukraine Vietnam

Oxford is a registered trade mark of Oxford University Press
in the UK and in certain other countries

Published in the United States
by Oxford University Press Inc., New York

British Library Cataloguing-in-Publication Data
Data available

Library of Congress Cataloging in Publication Data
Data available

Typeset by MPS Limited, A Macmillan Company
Printed in Great Britain on acid-free paper by
CPI Group (UK) Ltd., Croydon, CR0 4YY

ISBN 978–0–19–958500–7
ISBN 978–0–19–965199–3 (pbk.)

1 3 5 7 9 10 8 6 4 2

Contents

Acknowledgements

The origins of this book lie in a proposal by Dieter Grimm to convene a focus group at the *Wissenschaftskolleg zu Berlin* (the Berlin Institute of Advanced Study) for the academic year 2007–8 on the subject of constitutions beyond the nation state. The group consisted of Petra Dobner (Halle), Dieter Grimm (Berlin), Bogdan Iancu (Bucharest), Martin Loughlin (London), Fritz Scharpf (Cologne), Alexander Somek (Iowa), Gunther Teubner (Frankfurt), and Rainer Wahl (Freiburg). The group met weekly throughout the year to discuss this wide-ranging topic and in June 2008, towards the end of the session, convened a workshop to which leading scholars on various aspects of this theme were invited. The book is the product of those focus group discussions at the *Wissenschaftskolleg* and the workshop presentations.

For support in this venture, we must first thank Dieter Grimm for proposing the study and the Board of the *Wissenschaftskolleg* for accepting his request. We are also most grateful to Luca Guiliani, the Rector, and his dedicated staff at the *Wissenschaftskolleg* who provided a remarkably congenial environment in which the group were able to pursue their individual and collective projects. For financial support for the end-of-session workshop, we wish to express our gratitude to the *Otto und Martha Fischbeck-Stiftung*. Finally, our thanks go to Christoph Möllers (Göttingen) and Christian Walter (Münster), who participated in the workshop proceedings but were unable to contribute to this resulting work.

Petra Dobner (*Berlin*)
Martin Loughlin (*London*)
JULY 2009

Contributors

Tanja A. Börzel	Professor of Political Science, Freie Universität Berlin, Germany
Hauke Brunkhorst	Professor of Sociology, University of Flensburg, Germany
Petra Dobner	Associate Professor of Political Science, Martin-Luther-University of Halle-Wittenberg, Germany
Dieter Grimm	Professor of Public Law, Humboldt University, Berlin; Permanent Fellow, *Wissenschaftskolleg zu Berlin*; former Justice, Federal Constitutional Court of Germany
Nico Krisch	Professor of International Law, Hertie School of Governance, Berlin, Germany
Mattias Kumm	Professor of Law, New York University, USA
Marcus Llanque	Professor of Political Theory, University of Augsburg, Germany
Martin Loughlin	Professor of Public Law, London School of Economics and Political Science, UK
Riccardo Prandini	Associate Professor in Sociology of Cultural and Communicative Processes, University of Bologna, Italy
Ulrich K. Preuss	Professor of Law and Politics, Hertie School of Governance, Berlin, Germany
Sonja Puntscher Riekmann	Professor of Political Science, University of Salzburg, Austria
Fritz W. Scharpf	Director emeritus, Max Planck Institute for the Study of Societies, Cologne, Germany
Alexander Somek	Charles E. Floete Chair in Law, University of Iowa, USA
Gunther Teubner	Professor of Private Law and Legal Sociology, J. W. Goethe University of Frankfurt, Germany

Rainer Wahl   Professor of Public Law, University of Freiburg,
                          Germany

Neil Walker   Regius Professor of Public Law, University of
                          Edinburgh, UK

Introduction

Petra Dobner and Martin Loughlin

The twilight of constitutionalism? Surely not. Constitutionalism is a modern phenomenon, a feature of political life over the last 250 or so years, but one which in recent decades has been enjoying a greater influence in public discourse than ever before. Under its influence, modern constitutions have established a set of governmental institutions that provide the necessary conditions for the realisation of a democratic *Rechtsstaat*. Such constitutions constrain politics by legal means, structure power relations comprehensively, help normatively to integrate societies, and offer a practical account of legitimate democratic rule within the state. While these achievements cannot be denied, the fact is that this period of maturation of constitutionalism coincides with the erosion of some of the basic conditions on which those achievements have rested. Foremost amongst these conditions are those of statehood and a concept of democracy generated from the claim that 'we the people' are the authorising agents of the constitutional scheme. Constitutionalism is increasingly being challenged by political realities that effect multiple transgressions of the notion of democratic statehood. It is in this sense that constitutionalism can be understood to be entering a twilight zone.

The combination of these diverging trends of triumph and demise offers one powerful reason why interest in theorising about constitutions has recently gained a new momentum. However ambiguous the term 'globalisation' may be, among the few certainties is an acknowledgement of a growing incongruity between the political (ie the world of things that need to be ordered collectively in order to sustain society) and the state (ie the major institution for political decision making during modern times). And it is this incongruity that presents a serious challenge to the practices of constitutionalism. The far-reaching consequences and possible remedies of this double disjunction of politics and state and of state and constitution form the centre of an ongoing debate about 'constitutionalism beyond the state'. Whether the processes of constitutionalisation at the transnational level are to be seen as compensating for losses at the national level or as an enhancement by adding a new layer of constitutional ordering, these contemporary developments offer strong incentives for revisiting the achievements of constitutionalism, analysing its current modes of transmutation, and debating its future prospects. These are the issues that the chapters in this collection address.

The book investigates these issues in six parts. The first part deals with perhaps the most critical question concerning the character of modern constitutionalism, that of the mutual dependency (or possible independency) of statehood and constitutionalism. Dieter Grimm provides an overview of the achievements of constitutionalism, and outlines its central elements of democracy, limited government, and the principle of the rule of law. He argues that the achievements of constitutionalism are tied to an acknowledgement of its constitutive conditions— the boundary distinctions between public and private, and between internal and external. For this reason, Grimm contends that, to the extent that statehood is being eroded as a result of the blurring of these boundaries, then constitutionalism must be seen to be in decline. Internationalisation is opening up a gap between the exercise of public power and its modes of legitimation which constitutionalism is unable to close. Constitutionalism, in short, cannot be reconstructed on the international level.

Ulrich K. Preuss reworks Grimm's account of the achievement of constitutionalism and, in contrast to Grimm's analysis, argues that the essence of constitutionalism is misunderstood if it is too directly linked to the concept of statehood. In Preuss's view, the principle of territoriality—which is, he claims, the essence of statehood—was made effective by the absolutist state and that the key feature of constitutionalism has been to overcome the logic of the absolutist state. This has been done by linking sovereignty not so much to territory as to a people. Exploring this latter relation, Preuss argues that constitutionalism maintains the potential to overcome its historic links with statehood and to provide a means of normative integration of institutional arrangements at the transnational level. Martin Loughlin's response to the possibilities of transnational constitutionalisation is more sceptical. For Loughlin, the emergence of the novel concept of constitutionalisation is associated with certain social and economic processes that presently are affecting government at both the national and international levels. Constitutionalisation is the product of a reconfiguration of the values of constitutionalism; it promotes a merely legalistic understanding of constitutionalism and deflects from a broader notion of political constitutionalism, ie a form of constitutional thinking directed not only at the legal order but at political organisation in general.

To the extent that recent trends have led to a search for functional equivalents to the state at the transnational level, then this has been most clearly visible in the development of the European Union (EU). The ongoing process of European integration has fuelled a number of attempts to conceptualise this specific multi-level system of constitutions on the regional, the federal, and the European levels. Among the many questions which are raised, the mutual relationship between political and legal autonomy of the member states, their political and legal cooperation on the European level, and the independence of some genuinely European institutions may be highlighted. The constitutional question has arisen in part because of efforts to understand the *sui generis* character of the EU itself. But it also arises because power-sharing arrangements within the EU have touched on crucial aspects of democratic governance and raised questions about the legitimacy of EU actors. These developments provide the focus for the chapters in Part II.

Tanja A. Börzel offers an account of the nature of the structure of governance of the EU. In contrast to understandings of the EU as a prototype of 'network governance' or as 'governance without government', she argues that empirically the EU is best characterised as a form of 'governance *with* the state'. Börzel argues that the governing arrangements of the EU most closely resemble the German model of cooperative federalism; the EU has developed a supranational constitutional system, but this constitution, far from being autonomous, is interlocked with national constitutions. Fritz W. Scharpf advances this discussion by developing a theoretical framework which distinguishes between the sources for legitimation in European politics, which he argues lie entirely within the state, and the exercise of public authority, which by contrast is often located on the European level. Scharpf's model of a two-level polity parallels Börzel's. But Scharpf takes the constitutional analysis further by suggesting that this model imposes specific limits to the legitimacy of EU institutional action.

In the final chapter of this part of the book, Sonja Puntscher Riekmann argues that a core concept of modern constitutionalism is that of representation. In the European tradition, this concept is expressed mainly through the existence of parliaments as institutions that, acting as representative forums of the people, provide a vital source of constitutional legitimacy. Maintaining that the EU contains important federative elements, Puntscher Riekmann contends that constitutionalisation of the EU is a necessary process but that serious problems of representation exist. In the context of the failed Constitutional Treaty, she thus explores the potential role of parliaments to provide the means of enhancing representation within EU governing arrangements.

Whereas Part I focuses on the erosion of statehood, Part III addresses the other main plank of modern constitutionalism: the question of democracy. From different perspectives, the essays in this part converge on one central question: in what ways, if at all, can transnational constitutionalism be reconciled with the claims of democratic legitimacy? Petra Dobner examines the growing tension between the normative desirability of democratised law and the practical dissolution of the relation between law and democracy at the transnational level. She argues that the transformation of statehood leads simultaneously to forms of deconstitutionalisation and losses of democratic control. The emergence of global law, she contends, has yet to account for these losses, and present trends generally compound the challenge of finding democratic ways of living. Marcus Llanque takes a different tack. Examining the genealogy of citizenship, he seeks to broaden the meaning of the concept to render it more useful to contemporary circumstances. Distinguishing citizenship from such concepts as 'the people' and 'nationality', he adopts a notion of citizenship founded on the idea of constitutional membership. Starting from experience on the national level, Llanque rests his case with a plea for further explorations of the meaning of constitutional membership with respect to a future polity which is able to balance national, transnational, supranational, and cosmopolitan claims of allegiance and loyalty.

Hauke Brunkhorst closes this part of the book with a broad-ranging account of the impact of the emergence of 'world society' on the ideals of constitutional democracy. Brunkhorst bases his argument on the premiss that constitutionalism has always maintained the Janus-face of inclusion and exclusion, emancipation and oppression. Although Western constitutionalism has acquired its inclusive qualities at the price of its cosmopolitan claims, he suggests that it has nevertheless been able to provide a legal means of coordinating conflicting powers within nation-state systems. Brunkhorst argues finally that the democratic possibilities which are inherent in the emergence of a world society can be realised only by promoting an agenda of radical reform which, in conceptual terms, requires us to overcome the limitations of dualistic and representational thinking (an argument that would appear to run counter to those of Grimm and Puntscher Riekmann).

The remaining parts address three of the main approaches to transnational law that arise from a constitutional perspective. Part IV explores the changing relationship between national constitutional law and public international law, with the two chapters in this part offering alternative explanations of the prospects of extending constitutionalism beyond the borders of the nation state. Mattias Kumm suggests that progress can be made with understanding the emerging relationship between national constitutional law and public international law only if we move beyond the crude division between the triumphalists, who see the present era as marking a radical extension of constitutionalism's claims in the international arena, and the nostalgists, who believe constitutionalism can only be realised in a world of sovereign nation states. Critiquing the position of 'constitutional nostalgia', a stance that underpins many advocating what he calls 'democratic statism', Kumm proposes in its place 'the practice conception of constitutionalism'. The practice conception is, he argues, a conceptual arrangement that is better fitted to adequately address the constitutional challenges that emergent transnationalism presents. In his contribution to this part, Rainer Wahl, by contrast, vigorously defends the conceptual use of 'constitution' as a state-centred concept. Wahl presents the case that the extension of the usage of the concept, whether as a form of 'higher law' in the international arena or as a species of 'societal law', amounts to a political emptying of the concept. Those who use the language of constitutionalism in such circumstances, he claims, are seeking to exploit the 'noble aura' of the term without being able to realise its necessary prerequisites.

Part V marks a slight detour. It considers the attempt to evade many of these conceptual intricacies by the suggestion that the evident tendencies towards global governance do not of themselves raise issues of constitutional quality. This part focuses on the concept of Global Administrative Law (GAL), and highlights the perception that the evolution of global law mostly engages issues of administrative rather than constitutional law. Nico Krisch weighs the pros and cons of applying the insights of constitutionalism to issues of global law. He argues that the modest scale and narrower reach implied when one talks about the globalisation of administrative law offers a more suitable model both for scholarship and political reform than constitutionalist approaches with their holistic vision. Alexander Somek does not challenge Krisch's observation that recent trends are better understood from an administrative rather than a constitutional perspective. But Somek draws out some of the issues raised by the ostensibly modest ambition of the GAL project. He is, in particular, critical of the claim that the project amounts only to a redescription of modern international law under the dominating influence of administrative rationality. Rather, he claims, it marks the triumph of administrative rationality over the legal form itself. The world that GAL describes, Somek concludes, is not that of the demise of the state under globalising pressures; it marks instead the triumph of the state (the state as administration) over both politics and law.

Finally, Part VI offers three accounts of the way in which the fragmentation of law and constitution under globalising pressures can be addressed only by analysing the emergence of norm production from the societal periphery. This is the driving theme of the concept of societal constitutionalism. Neil Walker returns to the themes of Part I, dealing with the constitutional consequences of the erosion of statehood. He does so by considering whether—and, if so, on what terms—constitutionalism can remain a viable concept in the old state setting. And he asks whether—and, if so, on what terms—constitutionalism could possibly be adapted to new settings. His reconciling conclusion is that the use of the term constitutionalism should be retained, and it should be used to serve as a placeholder for exactly those concerns with respect to which others reject the use of the constitutional language when speaking about the transnationalisation of law. Constitutionalism, Walker argues, serves a crucial longstop function of providing a medium for dealing with the abiding concerns we still have, and ought to have, about our ideas of the common interest.

Riccardo Prandini frames the question of societal constitutionalism in rather different terms. In Prandini's account, the evolution of constitutionalism is to be seen in the mode of morphogenesis, that is, as a socio-cultural cycle in which a given institutional and cultural structure through cultural and structural interactions activated by societal actors gives rise to new forms. Prandini's approach displaces the centrality of the political in discussions of constitutions and offers an analysis of constitutionalisation as a specific movement generated by the proliferation of legal orders operating, both privately and publicly, at subnational, national and transnational levels. Finally, Gunther Teubner, beginning from the empirical observation that transnational private actors intensively regulate entire areas of life through their own private governance regimes, seeks to reposition the main constitutional question we face today. According to Teubner, the critical questions are raised by asking how legal theory should react to these major trends of privatisation and globalisation: how can nation-state constitutionalism be redesigned in a way that might enable constitutionalism's achievements to cope with these developments? Overcoming state-centrism and accepting the polycentric form of globalisation, he argues, are two sides of the same coin, and they result in the need to accept that the world of nation-state constitutionalism finds a functional equivalent in the emerging production of a global societal law.

It cannot be denied that the production of law, which used to be reserved to governmental institutions, has increasingly been complemented by forms of private regulation. And while the legitimacy of this production may well be questioned, its existence does call for theoretical conceptualisation and also integration into

xvi   ⌒   *Introduction*

the framework of constitutional thinking. The developments that the chapters in this book examine pose some basic questions about the foundations of modern constitutionalism, have provoked calls for a revision of that heritage, and evoked a lively debate about the future of constitutionalism. Constitutionalism is changing—that is beyond question. But the direction of change remains an open issue.

PART I

CONSTITUTIONALISM AND THE EROSION OF STATEHOOD

The Achievement of Constitutionalism and its Prospects in a Changed World

Dieter Grimm

I. EXTERNAL CULMINATION—INTERNAL EROSION

Constitutionalism is a relatively recent innovation in the history of political institutions. It emerged in the last quarter of the eighteenth century from two successful revolutions against the hereditary rulers, first in the British colonies of North America, then in France. Immediately understood as an important achievement, it appealed to many people outside the countries of origin, and attempts to introduce modern constitutions started all over Europe and soon also in other parts of the world. The nineteenth century was a period of struggle for constitutionalism in a lot of countries. But after many detours and setbacks constitutionalism had finally gained universal recognition by the end of the twentieth century. Today, only a handful of the nearly 200 states in the world is still without a constitution.

This is not to say that these constitutions are everywhere taken seriously, or that constitutional norms always prevail in cases of conflict with political intentions. But the universal recognition of constitutionalism as a model for the organisation and legitimation of political power is shown by the fact that even rulers who are not inclined to submit themselves to legal norms feel compelled at least to pretend to be exercising their power within the constitutional framework. Further, the general willingness of rulers to govern in accordance with the provisions of the constitution has recently increased considerably, as is indicated by the great number of constitutional courts or courts with constitutional jurisdiction that were established during the last quarter of the twentieth century. After 225 years, constitutionalism seems now to have reached the peak of its development.

This external success of constitutionalism, however, should not mislead the observer. It is accompanied by an internal erosion that started almost unnoticed in the wake of a transformation of statehood, domestically as well as internationally, and eventually cost the state the monopoly of public power over its territory.[1] Today,

---

[1] For the domestic causes and effects, which are not the central concern of this chapter, see D. Grimm, *Die Zukunft der Verfassung* (Frankfurt: Suhrkamp, 1991; 3rd edn, 2002), 399; D. Grimm, 'Ursprung und Wandel der Verfassung', in J. Isensee and P. Kirchhof (eds), *Handbuch des Staatsrechts* (Heidelberg: C. F. Müller, 3rd edn, 2003), i. 22 et seq.

the state shares its power with a number of non-state actors, most of them international organisations to whom sovereign rights have been transferred and whose exercise escapes the arrangements of national constitutions. This differs from the fact that constitutional norms may be violated or have little impact on political action; such a gap between norm and fact has always existed, but does not of itself undermine the potential of constitutionalism. The internal erosion, by contrast, endangers the capacity of the constitution to fulfil its claim of establishing and regulating all public power that has an impact on the territory where the constitution is in force. This is why the erosion not only affects this or that constitution, but the achievement of constitutionalism altogether.

One response to this development has been the attempt to elevate constitutionalism to the international level. The recent boom of the term 'constitutionalisation' is an indicator of this tendency. Different from traditional constitution-making, it describes not an act by which a constitution takes legal force, but a process which eventually ends up in a constitution. Such processes can already be seen underway in Europe, where the European Convention on Human Rights (ECHR) and the primary law of the European Union are analysed in terms of constitutional law, but also globally. For many authors, public international law is acquiring constitutional status. The Charter of the United Nations as well as the statutes of other international organisations such as the World Trade Organization are interpreted as constitutions. Even global public policy networks and self-organisation processes of private global actors are discussed in terms of constitutionalism—all objects not regarded as constitutions just a few years ago.[2]

---

[2] The literature is increasing rapidly. See in general R. St J. Macdonald and D. M. Johnston (eds), *Towards World Constitutionalism* (Leiden: Brill, 2005); A. Peters, 'Compensatory Constitutionalism: The Function and Potential of Fundamental International Norms and Structures' (2006) 19 *Leiden Journal of International Law* 579; E. de Wet, 'The International Legal Order' (2006) 55 *International & Comparative Law Quarterly* 51; R. Uerpmann, 'Internationales Verfassungsrecht' (2001) *Juristenzeitung* 565; M. Knauff, 'Konstitutionalisierung im inner- und überstaatlichen Recht' (2008) 68 *Zeitschrift für ausländisches öffentliches Recht und Völkerrecht* 453; M. Rosenfeld and H. R. Fabri, 'Rethinking Constitutionalism in an Era of Globalization and Privatization' (2008) 6/3–4 *International Journal of Constitutional Law* 371; C. Walter, 'Constitutionalizing International Governance' (2001) 44 *German Yearbook of International Law* 170; R. Kreide and A. Niederberger (eds), *Transnationale Verrechtlichung* (Frankfurt: Campus, 2008). For public international law, see: J. A. Frowein, 'Konstitutionalisierung des Völkerrechts' (1999) 39 *Berichte der Deutschen Gesellschaft für Völkerrecht* 427. For the UN, see B. Fassbender, 'The United Nations Charter as Constitution of the International Community' (1998) 36 *Columbia Journal of Transnational Law* 529. For the WTO, see D. Cass, *The Constitutionalization of the World Trade Organization* (Oxford: Oxford University Press, 2005); J. P. Trachtman, 'The Constitution of the WTO' (2006) 17 *European Journal of International Law* 623. For the European Convention on Human Rights, see C. Walter, 'Die EMRK als Konstitutionalisierungsprozess' (1999) 59 *Zeitschrift für ausländisches öffentliches Recht und Völkerrecht* 961. For the EU, the literature is immense: see, eg J. Weiler, *The Constitution of Europe* (Cambridge: Cambridge University Press, 1999); I. Pernice, 'Multilevel Constitutionalism and the Treaty of Amsterdam' (1999) 36 *Common Market Law Review* 703; A. Peters, *Elemente einer Theorie der Verfassung Europas* (Berlin: Duncker & Humblot, 2001).

In order to realise the extent to which the development affects the constitution on the national level one needs a clear notion of what constitutionalism entails. This is not always present in discussions over the process of constitutionalisation and the future of constitutionalism. Many authors tend to identify constitutionalism as involving a submission of politics to law. This is not wrong, but it is not the whole story. Legalisation of politics is nothing new; it existed long before the constitution emerged. A clear notion of constitutionalism can therefore be best obtained if one tries to determine what was new about the constitution when it emerged from the two revolutions, and which conditions had to be present before it was able to emerge.[3] This, in turn, will allow a comparison of constitutionalism in the traditional sense with new developments on the international level and permit an assessment to be made of the possibility of its reconstruction at the global level.

II. THE ACHIEVEMENT AND ITS PRECONDITIONS

The emergence of the modern constitution from revolution is not accidental. The American and the French Revolutions differed from the many upheavals and revolts in history in that they did not content themselves with replacing one ruler by another. They aimed at establishing a new political *system* that differed fundamentally from the one they had accused of being unjust and oppressive. In order to achieve this, they devised a plan of legitimate rule, with persons being called to govern on the basis of and in accordance with these pre-established conditions. The historic novelty of this step is often obscured by the fact that the legalisation of politics did not start with the first constitutions. Neither was the term 'constitution' new. It had been in use long before constitutionalism emerged. But the earlier legal bonds of politics were of a different kind and the term 'constitution' had a different meaning before and after the revolutionary break.[4]

In its traditional meaning, the term referred to the state of a country as determined by various factors, such as the geographical conditions, the nature of its population, and the division of power. Also among these factors were the fundamental

---

For societal constitutionalism, see: G. Teubner, 'Globale Zivilverfassungen: Alternativen zur staatszentrierten Verfassungstheorie' (2003) 63 *Zeitschrift für ausländisches öffentliches Recht und Völkerrecht* 1; A. Fischer-Lescano and G. Teubner, *Regimekollisionen* (Frankfurt: Suhrkamp, 2006); H. Schepel, *The Constitution of Private Governance* (Oxford: Hart, 2005). For some critical voices, see R. Wahl, 'Konstitutionalisierung: Leitbegriff oder Allerweltsbegriff?' in C.-E. Eberle (ed), *Der Wandel des Staates vor den Herausforderung der Gegenwart: Festschrift für W. Brohm* (Munich: Beck, 2002), 191; U. Haltern, 'Internationales Verfassungsrecht?' (2003) 128 *Archiv des öffentlichen Rechts* 511; P. Dobner, *Konstitutionalismus als Politikform* (Baden-Baden: Nomos, 2002); D. Grimm, 'The Constitution in the Process of Denationalization' (2005) 12 *Constellations* 447.

[3] See D. Grimm, *Zukunft der Verfassung*, above n 1, 31; D. Grimm, *Deutsche Verfassungsgeschichte* (Frankfurt: Suhrkamp, 3rd edn, 1995), 10 et seq.

[4] See H. Mohnhaupt and D. Grimm, *Verfassung* (Berlin: Duncker & Humblot, 2nd edn, 2002); C. H. McIlwain, *Constitutionalism, Ancient and Modern* (Ithaca, NY: Cornell University Press, 1940).

legal rules that determined the social and political structure of a country. Later in the eighteenth century the notion was used in a narrower sense, referring to the country's state as formed by the fundamental rules. But still the term 'constitution' did not designate these rules. It was an empirical rather than a normative notion. Understood in a descriptive sense, every country had—or more precisely was in—a constitution. If used in a normative sense, constitution designated some specific laws, such as laws enacted by the Emperor in the Holy Roman Empire (*Constitutio Criminalis Carolina*). On the other hand, there existed laws regulating the exercise of public power, though these were not called 'constitutions', but forms of government, *leges fundamentales*, etc.

In the medieval era, these fundamental laws were regarded as of divine origin. They were by definition higher law and the political powers could not dispose of them. The function of politics consisted in enforcing God's will. Legislation, if it occurred, was not understood as law creation, but as concretisation of eternal law, adapting it to exigencies of time and space. This understanding lost its ground with the Reformation of the early sixteenth century. The devastating civil wars that followed the schism made the restoration of social peace the ruler's primary function. This required a concentration of all powers and prerogatives, which in the medieval order had been dispersed among many independent bearers who exercised them not as a separate function but as an adjunct of a certain status, eg that of a landowner. In addition, this power did not extend to a territory; it referred to persons so that various authorities coexisted on the same territory, each of them exercising different prerogatives.

Restoration of internal peace seemed possible only if all holders of prerogatives were deprived of their power in favour of one single ruler, historically the prince, who combined them in his person and condensed them to the public power in the singular. This power was no longer limited to law enforcement. It included the right to create a legal order that was independent of the competing faiths and secular in nature. Eternal law thereby lost its legal validity and retreated to a moral obligation. In order to enforce the law against resisting groups in society the prince claimed the monopoly of legitimate use of force, which entailed on the other side a privatisation of civil society. A new notion for this completely new type of political rule soon came into use: the *state*, whose most important attribute was sovereignty, understood since Bodin's seminal work as the ruler's right to dictate law for everybody without being bound by law himself.[5] The state originated as an absolute state.

Absolutism nevertheless remained an aspiration of the rulers that was nowhere completely fulfilled before the French Revolution ended this period. Sovereignty, although defined as highest and indivisible authority over all subjects, was but relative in practice. Old bonds dating from the medieval period survived, new ones were established. But they did not form an integral whole. Most of these laws had a contractual basis. They took the form of agreements between the ruler and the privileged estates of a territory on whose support the ruler depended. They were

---

[5] Jean Bodin, *Les six livres de la République* (Paris: Du Puys, 1576).

regarded as mutually binding and could sometimes even be enforced by courts. Yet none of these legal norms questioned the ruler's right to rule. Based on transcendental or hereditary legitimation this right preceded the legal bonds. They merely limited the right in this or that respect, not comprehensively, and in favour of the parties to the agreement, not universally.

The existence of such legal bonds, first eternal and then secular, indicates that it would not be sufficient to characterise constitutionalism as a submission of politics to law. Different from the older legal bonds of political power, the new constitutions did not modify a pre-existing right to rule: they preceded the ruler's right to rule. They created this right, determined the procedure in which individuals were called into office, and laid down the conditions under which they were entitled to exercise the power given to them. In contrast to the older legal bonds, the constitution regulated public power coherently and comprehensively. This is not to say that political power was again reduced to law enforcement, as with the medieval order. It means, rather, that constitutionalism neither recognised any extra-constitutional bearer of public power, nor any extra-constitutional ways and means to exercise this power vis-à-vis citizens. Finally, the legal regulation of public power not only favoured certain privileged groups in society who possessed sufficient bargaining power, but society as a whole.

These differences had some consequences that further characterise the constitution. As an act that constituted legitimate public power in the first place, the constitution could not emanate from the ruler himself. It presupposed a different source. This source was found in the people that had decided to form a polity. The legitimating principle of the modern constitution was popular rather than monarchical sovereignty. This was by no means an original idea of the American and the French revolutionaries. It had older roots and gained widespread recognition when religion no longer served as the basis of the social order after the Reformation. In the absence of a divine legitimation the philosophers of the time turned to reason as a common endowment of mankind, independent of religious creeds. In order to find out how political rule could be legitimised, they placed themselves in a fictitious state of nature where everybody was by definition equally free. The question, then, was why and under which conditions reasonable people would be willing to leave the state of nature and submit themselves to a government.

The reason for this was the fundamental insecurity of life and limb in the state of nature. Leaving the state of nature became a dictate of reason. Given the equal freedom of all individuals, the step from the state of nature to government called for a general agreement. Legitimacy could be acquired only by a government based on the consent of the governed. It was also up to the governed to determine the conditions under which political power could be exercised. These conditions varied over time. For those philosophers who elaborated their theory against the backcloth of the religious wars of the sixteenth and seventeenth centuries, ending civil war and enabling peaceful coexistence of believers in different faiths enjoyed absolute priority. For them, this goal could be achieved only if individuals handed over all their natural rights to the ruler in exchange of the overarching good of security. Here, the theory of the social contract justified absolutism.

The better the absolute ruler fulfilled his historical function of pacifying society, the less plausible seemed the claim that peaceful coexistence in one society required a total relinquishment of all natural rights. The ruler's task was now seen to be the protection of individual freedom, which required no more from the individuals than handing over the right to self-justice. From the mid-eighteenth century, the treatises of natural law contained growing catalogues of fundamental rights that the state was obliged to respect and protect. This coincided with the economic theory that freedom of contract and property would be a better way of achieving justice and welfare in society than feudalism and state regulation of the economy. The idea that individual freedom remained endangered vis-à-vis a concentrated governmental power also gained ground. To guarantee that the state respected individual rights, some separation of powers and certain checks and balances were regarded as indispensable.

Although these theories contained all the ingredients that later appeared in the constitutions, they were not pushed forward to the postulate of a constitution by the philosophers. For them, they functioned as a test of the legitimacy of a political system: a political system was deemed legitimate if it could be considered *as if* established by a consensus of the governed. Like the state of nature, the social contract was fictitious. With the sole exception of Emer de Vattel,[6] neither a document nor a popular decision was required. The social contract served as a regulative idea. It was not considered to be the result of a real process of consensus building. Its authority was based on argumentation, not on enactment. No ruler before the revolution had been willing to adopt it, and most rulers had explicitly rejected it. Natural law and positive law contradicted each other.

Only after the revolutionary break with traditional rule were these ideas able to become a blueprint for the establishment of the new order needed to fill the vacuum of legitimate public power. By their very nature they worked in favour of a constitution. Popular sovereignty was the legitimating principle of the new order. But unlike the sovereign monarch, the people were incapable of ruling themselves. They needed representatives who governed in their name. Democratic government is government by mandate and as such stands in need of being organised. In addition, the mandate was not conferred upon the representatives unconditionally. In contrast to the unlimited power of the British Parliament and the French monarch, the revolutionaries wanted to establish a limited government. The limits in scope and time as well as the division of power among various branches of government also required a determination in the form of rules.

Hence, the contribution of the American and French revolutionaries was to turn the idea from philosophy into law. Only law had the capacity to dissolve the consensus as to the purpose and form of government from the historical moment and transfer it into a binding rule for the future, so that it no longer rested on the power of persuasion but on the power of a commitment. There was, however, the problem that, after the collapse of the divinely inspired medieval legal order, all law had

[6] E. de Vattel, *Le Droit des gens ou principe de la loi naturelle* (Leiden, 1758), i. 3 § 27.

become the product of political decision. Law was irreducibly positive law. Nothing else could be true for the law whose function it was to regulate the establishment and exercise of political power. The question that emerged from this positivisation of law was how a law that emanated from the political process could at the same time bind this process.

This problem was solved by taking up the old idea of a hierarchy of norms (divine and secular) and re-introducing it into positive law. This was done by a division of positive law into two different bodies: one that emanated from or was attributed to the people and bound the government, and one that emanated from government and bound the people. The first one regulated the production and application of the second. Law became reflexive. This presupposed, however, that the first took primacy over the second. The revolutionary theoreticians had a clear notion of this consequence of constitution making. The Americans expressed it as 'paramount law' and deployed the distinction between master and servant or principal and agent, while Sieyes conceptualised it in the dichotomy of *pouvoir constituant* and *pouvoir constitué*.[7] Without this distinction and the ensuing distinction between constitutional law and ordinary law and of the subordination of the latter to the former, constitutionalism would have been unable to fulfil its function.

Constitutionalism is therefore not identical with legalisation of public power. It is a special and particularly ambitious form of legalisation. Its characteristics can now be summarised:

1. The constitution in the modern sense is a set of legal norms, not a philosophical construct. The norms emanate from a political decision rather than some pre-established truth.
2. The purpose of these norms is to regulate the establishment and exercise of public power as opposed to a mere modification of a pre-existing public power.
3. The regulation is comprehensive in the sense that no extra-constitutional bearers of public power and no extra-constitutional ways and means to exercise this power are recognised.
4. Constitutional law finds its origin with the people as the only legitimate source of power. The distinction between *pouvoir constituant* and *pouvoir constitué* is essential to the constitution.
5. Constitutional law is higher law. It enjoys primacy over all other laws and legal acts emanating from government. Acts incompatible with the constitution do not acquire legal force.

These five characteristics refer to the function of the constitution. As such they differ from the many attempts to describe the modern constitution in substantive terms: democracy, rule of law, separation of powers, fundamental rights. The reason is that constitutionalism leaves room for many ways of establishing and organising political

---

[7] James Madison, Alexander Hamilton, and John Jay, *The Federalist Papers* (1788), No 78; E. Sieyes, *Qu'est-ce le Tiers État?* (Paris: 1789).

power: monarchical or republican, unitarian or federal, parliamentarian or presidential, unicameral or bicameral, with or without a bill of rights, with or without judicial review, etc. All this is left to the decision of the *pouvoir constituant*. But this is not to say that the constitution in the modern sense is compatible with any content. The reason is supplied by the function of the constitution, namely to establish legitimate rule and to regulate its exercise by the rulers comprehensively. A system that rejects the democratic origin of public power and is not interested in limited government does not meet the standards of the modern constitution.

The two elements of constitutionalism, the democratic element and the rule of law element, cannot be separated from each other without diminishing the achievement of constitutionalism. It is widely accepted that a document which does not attempt to submit politics to law is not worth being called a 'constitution'. But it is not so clear with regard to democracy as a necessary principle to *legitimise* public power. Yet, every principle of legitimacy other than democracy would undermine the function of the constitution. If political power is based on some absolute truth, be it religious or secular, the truth will always prevail in cases of conflict with positive law. This will also happen if an elite claims superior insight in the common good and derives from this insight the right to rule independently of popular consent. For this reason, it would be wrong to recognise two types of constitutions as equally representing the achievement of constitutionalism: a democratic type and a rule of law type.[8] In terms of achievement only a constitution that comprises both elements is capable of fulfilling the expectations of constitutionalism fully.

Constitutionalism in this sense deserves to be called an achievement,[9] because it rules out any absolute or arbitrary power of men over men. By submitting all government action to rules, it makes the use of public power predictable and enables the governed to anticipate governmental behaviour vis-à-vis themselves, and to face public agents without fear. It provides a consensual basis for persons and groups with different ideas and interests to resolve their disputes in a civilised manner. And it enables a peaceful transition of power to be made. Under favourable conditions it can even contribute to the integration of a society.[10] Although there is no achievement without shortcomings, constitutionalism as characterised by the five features is not an ideal type in the Weberian sense that allows only an approximation, but can never be completely reached. It is a historical reality that was in principle already fully developed by the first constitutions in North America and France and fulfilled its promise in a number of countries that had adopted constitutions in this sense.

---

[8] For this attempt, see C. Möllers, 'Verfassunggebende Gewalt—Verfassung—Konstitutionalisierung', in A. von Bogdandy (ed), *Europäisches Verfassungsrecht* (Baden-Baden: Nomos, 2003), 1.

[9] See N. Luhmann, 'Die Verfassung als evolutionäre Errungenschaft' (1990) 9 *Rechtshistorisches Journal* 176.

[10] See D. Grimm, 'Integration by Constitution' (2005) 3 *International Journal of Constitutional Law* 193; H. Vorländer (ed), *Integration durch Verfassung* (Wiesbaden: Westdeutscher Verlag, 2002).

Yet, the five characteristics do *not* describe everything that in constitutional history or in present times presents itself under the name 'constitution'. There are many more legal documents labelled 'constitution' or considered as constitutions than constitutions in the full sense of the achievement. The reason is that once the constitution was invented and inspired many hopes, it became possible to use the form without adopting all of the features that characterise the achievement. There were constitutions that left a pre-constitutional right to rule untouched. There were constitutions without a serious intention to limit the ruler's power. There were constitutions whose rules did not enjoy full primacy over the acts of government, but could legally be superseded by political decisions. But to the extent that these constitutions lacked some of the essential features of constitutionalism they failed to meet the achievement and were regarded as deficient.

The fact that the achievement was reached rather late in history nourishes the presumption that additional preconditions had to exist before a constitution in the sense described here, ie different from a mere legalisation of public power, could arrive. Although the first constitutions were a product of revolutions, a revolutionary break is not an indispensable precondition of the constitution. For the invention of the constitution the break with the traditional rule, combined with a new imagination of legitimate government, may have been necessary. But once invented the constitution no longer depends on a revolutionary origin. It can be adopted in an evolutionary way. It is sufficient that questions of legitimacy and organisation of political power are open to political decision. If the political order is predetermined independently of a consensus of the people, there is no room for a constitution. A document that bears this name is unlikely to enjoy primacy, but will be subordinated to an ultimate truth.

However, understood as a coherent and comprehensive regulation of the establishment and exercise of public power, the constitution could not emerge unless two further preconditions were in place. First, there has to be an object capable of being regulated in the specific form of a constitution. Such an object did not exist before the emergence of the modern state in the sixteenth and seventeenth centuries. Different from the medieval order, the state was characterised by a concentration of all prerogatives on a certain territory in one hand. Only after public power had become identical with state power could it be comprehensively regulated in one specific law. The medieval world did not have a constitution, and it could not have had one.[11] All talk about the constitution of the ancient Roman Empire, or of medieval kingdoms, or of the British constitution refers to a different object.

Although a necessary condition for the realisation of the constitution, the state was not a sufficient condition. For historical reasons, the state emerged on the European continent as the absolute state. This meant that it did not depend on the consent of its citizens; it claimed unlimited power over them. Different from political

---

[11] See H. Quaritsch, *Staat und Souveränität* (Frankfurt: Athenäum, 1970), 184; E. W. Böckenförde, 'Geschichtliche Entwicklung und Bedeutungswandel der Verfassung', in *Festschrift für R. Gmür* (Bielefeld: Gieseking, 1983), 9; D. Grimm, *Zukunft der Verfassung*, above n 1, 37 et seq.

power that is exercised in the form of a mandate, power that a ruler claims of his own right requires no regulation of the relationship between principal and agent. Omnipotence is then the only rule of constitutional rank. But even if the ruler has a mandate but it is unconditional, no regulation is necessary. Unlimited government stands opposed to constitutional government. Only when the idea had taken root that the power of the state should be limited in the interest of individual freedom and autonomy of various social functions was a constitution needed.

The concentration of all public power in the hands of the state has a corollary: the privatisation of society. The constitution did not change this. It only changed the order between the two. Individual freedom takes primacy while the state's task is to protect it against aggressors and criminals. In order to fulfil this limited function the state continued to claim the entire public power and the monopoly of legitimate force. Only the purpose for which and the conditions under which it might be used were limited. The border between public and private is thus constitutive for the constitution.[12] A system where the state enjoys the freedom of private persons would have as little a constitution as a system in which private persons may exercise public power. If private persons gain a share in public power, the constitution can no longer fulfil its claim to regulate the establishment and exercise of public power comprehensively unless the private actors submit to constitutional rules whereby they would lose their status as free members of society.

The fact that an object capable of being constitutionalised emerged in the form of the territorial state had the consequence that a plurality of states existed side by side. A second precondition for the constitution's claim to comprehensive validity was therefore that the public power of the state was without an external competitor within the territory. Consequently its legal force ended at the border of the territory. No constitution submitted domestic power to a foreign power or granted acts of a foreign power binding force within the domestic sphere. Just as the boundary between public and private is of constitutive importance for the constitution, so too is the boundary between external and internal.[13] A state that was unable to shield its borders from acts of a foreign public power could not secure the comprehensive functioning of its constitution.

Above the states there was no lawless zone. Rather the rules of public international law applied. But public international law rested on the basic assumption of the sovereignty and integrity of the states. It regulated their relationship based on the prohibition of intervention in the internal affairs of states. Legal bonds among states were therefore recognised only if they emanated from a voluntary agreement that was limited to the external relations of states. Only the precondition of this order, the rule *pacta sunt servanda*, was valid independently of consent. But the international order lacked the means to enforce contractual obligations. This is why war

---

[12] See Grimm, 'Ursprung und Wandel', above n 1, 18 et seq; S. Sassen, *Territory, Authority, Rights* (Princeton: Princeton University Press, 2008).

[13] Grimm, 'Ursprung und Wandel', above n 1, 18; R. Walker, *Inside/Outside* (Cambridge: Cambridge University Press, 1993).

could not be ruled out. But there were no legal means for states or the international community to interfere with the internal affairs of a state. The two bodies of law—constitutional law as internal law and international law as external law—could thus exist independently of one another.

III. PROSPECTS UNDER CHANGED CONDITIONS

If the modern constitution could only come into existence because of the prior development of certain conditions, it cannot be denied that these conditions may disappear, just as they once arrived. This does not necessarily mean that the constitution will cease to exist. The disappearance of such conditions is unlikely to be a sudden event. If it occurred it would most probably be a long process with remote rather than immediate consequences. But should the constitution survive, it is almost certain that it would acquire a new meaning and produce different effects. It is therefore of crucial importance for the future of constitutionalism to inquire whether, or to what extent, the situation that brought forth the constitution has changed, and to gauge how this affects the achievement of constitutionalism. The question of the prospects of the constitution is a question concerning the continued existence of its preconditions.

For two of these preconditions the answer seems straightforward. They do not pose a problem, at least in most parts of the world. Questions of political order continue to be open to political decision. They are not regarded as pre-determined by some transcendental will and removed from political influence. Furthermore, the idea of limited government is still the leading concept in countries in the Western tradition. The problem rather arises in relation to the state and its two constitutive borders: the boundary between internal and external and between public and private. It is generally observed that we are living in a period of erosion of statehood,[14] although it is not always precisely determined of what that consists. If the feature that distinguished the state from previous political entities was the concentration of public power in a given territory and the fact that this power was not submitted to any external will, it seems likely that here the source of the erosion has to be sought.

In fact, both boundaries become blurred. The boundary between public and private has become porous as a consequence of the expansion of state tasks. No longer only a guardian of individual freedom and market economy, the state regulates the economy, engages in social development and welfare politics, and tries to protect society against all sorts of potential risks. Many of these tasks cannot be carried out with the traditional instruments of order and enforcement. In a growing number of cases the state

---

[14] See, eg S. Leibfried and M. Zürn (eds), *Transformationen des Staates?* (Frankfurt: Suhrkamp, 2006); M. Beisheim et al, *Im Zeitalter der Globalisierung? Thesen und Daten zur gesellschaftlichen und politischen Denationalisierung* (Baden-Baden: Nomos, 1999); D. Held et al, *Global Transformations* (Stanford, Calif.: Stanford University Press, 1999); S. Sassen, *Losing Control? Sovereignty in an Age of Globalization* (New York: Columbia University Press, 1996); Sassen, above n 12.

relies on negotiations with private actors rather than legal orders addressed to them: agreements replace laws. This means that private actors gain a share in public power, yet without being integrated into the framework of legitimation and accountability that the constitution establishes for public actors. In addition, there are modes of decision making that are not submitted to the requirements prescribed by the constitution for acts of public authority. Since there are structural reasons for this development, it can neither be simply prohibited nor fully constitutionalised.[15]

The same is true for the boundary between inside and outside. After having been unchallenged for almost 300 years, the border became permeable when, in order to enhance their problem-solving capacity, the states began to establish international organisations to whom they transferred sovereign rights which these organisations exercise within the states and unimpeded by their right to self-determination. The first step in this direction was the foundation of the United Nations in 1945, whose task it was not only to coordinate state activities but also to fulfil a peace keeping mission of its own. To reach this end, member states not only gave up the right to solve their conflicts by means of violence, except in cases of self-defence (as a self-limitation this would have remained within the framework of traditional international law and left their sovereignty intact), they also empowered the UN to enforce the prohibition, if necessary by military intervention. As a consequence, the right to self-determination is limited to the relationship among states, but cannot be invoked against the public power exercised by the international organisation.

This development has meanwhile progressed further. It is no longer doubtful that, if a state completely disregards the human rights of its population or of minorities within the population, the UN has in principle the power of humanitarian intervention. Moreover, international courts have been established that can prosecute war crimes and crimes against humanity. Some of these courts, the criminal courts for the former Yugoslavia and for Rwanda, were established not by way of treaties, but by a decision of the Security Council and may act on the territory of the states independently of their permission. Beyond that, under the umbrella of the UN, a *jus cogens* has developed that claims validity independently of the state's consent, but which, in turn, limits them in their treaty-making power. Similar effects went along with the foundation of the World Trade Organization, basically a forum for negotiations and agreements of states, but independent from these states through its court-like treaty enforcement mechanism.

As a consequence, no state remains sovereign to the extent states used to be before 1945.[16] But nowhere has this development progressed as far as in Europe. It is true that UN interventions, if they occur, can be much more substantial than acts of European institutions. But they do not occur frequently, in part because the great majority of member states provide no reason for an intervention, and also because some states are permanent members of the Security Council and thereby enjoy a

[15] See D. Grimm, 'Lässt sich die Verhandlungsdemokratie konstitutionalisieren?' in C. Offe (ed), *Demokratisierung der Demokratie* (Frankfurt: Campus, 2003), 193.

[16] See D. Grimm, *Souveraenitaet* (Berlin: Berlin University Press, 2009).

veto-right that they can use to prevent interventions. Unlike the sovereign power of states, the UN power actualises itself very rarely and only vis-à-vis states that disregard their treaty obligations and provoke UN actions. The majority of states have never been subjected to measures of the UN. For them, the change that occurred with the founding of the UN is less visible, the loss of sovereignty not obvious.

This is different on the European level. Although no European organisation has yet acquired the power to use physical force vis-à-vis its members, the states are constantly subject to European legal acts which they have to observe. Only the degree varies. So far as the Council of Europe is concerned, these are judicial acts. The Council of Europe exercises public power solely through the European Court of Human Rights (ECtHR). Its judgments are binding for the forty-six member states, but they do not take direct effect within them. The ECtHR is not an appellate court with the power to reverse judgments of national courts. It can only state a violation of the ECHR, but has to leave the redress to the states themselves. Still, the effects on member states' legal systems are far-reaching. They may even include an obligation to change the national constitution.

The power of the EU is broader in scope and deeper in effect on the member states' sovereignty. It includes legislative, administrative, and judicial acts. It is true that the EU has only those powers that the member states have transferred to it. As far as the transfer of sovereign rights is concerned they retain their power of self-determination. They remain the 'masters of the treaties'. Once transferred, however, the powers are exercised by organs of the EU and claim not only direct effect within the member states but also primacy over domestic law, including national constitutions. Although this lacks an explicit basis in the Treaties, it has been accepted in principle as a necessary precondition of the functioning of the EU. Only the outer limits remain controversial, as both the European Court of Justice (ECJ) and some constitutional courts of the member states each claim the last word concerning *ultra vires* acts of the EU.[17]

Hence, the state is no longer the exclusive source of law within its territory. Laws and acts of law enforcement claim validity within the state that emanate from external sources and prevail over domestic law. The identity of public power and state power that was implied in the notion of sovereignty and had been the basis of the national as well as the international order is thus dissolving. This development cannot leave the constitution unaffected.[18] Since the constitution presupposed the state and referred to its power, the fragmentation of public power inevitably entails a

---

[17] See F. C. Mayer, *Kompetenzüberschreitung und Letztentscheidung* (Munich: Beck, 2000); M. Claes, *The National Courts' Mandate in the European Constitution* (Oxford: Oxford University Press, 2006); A. M. Slaughter et al (eds), *The European Court and National Courts* (Oxford: Oxford University Press, 1998).

[18] See D. Grimm, 'Zur Bedeutung nationaler Verfassungen in einem vereinten Europa', in D. Merten and H. J. Papier (eds), *Handbuch der Grundrechte* (Heidelberg: Müller, 2009), vi. 1; M. Ruffert, *Die Globalisierung als Herausforderung des Öffentlichen Rechts* (Stuttgart: Boorberg, 2004); R. Wahl, *Herausforderungen und Antworten: Das Öffentliche Recht der letzten fünf Jahrzehnte* (Berlin: De Gruyter, 2006).

diminution of the constitution's impact. Of course, the loss did not occur contrary to the will of the states. Sovereign rights were given up voluntarily because they expected something in return: an increase in problem-solving capacity in matters that could no longer be effectively handled on the national level. In addition, the states usually retain a share in the decision-making processes of the international institutions that now exercises these rights. But this cannot compensate for the decrease in constitutional legitimation and limitation of public power.

With respect to the five criteria that were found to be constitutive for the modern constitution the consequences are the following:

1. The constitution remains a set of legal norms which owe their validity to a political decision.
2. Their object continues to be the establishment and exercise of the public power, but only insofar as it is state power.
3. Since public power and state power are no longer congruent, the constitution ceases to regulate public power coherently and comprehensively.
4. Consequently, the primacy of constitutional law is no longer exclusive. It prevails over ordinary domestic law and acts applying domestic law, not in general.
5. The constitution still emanates from or is attributed to the people. But it can no longer secure that any public power taking effect within the state finds its source with the people and is democratically legitimised by the people.

In sum, the emergence of an international public power does not render the constitution obsolete or ineffective. But to the extent that statehood is eroding, the constitution is in decline. It shrinks in importance since it can no longer fulfil its claim to legitimise and regulate all public authority that is effective within its realm. Acts of public authority that do not emanate from the state are not submitted to the requirements of the state's constitution, and their validity on the state's territory does not depend on their being in harmony with the domestic constitution. The constitution shrinks to a partial order. Only when national constitutional law and international law are seen together is one able to obtain a complete picture of the legal conditions for political rule in a country. The fact that many constitutions permit the transfer of sovereign rights prevents the situation from being unconstitutional. But it does not close the gap between the range of public power on the one hand and that of constitutional norms on the other.

This gives rise to the question of whether the loss of importance that the constitution suffers at the national level can be compensated for at the international level. Public power stands in need of legitimation and limitation regardless of the power holder. The constitution has successfully solved this problem vis-à-vis the state. It therefore comes as no surprise that the question is posed whether the achievement of constitutionalism can be elevated to the international level.[19] This, in fact, is the reason why the new term 'constitutionalisation' has acquired its current popularity in academic writing and public discourse. 'Constitutionalisation' means a

---

[19] See the indications suggested in n 2 above.

constitution-building process beyond the state.[20] It applies to international political entities and international legal documents and is even extended to rule making of public-
private partnerships on the international level and of globally active private actors.

In view of the preconditions that had to be fulfilled before national constitutions
became possible, the question is whether an object capable of being constitutionalised
exists at the international level. The answer cannot be the same for all international
organisations, the differences between them being too big. This is even more true if
societal institutions are included in the consideration. The easiest case seems to be
the EU. The EU is certainly not a state, but neither is it an international organisation
within the usual meaning. It differs from other international organisations first in its
range of competencies which are not limited to a single issue but cover an increasing
variety of objects. It differs secondly in the density of its organisational structure,
comprising all the branches of government possessed by a state. And it differs finally
in the intensity of the effects that its operations have on the member states and their
citizens. Given all these features, the EU comes quite close to comparison with the
central unit of a federal state.

The power of the EU is by no means unregulated. It is, on the contrary, embedded in a closely meshed net of legal norms. Although these legal norms are not
contained in a constitution but in international treaties concluded by the member
states, the treaties fulfil within the EU most of the functions that constitutions fulfil
in states. The European treaties established what is today the EU. They created the
organs of the EU, determine their powers and procedures, and regulate the relationship between the EU and the member states as well as the citizens—all rules that in
the state one would find in the constitution. The Treaties are also higher law: all legal
acts of the EU must comply with the provisions of the Treaties. This is why many
authors do not hesitate to call the Treaties the constitution of the EU, and neither
does the ECJ.

However, this mode of speaking neglects one of the elements that characterise a
constitution in the full sense of the notion.[21] Different from constitutions, the Treaties are not an expression of the self-determination of a people or a society about the
form and substance of their political union. The EU does not decide upon its own
legal foundation. It receives this foundation from the member states which create it
by an agreement concluded according to international law. Consequently, the Treaties lack a democratic origin. This does not make them illegitimate. But they do not
enjoy the democratic legitimacy that characterises a constitution. The citizens of the
EU have no share in making the basic document. They do not give a mandate to a
constitutional assembly. They do not adopt the text. Ratification within the member
states, even if it happens by a referendum, is not a European but a national act deciding

---

[20] Cf Loughlin in this volume.

[21] See D. Grimm, *Braucht Europa eine Verfassung?* (Munich: Siemens, 1995) (Eng. trans. (1995)
1 *European Law Journal* 278); D. Grimm, 'Entwicklung und Funktion des Verfassungsbegriffs',
in T. Cottier and W. Kälin (eds), *Die Öffnung des Verfassungsstaats, Recht-Sonderheft* (2005);
D. Grimm, 'Verfassung—Verfassungsvertrag—Vertrag über eine Verfassung', in O. Beaud
et al (eds), *L'Europe en voie de constitution* (Bruxelles: Bruylant, 2004), 279.

whether a state approves of the treaty. The document is not even attributed to the citizens as the source of all public power.

Nevertheless, there are examples in history in which a constitution in the full sense originates in the form of a treaty concluded by states which unite into a greater state. But in these cases the founding treaty is only the mode to establish a constitution. As soon as the treaty is adopted as the legal foundation of the new political entity, the founding states give up the power to determine the future fate of the text and hand this power over to the new entity which thereby gains the full authority to maintain, change, or abolish it. It is a treaty by origin, but a constitution by legal nature. The test is the provision for amendments. If the amendment power remains in the hands of the member states and is exercised by way of treaties, the transition from treaty to constitution has not taken place. If the newly created state has gained the power of self-determination (even if the member states retain a share in the decision of the new entity) the legal foundation has turned into a constitution.

Such a transfer has not taken place in the EU. It was not even provided for by the failed Constitutional Treaty. Even if ratified in all member states, it would not have acquired the quality of a constitution. However, this does not deprive the EU of its capacity to be a potential object of constitutionalisation. Its status as an entity comparable to the central unit of a federation qualifies the EU to a legal foundation in the form of a constitution. The member states would simply have to give up their power to determine for themselves the legal foundation of the EU. The question is not one of possibility but of desirability. However, by doing so they would inevitably transform the EU into a federal state. It is here that doubts arise. Would the formal democratisation of the EU be accompanied by a gain in substantive democracy, or does it serve the democratic principle better if the decision about the legal foundation of the EU remains in the hands of the states where the democratic mechanisms work better than in the EU? Would it deprive the EU of its innovative character as a genuine entity between an international organisation and a federal state?

The issue is different at the global level. Here, no organisation exists whose range of powers and organisational density is comparable to that of the EU. There are some isolated institutions with limited tasks, most of them single-issue organisations, and with correspondingly limited powers. They are not only unconnected, but sometimes even pursue goals that are not in harmony with each other, such as economic interests on the one hand and humanitarian interests on the other. Rather than forming a global system of international public power they are islands within an ocean of traditional international relations. In this respect, the international order currently resembles the pre-state medieval order with its many independent bearers of dispersed powers.[22] Like medieval ordering, the international level is not susceptible to the type of coherent and comprehensive regulation that characterises the constitution.

The UN is no exception. It stands out among international organisations because of its all-encompassing nature, its peacekeeping purpose, and its corresponding powers.

---

[22] See Sassen, above n 12.

But it is far from aggregating all public power exercised on the global level and even farther from the concentrated and all embracing public power of the state. Its charter therefore does not come close to a world constitution. It marks an important step in legalising international relations but does not go beyond that. This is doubly so with respect to institutions like the World Trade Organization, the International Monetary Fund, the International Labour Organization, and such like. Their statutes regulate the powers of these institutions and guide them in the exercise of their functions. But their limited competencies and their non-democratic structure do not qualify them for the specific form of regulation that is characteristic of the constitution.

It has nonetheless become quite common to see constitutionalising processes at work also on this level and to call the statutes or charters of international organisations or the *jus cogens* within public international law a constitution. The term is, of course, not reserved to one single meaning. As could be seen, the notion 'constitution' has covered a number of phenomena in the past.[23] But if it is applied to international institutions and their legal foundation one should not forget that it does not have much in common with the *achievement* of constitutionalism. Without doubt, international law is undergoing important changes, covering new ground, and becoming more effective.[24] But calling it a constitution empties the notion and reflects a very thin idea of constitutionalism. Basically, it identifies constitutionalisation with legalisation of public power, a phenomenon that existed long before the constitution emerged and from which the constitution differed considerably. This difference is levelled by the new use of the term which does not contribute to a clarification of the current state of affairs.

This argument applies with even greater force to so-called societal constitutionalism.[25] This type of constitutionalism is not only disconnected from the state but also from international organisations created by states. The proponents of societal constitutionalism realise on the one hand that the state is unable to regulate the transactions of global actors. On the other hand they do not believe either that international organisations have sufficient regulatory power to provide a legal framework for the operations of global actors that would prevent them from pursuing their own interests in an unihibited way. At best, international organisations could 'constitutionalise' themselves, ie submit their actions to self-created standards. The gap between international rule making and transnational operations of private actors could only be closed if the idea of constitutionalism is disconnected from its

[23] See Mohnhaupt and Grimm, above n 4.

[24] See B. Zangl and M. Zürn (eds), *Verrechtlichung: Bausteine für Global Governance?* (Bonn: Dietz, 2004); B. Zangl, *Die Internationalisierung der Rechtstaatlichkeit* (Frankfurt: Campus, 2006).

[25] See D. Sciulli, *Theory of Societal Constitutionalism* (Cambridge: Cambridge University Press, 2005); G. Teubner, 'Global Private Regimes: Neo-Spontaneous Law and Dual Constitution of Autonomous Sectors?', in K. H. Ladeur (ed), *Public Governance in the Age of Globalization* (Aldershot: Ashgate, 2004), 71; see also Teubner and Fischer-Lescano, and Teubner, above n 2. For comment see D. Grimm, 'Gesellschaftlicher Konstitutionalismus: Eine Kompensation für den Bedeutungsschwund der Staatsverfassung?' in *Festschrift für R. Herzog* (Munich: Beck, 2009), 67.

traditional link with politics and adapted to the societal sphere. In this case a body of transnational law would emerge alongside national and international law.

This law is seen as being capable of fulfilling the function of constitutions vis-à-vis private global actors. However, this requires an adaptation of the notion 'constitutionalism' to its object, the global private actors. In contrast to state constitutions, societal constitutions do not take legal force by an authoritative act of a constitution maker. They emerge from a long-lasting evolutionary process, even though this process may be stimulated by political incentives or supported by formal legal requirements. Societal constitutions are neither mere legal texts, nor simply reflections of the factual situation. And, more importantly, they do not encompass the internationally exercised private power in its totality. In contrast to traditional state constitutions that cover public power comprehensively but are territorially limited, societal constitutions claim global validity but are limited to certain sectors of society. The territorial differentiation of national law is relativised by the sectoral limitation of global law.

In order to deserve the name 'constitution', societal law must show in addition some of the structural elements of state constitutions. First, societal constitutions must function as higher law that regulates the making of ordinary law. Secondly, this higher law must contain provisions that regulate the organisation and the procedures of the global actors. Thirdly, it must limit the scope of action of the private global actors, just as fundamental rights limit the scope of action of state actors in domestic law. Finally, it must provide control mechanisms similar to constitutional adjudication that guarantee an effective review of the acts of global organisations with respect to their compliance with higher law. The proponents of this idea concede that up to now societal constitutionalism exists only in rudimentary form. But they believe in its potential for institutionalising within these global sectors respect for the autonomy of other social sectors and their needs as well as recognition of areas where the behaviour of global actors can be observed independently and criticised freely.

However, this potential, if it exists, depends on some preconditions which cannot be taken for granted. In the absence of a global legislator, the limitation by societal constitutions will always be self-limitation guided by the actor's interest, not the common interest. Both interests may partly coincide, but not completely. Hence, self-limitation capable of harmonising actors' own interests with the interests of those affected by their actions and the communal interests is unlikely if not imposed by a public authority whose task it is to keep the self-interest of the various sectors of society within the limits of the common best. On the national level, government fulfils this function. But how can the same result be reached on the international level in the absence of an equivalent of the state or of other institutions with sufficiently broad regulatory power? And even if existing international institutions possessed this power, how effectively would they use it without the democratic and representative element that guarantees participation of those affected by the decisions and thus enables a perception of problems beyond the institutional interests of the actors? No so-called constitution on the international and transnational level is yet capable of fulfilling only minimal democratic demands.

IV. WHICH CONCLUSION?

This analysis suggests that the gap between public power and its constitutional legiti-mation and limitation, which is opening up as a result of the erosion of statehood and transfer of public power to the international level, cannot for the time being be closed. On the one hand, it seems neither possible nor desirable to return to the Westphalian system. On the other, the achievement of constitutionalism cannot be reconstructed on the international or transnational level. National constitutions will not regain their capacity to legitimise and regulate comprehensively the public power that takes effect within the territory of the state. The regulation of interna-tionally exercised public power is expanding, but remains a legalisation unable to live up to the standard of constitutionalism. Whoever invokes constitutionalism in this connection uses a thin notion of constitutionalism with its democratic element almost always left out.

If a full preservation of constitutionalism is not available, the second best solu-tion would be to preserve as much of the achievement as possible under given conditions. In principle, this can occur in two directions: by striving for a greater accumulation of public power on the international level,[26] or by limiting the erosion of statehood on the national level. Strengthening the international level would be a solution only if the international order could develop into an object capable of being constitutionalised in the sense of the achievement, ie as differ-ent from mere legalisation. This is neither likely in a medium-term perspective, nor are there convincing models for democratic governance on the global level.[27] A democracy that is not deprived of its participatory element, but maintains a substantive rather than a purely formal outlook including the societal precondi-tions of democratic government such as a lively public discourse, is already diffi-cult to realise within the EU. On the global level even a democracy reduced to the formal element of free elections seems unlikely.

The consequence would be to put the emphasis on states where constitutional-ism still finds more favourable conditions and where the potential for democratic legitimisation and accountability of public power remains greater than on the inter-national level. This should not be misunderstood as a call to restore the traditional nation state. On the contrary, the international turn of politics is in need of further development. An approximation of the scope of politics to the scope of action of private global actors seems an urgent postulate. But it is likewise important that democratic states remain the most important source of legitimation, including the

---

[26] See M. Lutz-Bachmann and J. Bohman (eds), *Weltstaat oder Staatenwelt?* (Frankfurt: Suhrkamp, 2002); M. Albert and R. Stichweh (eds), *Weltstaat und Weltstaatlichkeit* (Wiesbaden: Westdeutscher Verlag, 2007).

[27] See A. Kuper, *Democracy Beyond Borders* (Oxford: Oxford University Press, 2004); J. Anderson (ed), *Transnational Democracy: Political Spaces and Border Crossings* (London: Routledge, 2002); A. Niederberger, 'Wie demokratisch ist die transnationale Demokratie?' in Albert and Stichweh, above n 25, 109; G. de Burca, 'Developing Democracy beyond the State' (2008) 46 *Columbia Journal of Transnational Law* 221.

legitimation of international organisations. They must be prevented from becoming self-supporting entities distant from the citizenry and largely uncontrollable in their activities and unaccountable for the results.

In fact, states are by no means out of the international and transnational game. Up to now the process of internationalisation has not touched the monopoly of the legitimate use of force. No international organisation possesses its own means of physical force, let alone a monopoly. The fragmented global society has no enforcement mechanisms per se. International courts and even more so private arbitration bodies depend on states when it comes to enforcing judgments against reluctant parties. In addition the states retain a share in the direction and control over the international organisations they have formed. This is as important in the EU as it is on the global level. In all these matters they are subservient to the requirements of their national constitutions. These bonds should neither be prematurely relinquished, nor severely weakened.

Regarding the supranational level, it seems preferable to leave the constitutional path and drop the notions of constitutionalism and constitutionalisation altogether. They are misleading insofar as they nourish the hope that the loss national constitutions suffer from internationalisation and globalisation could be compensated for on the supranational level. This would, however, be an illusion. The submission of internationally exercised public power to law will always lag behind the achievement of constitutionalism on the national level. The conditions that would allow a reconstruction of the achievement beyond the nation state are not given. The internationalisation of public power is a new phenomenon that poses new challenges. The illusion that these challenges could be met by using a model that was invented for a different object tends to obstruct the search for solutions that are oriented towards the new situation and will suit it better.

2

Disconnecting Constitutions from Statehood

Is Global Constitutionalism a Viable Concept?

Ulrich K. Preuss

I. INTRODUCTION

Our conventional wisdom teaches us that constitutions are essentially linked with the concept of statehood, more specifically with the state's sovereign power. This perception is quite persuasive, given the established meaning of sovereignty as absolute and exclusive power within a territory.[1] From the sixteenth century on, sovereignty—in Bodin's famous definition the 'power … of giving the law to subjects in general without their consent'[2]—became the defining feature of a new concept of politics which superseded the medieval patterns of interpersonal reciprocity.[3] The conversion of the socially and culturally embedded medieval individual and his or her particular community-linked status with the levelled equal status of subjection to the sovereign state, triggered a desire for protection against this almost context-less coercive and unilaterally imposed power. Consequently, curbing the ostensibly limitless sovereign power was the obvious remedy against absolutist rule.

In fact, liberal reasoning dominated the constitutional discourse in the eighteenth and nineteenth centuries. When the French Declaration of the Rights of Man and Citizen of 1789 asserted in Article 16 that 'a society in which the guarantee of rights is not assured and the separation of powers not established has no constitution', it identified two prerequisites as defining elements of a constitution which could easily be understood as power-limiting devices. As I shall argue below, this was a misunderstanding, and a far-reaching one at that. In countries influenced by US constitutionalism, fundamental rights and separation of powers were mainly seen

---

[1] D. Philpott, *Revolutions in Sovereignty: How Ideas Shaped Modern International Relations* (Princeton: Princeton University Press, 2001), 16 et seq.

[2] Jean Bodin, *On Sovereignty* (Cambridge: Cambridge University Press, 1992), i., ch 8, 23.

[3] U. K. Preuß, 'Souveränität: Zwischenbemerkungen zu einem Schlüsselbegriff des Politischen', in T. Stein, H. Buchstein, and C. Offe (eds), *Souveränität, Recht, Moral: Die Grundlagen der politischen Gemeinschaft* (Frankfurt am Main: Campus, 2007), 313–35.

as establishing limited government until well into the twentieth century.[4] In this view, the taming of the Leviathan is the essential function of constitutions. Without devices which restrain sovereignty, or so reads the argument, government tends to become oppressive and despotic, irrespective of who governs. Obviously, the shift of sovereignty from the absolutist monarch to the people did not calm the fears that sovereignty is inherently predisposed to despotism. As we know, the Founders of the US constitution were sceptical about the democratic version of unrestricted sovereign power,[5] which Tocqueville, two generations later, famously labelled the tyranny of the majority.[6]

In Europe, the historical development of modern constitutionalism was closely linked to the emergence and development of the modern state. In the early stages of the evolution of statehood, between the twelfth and sixteenth centuries, three main institutional devices restrained the state's power, namely urban autonomy, parliamentarianism, and constitutionalism.[7] The latter consisted mainly of charters in which monarchs 'promised to eliminate specifically named abuses and to treat their subjects according to the law'.[8] Those institutional devices converged on the issue of finding an institutional balance between the benefits of an efficient central government and the individual's quest for freedom, ie 'between utter subjection and complete anarchy'.[9] A major shift in the relative importance of these three restraining devices occurred in the period of high absolutism, where 'unfettered personal rule was eventually contested everywhere'.[10] However, as the cases of England, France, and the Netherlands—the most important European states which overcame or avoided absolutism through constitutions—attest, the struggle over the distribution and the appropriate institutionalisation of power among the political, economic, social, and religious elites played a major role. A purely negative understanding of the constitution as a mechanism of limiting government was not prevalent.[11] In the emerging United States of America, by contrast, 'the Americans' inveterate suspicion and jealousy of political power, once concentrated almost exclusively on the Crown

---

[4] For instance, C. J. Friedrich gave his influential comparative account of constitutional history the title 'limited government': C. J. Friedrich, *Limited Government: A Comparison* (Englewood Cliffs, NJ: Prentice-Hall, 1974).

[5] See *The Federalist Papers*, Nos 1, 9, 10.

[6] A. de Tocqueville, *Democracy in America* (New York: Vintage Books, [1848] 1990), i., ch 15, 258 et seq.

[7] R. C. van Caenegem, *An Historical Introduction to Western Constitutional Law* (Cambridge: Cambridge University Press, 1995), 78 et seq.

[8] Ibid 80.

[9] Ibid 98.

[10] Ibid 108.

[11] See the respective accounts of Caenegem, ibid at 108 et seq (England), 142 et seq (Netherlands), and 174 et seq (France).

and its agents, was transferred to the various state legislatures'[12] and remained a dominant motif in the debates on the Federal Constitution. In this respect the US model of constitutionalism seems to resemble a *Sonderweg*.[13]

Be this as it may, it is beyond question that modern constitutions have evolved as a concomitant element of the modern sovereign state,[14] at least in the Western hemisphere. To be sure, this close relationship of constitutionalism and statehood applies only to the states' internal formation; it is absent in the sphere of their external relations. Due to their territorial character, states are political entities which necessarily exist as a plurality. They interact on the basis of mutual independence and equality and form an unorganised international society,[15] which Hedley Bull rightly qualified as an anarchical society.[16] Independence is a synonym for sovereignty or, for that matter, for sovereign equality, one of the basic principles of the UN Charter (Article 2, para 1). Independence and integration into a constitutionalised system are mutually exclusive. Thus, it seems that the idea of constitutionalism as a pattern of order is only meaningful within states, rendering any concept of constitutional order beyond the states' internal sphere, let alone of a global constitution, futile from the very outset.

In the following I reassess these assumptions. How can we explain the close relationship between statehood and constitutionalism in the first place? Can we substantiate the claim that the states' sovereign equality and global constitutionalism are incompatible? I will discuss these questions in turn, starting with an analysis of the significance of the territorial character of the modern state and its connection with the concept of sovereignty (II). I will then deal with the consequences of the state's territoriality for the character of the law (III). The main section deals with the analysis of the relationship between the territorial character of the state and constitutionalism, where I will argue that the essence of modern constitutionalism is not to be found in the imposition of restraints on the absolutist state but in the constitution of a thoroughly new kind of polity (IV). In the following section I will discuss a hypothesis which posits a three-stage model of the development of sovereignty (V), followed by an attempt to reconceptualise the notion of constitution in the light of a constructivist approach (VI). Finally, I offer some concluding remarks about certain embryonic elements of a constitutionalisation of the international community (VII).

[12] G. S. Wood, *The Creation of the American Republic, 1776-1787* (New York: Norton, 1972), 409.

[13] See U. K. Preuß, 'Der Begriff der Verfassung und ihre Beziehung zur Politik', in Preuß (ed) *Zum Begriff der Verfassung: Die Ordnung des Politischen* (Frankfurt am Main: S. Fischer, 1994), 7–33.

[14] See D. Grimm, 'Does Europe need a Constitution?' (1995) 1 *European Law Journal* 282–302, at 284–8.

[15] U. K. Preuss, 'Equality of States: Its Meaning in a Constitutionalized Global Order' (2008) 9 *Chicago Journal of International Law* 17–49.

[16] H. Bull, *The Anarchical Society: A Study of Order in World Politics* (London: Macmillan, 1977).

II. STATEHOOD AND TERRITORIALITY

A prominent characterisation of the state is Max Weber's contention that from a sociological perspective the modern state can only be defined by a specific means, namely its exclusive control of the means of coercion. Weber admitted that in the past very disparate associations—eg families, clans, tribes—had used violence as a means of imposing social discipline upon their subordinates. But he insisted that the state is unique because it is the only human association which successfully claims the monopoly of physical force 'within a defined territory'.[17] In fact, the element of territoriality is essential for the proper understanding of the state. It implies a profound transformation in the structure and significance of physical force within a given social structure. In pre-state political associations, coercive, ultimately physical, force was a mere instrument in the hands of rulers whose authority was rooted in their social status based on age, divine descent, dynastic tradition, religious charisma, military virtues, and the like. In contrast, in the modern state coercive force is itself not *a*, but *the* source of political authority. It becomes the key factor of societal integration. The reason is that the political entity, 'state', is defined in physical terms, that is, as a bounded territory.

There are two different kinds of territoriality: one is a means of assigning things to persons, to confer control over physical objects and to exclude others from their use. This kind of territoriality is embodied in the concept of property. The other is the exercise of authority over human individuals. Both institutions are based upon territorial boundaries. Whereas the territorial character of property is limited to merely excluding others from access to the demarcated space, the territorial character of jurisdiction is more complex, as it involves claims to the obedience of 'whoever is physically in that area'.[18]

Thus, territoriality in this latter sense is by no means a purely spatial category. Space becomes a territory when it is combined with the exercise of authoritative power: that is, by controlling the access to or departure from the area, by the exclusion from or access to the use of the resources available there, or by the control over the social interactions within this area.[19] In the latter case in particular, it becomes clear that territoriality involves a type of generalisation of authoritative power. Instead of exercising control over each individual action or event case by case, the master of the territory is able to subject everything to his rule, including the various present and future events of which he largely is not even aware. This comprehensive and exclusive control of a territory is what we call sovereignty.

---

[17] Max Weber, *Wirtschaft und Gesellschaft: Studienausgabe. Zwei Halbbände* (Cologne: Kiepenheuer & Witsch, 1964), 1043 (not included in the American translation of Roth/ Wittich).

[18] D. Miller and H. Sohail, *Boundaries and Justice: Diverse Ethical Perspectives* (Princeton: Princeton University Press, 2001), 4.

[19] On this and on the following, see R. D. Sack, *Human Territoriality: Its Theory and History* (Cambridge: Cambridge University Press, 1986), 19, 31 et seq.

The territorial dimension of sovereignty has several important implications. First and foremost, authoritative power becomes impersonal because the subordination under the will of a ruler is not based on personal relations and therefore does not have to be secured and affirmed for each individual person. It is valid for each person within the borders of the territory, irrespective of his or her social status or individual attributes (such as religious belief or ethnic belonging). Note, however, that the European states in their early developmental stage had still to learn about their potential for ethnic or religious neutrality, as the enforcement of the principle of *cuius regio, eius religio*, established in the Augsburg and the Westphalian Peace Treaties of 1555 and 1648 respectively, attest.

Secondly, authoritative power by virtue of territoriality requires only a minimum of communication regarding object and limits of the ruler's powers. The clear and easily discernible limits of the space which constitutes the territory are sufficient to set a purely spatio-physical, evident demarcation of subordination. Ideally, the ruler does not need more than a fence, though the capacity to set up the fence may be extremely demanding in terms of material resources, power, political skills, and legitimacy.[20]

Thirdly, the depersonalisation of rule entails that the scope and intensity of domination is standardised according to the pattern: each person in territory X has the duties Y irrespective of their individual merits, attitudes, or capacities. It enables a master to rule over a multitude of individuals according to general standards. This quality of domination transforms interpersonal domination into impersonal order; it is an essential element of sovereignty. Sovereignty does not relate to individuals but to the impersonal order of a territory. It is not accidental that an early definition of a ruler's supreme power—the above-quoted principle of *cuius regio, eius religio*—had an explicitly territorial character. The dominant conflict of the early modern era was redefined in spatial terms. This depersonalisation of religion strikes us as strange because history teaches us that religion is the primary source of commonness and a pivotal emblem of social and cultural embeddedness of individuals. Statehood, ie the spatial organisation of authority, changed that status of religion profoundly, in that it gave rise to the idea of religious toleration and finally the individual right to religious freedom—at the price of opening the path to the privatisation of religion. However this may be, the structural relevance of the state's territorial character is best articulated in the assertion of Poggi: 'The state does not *have* a territory, it *is* a territory.'[21]

---

[20] See, eg the Advisory Opinion of the ICJ of 9 July 2004 and the Separate Opinions of several Judges regarding Legal Consequences of the Construction of a Wall in the Occupied Palestinian Territory <http://www.icj-cij.org/docket/index.php?p1=3&p2=4&k=5a&case =131&code=mwp&p3=4> (accessed 15 April 2009).

[21] G. Poggi, *The State: Its Nature, Development and Prospects* (Stanford, Calif.: Stanford University Press, 1994), 22.

Thus, territoriality defines sovereignty. Jean Bodin stated that 'there is nothing greater on earth, after God, than sovereign princes'.[22] But their majesty, their status, and their attributes 'which are properties not shared by subjects'[23] are just consequences of the impersonal concept of sovereignty which Bodin conceives as 'the absolute and perpetual power of a commonwealth'.[24] As is well known, Bodin developed the concept of sovereignty as a conceptual weapon against the religious wars in France which threatened to destroy the unity of the French kingdom. The justification of the right of the prince to issue laws without the consent of his subjects was a barely concealed legitimisation of the French monarchy's claim to superiority over the estates and other local and particularistic forces which prevented the king from safeguarding the peace and security of the kingdom. Overcoming the intermediary forces of the medieval society—the estates, local parliaments, and cities—was tantamount to the transformation of the kingdom into one territory controlled by the monarch; creating this territory was tantamount to establishing sovereignty.[25]

The conception of sovereignty as supreme, undivided, absolute, and exclusive power attributed to the state was a radical rupture with the traditional understanding of power as being embedded in a hierarchical order of social relations. In an interpersonal affiliation, power relations are reciprocal—not necessarily symmetric—balanced, divided, relative, inclusive, and hence limited. However, sovereign power also has its limits, which Bodin addresses in a separate chapter when he expounds the relationship of the sovereign princes among each other.[26] He takes it for granted that there is a plurality of princes each of whom has, after God, supreme power. This can only mean that each of them is sovereign within a demarcated space on earth, ie within a territory. In fact, power can be supreme, undivided, absolute, and exclusive only within a demarcated territory—without this spatial limitation it would simply water down and diffuse in the vastness and the complexities of the world. It would be altogether impossible. While the plurality of independent territories transformed the world of empires into the international society of states,[27] within the territories the social disembeddedness of power generated a new mode of sociality which C. B. Macpherson, in his analysis of the political philosophy of Hobbes

---

[22] Bodin, above n 2, i., ch 10, at 46.

[23] Ibid.

[24] Ibid, i., ch 8, at 1.

[25] A thorough analysis of the complex relation between land and lordship which is inherently connected with the process of territorialisation of medieval Austrian lands is provided by O. Brunner, *Land and Lordship: Structures of Governance in Medieval Austria* (Philadelphia: University of Pennsylvania Press, 1992) (Eng. trans. of Otto Brunner, *Land und Herrschaft: Grundfragen der territorialen Verfassungsgeschichte Österreichs im Mittelalter* (Darmstadt: Wissenschaftliche Buchgesellschaft, 1965), see especially section V.i.).

[26] Bodin, above n 2, i., ch 9 (not included in the edition cited).

[27] For a thorough analysis of its implications, see Bull, above n 16.

and Locke, called 'possessive individualism'.[28] This was an impersonal and abstract pattern of interactions by a multitude of atomised individuals, each of whom strove separately for his and her survival. And the state was the container of this society.[29] Two brief remarks about the implications of the state-contained kind of sociality may be appropriate, before I turn to the relationship between constitutionalism and territoriality.

III. LEGALITY AND TERRITORIALITY

The character of the social discipline which is required in this territorially defined order undergoes a fundamental change. The individuals' subordination no longer consists in their posture of loyalty towards their superiors of the social hierarchy but in a behavioural attitude of conformity to the requirements of the abstract order. Loyalty to persons gradually metamorphoses into obedience to law. The traditional Christian natural law doctrine as developed by Thomas Aquinas—natural law is given by God, hence its commands are inherently right, it is eternally valid and immutable, and it is binding upon every human being due to its inherent rightfulness—is replaced with a new concept of law which has been posited by man. Its binding force is content independent, based upon social facts which are recognised in the society as duty engendering: the fact that an authority has enacted the law in a procedure which is recognised as authoritative—*auctoritas, non veritas facit legem*.

This means that obedience is owed to the mere existence of the law whose fundamental nature is a command. The correlative obedience of the ruled requires the attitude 'as if [they] had made the content of the command the maxim of their conduct for its very own sake'.[30] This is the rationale of positive law: it is binding because it is the law. Irrespective of its source—a dictator or a democratically elected representative body—positive law constitutes a vertical and unilateral relationship of command and obedience. Bodin is fully aware of the importance of this attribute of the law when he states that 'the very word "law" in Latin implies the command of him who has the sovereignty'.[31] He cautions his readers 'not to confuse a law and a contract. Law depends on him who has the sovereignty and he can obligate all his subjects (by a law) but cannot obligate himself', while a contract as a mutually binding scheme 'obligates the two parties reciprocally and one party cannot contravene it to the prejudice of the other and without the other's consent'.[32] Obviously, Bodin foreshadowed John Austin, the leading theorist of nineteenth-century

---

[28] C. B. Macpherson, *The Political Theory of Possessive Individualism: Hobbes to Locke* (Oxford: Oxford University Press, 1979).

[29] P. J. Taylor, 'The State as Container: Territoriality in the Modern World-System' (1994) 18 *Progress in Human Geography* 151–62.

[30] Max Weber, *Economy and Society: An Outline of Interpretive Sociology,* ed G. Roth and C. Wittich (Berkeley: University of California Press, 1978), 946.

[31] Bodin, above n 2, i., ch 8, at 11.

[32] Ibid 15.

legal positivism, who stated: 'Every law or rule … is a command … A command is distinguished from other significations of desires … by the power and the purpose of the party commanding to inflict an evil or pain in case the desire be disregarded.'[33]

Law-as-command bears a structural resemblance to the territory: it requires only a minimum of communication because its binding character is not dependent upon its content but exclusively upon the lawgiver's authoritative power. It is impersonal because its authoritative power is independent of any particular characteristics of the addressee and therefore can be imposed upon everyone within the territory. Its formal character as a command achieves the generalisation of authoritative power to the effect that sovereignty and territoriality complement and reinforce each other. One of its major benign effects was its neutrality vis-à-vis questions of religious rightness. In the emerging world of sectarian strife among the Christian denominations and the pluralisation of normative principles, the separation of the concept of law from any kind of concept of what is good and right was an important step towards the idea of individual religious and spiritual freedom. Moreover, in the long run the abstract character of the law generated the potentiality of associating individuals who were also alien to each other in non-religious aspects, as for instance in terms of social status, geographical origin, ethnic identity, or economic success. The reduction of the disembedded individuals' obligations to mere obedience to the sovereign's commands thus facilitated the emergence of social spaces in which diverse individuals could autonomously pursue their life plans.

IV. TERRITORIALITY AND CONSTITUTIONALISM

The concept of law is a significant exemplar of the deep political and cultural impact which the territorial character of the state has had on the character of Western societies, in particular on most continental European societies. During the nineteenth and well into the twentieth century, particular social formations, cultural practices, and national identities developed within the security of the territorial borders and left deep cultural imprints on the European nation states. Arguably, the idea of constitutionalism has been one of the furthest-reaching corollaries of statehood; it mirrors the idea of 'founding the order of society through the state'.[34]

Constitutions for the state or for society?

State-centred societies need other forms and institutions of self-determination than societies which are not integrated through the coercive means of sovereign power. Still, even if the constitution of a statist society appears to be merely focused upon the state, it is actually a constitution of the society. Take Article 16 of the French

---

[33] J. Austin, *The Province of Jurisprudence Determined* [1832/1863], ed D. Campbell and P. Thomas (Aldershot: Dartmouth, 1998), 11.

[34] A. Supiot, *Homo Juridicus: On the Anthropological Functions of the Law* (London: Verso, 2007), 52 et seq.

Declaration of the Rights of Man and Citizen, which is frequently invoked as the quintessential definition of a constitution. It stipulates that 'a society in which the guarantee of rights is not ensured, nor a separation of powers is worked out, has no Constitution'. Note that it is the *society*, not the state, whose order is secured by a constitution; after all, it is the liberty in the *society* which is the aim of the political association.[35]

This reference to the society rather than to the state was not an inadvertence in the drafters' editing. Rather, it articulated the particular French concept of constitutionalism, whose essence has remained effective up to the present. As Michel Troper has pointed out, Article 16 must not be understood as a model of the American principle of limited government.[36] In the framework of the French Declaration, the state is not a threat to the citizens' liberties but a device which enables the enjoyment of these very liberties. Liberty as defined in Article 4 of the Declaration—'Liberty consists in the freedom to do everything which injures no one else; hence the exercise of the natural rights of each man has no limits except those which assure to the other members of the society the enjoyment of the same rights. These limits can only be determined by law'—is a liberty of associates.

The limits of these liberties do not derive from some collective good, interest, or value; rather, they originate in the fabric of the society itself, namely in the equal liberty of all members of the society. The contention of Article 2 of the Declaration—'The aim of all political association is the preservation of the natural and imprescriptible rights of man'—postulates that the natural freedoms of the individuals be compatibilised under the conditions of political association, ie transformed into freedom *inter socios*. Thus, setting limits to natural freedom through law is tantamount to defining freedom *inter socios*.[37] It is by defining freedom *inter socios* that the basic institutional fact of the society is established—and this is an essential part of the constitution of the society. When the law defines the concrete content of a freedom it does not interfere with the natural freedoms of the individuals, but organises freedom as a mode of societal communication and interaction, that is, it enables their freedoms in the society. Thus, the 'guarantee of rights' in Article 16 of the Declaration is based upon two interdependent presuppositions: first, rights specify demarcated spheres of action *inter socios* (as opposed to boundless natural freedoms and rights); secondly, these demarcations which are by necessity definitions of rights 'can only be determined by law' (as opposed to decrees, contracts, local conventions, customary law, and the like). In one word, the 'guarantee of rights' in Article 16 of the Declaration is an essential element of the constitution of a society which determines its freedom through collective law-making acts of the nation.

---

[35] See Art 1: 'Men are born and *remain* free and equal in rights. *Social distinctions* may be founded only upon the general good' (emphasis supplied).

[36] M. Troper, 'Who Needs a Third Party Effect Doctrine? The Case of France', in A. Sajó and R. Uitz (eds), *The Constitution of Private Relations: Expanding Constitutionalism* (Utrecht: Eleven International Publishing, 2005), 115–28, at 121 et seq.

[37] Ibid 120.

Likewise, the separation of powers—the second essential of a constitution pursuant to Article 16 of the Declaration—can be understood as a case of the application of a broader principle of societal organisation—the division of labour—in the political sphere. Here the specialisation of functions and agencies enhances the government's capacity to cope with a growing number and diversity of problems with which the society is confronted.[38] Unsurprisingly, Tocqueville, the clear-sighted analyst of the inherent logic of the relationship of society and political institutions, observed that 'extreme centralization of government ultimately enervates society and thus, after a length of time, weakens the government itself'.[39] Here, too, Article 16 of the Declaration addresses an issue of the constitution which is only indirectly related to the state.

This does not mean that the state does not play a role in this conception of the constitution. The concepts of political association, of sovereignty, and of law clearly point to the contrary. The state is an essential element of the constitution of the society which is imbued, as it were, with statist elements. In fact, for modern Western societies the state has served as a container which—through its sovereign power in a particular territory—confined and shaped all social relations within its boundaries.[40] Yet the main purposes of a constitution—which is to reconcile 'the will of one person ... with the will of another in accordance with the universal law of freedom'[41] through legislation, adjudication, or defining and protecting individual rights—have to be performed also in societies which are not 'contained' through a sovereign state. Think of any kind of private association with a great number of voluntary members whose actions have to be coordinated in order for the association to pursue its objectives. A voluntary association also needs rules on the formation of its corporate will, the creation of its various organs and their respective functions, and the determination of the rights and duties of its members. These requirements are by no means occasioned by the coercive character of the territorially defined political association.

There is one open question, however, which has to do with the relationship of a constitution and the power of an association which it constitutionalises. Constitutions of non-statist associations generate, organise, channel, and distribute the collective (or corporate) power of the association which they put in order. This follows from their function to enable a collectivity to organise itself or, for that

---

[38] See S. Holmes, 'Precommitment and the Paradox of Democracy', in J. Elster and R. Slagstad (eds), *Constitutionalism and Democracy* (Cambridge: Cambridge University Press, 1988), 195–240, at 228 et seq; U. K. Preuss, *Constitutional Revolution: The Link between Constitutionalism and Progress* (Atlantic Highlands, NJ: Humanities Press, 1995), 112 et seq.

[39] Tocqueville, above n 6, ii. 300.

[40] A. Giddens, *The Nation-State and Violence* (Berkeley: University of California Press, 1987), 12 et seq; Taylor, above n 29; N. Brenner, *State/Space: A Reader* (Malden, Mass.: Blackwell, 2004).

[41] Immanuel Kant, 'The Metaphysics of Morals', in his *Political Writings* (Cambridge: Cambridge University Press, 1991), 133.

matter, its Self.[42] As I will argue below more elaborately, constitutions are instruments of collective self-determination. They do not limit a pre-existing unlimited power; rather, by transforming a multitude into a collective or corporate entity they create the collective power of that multitude in the first place. But does this apply to societies organised through the territorial container of the state? Here it seems that the sovereign power of the state exists prior to the association created by the constitution. After all, it is the sovereign state which creates the 'statist' society, ie a society moulded by the territorial character of the state. The Self of this society is always in danger of being absorbed by the sovereign state; consequently, the constitution can only serve to protect the endangered society against the sovereign power of the state. Or so the argument is made.

Sovereignty as the power of the polity

But this is not quite the case. True, sovereign power is a constitutive attribute of the state which permeates and shapes the society contained in its territory, but it does not exist prior to and independently of the society. This would presume a state which has supreme power also in the absence of a society. But what could the term supreme power then mean? Supreme power presupposes a plurality of potential or actual powers, with one supreme because it is superior to all others. Sovereign power is not merely relatively greater than the other powers to which it is superior; it is also qualitatively different. As Bodin unmistakably and succinctly defined: 'Sovereignty is the *absolute* and perpetual power of a *commonwealth*'[43]—sovereignty is absolute power because it is the power of the commonwealth (*République*). In other words, the power which combines, centralises, and embodies the capabilities of the collectivity as such is absolute: this is the meaning of sovereignty.

Sovereignty is not defined as the greatest quantity of power in proportion to other power holders; rather, its quality of embodying the power of the polity as a distinct collective entity defines it. Bodin emphasises this attribute of sovereignty when he specifies that the law is not just a command of the sovereign, but that it 'is the command of the sovereign *affecting all the subjects in general*, or dealing with *general interests*'; when he refers, as usual, to the constitution and the politics of the ancient Romans and their legislation he stresses the point that the laws were commands of 'the entire people', and that 'the nobility and the Senate as a whole, and each one of the people taken individually, should be bound' by them.[44] In other words, the superiority of sovereign power over the power of the particular forces within the polity originates in its attribution to the whole of the society. Those forces are not simply less powerful than the sovereign, which is not necessarily the case. They are

---

[42] H. Lindahl, 'Constituent Power and Reflexive Identity: Towards an Ontology of Collective Selfhood', in M. Loughlin and N. Walker (eds), *The Paradox of Constitutionalism: Constituent Power and Constitutional Form* (Oxford: Oxford University Press, 2007), 9–24, at 14 et seq.

[43] Bodin, above n 2, at 1 (emphases supplied).

[44] Ibid 51.

the sovereign's subjects, and this unique status of superiority justifies Bodin's characterisation as 'absolute'. Consequently, states with relatively small power resources can be sovereign if they are able to embody the whole of the society. To paraphrase Poggi's statement, one can say that the state does not have power but is a power (as is the common saying in international relations).

Note that there is a circular and mutually reinforcing relationship between sovereign power and the quality of a commonwealth: not only is a power absolute, ie sovereign because it is the power of a commonwealth, but at the same time an entity is a commonwealth because it has absolute power, or, for that matter, because it is a power. The turn from having power to being a power constitutes a polity. This step is not contingent upon the increase of the quantity of power in the hands of any individual who happens to outrival all other power holders within a collectivity. It depends upon an individual's or a group's capacity to represent the whole of the collectivity (which, of course, presupposes a certain amount of material power resources from the elites which represent this collectivity).

When, in the dusk of European absolutism, the state subjects' belief in the capacity of the monarchs to represent the whole of the society declined, their power faded although for a considerable period their tangible power resources remained. At the end of the eighteenth century, the French monarchy (and most of the absolutist regimes in Europe) had depleted their moral and political capital which had allowed them to embody the whole of the polity for some 200 years. We may assume that the discrepancy between the function of the absolutist princes to represent the whole of the polity—which soon after became called the nation—and the frequently debauched lifestyle of the princes and their courts contributed to their eventual delegitimisation. After all, representing the polity requires the embodiment of such common values as dignity, honour, and self-respect, which can only be credibly achieved by characters who themselves command respect. Nevertheless, the main reason was their failure to facilitate the creation of institutions through which new and resourceful social forces could represent the whole of the polity.

Obviously, the institution which made that possible was the constitution. The constitution—not accidentally an 'object of all longing' at the end of the eighteenth century both in Continental Europe and in the United States[45]—embodied the claim that the sovereign power of the state was no longer to be attributed to dynastic families but to 'the people'. What at a first glance seems to represent no more than a mere replacement of one holder of the state's sovereign power with another—the prince with the people—in fact amounted to a genuine revolution which profoundly changed the concept of the polity.

The reason is that power in general, and political power in particular, is not a thing which can be transferred from one owner or holder to another. Power designates a social relationship, and among the varieties of social power political power is characterised by what Max Weber called 'domination by virtue of authority' which he defined as the 'authoritarian power of command' of a ruler over the ruled. In

---

[45] Preuss, above n 38, 25 et seq.

essence, rule is a relationship of command and obedience.[46] Whilst the sovereign power of the absolutist prince over his subjects clearly is a variety of domination of a ruler over the ruled, this pattern obviously does not apply when sovereign power is claimed for the people (as a multitude). In this case, ruler and ruled are (or at least appear to be) identical, and domination can no longer be defined in terms of the polarity of rulers and ruled. Rather, it has become the problem of an appropriate self-organisation of the people.

In order to acquire sovereign power, the multitude had to become a collective entity which embodied the unity of the multitude; at the same time, this collective entity could not come into being as long as sovereign power had not been arrogated by the multitude. The many atomised individuals are powerless, as they lack the resources to transform themselves into an organised collectivity. The circular causation which we observed with respect to the relationship between sovereignty and commonwealth in the framework of Bodin's theory resurfaces in the relation between sovereignty and people. They are interdependent in that the processes of collective self-organisation and the arrogation of sovereign power mutually constitute each other. In fact, the formation of a corporate body which includes all members of the society is tantamount to the people's acquiring sovereign power. As the only purpose of uniting the multitude in one body is the goal of creating their capacity to act collectively and, consequently, to subject the individuals to the will of the collectivity, the achievement of corporate unity means the achievement of the capacity and authority to impose the collective will on all individuals. This is nothing other than Bodin's concept of absolute power which he labelled sovereignty.

V. CONSTITUTIONS CONNECT SOVEREIGNTY WITH THE PEOPLE AND LOOSEN ITS LINK TO TERRITORY

There is an obvious analogy to the relationship between territory and sovereignty which I indicated above: just as the territorialisation of the French kingdom, fragmented by particularist feudal forces, meant the establishment of the monarchy's sovereignty, so was the unification of the individualised multitude to one collective body identical with the constitution of the people's sovereignty. At the same time there is a profound difference between the concept of sovereignty attached to territoriality and sovereignty embodied in the corporate unity of the people. In both cases, sovereignty means absolute power in the sense established by Bodin. But whilst absolute power as a defining element of territoriality means comprehensive and exclusive control of all social interactions within the territory, including all transborder activities, absolute power as a defining element of the corporate unity of the people means the multitude's capacity of self-rule.

The transition from the territorially defined concept of sovereignty to popular sovereignty entails a change in the significance of the territory. For the former, the

---

[46] Weber, above n 30, 941–8, especially at 943, 946.

territory is essential for the very existence of the polity—the state—as it defines not only the mode of domination but also the identity of the polity itself. In order to preserve the existence of the polity, it is necessary to maintain the coherence and continuity of a territory. For this, the ruler needs to have the monopoly of coercive power, including the control of the means of extraction and of violence in the hands of a power elite. This is the pattern of the absolutist state.[47] Its functioning is based upon the status of its subjects as a passive and subaltern mass unable to govern itself.

For the latter—the unity of the multitude—the territory is still of great importance, as it continues to serve as a container which defines the boundaries of who belongs to the multitude and hence who qualifies as belonging to the people. But it is a defining element of the multitude, not of 'the people'; the transformation of the multitude into 'the people' is due to forces which have nothing to do with the territory and the means of its ruler to control it. Sovereignty of the people means their collective capacity to rule themselves, which means to be obligated only by laws which they have given to themselves.

Basically, there are two methods to qualify a multitude to rule itself: the 'sovereigntist' and the 'constitutionalist' approaches. I call 'sovereigntist' a conception of self-rule which is understood as collective self-determination requiring no more and no less than the institutionalised absolute power of the collectivity over its constituent parts—unity and sovereignty of the people are identical. Acts of rule consist of the willpower of the collectivity. 'Constitutionalist' is a notion of self-rule according to which the will of the united body is embodied in a system of rules, institutions, and procedures which determine the principles of how a free society wants to be ordered. Here, too, the multitude is transformed into 'the people'; but 'the people' do not rule by joining the individual wills to one collective will but by the application of those rules to the relevant cases through the competent institutions. The effectiveness of this sovereignty, embodied in the constitution, is not dependent upon the actuality of a collective will but upon the functioning of the constitutional institutions.

For Rousseau, the forefather of the 'sovereigntists', the constitutional mediation of sovereignty was tantamount to the dissolution of the unified body of the people and, consequently, of its sovereignty. He thought that 'it would be against the very nature of a political body for the sovereign to set over itself a law which it could not infringe'.[48] He was right to realise that constitutions serve the function to set limits to the powers of governments, but he was wrong to assume that a constitution binds the sovereign and hence is doomed to undermine sovereignty

---

[47] See among the rich literature C. Tilly, 'Reflections on the History of European State-Making', in Tilly (ed), *The Formation of National States in Western Europe* (Princeton, NJ: Princeton University Press, 1975), 3–83; C. Tilly, *Coercion, Capital, and European States, AD 990-1990* (Cambridge, Mass.: Blackwell, 1990); Giddens, above n 40; M. Mann, *The Sources of Social Power*, i: *A History of Power from the Beginning to A.D. 1760* (Cambridge: Cambridge University Press, 1986); T. Ertman, *Birth of the Leviathan: Building States and Regimes in Medieval and Early Modern Europe* (Cambridge: Cambridge University Press, 1997).

[48] Rousseau, *The Social Contract*, i., ch 7.

altogether. A constitution 'should pattern a political system'[49] in the first place, not limit any kind of power which allegedly exists prior to the constitution. Otherwise, the idea of constitutionalism would have been valid also as a means of limiting the power of the absolutist princes. This, however, was not the case; nowhere did constitutions exist which were limited to the function of imposing restrains upon autocratic rulers.[50] Ever since the emergence of the modern concept of constitutionalism, constitutions were inseparably connected with the idea of popular sovereignty, ie with the elimination of the sovereign power of the absolutist princes and the establishment of the absolute power of the people by means of a government. The creation of constitutions was identical with the creation of the constituent power of the people. This amounted to the transition from sovereignty attached to territory to sovereignty attributed to the people. More precisely, it was the changeover from comprehensive and exclusive control of the 'negative community'[51] to a system of popular self-rule.

This change has far-reaching consequences for our understanding of constitutions. It means that the idea of the constitution is not intrinsically bound to the concept of the territorially bounded state. The modern constitutions which, since the end of the seventeenth (England) and the eighteenth centuries (France and the other monarchies of the European continent), replaced the absolutist systems of domination based upon the territorial character of the modern state, established an alternative mode of rule. They disconnected the idea of sovereignty from the control over a territory and connected it with the idea of collective self-rule of a multitude. This does not mean that the modern concept of constitution has completely severed its link to the territory; until the present day, constitutions have been established to enable the self-rule of multitudes contained in and by state territories. But, as mentioned, the factor which affects the metamorphosis of a multitude into a nation or a people—the corporate unity of the multitude—is not the control over the coherence and continuity of the territory, but the constituent power of the people themselves.

This developmental step of loosening the connection of sovereignty with the territory to attaching it to the people has been the great achievement of the democratic revolutions at the end of the eighteenth century. The essential embodiment

---

[49] W. F. Murphy, 'Constitutions, Constitutionalism, and Democracy', in D. Greenberg et al (eds), *Constitutionalism and Democracy: Transitions in the Contemporary World* (New York: Oxford University Press, 1993), 3–25, at 7.

[50] In Germany, where in the nineteenth century attempts were made to use the concept of the constitution as an instrument of power sharing between the absolutist princes and representatives of the rising bourgeois class, these efforts ultimately failed (see the analysis of Carl Schmitt, *Constitutional Theory* [1928] (Durham, NC: Duke University Press, 2008), 331 et seq; E.-W. Böckenförde, 'Die verfassunggebende Gewalt des Volkes: Ein Grenzbegriff des Verfassungsrechts', in Böckenförde, *Staat, Verfassung, Demokratie: Studien zur Verfassungstheorie und zum Verfassungsrecht* (Frankfurt am Main: Suhrkamp, 1998), 90–112.

[51] F. Kratochwil, 'Of Systems, Boundaries and Territoriality: An Inquiry into the Formation of the State System' (1986) 39 *World Politics* 27–52, at 33.

is the nation state, ie the people that rules itself in and through the state. In the last two decades this concept of sovereignty has come under stress through phenomena which threaten to undermine the capacity of a state-contained multitude to rule themselves, ie to control the main conditions of their lives. The container is now leaking.[52] As is now commonplace, the porosity of state boundaries and the extensity and intensity of trans-border interactions and movements of capital, people, goods, services, information, symbols, and ideas have generated transnational social patterns and institutions which stretch the spatial dimension of social relations across state borders; in many respects it has become global.[53] The inside/outside distinction of what is usually called the Westphalian system—the coexistence of 'territorially disjoint, mutually exclusive, functionally similar, sovereign states'[54]—is, at least in the world of the Organisation for Economic Co-operation and Development, blurring. The discrepancy between the territorially defined range of the states' sovereign power and their effective influence upon the living conditions of their populace reveals a significant decrease in their capacity to shape and to control the society. The decision-making power is no longer exclusively distributed along the lines of state borders which are no longer 'meaningful dividers between social, economic, and cultural systems'.[55]

What has been evolving instead are patterns of decentralised social regulation in which law—both national and international—originates from a plurality of sources, among which the sovereign state remains a vital actor; but by and large it has lost its traditional structural superiority over the social world and must learn to communicate with its agents in modes of cooperation and sharing resources and influence. It has become a mere component of a broad variety of legal authors, including, aside from states and international organisations, a growing number of national and transnational civil society actors, such as transnational chambers of commerce, economic interest groups, trade unions, environmental and human rights groups, law firms, churches, sports associations, university and other academic associations and networks, which create legal and para-legal rules for different spatial levels, functionally defined social spheres, and specific categories of individuals. They coexist, partly overlap, compete and conflict, and form a non-hierarchical pattern of transborder regulation in which no single ruler can be identified and held responsible for the quality of the social order.

The European Union (EU) is an obvious case in point. Due to the direct effect upon the citizens of the member states, EU law and the national law of the

---

[52] See Taylor, above n 29, 157 et seq.

[53] D. Held et al, *Global Transformations: Politics, Economics and Culture* (Cambridge: Polity Press, 2000), 14–15.

[54] J. G. Ruggie, 'Territoriality and beyond: Problematizing Modernity in International Relations' (1993) 47 *International Organization* 139–74, at 151.

[55] A. B. Murphy, 'The Sovereign State System as Political-Territorial Ideal: Historical and Contemporary Considerations', in T. J. Biersteker and C. Weber (eds), *State Sovereignty as a Social Construct* (Cambridge: Cambridge University Press, 1996), 81–120, at 90.

member states coexist side by side. Although the former claims primacy over the latter, this does not mean that the EU has sovereign power over the domestic sphere of its member states; nor is the relationship of EU law and national law hierarchical. The primacy of EU law does not refer to the validity of the involved legal norms (*Geltungsvorrang*), but merely to their application when conflicting EU and national legal rules exist for the same facts of a case (*Anwendungsvorrang*). This, then, is a matter of interpretation through courts with different, potentially overlapping jurisdictions which have to be adjusted to each other in a non-hierarchical institutional setting.

These phenomena give rise to the question of whether we are entering a third historical phase of the concept of sovereignty—the first being characterised by exclusive territorial control, the second by collective self-rule of a multitude through a constitution which constitutes them as a 'We the people', and the third by the reconceptualisation of the idea of collective self-rule as the capacity of a collective to interact with other communities and share with them the control of their life conditions on a global scale irrespective of territorial boundaries. If this were the case, the traditional concept of the constitution—the institutional device which constitutes a territory-bound multitude as a political body capable of self-rule—would no longer fit the requirements of a political universe in which state borders have lost much of their structural importance. Would such a developmental step render the concept of constitution meaningless?

Before having a closer look at the inherent logic of constitutions a brief comparative remark about the three conceptions of sovereignty seem appropriate. Note that the first and the second developmental forms of sovereignty have an inherently coercive character. This is obvious for the control of the territory. With respect to the concept of collective self-rule it follows from the principle of the superiority of the collective will over the constituent members of the multitude; the option of a merely voluntary compliance would undermine the generality of the authority of the collective will and hence destroy it altogether. Even Rousseau, who claimed that the individuals' participation in the formation of the general will become free because they share in the sovereign power, admitted that those who refuse to obey the general will must be 'forced to be free',[56] which ultimately means: coerced. By contrast, the third developmental model of sovereignty is not intrinsically connected with coercion. As it is based on the capacity to interact and to share responsibilities it needs other instruments for the achievement of common goals. Horizontal modes of amalgamating discrete agents seem to be more promising. Here too the institutional construction of the EU can serve as a relevant example. It gives rise to a more detailed view on the constitutive character of constitutions.

---

[56] Rousseau, above n 48.

VI. THE CONSTITUTIVE ROLE OF CONSTITUTIONS

If a constitution 'is that which results from an effort to constitute',[57] how can a constitution transform a multitude into one unified body, 'the people' or 'the nation'? Murphy, who discussed this question, denied this possibility. He argues that 'to agree in their collective name to a political covenant, individuals must have already some meaningful corporate identity *as a people*' and concludes that 'the notion of constitution as covenant must mean it formalizes or solidifies rather than invents an entity'.[58] Indeed, this conceptual enigma exists if we conceive of individuals as socially isolated atomised beings in a state of nature as hypothesised in Hobbes's construction of the social contract. But this is not what constitutions are all about. They are not supposed to be social contracts; rather, they are rules through which individuals who are thoroughly familiar with social relations and social facts create a new social reality for themselves by constituting themselves as a body which commits them permanently to common ventures. Constitutions are not restricted to merely forming 'a more perfect union', as the preamble of the US constitution declares; rather, they are institutional devices which constitute a union among discrete natural or corporate individuals who live in a society.

In fact, constitutions are constitutive norms in that they create an institutional reality in which hitherto purely physical facts are transformed into institutional facts and gain a specific meaning through this metamorphosis. They are important elements of what the philosopher John Searle called the construction of social reality. Such a metamorphosis occurs when a plurality of people agree that a physical fact shall have a particular meaning and count as a normatively relevant fact. Take one of Searle's examples: 'Bills issued by the Bureau of Engraving and Printing ... count as money ... in the United States.'[59] An empirical fact—the issuance of pieces of paper—acquires a particular social significance in that it is transformed into an institutional fact which consists in the recognition of this fact as constituting money. Likewise, the rule 'a piece of land recorded in a special register counts as private property' is a constitutive norm which does not refer to an antecedent social reality but creates an institutional reality in the first place. Constitutive norms are different from regulative norms which do not create possibilities of action but rather regulate an antecedently existing activity by establishing dictates, prohibitions, permissions, etc.[60]

---

[57] S. L. Elkin, 'Constitutionalism: Old and New', in S. L. Elkin and
K. E. Soltan (eds), *A New Constitutionalism: Designing Political Institutions for a Good Society* (Chicago, Ill.: University of Chicago Press, 1993), 20–37, at 32.

[58] Murphy, above n 49, at 9.

[59] J. R. Searle, *The Construction of Social Reality* (New York: Free Press, 1995), 28, 43 et seq.

[60] Ibid 27 et seq; see also G. Boella and L. van der Torre, 'Regulative and Constitutive Norms in Normative Multiagent Systems' in *Proceedings of 9th International Conference on the Principles of Knowledge Representation and Reasoning* (Menlo Park, Calif., 2004), 255–65. This distinction between constitutive and regulative norms was at the beginning of the twentieth century developed, if in a different language, by Georg Jellinek, *System der subjektiven*

Obviously constitutive norms presuppose a plurality of agents who agree that some particular fact 'counts as' an institutional fact. The sentence of Article 78 of the German Basic Law: 'A bill adopted by the Bundestag shall become law if the Bundesrat consents to it' constitutes the institution of the federal law, referring to a plurality of addressees who share the understanding of what the concept 'law' means. With respect to constitutions and constitutionalism we should distinguish three levels of meaning: (1) constitutive norms create institutional facts; (2) at the same time they create and corroborate the interactive normative system in which those facts have a particular meaning, whereby the term 'interactive normative system' is just a more neutral expression for the more traditional, but frequently normatively overloaded phrase 'legal community'; (3) moreover, they create the norms which specify the conditions under which constitutive norms can be created, abolished, or altered. They belong to the category of secondary rules of H. L. A. Hart's concept of law: rules of recognition, change, and adjudication.[61] Rules about making, unmaking, and changing rules exhibit the capacity of reflexivity of the interactive normative system. Thus, it is an inherently dynamic system.

This sounds trivial as we normally know the structure of a modern constitution. We also know that, for instance, an order which any assembly may proclaim as binding upon everybody is not a law but a mere utterance of an opinion without authority, even if these people have power and can force us to comply with that order. We 'do not just accept that somebody has power, but we accept that they have power in virtue of their institutional status'[62] which has been created through constitutive rules beforehand. Even the constituent power of the people which constitutional theory constructs as the source of the constitution is by no means merely an empirical fact; rather, it is a power which exists only by virtue of being constructed as the ultimate author of the constitution, that is, as an institutional phenomenon. Hence, the act of constitution making must be understood as an act of 'collective self-attribution' through which a multitude defines 'an interest that is held to be common' to all members of that multitude and thereby constitute themselves as a political community.[63] Paradoxically this act of self-constitution of an unconstituted multitude can only occur 'if individuals retroactively identify themselves as the members of a polity in constituent action by exercising the powers granted to them by a constitution'.[64]

öffentlichen Rechte [1905] (Darmstadt: Wissenschaftliche Buchgesellschaft, 1963). Jellinek made the distinction between norms which create a 'Können' [can] which equate to constitutive norms and 'Dürfen' [may] which equate to regulative norms.

[61] H. L. A. Hart, *The Concept of Law* (Oxford: Clarendon Press, 1961), 91 et seq.

[62] J. R. Searle, 'Social Ontology: Some Basic Principles' (2006) 6 *Anthropological Theory* 12–29, at 18.

[63] Lindahl, above n 42, at 19; see also U. K. Preuss, 'The Exercise of Constituent Power in Central and Eastern Europe', in Loughlin and Walker (eds), above n 42, 211–28, at 213 et seq.

[64] Lindahl, above n 42, at 19.

This paradox can be explained by the inherent logic of our social world which presupposes that we interact on the basis of a construction of reality. It is not only the case that we accept someone's power only by virtue of its institutional character. Our social actions are contingent upon the capacity of institutional facts and statuses to generate obligations, rights, responsibilities, and authorisations and thereby to expand the reach of human actions.[65] For instance, civil laws establish powers of individuals, eg the power to conclude a contract or to acquire property; contracts and property in their turn entail rights, duties, responsibilities, and powers of further individuals and give rise to new transactions which involve new agents. A familiar example is the legal creature of a corporation which has a distinct legal personality and thus allows the collection and investment of capital—which means new social relations—in an amount which otherwise would not be available. In a word, rules which create hitherto unknown or unavailable opportunities for social actions are constitutive rules.

Not all constitutive rules are constitutions, but all constitutions are constitutive rules plus some additional attributes. Grimm, who defines constitutions as 'deriving from the people and directed at the State power', affirms that they do not 'modify rule but establish it, not particularly but universally, not here and there, but comprehensively'[66] and thus acknowledges their constitutive character. While I share this analysis, I disagree with the underlying premiss that constitutions must originate from the constituent power of a people and that they are directed at binding state power.

True, the territorial character of the state has been an essential element of demarcating the boundaries of the multitude who transform themselves into the corporate entity of the people; but this transformation is directed at collective self-rule which, admittedly, occurred within the territorial boundaries of the state. Yet the primary function of the constitution—to establish a regime of collective self-rule by constituting 'We the people'—can be disconnected from the territory without destroying the meaning of the constitution. Note that the 'We' which is generated in and through the process of constitution making is the first-person plural, ie a collective singular. This means that the many have the self-referential qualities and capacities of a single entity. The multitude of individuals who form the 'We' of a people or a nation are able to recognise themselves as a body that is able to act, to deliberate, and to understand itself *as* an artificial body which is able to act upon itself. More precisely, the many are able to act *as if* they were *one entity*. This is what enables them to rule themselves—the 'We' is the result of the self-empowerment of a multitude to a reflexive collective actor. It is this reflexive character of the 'We' which is created through the constitution.[67]

---

[65] Searle, above n 62, at 18.

[66] Grimm, above n 14, at 287.

[67] See the remark of Grimm and his reference to Luhmann with respect to the reflexive character of constitutional law, ibid at 286; Lindahl, above n 42, at 15 et seq.

In practical terms that means that constitutions establish a political system which provides an institutional space in which the affairs of a multitude as such become the matter of collective deliberation and action and are separated from the spheres of its individual members. They determine the elements of collective will formation, the conditions under which the collective has supremacy over the individuals' spheres and the procedures through which individual obligations are created and their enforcement guaranteed. Moreover, they establish rules of accountability of those who act on behalf of the collective and finally stipulate rules about changing the rules of the constitution.

This rough definition of constitutions fits well together with constitutions of states. But they may well cover political formations which, unlike nations or peoples, do not incorporate territorially defined multitudes. When I speak of political formations I mean those entities which provide the common security and welfare of a group—purposes which require a thorough control of the group and which in the past have been performed most effectively and efficiently by states.[68] Since states have no longer the monopoly in fulfilling these functions, a modern-day definition of a constitution as the fundamental source of authority must include both states and new political formations not based upon territoriality. For the present I submit that, whenever a multitude whose members are demarcated against the outside world establish a regime through which they pursue the goals of common defence and/or common welfare and establish rules about the formation of a common will which are able to generate obligations and responsibilities for the individual members this multitude has constituted itself as a distinct entity shaped by a constitution.

On this view constitutions are norms which create institutional facts that are meaningful for the social actions and interactions of natural or artificial individuals and allow them to act commonly in a frame of interdependence. As a result, a subjectless process of establishing rules of shared responsibility may arise. This interactive process may be able to produce not a collective will, but commonly shared rules and principles which are binding upon the constituent parts not because they are imposed on them, but because they are recognised by them. The rules pursuant to which this process takes course may at times be implemented by some forms of coercion—eg by rendering non-compliance costly—but other than in the framework of traditional, state-centred constitutionalism coercion is not an essential element.

Thus, although this institutionalised scheme of horizontal and non-coercive social coordination and cooperation has little if any connection with the traditional idea of constitutionalising a multitude of socially disembedded, free, and autonomous individuals in order to enable them to form a collective, it seems reasonable to include it in the concept of the constitution. The reason is not to exploit the aura of the term constitution; rather, it is the objective to transfer the intellectual and moral power which created the aura of the constitution in the first place into spheres where the essential promises of constitutions—namely to establish systems of collective action

[68] See Murray Forsyth, *Unions of States: The Theory and Practice of Confederation* (New York: Leicester University Press, 1981), 160 et seq.

based on principles of equal participation, accountability, and rule of law—are still largely lacking. The international community is an obvious case in point.

VI. CONCLUDING REMARKS: THE INTERNATIONAL COMMUNITY AS A CONSTITUTIONALISED ACTOR?

In fact, some recent developments in international law can be read and have rightly been read by several scholars as indicators of a process of international constitutionalisation.[69] Let me briefly mention four of them.[70]

First, the existence of legal norms, which stipulate obligations of states not only or not primarily towards other states but towards the international community as such, indicates a new status of states, namely their membership status in the international community.[71] This status change entails relationships of interdependence and mutual responsibility alien to the traditional understanding of the states' sovereignty. In the doctrine of international law the relevant obligations are called 'obligations *erga omnes*'.[72]

Secondly, closely related to *erga omnes* rules is the corpus of international legal rules which are considered as so fundamental that they cannot be derogated by the states. They are peremptory norms or *ius cogens*.[73] Peremptory rules are as much binding upon the states without or even against their will[74] as norms *erga omnes*. Both *erga omnes* norms and *ius cogens* presuppose and refer to a sphere of common matters of mankind as embodied in the international community; they are the sources of obligations and responsibilities of states and have a different normative status than rules regulating interstate relations.

---

[69] See the accounts of B. Fassbender, 'We the Peoples of the United Nations: Constituent Power and Constitutional Form in International Law', in Loughlin and Walker (eds), above n 42, 269–90; for a more sceptical view, see Krisch in this volume.

[70] In what follows I largely refer to parts of my previous article, Preuss, above n 15, at 35 et seq.

[71] See the account of B. Fassbender, 'The Meaning of International Constitutional Law', in R. S. J. Macdonald and D. M. Johnston (eds), *Towards World Constitutionalism: Issues in the Legal Ordering of the World Community* (Leiden: Martinus Nijhoff Publishers, 2005), 837–51; B. Simma, 'From Bilateralism to Community Interest in International Law' (1994) 250 *Recueil des Cours de l'Académie de Droit International* 217–384, at 285 et seq; C. Tomuschat, 'International Law: Ensuring the Survival of Mankind on the Eve of a New Century' (1999) 281 *Recueil des Cours de l'Académie de Droit International* 9–438, at 72 et seq.

[72] *Barcelona Traction, Light and Power Company, Limited*, 1970 ICJ (5 February 1970), at 3, ¶ 33.

[73] See Art 53 of the Vienna Convention on the Law of Treaties which defines a peremptory norm as 'a norm accepted and recognized by the international community of States as a whole as a norm from which no derogation is permitted and which can be modified only by a subsequent norm of general international law having the same character'.

[74] C. Tomuschat, 'Obligations Arising for States without or against their Will' (1993) 241 *Recueil des Cours de l'Académie de Droit International* 195–374.

Thirdly, there are profound changes in international law-making. Doubtless the main traditional sources of international law—international treaties and international customary law—still predominate. They guarantee that states can only be bound by obligations to which they have given their consent. Yet this principle has become quite hole-riddled[75] without, however, being superseded by mechanisms of a unilateral creation of obligations through a centralised law-giving authority characteristic of the municipal law of the states.[76] The main indicator is the surfacing of the category of world order treaties, a hybrid of treaty and law. World order treaties are multilateral international treaties with a 'quasi-universal membership', the UN Charter being the obvious primary example,[77] although many others are hardly less important, as for instance the international human rights covenants or the UN Convention on the Law of the Sea. The more comprehensive a multilateral treaty is, the more costly it is for a state to stay aside, an option which only few great powers or outlaw states can afford for a certain period of time. So world order treaties represent widely or even universally shared interests and values and can be regarded as embodying the collective will of mankind. In other words, an institutional mechanism of international law-making is emerging which meets the above criterion of a modern-day concept of a constitution, namely the cooperative and horizontal mode of creating collectively binding obligations.

Fourthly and finally, next to international legislation the institution of an independent compulsory judiciary would be a major step towards the constitutionalisation of the international community. More than sixty years ago Kelsen contended that international peace and security could only be maintained efficiently by 'the establishment of an international community whose main organ is an international court endowed with compulsory jurisdiction'.[78] Although until our times a compulsory international judiciary has not yet been established, there are clear tendencies which point in that direction. In the field of international crimes the Statute of Rome, a multilateral treaty concluded on 17 July 1998 and effective since 1 July 2002 has established an International Criminal Court and laid down the substantive and procedural rules for the exercise of its 'jurisdiction over persons for the most serious crimes of concern to the international community as a whole'.[79] With 110 countries (as of 21 July 2009) having become States Parties to the Statute it can be seen as a world order treaty in the above sense, although some important countries like, for instance, the USA, China, India, and most countries of the Middle East have so far failed to join

---

[75] Ibid, at 248 et seq.

[76] See C. Tomuschat, 'Multilateralism in the Age of US Hegemony', in Macdonald and Johnston (eds), above n 71, 31–75, at 43.

[77] Tomuschat, above n 74, at 248 et seq; A. Peters, 'Global Constitutionalism in a Nutshell', in K. Dicke et al (eds), *Weltinnenrecht: Liber Amicorum Jost Delbrück* (Berlin: Duncker & Humblot, 2005), 535–50.

[78] H. Kelsen, 'The Principle of Sovereign Equality of States as a Basis for International Organization' (1944) 53 *Yale Law Journal* 207–20, at 214.

[79] Arts 3 and 5.

the treaty.[80] Still, the recognition of 'crimes of international concern' and the estab-lishment of a permanent international criminal court—prefigured after the Second World War in the Tribunals of Nuremberg and Tokyo against the main war crimi-nals of Germany and Japan—is in itself a major step towards the constitution of the international community as an entity which is able to establish rules which secure basic principles of global responsibility.

As a preliminary conclusion I submit that the idea of constitutionalism, although in its historical origin inherently tied to the structure of the modern sovereign state, remains a viable concept for modes of social organisation which are not intrinsically based on the use of the coercive means of the state. Both the EU and the inter-national community are examples to that effect. Constitutions can create schemes of cooperation across physical, social, and cultural boundaries because they do not presuppose shared values or shared understandings of social practices. They may produce a common cognitive and normative horizon in that they create institutional facts which generate new possibilities of action among aliens who otherwise would be relegated to largely ineffective forms of purely voluntary cooperation. Between the extremes of the constitution of the vertical integration through coercive state power and the mere contractualism of voluntary social coordination and coopera-tion, new modes of non-coercive, though nevertheless obligatory cooperation, both in and beyond the boundaries of the state, are evolving which are susceptible to being ordered by constitutions.

---

[80] See the website of the ICC <http://www.icc-cpi.int/Menus/ASP/states+parties/> (accessed 10 November 2009).

3

What is Constitutionalisation?

Martin Loughlin

I. INTRODUCTION

A new term has recently entered the vocabulary of politics: constitutionalisation. It stands as an expression of a set of processes that are now having a significant impact on decision making at all levels of government—local, regional, national, transnational, international. Constitutionalisation involves the attempt to subject all governmental action within a designated field to the structures, processes, principles, and values of a 'constitution'. Although this phenomenon is having an impact across government, its prominence today is mainly attributable to the realisation that the activity of governing is increasingly being exercised through transnational or international arrangements that are not easily susceptible to the controls of national constitutions. Constitutionalisation is the term used for the attempt to subject the exercise of all types of public power, whatever the medium of its exercise, to the discipline of constitutional procedures and norms.

In this chapter, I aim to specify the character of this phenomenon, offer an account of its dynamic, and raise some questions about the processes it engenders. Constitutionalisation is, I believe, best understood by reference to the related concepts of constitution and constitutionalism. I therefore begin by considering the eighteenth-century movements that gave rise to the modern idea of a constitution and its associated political theory, that of constitutionalism. By situating constitutionalisation in this context, I aim to offer a perspective that will help us to reach a judgment on the question of whether this emerging phenomenon of constitutionalisation signals the global triumph of constitutionalism, its demise, or its transmutation.

II. CONSTITUTIONS

The concept of the constitution today generally refers to a formal contract drafted in the name of 'the people' for the purpose of establishing and controlling the powers of the governing institutions of the state. This concept came to be delineated only in the late eighteenth century and mainly as a consequence of the American and French Revolutions. This modern idea of the constitution results from a basic shift that took place in conceiving the relationship between government and people: rejecting traditional orderings based on status and hierarchy, it expressed the conviction that government, being an office established for the benefit of the people, must be based on their consent.

This modern concept emerged alongside social contract theories that were circulating in Western political thought during that critical period. Shaped by the philosophy of the Enlightenment, such theories imagined a situation in which somehow the people would come together to reject their traditional constitutions, the products of 'accident and force', and would deliberate and devise a new framework of government from 'reflection and choice'.[1] The new type of constitution that results takes the form of a written document establishing the main institutions of government, enumerating their powers, and specifying the norms that would regulate their relations.

Since the late eighteenth century, many states across the world have adopted modern constitutions. These written constitutions were generally devised at critical moments in their history, often with the aim of protecting the people from regimes of absolute, authoritarian, or arbitrary rule that had preceded them. Their adoption marked the attempt to open a new chapter in the nation's political development. The constitution often signalled the intention to institute a republican scheme of government, with the constitution performing the function of establishing a framework of limited, accountable, and responsive government. Constitutions were therefore linked to the promotion of a particular theory of government: based on contract, enumeration of powers, institutionalisation of checks over the exercise of powers, and protection of the individual's basic rights, they were founded on a theory of limited government. This is the theory of constitutionalism. It has exerted such an impact on the drafting of written constitutions since the late eighteenth century that the theory has almost become synonymous with the modern concept of the constitution itself.

Before discussing constitutionalism, however, I must briefly consider three issues relating to modern constitutions: how they differ from the older idea of the constitution, their key characteristics, and the basic changes in social life that have tended to accompany the establishment of modern constitutional arrangements.

Constitutions, ancient and modern

The ancient sense of the constitution treats the state as an organic entity. Just as the body has a constitution, so too does the body politic. Drawing on this metaphor, the ancient idea of the constitution expressed the health and strength of the nation, and the constitution evolved as the nation itself increased in vitality. This was the meaning Burke drew on when he argued, against French revolutionary developments, that 'the state ought not to be considered as nothing better than a partnership agreement in a trade of pepper and coffee, calico, or tobacco, or some other such low

---

[1] James Madison, Alexander Hamilton, and John Jay, *The Federalist Papers* [1788], ed I. Kramnick (London: Penguin, 1987), 87.

concern'.[2] A constitution must be revered precisely because 'it is not a partnership in things subservient only to the gross animal existence of a temporary and perishable nature'. It has evolved through the life of a nation and 'becomes a partnership not only between those who are living, but between those who are living, those who are dead, and those who are to be born'.[3]

In this ancient sense, the constitution expressed a political way of being. Understood as such, constitutions can no more be made than language is made: like language, constitutions evolve from the way of life of certain groups that come to conceive of themselves as 'a people' or 'nation'. There may come moments when attempts are made to specify some of the basic rules of political existence in a text, but this document no more provides the source of the nation's constitution than a grammar book is the authoritative source of a language. In this understanding, written constitutions cannot provide the foundation of governmental authority.[4]

It was this ancient understanding which the modern concept sought to replace. In *Rights of Man* in 1791, Paine specified the innovations brought about by the late eighteenth-century revolutions. Expressing frustration about disputes over the significance of the changes, Paine stated that 'it will be first necessary to define what is meant by a *constitution*'. 'It is not sufficient that we adopt the word', he explained, 'we must fix also a standard specification to it.'[5] Paine provides us with the first clear statement of the character of modern constitutions.

Characteristics of modern constitutions

Constitutions, wrote Paine, have four key elements. First, a constitution 'is not a thing in name only, but in fact'. That is, it has not merely 'an ideal, but a real existence' and therefore, 'whenever it cannot be produced in a visible form, there is none'. A constitution, in short, is a thing—and specifically it is a *document*. Secondly, 'it is a thing antecedent to a government, and a government is only the creature of a constitution'. A constitution 'is not the act of its government, but of the people constituting a government'. Paine here draws a distinction between the constituted power (the government) and the constituent power (vested in the people), and fixes the *primacy of the people* over their government. Thirdly, Paine highlights the *comprehensive nature* of the constitution. It is, he states, 'the body of elements … which contains the principles on which the government shall be established,

---

[2] Edmund Burke, *Reflections on the Revolution in France* [1790], ed C. C. O'Brien (London: Penguin, 1986), 194.

[3] Ibid 194–5.

[4] A country's constitution, Maistre noted, cannot be known from its written laws 'because these laws are made at different periods only to lay down forgotten or contested rights, and because there is always a host of things which are not written' (Joseph de Maistre, 'Study on Sovereignty' [1794–5] in J. Lively (ed), *The Works of Joseph de Maistre* (New York: Macmillan, 1965), 93–129, at 103–4).

[5] Thomas Paine, *Rights of Man* [1791–2] in his *Rights of Man, Common Sense and other Political Writings*, ed M. Philp (Oxford: Oxford University Press, 1995), 83–331, at 122.

the manner in which it shall be organized, the powers it shall have, the mode of elections, the duration of parliaments, or by what other name such bodies may be called; the powers which the executive part of the government shall have; and, in fine, everything that relates to the compleat organization of a civil government, and the principles on which it shall act, and by which it shall be bound'. Finally, Paine refers to its status as *fundamental law*: a constitution 'is to a government, what the laws made afterwards by that government are to a court of judicature'. That is, the court 'does not make the laws, neither can it alter them; it only acts in conformity to the laws made: and the government is in like manner governed by the constitution.' Similarly, he suggests that the government neither makes nor can alter the constitutional laws which bind it; these can only be altered through an exercise of the constituent power of the people.[6] Although each of these elements was controversial at that time,[7] they have now become widely accepted principles of modern constitutions.[8]

Modern constitutions, based on these key features, have since—in stages—acquired an enhanced authority in public life. To the extent that this has occurred, it is related to the modern processes of positivisation and juridification. Not only are constitutional norms today accepted as being 'fundamental law', but this fundamental law is now conceived as a category of positive law, and the judiciary have asserted their authority to act as ultimate interpreters of its meaning. The modern constitution is now widely accepted as providing the foundation of legal order, not only by establishing the authoritative law-making institutions of the state but also in laying down the basic norms that guide law-making. The constitution is now perceived as providing the basis of the legitimacy of legality.

These claims are controversial. If the constitution is simply a document why should we have reason to believe in its power-conferring character? One answer is that the document was 'authorised' by 'the people'. But if so, then 'the people' must not only be anterior to, but also superior to, the document. This leads certain social contract theorists to postulate two different contracts: with the first, the multitude constitute themselves as a collective entity (the people, the nation, the state) and with the second this collective entity then agrees a framework of government (the constitution).[9]

---

[6] Ibid 122–3.

[7] See, eg Maistre, above n 4, at 107: 'In his evil book on the rights of man, Paine said that a constitution is antecedent to government [etc] ... It would be difficult to get more errors into fewer lines.'

[8] See, eg D. Grimm, 'Verfassung—Verfassungsvertrag—Vertrag uber eine Verfassung', in O. Beaud et al (eds), *L'Europe en voie de Constitution* (Brussels: Bruylant, 2004), 279–87, at 281–2 (identifying as the five key characteristics of modern constitutions: (1) a set of legal norms, (2) establishing and regulating the exercise of public power, (3) founded on an agreement of the people, (4) that forms a comprehensive framework, and is (5) erected on the principle of the primacy of constitutional law). See also Grimm in this volume.

[9] See Samuel Pufendorf, *On the Duty of Man and Citizen According to Natural Law* [1673], trans M. Silverthorne, ed J. Tully (Cambridge: Cambridge University Press, 1991), ii., ch 6.

What is presented as the fundamental law with respect to positive law (ie the written constitution) cannot bind 'the people'.

This type of argument poses specific difficulties for those who would argue that, once adopted, the constitution binds future generations.[10] But it also raises more general complications. In particular, since 'the people' is to be distinguished from a multitude, that concept is itself a legal construction. The modern constitution is a constitution of government, but it cannot be the constitution of the state.[11] That being so, the question arises: is there a fundamental law—that which constructs the people (the original compact)—which lies behind the fundamental law that authorises positive law?

One alternative to the postulation of sequential contracts is to reject the historical claims being made of the foundation and assert its hypothetical character. Since 'the people' comes into existence only by virtue of the basic contract, it is difficult to envisage how the multitude—with their differing interests and conflicting needs— could ever transcend their differences and come together to devise an agreement that creates political unity.[12] Recognising the virtual character of the basic contract, some scholars argue that—paradoxically—'the people' who supposedly agree the contract come into existence only by virtue of the contract.[13] That is, the foundation can only be understood as a reflexive construct.

However those matters are resolved, examination of the foundation seems to reveal that the modern constitution is fundamental only with respect to the office of government, and the constitution's authority derives from a more basic construct, that of the people (however conceptualised). Once this is recognised, however, the

---

[10] Paine recognised this, arguing against constitutional entrenchment: 'Every age must be as free to act for itself, *in all cases*, as the ages and generations which preceded it. The vanity and presumption of governing beyond the grave, is the most ridiculous and insolent of all tyrannies. ... That which the whole nation chooses to do, it has a right to do. ... I am contending for the rights of the *living*, and against their being willed away, and controuled and contracted for, by the manuscript assumed authority of the dead' (Paine, above n 5, 92 (emphasis in original)).

[11] See Emmanuel Joseph Sieyès, *What is the Third Estate?* [1789], trans M. Blondel (London: Pall Mall Press, 1963), 124: 'The nation is prior to everything. It is the source of everything. Its will is always legal; indeed, it is the law itself.'

[12] See Jean-Jacques Rousseau, *The Social Contract* [1762] in *The Social Contract and Other Later Political Writings*, ed V. Gourevitch (Cambridge: Cambridge University Press, 1997), 39–152, at 71: 'For a nascent people to be capable of appreciating sound maxims of politics and of following the fundamental rules of reason of State, the effect would have to become the cause, the social spirit which is to be the work of the institution would have to preside over the institution itself, and men would have to be prior to the laws what they ought to become by means of them.'

[13] P. Ricoeur, 'The Political Paradox', in his *History and Truth*, trans C. Kelbley (Evanston, Ill.: Northwestern University Press, 1965), 247–70; L. Althusser, 'Rousseau: *The Social Contract* (the Discrepancies)' in his *Politics and History: Montesquieu, Rousseau, Marx*, trans B. Brewster (London: Verso, 2007), 113–60; J. Derrida, 'Declarations of Independence' (1986) 15 *New Political Science* 7–15.

attempt to forge a sharp distinction between the ancient and modern concepts of the constitution is less convincing; while the modern concept is directed to the constitution of government, the ancient concept addresses itself to the constitution of the nation—and this is the issue that modern constitutions tend to suppress. When questions are asked about the authority of the written constitution, however, it is precisely these more basic considerations that come to the surface. The point of Burke's analysis was to indicate that, to be able to command authority, the constitution must be treated as a sacred thing worthy of reverence, and the ancient understanding carries its power precisely because it is not, at least in any simple sense, a man-made instrument.[14]

We are now able to grasp the ambition that underpins modern constitutions: specifying the structure of the office of government is one matter, but forging the bonds of unity of the nation is quite another. Yet this is what modern constitutions are expected to do. Modern constitutions are required to serve both instrumental and symbolic purposes. In its instrumental role, the constitution gives guidance for the future by establishing the authoritative modes of collective decision making of a nation. In its symbolic function, it provides a point of unity; the constitution must operate in such a way as to bolster the established order of things. The instrumental aspect, which expresses the principle of legality, looks primarily to the future, whereas the symbolic, drawing on custom and myth and expressing the principle of legitimacy, primarily makes an appeal to the past. The latter is a sacred task and, when no longer able to rely on the power of religion or the authority of the 'eternal past', this task is incapable of being fulfilled without developing a civil religion.[15]

It is evident, then, that although presenting themselves as instrumental documents, modern constitutions must also perform the function—similar to that of the ancient understanding—of nation building. This is often a delicate task, especially since much of modern constitution making takes place under circumstances in which the new settlement seeks to draw a line under the past. This task is often advanced by the adoption, as part of the constitutional settlement, of new symbols of nationhood (flags, anthems, special anniversary dates, etc.)[16] or in an exercise of ideological re-traditionalisation, invoking an idealised version of an earlier narrative about the customs and values of the people.[17] In certain cases, however, the past is such a barrier that reverence of the constitution must in itself provide a substitute for reverence of

---

[14] Maistre makes a similar point to Burke: 'One of the greatest errors of this age is to believe that the political constitution of nations is the work of man alone and that a constitution can be made as a watchmaker makes a watch ... Men never respect what they have made.' Joseph de Maistre, 'Study on Sovereignty' [1794–5], in *The Works of Joseph de Maistre*, ed J. Lively (London: Allen & Unwin, 1965), 93–129, at 102–4.

[15] See Rousseau, above n 12, iv., ch 8.

[16] R. Smend, *Verfassung und Verfassungsrecht* (Munich: Duncker & Humblot, 1928), 48; D. Grimm, 'Integration by Constitution' (2005) 3 *International Journal of Constitutional Law* 193–208.

[17] See W. Kymlicka and M. Opalski (eds), *Can Liberal Pluralism be Exported? Western Political Theory and Ethnic Relations in Eastern Europe* (Oxford: Oxford University Press, 2002).

a political way of being of a people. And in this situation, as is illustrated by the case of the post-war Federal Republic of Germany,[18] it leads to the claim—exemplified by Habermas—that we are now living in a post-metaphysical age orientated to the future, where the only justifiable source of allegiance is to the set of principles of liberty and equality that the constitution declares.[19]

Civil society and government

The role of modern constitutions in bolstering contemporary political identity brings us to the third issue to consider in relation to modern constitutions: the way in which modern constitutional relationships reflect more basic changes in modern social life. The essential question is highlighted by asking: how in modernity is the public sphere to be characterised?

Although social contract theories continued to use the language of sovereignty, it seems clear that Paine was seeking to move beyond that conceptual scheme. When arguing in defence of French revolutionary principles, he occasionally referred to sovereignty as appertaining to the entire nation.[20] But he believed that the envisaged 'universal reformation' would result in a radical shift in the nature of modern political discourse, in which the concept of sovereignty could no longer stand as an adequate representation of the public sphere.

Paine argued that this reformation was being driven by natural laws of social development. These natural laws were operating to reorder governmental regimes not because of the action of some revolutionary vanguard but as expressions of fundamental laws of social development. This natural law 'does not gain its validation subjectively through the consciousness of politically active citizens'; it achieves this objectively 'through the effect of the uninhibited workings of society's immanent natural laws'.[21] Building on the natural jurisprudence of Adam Smith, Paine argued that the workings of 'society's immanent natural laws' was leading to the opening up of trade and commerce and, in its train, the formation of what might be called 'civil society'.[22]

---

[18] See, eg J. Habermas, 'A Kind of Settlement of Damages: The Apologetic Tendencies in German History Writing' in *Forever in the Shadow of Hitler?*, trans J. Knowlton and T. Cates (Atlantic Highlands, NJ: Humanities Press, 1993), 30–43, at 43: 'The unconditional opening of the Federal republic to the political culture of the West is the greatest achievement of the postwar period.'

[19] J. Habermas, 'On the Relation between the Nation, the Rule of Law and Democracy', in his *The Inclusion of the Other* (Cambridge: Polity Press, 2002), 129–54.

[20] See, eg Paine, above n 5, 140, 193. Art III of the French Declaration of the Rights of Man and Citizen, 1789, stated: 'The Nation is essentially the source of all Sovereignty.'

[21] J. Habermas, 'Natural Law and Revolution', in his *Theory and Practice*, trans J. Viertel (Boston, Mass.: Beacon Press, 1973), 82–120, at 94.

[22] Adam Smith, *The Theory of Moral Sentiments* [1759], ed K. Haakonssen (Cambridge: Cambridge University Press, 2002); id, *An Inquiry into the Nature and Causes of the Wealth of Nations* [1776]; K. Haakonssen, *Natural Law and Moral Philosophy: From Grotius to the Scottish Enlightenment* (Cambridge: Cambridge University Press, 1996).

In *Rights of Man*, Paine remarks that the 'great part of that order which reigns among mankind is not the effect of government' but has its origins in 'the principles and natural constitution of man'. This order pre-dates government and would continue to exist even 'if the formality of government was abolished', because human interdependence and reciprocal interest form a 'chain of connection' which holds together all the parts of civilised community. And it is through the workings of these natural laws, rather than any social contract, that humans were led into society.

Substituting the distinction made in social contract theory between the state of nature and the civil state with that between society and government, Paine argues that mankind is elevated by society rather than government. Government 'makes but a small part of civilized life', and it is 'to the great and fundamental principles of society and civilization ... infinitely more than to any thing which even the best instituted government can perform, that the safety and prosperity of the individual and of the whole depends'. As civilisation evolves, Paine argues, government dissipates, since civil society becomes more able to regulate its own affairs and to govern itself.[23] Building on the work of Locke and Smith, Paine brings natural law into alignment with the laws of trade and commodity exchange. 'All the great laws of society', Paine proclaims, 'are laws of nature.' But these are laws of a different order; they are obeyed not because they are commands backed by sanctions, but because it is in the individual's interest to follow them. The laws of trade and commerce 'are laws of mutual and reciprocal interest'.[24]

In this world-view, society, not government, represents the public interest, and government acts legitimately only when promoting society's interests. The newly emerging regime of government—that of which the American republic provides the model—'promotes universal society, as the means of universal commerce'.[25] Paine here seeks to move beyond sovereignty as a representation of the autonomy of the public sphere and to replace it with the separate spheres of society and government. His argument marks the emergence of civil society as the paramount force in the public sphere. The universal reformation he envisages goes hand in hand with a limited role for government, and this limited role is to be defined in its constitution. One vital function of the constitution, Paine argues, is to protect certain rights enumerated in written constitutions—especially the rights of life, liberty, and property—which exist to protect the operation of the natural laws of the commercial republic from undue political interference by government.

From the perspective of public law, the critical issue is not the division of the public sphere into civil society and government since these are not separate entities but only distinctions in thought; the critical issue is whether or not civil society is able to offer an adequate expression of public reason. To this question, Hegel gave a robust answer. While acknowledging the emergence of civil society and the power of its laws—the laws of political economy—to meet particular social needs, Hegel also

---

[23] Paine, *Rights of Man*, above n 5, 216.

[24] Ibid.

[25] Ibid 223.

recognised that, far from addressing the natural inequality of man, these laws had the effect of reinforcing them.[26] Forming a sphere of competition and antagonism, civil society can express only particularistic interests. Contrary to Paine's claim that the rise of civil society will lead to a diminution in the power of government, Hegel demonstrated that this reformation would result in governments assuming a much greater role in the regulation of social life. Since the operation of the natural laws of civil society lead to disequilibrium and disorganisation, Hegel suggested that civil society stands in particular need of regulation by government.[27] Hegel's analysis gives a different twist to Paine's argument about the function of modern constitutions. If the modern constitution exists mainly to protect subjective rights exercised in civil society, then they are likely to act as barriers to the realisation of objective freedom.

III. CONSTITUTIONALISM

At its core, the modern concept of the constitution requires only the adoption of a formal document establishing a set of governmental institutions; constitutionalism is the political theory that generally accompanies the technique. Constitutionalism is a theory of limited government and is concerned mainly with the norms which modern constitutions should contain. These norms not only impose limits on the exercise of public power but also on the procedures through which such power should be exercised. Its key principles are independence of the judiciary, separation of governmental powers, respect for individual rights, and the promotion of the judiciary's role as guardians of constitutional norms.

The theory of constitutionalism has exerted such an impact on the drafting of constitutional documents that it is often assumed to be synonymous with the modern concept of the constitution itself. Although modern constitutions exhibit significant variation as to the particular form of their governing institutions, they increasingly seem to acquire legitimacy only to the extent that they measure up to the norms of constitutionalism. In this sense, the contemporary era would appear to be one marked by the triumph of constitutionalism. This, however, remains an ambiguous achievement. In part, this is because constitutionalism has, with justification, been called 'one of those concepts, evocative and persuasive in its connotations yet cloudy in its analytic and descriptive content, which at once enrich and confuse political discourse'.[28] But it may also be the case that its symbolic aspect has been enhanced as its instrumental aspect has declined. I will return to this point later. First, we should try more precisely to determine the content of these norms.

---

[26] G. W. F. Hegel, *Philosophy of Right* [1821], trans T. M. Knox (Oxford: Oxford University Press, 1952), § 200.

[27] Ibid § 236.

[28] T. C. Grey, 'Constitutionalism: An Analytical Framework', in J. R. Pennock and J. W. Chapman (eds), *Constitutionalism: Nomos XX* (New York: New York University Press, 1979), 189–208, at 189.

This issue can most concisely be addressed by highlighting two contrasting articulations of constitutionalism. Having informed deliberations over the US Constitution, these rival positions have been expressed from the originating moments of birth of modern constitutions. These positions are, in that context, exemplified in the writing of two *Federalist* colleagues, James Madison and Alexander Hamilton. For ease of exposition, I refer to these positions as republican and liberal variations.

Madison and Hamilton agreed that, once adopted, the Constitution must be protected from the people: modern republican government must be government of the people and for the people, but demonstrably not government by the people. Notwithstanding the rhetorical claim that government receives its authority from the people, the government must possess the capacity to control and manage the people. In framing a government, argued Madison, 'you must first enable the government to control the governed; and in the next place oblige it to control itself'.[29] Constitutionalism bases itself first on the necessity of accepting the authority of the Constitution and then on the necessity of creating institutional arrangements to ensure that the established government is able to control itself.

Republican constitutionalism

Madison and Hamilton both accepted the need for such 'auxiliary precautions', and both accepted that the constitutionalist objective was to establish an institutional configuration that would, through the reason of its principles, generate the allegiance of the nation. Their differences flow mainly from the type of safeguards each believed to be conducive to the realisation of that objective. Madison takes the institutional framework created by the Constitution—the establishment of checks and balances—as the primary mechanism of control, whereas Hamilton relies on a more centralist and rationalist solution which places greater faith in the special role of judicial review.[30]

Madison's position placed great importance on the necessity of 'so contriving the interior structure of the government as that its several constituent parts may, by their mutual relations, be the means of keeping each other in their proper places'.[31] And since the several departments of state are 'perfectly co-ordinate by the terms of their common commission, neither of them, it is evident, can pretend to an exclusive or superior right of settling the boundaries between their respective powers'.[32] The Constitution is thus conceived as establishing an elaborate institutional configuration through which all political action is channelled, but is held in tension—in a state

---

[29] *The Federalist*, above n 1, No 51 (Madison), at 320.

[30] Controversy continues over the extent to which the authors of the *Federalist* papers conceived their writings as a coherent whole: see D. F. Epstein, *The Political Theory of The Federalist* (Chicago, Ill.: University of Chicago Press, 1984), 2. Here, I use Madison and Hamilton's arguments in a stylised manner for the purpose of exposing two different strands of constitutionalist argument.

[31] Ibid at 320, 318–19.

[32] Ibid No 49 (Madison), at 313.

of irresolution. In the words of John Adams: 'Power must be opposed to power, force to force, strength to strength, interest to interest, as well as reason to reason, eloquence to eloquence, and passion to passion.'[33] By dividing, channelling, and opposing political power in this manner, constitutional meaning—the proper ordering of constitutional values—remains the subject of continuing structured political contestation. Constitutional maintenance is a political task.

Within this institutional arrangement, Madison accorded no special place to the judiciary. Believing that these checks should remain plural, this was not an oversight. Madison was sceptical about the desirability of vesting an appointed cadre of judges with the powers to fix constitutional meaning and enforce the Constitution as fundamental law. For similar reasons, he had initially been opposed to the inclusion of a bill of rights in the US Constitution: such rights are better protected, he maintained, by the structure of the federal system and also 'because experience proves the inefficacy of a bill of rights on those occasions when its controul is most needed'.[34] Madison presents us with an account of what may be called republican (or political) constitutionalism.[35]

Liberal constitutionalism

Madison's account of the nature of constitutionalism can be contrasted with that of Hamilton, who placed greater importance on the role of a small elite in maintaining political power and constitutional stability. For Hamilton, a strong, independent central government was essential, a position that led, for example, to a specific policy opposition between Hamilton and Madison over the necessity of establishing a national bank.[36] Within the structure of Hamilton's centralising philosophy, the judiciary was expected to perform a special role. This is most clearly expressed in Hamilton's analysis in *The Federalist* No 78, in which he argued that because the judiciary 'will always be the least dangerous to the political rights of the Constitution' they should be entrusted with the duty 'to declare all acts contrary to the manifest tenor of the Constitution void'.[37] Although constitutional judicial review is not explicitly provided for in the US Constitution, it is later claimed by the judiciary in *Marbury v Madison* (1803), in a judgment in which Chief Justice Marshall drew heavily on Hamilton's analysis.[38]

---

[33] Z. Haraszti, *John Adams and the Prophets of Progress* (Cambridge, Mass.: Harvard University Press, 1952), 219: cited in H. Arendt, *On Revolution* (Harmondsworth: Penguin, 1973), 152.

[34] Madison to Jefferson, 17 October 1788: cited in S. Snowiss, *Judicial Review and the Law of the Constitution* (New Haven, Conn.: Yale University Press, 1990), 91.

[35] See G. Thomas, 'Recovering the Political Constitution: The Madisonian Vision' (2004) 66 *Review of Politics* 233–56.

[36] *McCulloch v Maryland* 17 US (4 Wheat.) 316 (1819). See C. A. Sheehan, 'Madison v. Hamilton: The Battle over Republicanism and the Role of Public Opinion' (2004) 98 *American Political Science Review* 405–24.

[37] See especially *The Federalist*, above n 1, No 78 (Hamilton), at 438–9.

[38] *Marbury v Madison* 5 US (1 Cr) 137 (1803).

In Hamilton's constitutional philosophy, the Constitution is a type of positive law and the judiciary, as the institution charged with the responsibility of interpreting and enforcing the law, have the ultimate authority to determine the meaning of the Constitution. There was nothing inevitable about this development.[39] It had initially been recognised only that the judiciary had some role to play in the determination of unconstitutionality. Such unconstitutionality, however, was felt 'not to be determined by judicial exposition of written supreme law but to consist of violation of long-standing and publicly acknowledged first principles of fundamental law, written or unwritten'.[40] And there was no expectation that the judiciary would have a role in determining conflicting interpretations of general constitutional provisions.

Only during the nineteenth century did perceptions change. Much of this is attributable to Chief Justice Marshall's statecraft.[41] In the process, the US Constitution was transformed into a species of positive law, and the judiciary became impressed with the duty, through the forensic processes of judicial review, of determining its meaning and enforcing its provisions. But behind Marshall's statecraft lay Hamilton's analysis. In *The Federalist*, he had argued that, holding neither the power of the sword nor the purse, the judiciary possesses neither force nor will, but only judgment.[42] The authority of the judiciary thus rests on its relative weakness, and is sustained only by its independence and the integrity of its own judgment, that is, by adherence to 'strict rules and precedent'. Hamilton's argument reinforces the conviction amongst both the judiciary and the public that, in the exercise of constitutional review by the courts, a strict analytic logic must be seen to operate in preference to a demonstrable exercise in political prudence. Hamilton presents us with an account of what may be called liberal (or legal) constitutionalism.

Constitutional development

These accounts are presented as two stylised interpretations for the purpose of making a general claim. Although Hamilton and Madison's ideas draw from a common source, and although the detailed history reveals a considerable intertwining of their ideas, the general trajectory is fairly clear. Crudely expressed, the history of the development of the US Constitution is the history of the triumph of liberal-legal over republican-political constitutionalism. In the course of constitutional development, the US Constitution has become positivised, individualised,

---

[39] See G. S. Wood, *The Creation of the American Republic, 1776-1787* (Chapel Hill, NC: University of North Carolina Press, rev edn, 1998), 292: 'There was ... no logical or necessary reason why the notion of fundamental law, so common to Englishmen for over a century, should lead to the American invocation of it in the ordinary courts of law. Indeed in an important sense the idea of fundamental law actually worked to prohibit any such development, for it was dependent on such a distinct conception of public law in contrast to private law as be hardly enforceable in the regular court system.'

[40] Snowiss, above n 34, 37.

[41] See ibid ch 5.

[42] *The Federalist*, above n 1, No 78 (Hamilton), especially at 437.

and legalised. The critical technique in this evolution has been judicial review. 'What in the final analysis gave meaning to the Americans' conception of a constitution', comments Wood, 'was not its fundamentality or its creation by the people, but rather its implementation in the ordinary courts of law.'[43]

In this sense, the history of American constitutionalism is that of the diminution in authority of Madison's account and the augmentation of Hamilton's. This involves the replacement of a relational logic, in which the interpretations and claims of different institutions pull in different directions and it is the tautness of that arrangement that contains the essence of constitutionalism, with an analytical logic, in which the judiciary, through a forensic technique of textual interpretation, assert final and exclusive authority to resolve the Constitution's meaning. In contrast to the idea of constitutionalism as an evolving arrangement of institutional forms, this conception promotes the authority of an independent group to interpret and enforce the terms of the text of the constitutional document. The Hamiltonian position leads to a position in which the Constitution is what the judges say it is; the history of the Constitution is reduced to the history of the work of its Supreme Court.[44]

The question remains: to what extent does the development of Western constitutionalism follow a similar pattern to that of the American experience? To what extent is the history of Western constitutionalism a story about the ascendancy of liberal-legal constitutionalism over its rival form? These questions are best addressed with reference to the emergence of 'constitutionalisation'.

IV. CONSTITUTIONALISATION

Constitutionalism is a political theory that was developed as part of a liberal philosophy to guide the formation of modern constitutions. Predicating an arrangement of limited government constructed by free, equal, rights-bearing individuals, constitutionalism reflects the concerns of a particular time, place, and social situation. With the emergence of welfare-regulatory states during the twentieth century, it was often claimed that constitutionalism no longer carried much purchase. 'Many of the urgent problems of modern society have arisen after the heyday of constitutionalism', wrote Schochet in 1979, and these problems—economic inequalities, regulation of technologies, resource conservation, and so on—'require more decisive and resolute

---

[43] Wood, above n 39, 291.

[44] P. Bobbitt, *Constitutional Fate: Theory of the Constitution* (New York: Oxford University Press, 1982), 3: 'The central issue in the constitutional debate of the past twenty-five years has been the legitimacy of judicial review of constitutional questions by the United States Supreme Court.' See also M. Kammen, *A Machine that Would Go of Itself: The Constitution in American Culture* (New York: Knopf, 1987), 9: 'This propensity to conflate the Court and the Constitution is hardly limited to grass roots America. It seems to have been shared by a great many scholars because the constitutional history of the United States has been primarily written as the history of Supreme Court decisions, doctrines, procedures and personalities.'

action than limited constitutional government can provide'.[45] Whatever the symbolic function being performed by constitutionalism, from an instrumental perspective, the mid-twentieth century marked its twilight period.[46]

During the last twenty or so years, however, interest in the theory of constitutionalism has been rekindled. Some of this is attributable to the transitions made by post-fascist (Spain, Portugal), post-communist (central and eastern Europe) and post-Apartheid (South Africa) regimes towards the formation of market-based economies and liberal democratic constitutional regimes. At the same time, many constitutional democracies—new and old—have been reconfiguring their governmental arrangements in response to domestic and international changes. Domestically, many regimes have scaled back the public sector through privatisation of public service provision, and reordered governing arrangements through the formation of public–private partnership schemes, and the subjection of public processes to a range of market disciplines.[47] Internationally, governments are increasingly obliged to participate in a variety of transnational arrangements for the purpose of enhancing their ability to deliver their economic, social, and environmental objectives.[48]

These various developments have led to a complicated situation, with some trends strengthening constitutionalist values and others weakening them. Some domestic changes, for example, have strengthened modes of review and accountability of governmental action, while others, by blurring the public–private distinction, have done otherwise. International developments have also resulted in governmental action being undertaken through arrangements that are not easily susceptible to review and control through the procedures and standards of the national constitution. For many regimes, these changes appear to erode the constitution's status as the authoritative and comprehensive framework for guiding and regulating the exercise of public power.[49] One type of response has been to strengthen the processes by which governmental action can be subjected to the discipline of a constitution. This movement has led, in turn, to a rekindling of interest in the theory of constitutionalism, leading to the emergence of interest in the processes of constitutionalisation.

[45] G. J. Schochet, 'Introduction: Constitutionalism, Liberalism, and the Study of Politics', in Pennock and Chapman (eds), above n 28, 1–15, at 6.

[46] See, eg G. Teubner (ed), *Dilemmas of Law in the Welfare State* (Berlin: de Gruyter, 1986). In this extensive analysis of this problem by European and American scholars, constitutional issues are only briefly discussed (Preuss, 154; Habermas, 219; Wiethölter, 242). Teubner here introduces the idea of 'legal control of social self-regulation' (308), which later becomes the basis of his rather different concept of constitution: see Teubner in this volume.

[47] See, eg E. Suleiman, *Dismantling Democratic States* (Princeton, NJ: Princeton University Press, 2003).

[48] See D. Held and A. McGrew, *Governing Globalization: Power, Authority and Global Governance* (Cambridge: Polity Press, 2002).

[49] D. Grimm, 'The Constitution in the Process of Denationalization' (2005) 12 *Constellations* 447–65.

Constitutionalism reconfigured

Constitutionalisation, it is suggested, is a process born of a reconfiguration of the political theory of constitutionalism. Traditionally conceived as a loose template against which the framework of government of the modern state might be drafted, constitutionalism is now being repackaged purely as an expression of liberal-legal constitutionalism and it is presented as a more or less free-standing set of norms. Constitutionalism is no longer treated as some evocative but vague theory which expresses a belief in the importance of limited, accountable government, to be applied flexibly to the peculiar circumstances of particular regimes. It now is being presented as a meta-theory which establishes the authoritative standards of legitimacy for the exercise of public power wherever it is located. Once repackaged in this manner, and especially when harnessed to the socio-economic forces that have been driving recent governmental changes (ie liberalisation, marketisation, globalisation), it emerges as the phenomenon of constitutionalisation. Constitutionalisation refers to the processes by which an increasing range of public life is being subjected to the discipline of the norms of liberal-legal constitutionalism.

The contentious character of constitutionalisation can best be explained by bringing this process into alignment with the account of constitutions and constitutionalism. The concept of constitution here being invoked is much closer to that of the constitutional text rather than the way of being of a people. But the concept of constitution in this new account refers not so much to the text itself but rather the set of norms that are assumed to underpin it: it asserts a concept of constitution as a set of rational principles. Questions about the source of authority of these principles tend to be avoided; the norms of right conduct prescribed in these texts acquire their authority from precepts of reason rather than approval of 'the people'. It is the authority of these norms that is being asserted and these norms acquire the status of fundamental law not because they have been authorised by a people but because of the self-evident rationality of their claims.

The process of constitutionalisation tends not to endorse decentralisation, diversity, and the idea of constitutional meaning being derived from the competing political values being held in tension through a taut institutional configuration. Constitutionalisation expresses a centralising philosophy: it both proclaims basic rights as trump cards in the political game and maintains that the nature, scope, and status of these rights must be determined by a small cadre of judges, either in the rarefied atmosphere of supreme courts or, in the international arena, through a variety of tribunals of uncertain status. At its core, constitutionalisation presupposes legalisation; as greater swathes of public life are brought within the ambit of constitutional norms, so too are they disciplined by formal legal procedures. Constitutionalisation is the process of extending the main tenets of liberal-legal constitutionalism to all forms of governmental action.

There is one final, particularly contentious, aspect of constitutionalisation to be brought into the frame. In the form promoted today, constitutionalisation absorbs much of Paine's assumptions about the relationship between society and government. Hegel was right in his observation that the emergence of civil society would lead to a growth, not a diminution, in government; extensive governmental action has been required in the modern era, not least for the purpose of controlling and regulating the operation of market freedoms. Constitutionalism may have lived on as symbol but it ceased to be an effective instrument. Constitutionalisation as it is now emerging is part of a more basic set of changes driving governmental reform—those of privatisation, marketisation, and contractualisation—and which are designed to make government more limited in its reach, more focused in its goals, more responsive to its stakeholders, and more accountable to its citizens.[50] Constitutionalisation is required to ensure that public power, in whatever manifestation, is exercised in accordance with the canons of rationality, proportionality, and by means that involve the least restrictive interference with the enjoyment of the individual's basic rights.

Domestic constitutionalisation

Although the impact of constitutionalisation has most often been discussed with respect to international arrangements, its effect on national arrangements should not be overlooked. In many regimes, the written constitution has occupied an ambivalent status in national life, often owing to the existence of a significant gap between constitutional norms and the ways in which governmental decision making actually occurs. In this situation, the constitution may have performed a symbolic role in presenting the public face of the regime to the world, but it was not fulfilling its instrumental role of regulating government decision making. Here, the enactment of a written constitution formed only an initial stage in a more general process of making a reality of the constitution's claims to be higher-order law. This is what constitutionalisation has meant at the domestic level, and it is realised through political and cultural changes that have been spearheaded by an activist judiciary assuming the responsibility to enforce the provisions of the constitutional text.

At the domestic level, constitutionalisation has reached a mature stage only in recent years. This has been achieved primarily through the instigation of a 'rights revolution',[51] a movement that even in the United States—where the Constitution rapidly acquired a sacred character—has been essentially a post-war phenomenon.[52] Elsewhere, it has been a much more recent development,[53] though one which is

[50] See, eg D. Osborne and T. Gaebler, *Reinventing Government: How the Entrepreneurial Spirit is Transforming the Public Sector* (Harmondsworth: Penguin, 1993) and the plethora of studies falling under the umbrella of 'new public management' or 'new governance'.

[51] N. Bobbio, *The Age of Rights*, trans A. Cameron (Cambridge: Polity Press, 1996); C. R. Epp, *The Rights Revolution: Lawyers, Activists, and Supreme Courts in Comparative Perspective* (Chicago, Ill.: University of Chicago Press, 1998); M. Ignatieff, *The Rights Revolution* (Toronto: Anasi Press, 2000).

[52] See R. A. Primus, *The American Language of Rights* (Cambridge: Cambridge University Press, 1999).

[53] Epp, above n 51, chs 5–10.

rapidly gathering pace.[54] It is extending its reach both territorially and with respect to scope, that is, not only across the world but also beyond the sphere of individual rights to embrace judicial scrutiny of electoral processes, review of government policy making in such matters of high policy as national security and macroeconomic planning, and even judicial determination of major issues of nation building.[55] The movement entails the absorption of broader elements of the ancient idea of the constitution into the frame of the modern constitution, the conversion of the Constitution into a species of ordinary law (albeit with 'higher' status), and the consequent establishment of the judiciary as the authoritative determinants of its meaning. General aspirations in the Constitution are thus rendered justiciable, and the implicit values on which the Constitution rests are explicated as fundamental legal norms that govern all aspects of public decision making.[56]

The rapid advance of the process of constitutionalisation at the national level coincides with a growing recognition that, to an increasing extent, governmental decision making is occurring beyond the structures of the nation state. Public power is now being exercised by supranational bodies of regional or global reach. In fields such as financial regulation, competition policy, energy and trade policy, environmental protection, crime and security, and such like, governmental policy making is regularly formulated through transnational arrangements. These developments undermine the claims of modern constitutions to be comprehensive in their reach, not least because governmental decisions in these fields appear to be made through networks that are unknown to national constitutions and with respect to which existing accountability mechanisms seem ill-suited. One response to this situation has been to loosen the anchorage of these constitutional norms for the purpose of extending their reach.

Supranational constitutionalisation

The supranational aspect of constitutionalisation takes two main forms. One is to reform the basis on which various supra or transnational bodies currently operate: these bodies, it is suggested, should themselves become constitutionalised. A second

---

[54] R. Hirschl, 'The New Constitutionalism and the Judicialization of Pure Politics Worldwide' (2006) 75 *Fordham Law Review* 721–53. The British case provides an unusual but illustrative example: lacking a modern written constitution, it has operated as the epitome of political constitutionalism with constitutional values protected through a series of tensions in institutional arrangements that are not expressed in the law of the constitution. Since 1997, however, the Labour government has instituted a programme of modernisation, which incorporates devolution of governmental power, reform of the second chamber, enhanced human rights protection, and in which a central theme has been the formalisation of constitutional and governmental arrangements (which, of course, is the first step to their legalisation).

[55] Ibid at 729–43. See further Hirschl, *Towards Juristocracy: The Origins and Consequences of the New Constitutionalism* (Cambridge, Mass.: Harvard University Press, 2004).

[56] One manifestation of this movement has been the debates within various jurisdictions over what is generally called the horizontal effects of charters of rights, that is, the degree to which these charters may be used to regulate conduct between private actors.

type of response has been to argue that the emergence of networks of transnational governance has eroded the foundational elements of modern constitutions, thereby undermining their authority. The proposed solution involves a reconfiguration of the basis of constitutionalism in the light of late modern conditions. This type of reconfiguration is promoted under the label of 'multi-level constitutionalism'. Although these two aspects of supranational constitutionalisation are related, they need to be kept distinct.

Constitutionalisation of international, treaty-based bodies is a major topic in its own right. A great deal of scholarly attention has recently been devoted to the issue of the 'constitutionalisation' of such bodies as the World Trade Organization (WTO).[57] What this development is intended to signify, however, remains unclear. Having developed a set of binding rules enforced by an adjudicative body, the WTO has certainly become more legalised.[58] But the rights that the WTO promotes are essentially market freedoms and, while there have been claims that it promotes broader (liberal) constitutional functions,[59] such claims remain contentious.[60] While the WTO continues to conceive itself as developing a *lex specialis*, any constitutional claims for its status must remain highly speculative; in this sphere, the way in which the growth of constitutional rhetoric is altering the perception of the nature of the organisation's task is as important as the institutional changes that are occurring.

Such claims are not restricted to sectoral bodies like the WTO. A debate has also recently evolved over the question of whether the United Nations Charter should now be treated as the 'constitution' of the 'international community'.[61] This type of

[57] See, eg R. Howse and K. Nicolaidis, 'Enhancing WTO Legitimacy: Constitutionalization or Global Subsidiarity' (2003) 16 *Governance* 73–94; D. Z. Cass, *The Constitutionalization of the World Trade Organization* (Oxford: Oxford University Press, 2005); J. L. Dunoff, 'Constitutional Conceits: The WTO's "Constitution" and the Discipline of International Law' (2006) 17 *European Journal of International Law* 647–75.

[58] S. Picciotto, 'The WTO's Appellate Body: Legal Formalism as a Legitimation of Global Governance' (2005) 18 *Governance* 477–503; C. Carmody, 'A Theory of WTO Law' (2008) 11 *Journal of International Economic Law* 527–57.

[59] See, eg E.-U. Petersman, 'The WTO Constitution and Human Rights' (2000) 3 *Journal of International Economic Law* 19–25; Petersman, 'Human Rights, Constitutionalism and the World Trade Organization: Challenges for World Trade Organization Jurisprudence and Civil Society' (2006) 19 *Leiden Journal of International Law* 633–67.

[60] See, eg S. Picciotto, 'Constitutionalizing Multilevel Governance?' (2008) 6 *International Journal of Constitutional Law* 457–79, at 477–8: 'The strong vision of the constitutionalization of the WTO, as put forward especially by Petersman, ... seems to consider all politics—including the WTO's rules and procedures and its deliberative democratic discourse—as favouring a producer-biased mercantilism. ... However, giving individuals, including investors and corporations, rights they could enforce directly ... could work to exacerbate economic inequalities by handing a powerful weapon to those whose considerable economic power could be defended in terms of morally underpinned economic rights.'

[61] See B. Fassbender, 'The United Nations Charter as Constitution of the International Community' (1998) 36 *Columbia Journal of Transnational Law* 529–619; Fassbender, '"We the Peoples of the United Nations": Constituent Power and Constitutional Form in

analysis postulates the existence of an 'international community' as a surrogate for 'the people' and treats the legal framework through which this community acts as its constitution.[62] In this debate, the 'world constitution' is conceived as a set of norms which not only binds all states, but which also guarantee their claims to autonomy by protecting them from unauthorised invasions of their 'rights' by others. This, then, presents itself as a purely normativist claim, an assertion of the normative authority of general rules of international law. Without a 'world state', without some agency that guarantees enforcement, the power that underpins these norms remains ambiguous: constitutionalisation here presents itself as a free-standing process.

The most intense level of discussion on the subject of supranational constitutionalisation concerns the question of the constitution of the European Union (EU). It is impossible here to do justice to this issue. What is clear, nevertheless, is that our investigations should not come to rest on the failed venture of the EU Constitution, the attempt to agree a formal constitution to mark a process of evolution of a 'new legal order' for the benefit of which member states had conceded some of their governing rights.[63] It might focus instead on the ways in which the entity has grown incrementally in capacity and competence.[64] One important indicator of constitutionalisation concerns competence, shown by the way the EU has altered from being an international organisation creating duties and rights binding on member states to an entity which has established itself as a vertically integrated legal order that, within its jurisdictional limits, determines rights and duties that are binding on all legal persons within the EU territory. A second concerns capacity, by which is meant the way the EU has, through force of circumstance, acquired a capacity to extend its own remit.[65] The limits to the EU's competence and capacity are uncertain and contested, and while that is the

International Law', in M. Loughlin and N. Walker (eds), *The Paradox of Constitutionalism: Constituent Power and Constitutional Form* (Oxford: Oxford University Press, 2007), 269–90.

[62] See C. Tomuschat, *International Law: Ensuring the Survival of Mankind on the Eve of a New Century* (The Hague: Martinus Nijhoff, 2001), 72–90; J. Habermas, 'Does the Constitutionalization of International Law Still Have a Chance?', in his *The Divided West*, trans C. Cronin (Cambridge: Polity, 2006), 115–93.

[63] The draft European Constitution was signed in October 2004 but rejected by referendums in France and the Netherlands in 2005; for developments, see <http://europa.eu/institutional_reform/index_en.htm>.

[64] See especially J. H. H. Weiler, *The Constitution of Europe: 'Do the new clothes have an emperor?' and Other Essays on European Integration* (Cambridge: Cambridge University Press, 1999); J. H. H. Weiler and M. Wind (eds), *European Constitutionalism beyond the State* (Cambridge: Cambridge University Press, 2002); E. Stein, 'Lawyers, Judges and the Making of a Transnational Constitution' (1981) 75 *American Journal of International Law* 1–27.

[65] One illustration is the way in which respect for fundamental rights came to form part of the general principles of law protected by the European Court of Justice. See A. Stone Sweet, *Governing with Judges: Constitutional Politics in Europe* (Oxford: Oxford University Press, 2000), 172: 'Without supremacy, the ECJ had decided, the common market was doomed. And without a judicially enforceable charter of rights, national courts had decided, the supremacy doctrine was doomed.'

case constitutionalisation of the entity remains partial and similarly contested. But it is on the claim that the EU possesses its own autonomous power of innovation—the power unilaterally to extend its own competence and capacity—that the critical question of constitutionalisation revolves.

The crucial point to be made about constitutionalisation of the EU is that, to the extent it has been achieved, it is the epitome of liberal-legal constitutionalism.[66] The EU constitutionalisation project has been centrally devised, with the Court and Commission setting the pace. This process of what might be termed 'constitution-alisation through integration' is most evident in the work of the Court. Extending the scope of the 'new legal order' to claim that the founding treaties have become the Community's 'basic constitutional charter',[67] the Court has, through creative interpretation, created a hierarchy of 'constitutional' norms. But although a textual constitutional arrangement is being set in place, the question of political unity—which ultimately is the source of power of the entity—continues to confound.[68] As promoted by Commission and Court, constitutionalisation through integration has been a form of liberal-legal constitutionalism allied primarily to market freedoms. A critical constitutional tension point—one that expresses the underlying ideology of the constitutionalisation process—manifests itself whenever this normative authority is exercised in ways that undermine the social rights established in member states.[69]

Tensions between national and European authorities bring us to the second, more general, aspect of supranational constitutionalisation: the claim made by certain jurists that these internationally driven changes are on the brink of effecting a 'paradigm shift', in which the modern era of nation-state constitutionalism will be superseded by 'twenty-first century constitutionalism'. This movement presents itself under the banner of 'multi-level constitutionalism'.

Multi-level constitutionalism is founded on the notion that 'in the era of globalization a constitutionalist reconstruction [at the global level] is a desirable

[66] See Weiler, above n 64, 221: 'Constitutionalism is the DOS or Windows of the European Community'. When Weiler states this, it is legal constitutionalism he has in mind. He continues (ibid): 'The constitutionalism thesis claims that in critical aspects the Community has evolved and behaves as if its founding instrument were not a treaty governed by international law but, to use the language of the European Court, a constitutional charter governed by a form of constitutional law.' But this, it should be noted, is not Weiler's position on European constitutionalisation.

[67] Case 26/62 *Van Gend en Loos* [1963] ECR 1; Case 294/83 *Parti Ecologiste, Les Verts v Parliament* [1986] ECR 1339.

[68] D. Grimm, 'Does Europe need a Constitution?' (1995) 3 *European Law Journal* 282–302. Grimm concludes (at 299) that: 'Since this State would not … have the mediatory structures from which the democratic process lives, the Community would after its full constitutionali-zation be a largely self-supporting institution, farther from its base than ever.' See also Wahl in this volume (on the constitutional constellation).

[69] F. W. Scharpf, *Reflections on Multi-level Legitimacy* (Cologne: Max Planck Institut für Gesellschaftsforschung, 2007), Working Paper 07/03, especially 14–15. Scharpf (16) seeks solutions in the establishment of arrangements drawn from a tradition of republican-politi-cal constitutionalism. See further, Scharpf in this volume.

reaction to visible de-constitutionalization at the domestic level'.[70] It is claimed that at the domestic level non-governmental actors are now exercising governmental tasks and 'this means that state constitutions can no longer regulate the totality of governance in a comprehensive way and the states constitutions' original claim to a complete basic order is thereby defeated'.[71] The solution, argues Peters, must be found in 'compensatory constitutionalization on the international plane'.[72] Building on the arguments of de Wet and Cottier and Hertig, Peters contributes to an emerging group of scholars advocating multi-level constitutionalism.

The core thesis of multi-level constitutionalism is that there is 'an emerging international constitutional order consisting of an international community, and international value system and rudimentary structures for its enforcement' and this requires the concept of the constitution to be extended 'to describe a system in which the different national, regional and functional (sectoral) constitutional regimes form the building blocks of the international community'.[73] In de Wet's words, it 'assumes an increasingly integrated international legal order in which the exercise of control over the political decision-making process would be possible in a system where national and postnational (i.e. regional and functional) constitutional orders complemented each other in what amounts to a *Verfassungskonglomerat*'.[74] State-based constitutionalism, it is contended (this time in Cottier and Hertig's words), now needs to 'give way to a graduated approach' which extends 'to fora and layers of governance other than nations' and which treats these 'layers of governance … as on[e] overall complex'.[75]

The common feature of multi-level constitutionalism is its pervasive normativism.[76] Legal rules and values are treated as forming a set of rational moral principles implicitly located within legal constitutionalism, with constitutional values rooted in the constituent power of the people scarcely being mentioned.[77]

---

[70] A. Peters, 'Compensatory Constitutionalism: The Function and Potential of Fundamental International Norms and Structures' (2006) 19 *Leiden Journal of International Law* 579–610, at 580.

[71] Ibid.

[72] Ibid.

[73] E. de Wet, 'The International Legal Order' (2006) 55 *International & Comparative Law Quarterly* 51–76, at 51, 53.

[74] Ibid 53.

[75] T. Cottier and M. Hertig, 'The Prospects of 21st Century Constitutionalism' (2003) 7 *Max Planck Yearbook of United Nations Law* 261–328, at 264.

[76] This criticism is addressed in more detail in M. Loughlin, 'In Defence of *Staatslehre*' (2009) 48 *Der Staat* 1–27, especially at 17–23.

[77] Peters, above n 70, at 592, does refer to the need to establish transnational democratic structures (without details), but this concern does not seem to register on de Wet's horizon. Cottier and Hertig do address the point that state constitutionalism is authorised by 'the people' but they claim that this concept, being ethnic or cultural in character, ought simply to be transcended: 'This is not a constitutional model upon which the future can build' (ibid at 287–93). Peters shares such concerns, arguing that the claim that the Constitution is 'owned' by the people suffers 'from a gender bias and risks overstating the importance of irrational and mythological foundations of constitutional law' (ibid 608).

Peters offers the most reflective account of the thesis, noting the existence of certain anti-constitutionalist trends in the international arena and acknowledging that 'the constitutionalist reading of current international law is to some extent an academic artefact'.[78] But while accepting that objections to the thesis may come from 'the legal soundness of the reconstruction' and to 'arguably negative policy effects', there is no recognition that the most pressing objections to the project come from the basic assumptions that underpin the concept of liberal-legal constitutionalism itself.[79] The concept of multi-level constitutionalism being touted is an exemplary illustration of constitutionalisation: freed from the governing traditions of specific nation states, its advocates present constitutionalism as an autonomous set of rational legal norms of universal validity.

V. CONCLUSION

The process of constitutionalisation is born of the reconfiguration of the values of constitutionalism, an extension of their reach, and a loosening of the connection between constitutionalism and the nation state. The process draws on some of the achievements of modern constitutions and constitutionalism in regulating govern-ment, but it jettisons those aspects of these modern processes which have rested on the particularities of history and culture. In the frame of constitutionalisation, it is not the way of being of a people (ie culture) that provides the source of authority of constitutional norms, but neither is this authority attributable of the enactment of a constitutional text (ie historical fact). As a social philosophy, constitutionalisation marks the elevation of certain constitutional norms—those expressing the principles of liberal-legal constitutionalism—to the status of rational truths. As a social move-ment, constitutionalisation is allied to the restructuring forces of 'new governance' and, as such, forms a movement that extends specific types of discipline across the range of governmental action.

The effect of this process of constitutionalisation has recently been felt across all levels of government. It has been spearheaded domestically through a 'rights revolu-tion' that has sought to extend the reach of judicially enforced constitutional rights. But its work can also be seen, more generally, in the ways that recent government restructuring—privatisation, reform of the administrative arrangements of the welfare state, and emergence of the regulatory form of government—has enhanced the importance of those constitutional norms that promote governmental accountability

---

[78] Ibid 605.

[79] Ibid 606. Habermas, who in his advocacy of constitutionalisation of the world society is acutely conscious of issues of democratic legitimation, does appear to recognise the tension between the logics of legal and political constitutionalism: J. Habermas, 'The Constitutionalization of International Law and the Legitimation Problems of a Constitution for World Society' (2008) 15 *Constellations* 444–55, at 446: 'Whereas the world organization would have a hierarchical organization and its members make binding law, interactions at the transnational level would be heterarchical.' This is, however, the statement of a problem without any clear solution.

and responsiveness. The movement has generated most interest, amongst certain constituencies at least, in the international arena where, ironically, the loss of the 'comprehensive' authority of national constitutions becomes the justification for extending the processes of constitutionalisation to trans and supranational bodies. The fact is that, in the sense being suggested, national constitutions were never comprehensive in their reach: modern constitutions provide a general framework for resolving governmental issues but have been able to do their work mainly through their gaps and silences and the vagueness of their formulations rather than because of the precision of their normative commitments. International constitutionalisation actually follows the same trajectory as the domestic level: it is part of a general restructuring movement, founded on particular conceptions of liberty and equality, and promoted through a rights and responsiveness agenda.

It might be objected that this argument presents constitutionalisation as some clearly designed project with universalising objectives and that in reality the nature of the changes that are taking place in government are more nuanced, complex, ambiguous, and uncertain. The impact of the processes that have been outlined has been differentially experienced across various regimes and in this sense, any general claims made for constitutionalisation must remain qualified. Further, the impact of transnational developments has generated sophisticated analyses from scholars who, recognising the difficulties of bringing the assumptions of liberal-legal constitutionalism directly to bear on these initiatives, are searching for alternative frameworks of explanation.[80] There is a measure of force in such claims. But my objective here has been to present an account based on two assumptions: that beneath the variety and particularism of instantiations there is a common trajectory of change, and that before abandoning modern understandings in favour of a 'new pluralism' or some 'new paradigm', the extent to which an explanation of these developments within the terms supplied by modern discourse should first be examined.

---

[80] See, eg N. Walker, 'Postnational Constitutionalism and the Problem of Translation', in Weiler and Wind, above n 64, ch 2; Walker, 'Post-Constituent Constitutionalism? The Case of the European Union', in M. Loughlin and N. Walker (eds), above n 61, ch 13; M. Maduro, 'Contrapunctual Law: European Constitutional Pluralism in Action', in N. Walker (ed), *Sovereignty in Transition* (Oxford: Hart, 2003), 502–37; N. Krisch, 'The Open Architecture of European Human Rights Law' (2008) 71 *Modern Law Review* 183–216; Kumm in this volume; Teubner in this volume.

PART II

THE QUESTION OF EUROPE

4

European Governance

Governing with or without the State?

Tanja A. Börzel[*]

I. INTRODUCTION

The European Union (EU) used to be considered a unique system of multi-level governance that cannot be compared to any other form of political order at the national or international level.[1] There is broad agreement that the EU is and has always been more than an international organisation of states, but it is not and probably never will be a state of its own right.[2] Political scientists have shown a remarkable creativity in developing new concepts to capture the allegedly *sui generis* nature of the EU, describing it as a 'new, post-Hobbesian order',[3] 'a post-modern state',[4] or 'a network of pooling and sharing sovereignty'.[5] In recent years, students of the EU have started to adopt a more comparative approach. The governance literature appears to be particularly attractive for studying the political institutions and policy processes in

[*] I wish to thank Fritz Scharpf for his very helpful comments on a previous version of this chapter.

[1] D. J. Puchala, 'Of Blind Men, Elephants and International Integration' (1972) 10 *Journal of Common Market Studies* 267–84; J. A. Caparaso, 'The European Union and Forms of State: Westphalian, Regulatory or Post-modern?' (1996) 34 *Journal of Common Market Studies* 29–52.

[2] W. Wallace, 'Less than a Federation, More than a Regime: The Community as a Political System', in H. Wallace, W. Wallace, and C. Webb (eds), *Policy-Making in the European Community* (John Wiley: Chichester, 1983), 43–80; see also Puntscher Rieckmann in this volume.

[3] P. C. Schmitter, *The European Community as an Emergent and Novel Form of Political Domination. Working Paper No. 26* (Madrid: Juan March Institute, 1991).

[4] J. G. Ruggie, 'Territoriality and Beyond: Problematizing Modernity in International Relations' (1993) 47 *International Organization* 139–74; J. A. Caporaso, 'The European Union and Forms of the State: Westphalia, Regulatory or Post-Modern?' (1996) 34 *Journal of Common Market Studies* 29–52.

[5] R. O. Keohane and S. Hoffmann (eds), *The New European Community: Decisionmaking and Institutional Change* (Boulder, Col.: Westview Press, 1991).

the EU by offering concepts that can be equally applied to interstate institutions and national states. Thus, the EU has been frequently portrayed as a system of 'network governance',[6] where the authoritative allocation of values is negotiated between state and societal actors,[7] which have also been invoked in reference to the 'negotiating state'[8] and international politics as 'governance without government'.[9]

This chapter, by contrast, argues that the EU's 'nature of the beast'[10] is not to be captured by one particular type of governance. Rather, the EU combines forms of governance, which involve the member states to different degrees and are best characterised as 'governance with the state'. First, governance without the state, where state and non-state actors cooperate on a non-hierarchical basis or non-state actors coordinate among themselves to make public policies, is hard to find in the EU. EU policies are largely formulated and implemented by state actors. Secondly, the EU seems to have the power to govern without the state. Its supranational institutions allow the adoption and enforcement of legally binding decisions without the consent of (individual) member states. While this is often overlooked in the literature, the EU still lacks coercive power—otherwise it would be a state. Being able to adopt decisions against the will of the member states, the EU still relies on their voluntary compliance and the willingness of *their* courts and enforcement authorities to make EU decisions effective. Thus, the EU is first of all governance with the state rather than without it. This has serious implications for the constitutional structure of the EU, both with regard to its effectiveness and its legitimacy.

The chapter starts with conceptualising the relationship between state and governance. It draws on the distinction between government or governance by the state and governance without the state. The second part uses this typology to study European governance. The analysis will show that EU policies are largely formulated and implemented in multiple overlapping negotiation systems that mostly involve supranational and state actors and give little room for business and civil society. While forms of private self-regulation or public–private co-regulation abound in the member states as well as in global politics, we hardly find such forms of governance without the state at the EU level. Thus, the EU is best described as governance with the state, whereby the role of the state varies significantly across policy areas. The

[6] B. Kohler-Koch, 'Catching up with Change: The Transformation of Governance in the European Union' (1996) 3 *Journal of European Public Policy* 359–80.

[7] Cf B. Kohler-Koch and R. Eising (eds), *The Transformation of Governance in Europe* (London: Routledge, 1999); C. Ansell, 'The Networked Polity: Regional Development in Western Europe' (2000) 13 *Governance* 303–33; A. Schout and A. Jordan, 'Coordinated European Governance: Self-Organizing or Centrally Steered?' (2005) 83 *Public Administration* 201–20.

[8] F. W. Scharpf, *Games Real Actors Play: Actor-Centered Institutionalism in Policy Research* (Boulder, Col.: Westview Press, 1997).

[9] J. N. Rosenau and E.-O. Czempiel (eds), *Governance without Government: Order and Change in World Politics* (Cambridge: Cambridge University Press, 1992).

[10] T. Risse-Kappen, 'Exploring the Nature of the Beast: International Relations Theory and Comparative Policy Analysis Meet the European Union' (1996) 34 *Journal of Common Market Studies* 53–80.

chapter concludes by discussing some implications of this governance constellation for the European constitutional structure. Since questions of legitimacy are covered by the contributions of Scharpf and Puntscher Rieckmann, the focus will be placed on the 'problem-solving gap' caused by the lack of governance by the state and the challenges it poses for the constitutional design of the EU.

II. GOVERNANCE AND THE STATE

The *governance* concept has made quite a career in European Studies. It would go beyond the scope of this chapter to provide an overview of the European governance literature.[11] This section builds on existing concepts and develops a governance typology which allows for a classification of European governance and its systematic comparison with state and interstate systems.

Following the work of Renate Mayntz and Fritz W. Scharpf, this chapter understands governance as institutionalised modes of coordination through which collectively binding decisions are adopted and implemented.[12] Governance consists of both structure and process.[13] In terms of structure, governance relates to institutions and actor constellations. Here, the literature usually distinguishes between hierarchy, market (competition systems),[14] and networks (negotiation systems).[15] These are ideal types, which differ with regard to the type of actors involved and the degree of coupling between them. Governance as process, in turn, points to the

---

[11] Cf I. Bache and M. Flinders (eds), *Multi-level Governance* (Oxford: Oxford University Press, 2004); B. Kohler-Koch and B. Rittberger, 'The "Governance Turn" in EU Studies' (2006) 44 *Journal of Common Market Studies* 27–49; L. Hooghe and G. Marks, *Multi-Level Governance and European Integration* (Lanham: Rowman & Littlefield, 2001).

[12] R. Mayntz and F. W. Scharpf, 'Steuerung und Selbstorganisation in staatsnahen Sektoren', in R. Mayntz and F. W. Scharpf (eds), *Gesellschaftliche Selbstregulierung und politische Steuerung* (Frankfurt: Campus, 1995), 9–38; R. Mayntz, 'Governance im modernen Staat', in A. Benz (ed), *Regieren in komplexen Regelsystemen: Eine Einführung* (Wiesbaden: VS Verlag für Sozialwissenschaften, 2004), 65–75.

[13] Scharpf, above n 8; Mayntz and Scharpf, above n 12.

[14] In the political science literature, markets are not regarded as governance since they are a 'spontaneous order' (Hayek) that leaves 'no place for "conscious, deliberate and purposeful" effort to craft formal structures' (O. E. Williamson, *The Mechanisms of Governance* (Oxford: Oxford University Press, 1996), at 31). Yet, market mechanisms can be institutionalised to coordinate actors behaviour through competition (A. Benz, 'Politischer Wettbewerb', in A. Benz et al (eds), *Handbuch Governance Theoretische Grundlagen und empirische Anwendungsfelder* (Wiesbaden: VS Verlag für Sozialwissenschaften, 2007), 54–67). This chapter uses the concept of competition systems to describe the institutionalisation of market-based modes of political coordination.

[15] The governance literature has identified other forms of social order, such as clans (W. G. Ouchi, 'Market, Bureaucracies, and Clans' (1980) 25 *Administrative Science Quarterly* 129–41) and associations (P. C. Schmitter and G. Lehmbruch (eds), *Trends towards Corporatist Intermediation* (London: Sage, 1979); W. Streeck and P. C. Schmitter (eds), *Private Interest Government: Beyond Market and State* (London: Sage, 1985). Like networks, this chapter conceptualises them as negotiation systems (see below).

modes of social coordination by which actors seek to achieve changes in (mutual) behaviour. Hierarchical coordination usually takes the form of authoritative decisions (eg administrative ordinances, court decisions). Actors must obey. Non-hierarchical coordination, by contrast, is based on voluntary compliance. Conflicts of interests are solved by negotiations. Voluntary agreement is either achieved by negotiating a compromise and granting mutual concessions (side-payments and issue-linkage) on the basis of fixed preferences (bargaining), or actors engage in processes of non-manipulative persuasion (arguing), through which they develop common interests and change their preferences accordingly.[16]

Institutions are crucial in shaping both governance structures and governance processes. On the one hand, they determine the degree of coupling between actors by defining their relationships and allocating resources to them. On the other hand, institutions set the framework for the modes of coordination on which actors draw.[17] In hierarchical structures, for instance, hierarchical and non-hierarchical modes of coordination can be used. Institutions bestow upon state actors the power to unilaterally impose decisions, but they can refrain from invoking their hierarchical authority when they bargain or argue with others. Negotiation and competition systems, by contrast, can only rely on bargaining and arguing. Which mode of coordination actors choose within their institutional limits, is, again, influenced by institutions, which render certain modes more appropriate or socially acceptable than others.

A comprehensive concept of governance as structure and process helps us delineate governance by, with, and without the state.[18]

The essence of governance by the state is hierarchy.[19] Hierarchies are based on an institutionalised relationship of domination and subordination, which significantly constrains the autonomy of subordinate actors (tight coupling) and allows for hierarchical coordination. Hierarchy can force actors to act against their self-interest.[20] They may be either physically coerced by the use of force or legally obliged by legitimate institutions (law). Hierarchical coordination does not leave actors either the possibility of exit or voice.[21] Unlike arguing and bargaining, hierarchical coordination does not seek to influence actors' choices but to unilaterally constrain or nullify them. Thus, hierarchy is based on coercion. While the state has many attributes, the

---

[16] A. Benz, *Kooperative Verwaltung: Funktionen, Voraussetzungen, Folgen* (Baden-Baden: Nomos, 1994), at 118–27; T. Risse, ' "Let's Argue!" Communicative Action in International Relations' (2000) 54 *International Organization* 1–39.

[17] Scharpf, above n 8.

[18] The distinction draws on the work of Michael Zürn, who refers to governance by, with, and without government (M. Zürn, *Regieren jenseits des Nationalstaates* (Frankfurt am Main: Suhrkamp, 1998)).

[19] R. A. W. Rhodes, *Governing without Governance: Order and Change in British Politics* (Cambridge: Cambridge University Press, 1996); Scharpf, above n 8.

[20] Scharpf, above n 8, at 171.

[21] A. O. Hirschman, *Exit, Voice, and Loyalty: Responses to the Decline in Firms, Organizations, and States* (Cambridge, Mass.: Harvard University Press, 1970).

monopoly of coercive public power ultimately distinguishes it from other forms of political organisations.

Governance without the state, by contrast, is based on equal relations between actors and the absence of coercion. They may differ with regard to their bargaining power, but no actor is subject to the will of the other.[22] The institutions of competition systems do not provide for any structural coupling. Actors have full autonomy to coordinate themselves through the mutual adjustment of their actions. Negotiation systems, finally, are characterised by loose coupling. Social coordination is based on mutual agreement. Unlike in formalised negotiation systems, the symmetrical relations of networks are not defined by formal institutions, but constituted by mutual resource dependencies and/or informal norms of equality.[23]

In sum, governance without the state refers to the involvement of non-state actors (companies, civil society) in the provision of collective goods through non-hierarchical coordination. It ranges from consultation and co-optation, delegation, and co-regulation/co-production to private self-regulation in and outside the control of the state. Governance with and without the state, hence, can involve state actors as long as they refrain from using their coercive powers. In order to avoid conceptual overstretch, however, certain forms remain outside this definition (Fig 4.1). Governance without the state does not cover lobbying and mere advocacy activities of economic and social actors aimed at state actors or supranational and international organisations.[24] Non-state actors who are not active participants in negotiating or competition systems pose few challenges to existing concepts and theories in political science and international relations. Also excluded are those arrangements among non-state actors that

- are based on self-coordination and do not aim at the provision of common goods and services (markets);

---

[22] Heavy power asymmetries can, however, reduce the choices of actors (by imposing prohibitive costs) so much so that coordination becomes largely hierarchical.

[23] Networks are then informal, ie non-formalised negotiation systems (cf B. Marin and R. Mayntz (eds), *Policy Network: Empirical Evidence and Theoretical Considerations* (Frankfurt am Main: Campus, 1991)). The literature discusses other characteristics of networks, including actor constellations that equally involve public *and* private actors (R. Mayntz, 'Modernization and the Logic of Interorganizational Networks', in J. Child, M. Crozier, and R. Mayntz (eds), *Societal Change between Market and Organization* (Aldershot: Avebury, 1993), 3–18) or relations based on trust, which favour problem solving over bargaining as the dominant action orientation (Scharpf, above n 8, at 137–8; A. Benz, *Der moderne Staat: Grundlagen der politologischen Analyse* (Munich: Oldenbourg, 2001), at 171). However, such a narrow concept of network governance is flawed both in theoretical and empirical terms (cf T. A. Börzel, 'Organising Babylon: On the Different Conceptions of Policy Networks' (1998) 76 *Public Administration* 253–73).

[24] Cf T. A. Börzel and T. Risse, 'Public-Private Partnerships: Effective and Legitimate Tools of Transnational Governance?' in E. Grande and L. W. Pauly (eds), *Complex Sovereignty: On the Reconstitution of Political Authority in the 21st Century* (Toronto: University of Toronto Press, 2005), 195–216.

- produce public goods and services as unintended consequences (for example rating agencies) or provide public 'bads' (mafia, drug cartels, transnational terrorism).

This chapter argues that the EU hardly features any forms of governance without the state. Nor do we find much governance by the state. Rather, the EU mostly constitutes forms of governance with the state.

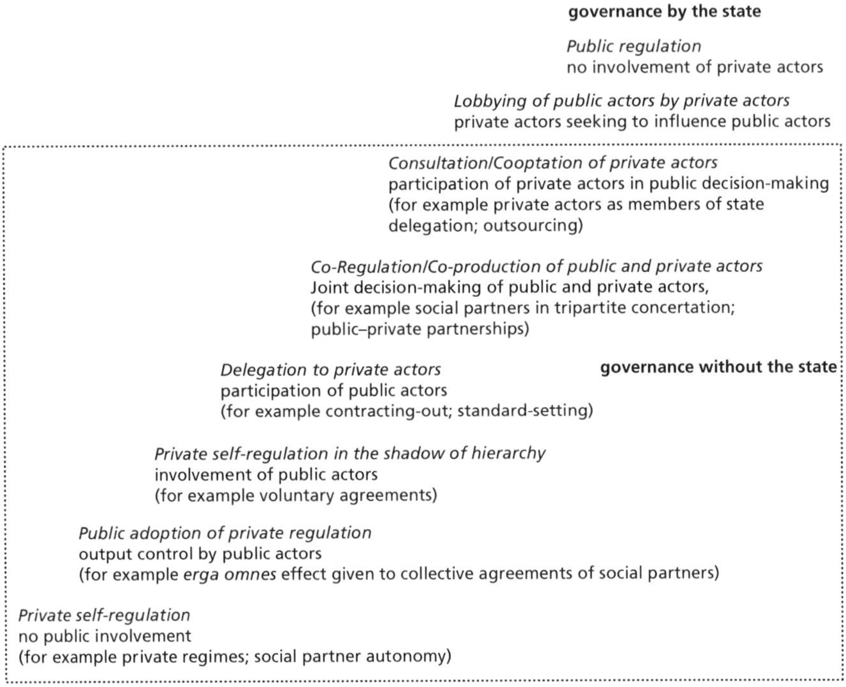

governance by the state

Public regulation
no involvement of private actors

Lobbying of public actors by private actors
private actors seeking to influence public actors

Consultation/Cooptation of private actors
participation of private actors in public decision-making
(for example private actors as members of state
delegation; outsourcing)

Co-Regulation/Co-production of public and private actors
Joint decision-making of public and private actors,
(for example social partners in tripartite concertation;
public–private partnerships)

Delegation to private actors   **governance without the state**
participation of public actors
(for example contracting-out; standard-setting)

Private self-regulation in the shadow of hierarchy
involvement of public actors
(for example voluntary agreements)

Public adoption of private regulation
output control by public actors
(for example *erga omnes* effect given to collective agreements of social partners)

Private self-regulation
no public involvement
(for example private regimes; social partner autonomy)

Source: based on Börzel and Risse, above n 24.

Figure 4.1

Governance with(out) the state: the non-hierarchical involvement of non-state actors.

III.   EUROPEAN GOVERNANCE: GOVERNANCE WITH RATHER THAN WITHOUT THE STATE

The following analysis draws on some of my previous work in which I attempt to map the governance in the EU.[25] For the purpose of this chapter, I have simplified my original typology collapsing the different forms of EU governance into governance by, with, and without the state.

[25] T. A. Börzel, 'European Governance: Markt, Hierarchie oder Netzwerk?' in
G. F. Schuppert, I. Pernice, and U. Haltern (eds), *Europawissenschaft* (Baden-Baden: Nomos,

Governance without the state

The EU is often treated as the prototype of governance without the state. Yet, if at all, we only find very weak forms of the non-hierarchical involvement of non-state actors in EU policy making. *Consultation and co-optation* of economic and social actors certainly abound in the EU, particularly in the committees and working groups of the Commission and the Council.[26] Yet, while non-state actors have some say in the formulation and implementation of EU policies, the member states and the Commission maintain a firm grip on the policy process and its outcomes.

Co-regulation is thus almost impossible to find. While non-state actors are regularly involved in EU policy-making, they are hardly engaged on 'a more equal footing'.[27] A rare exception is the partnership principle in structural policy, which explicitly requires the involvement of social partners in inter and transgovernmental negotiation systems. Their representatives are members of the management committee for the European Social Fund, in which the member states are represented as well and which is chaired by the European Commission.[28] There are also several EU regulations providing for the participation of the social and economic partners at the various stages of programming under the Social and the Regional Development Funds.[29] Moreover, a recent regulation extends the partnership principle to include civil society.[30] The extent to which business and civil society are actually involved, however, is contested in the literature and varies significantly across the member states. Overall, it seems that they still have a marginal role compared to national, regional, and local governments.[31]

Non-state actors are equally marginalised in the Open Method of Coordination (OMC), the epitome of so-called 'new' non-hierarchical modes of governance in the EU.[32] OMC was first applied in EU employment policy. It emerged as an innovative way to implement the so-called Lisbon Strategy, which the European Council

2005), 613–41; id, 'European Governance: Verhandlungen und Wettbewerb im Schatten von Hierarchie' (2007) *Politische Vierteljahresschrift, Sonderheft 'Die Europäische Union Governance und Policy-Making'* 61–91; cf T. A. Börzel, 'European Governance: Negotiation and Competition in the Shadow of Hierarchy' (forthcoming) *Journal of Common Market Studies*.

[26] T. Christiansen and S. Piattoni (eds), *Informal Governance in the European Union* (Cheltenham: Edward Elgar, 2003).

[27] B. Kohler-Koch, 'The Evolution and Transformation of European Governance', in B. Kohler-Koch and R. Eising (eds), *The Transformation of Governance in the European Union* (London: Routledge, 1999), 14–35, at 26.

[28] Treaty Establishing the European Community, Art 147.

[29] Cf European Council, Regulation 1260/99, Ch IV, Art 8.

[30] European Council, Regulation No 1083/2006.

[31] Cf Börzel forthcoming, above n 25.

[32] Cf D. Hodson and I. Maher, 'The Open Method as a New Mode of Governance: The Case of Soft Economic Policy Co-ordination' (2001) 39 *Journal of Common Market Studies* 719–46.

adopted in 2000 to promote economic growth and competitiveness in the EU.[33] OMC has facilitated the coordination of national policies in areas where member states have been unwilling to grant the EU political powers and additional spending capacity, particularly in the field of economic and social policy.[34] In the meantime, it has travelled beyond Lisbon and is applied in justice and home affairs,[35] health policy,[36] environmental policy,[37] and tax policy.[38] OMC is in principle open for the participation of non-state actors. Yet, in practice, they are neither involved in the formulation of joint goals at the EU level nor in their implementation at the national level.[39] This is not surprising since it is precisely the intergovernmental and volun-taristic nature that makes OMC an acceptable mode of policy coordination for the member states in sensitive areas.

Delegation is more prominent in the EU, although it has been around for quite some time, at least when it comes to technical standardisation. The setting of EU technical standards is mostly voluntary since supranational harmonisation of health and security standards is confined to national regulations concerning the public interest.[40] For other areas, the Council has delegated the task to develop technical standards to three European private organisations, which are composed of representatives from the member states. Since national standardising organisa-tions are mostly public, however, self-regulation is regulated by the EU and subject to the control of the member states through comitology. It hardly involves non-state actors.

This also holds for other areas of risk regulation, where regulatory networks have emerged in response to liberalisation and privatisation in the Single Market.

---

[33] Cf K. A. Armstrong, I. Begg, and J. Zeitlin, 'JCMS Symposium: EU Governance after Lisbon' (2008) 46 *Journal of Common Market Studies* 413–50.

[34] Hodson and Maher, above n 32.

[35] A. Caviedes, 'The Open Method of Co-ordination in Immigration Policy: A Tool for Prying Open Fortress Europe?' (2004) 11 *Journal of European Public Policy* 289–310.

[36] S. Smismans, 'New Modes of Governance and the Participatory Myth' (2006) 1 *European Governance Papers* <http://www.connex-network.org/eurogov/pdf/egp-newgov-N-06-01. pdf>.

[37] A. Lenschow, 'New Regulatory Approaches in "Greening" EU Politics' (2002) 8 *European Law Journal* 19–37.

[38] C. M. Radaelli and U. S. Kraemer, 'Governance Areas in EU Direct Tax Policy' (2008) 46 *Journal of Common Market Studies* 315–36.

[39] Hodson and Maher, above n 32; M. Rhodes, 'Employment Policy', in H. Wallace, W. Wallace, and M. A. Pollack (eds), *Policy-Making in the European Union* (Oxford: Oxford University Press, 2005), 279–304, at 295–300; S. Borrás and K. Jacobsson, 'The open Method of Co-ordination and New Governance Patterns in the EU' (2004) 11 *Journal of European Public Policy* 185–208, at 193–4; M. Büchs, 'How Legitimate is the Open Method of Co-ordination?' (2008) 46 *Journal of Common Market Studies* 765–86.

[40] T. Gehring and M. Kerler, 'Institutional Stimulation of Deliberative Decision-Making: Division of Labour, Deliberative Legitimacy and Technical Regulation in the European Single Market' (2008) 46 *Journal of Common Market Studies* 1001–23.

These market-making processes require some form of re-regulation at the EU and the national level to ensure fair competition and in order to correct or compensate undesired market outcomes. Since the member states have been reluctant to transfer regulatory powers to supranational institutions, particularly in the area of economic regulation, market-creating and market-correcting competencies are usually delegated to independent regulatory agencies or ministries at the national level.[41] To fill the 'regulatory gap' at the EU level, national regulatory authorities have established informal networks to exchange information and develop 'best practice' rules and procedures to address common problems.[42] We find these networks in an increasing number of sectors, such as pharmaceuticals and foodstuffs, but also beyond risk regulation, including competition, public utilities, financial services or data protection, and law enforcement. While these regulatory and operational networks may be open to the participation of non-state actors (eg providers and consumers), they are transgovernmental rather than transnational in character.

The strongest form of delegation in the EU is the Social Dialogue.[43] In selected areas of social policy, the social partners have the right to conclude agreements, which can be turned into European Law. Moreover, the EU cannot take legal action without consulting the social partners. If the latter abstain from collective bargaining, however, the EU is free to legislate. While this form of Euro-corporatism is unique, the negotiation procedure under the Social Dialogue has hardly been invoked.[44] Despite qualified majority voting in the Council, member states still are too diverse to agree on EU legal standards. In the absence of a credible shadow of hierarchy, employers had little incentive to negotiate with the trade unions. Moreover, the social partners themselves have faced problems in reaching agreement among their members since industrial relations are still organised along national lines. As a result, delegation has hardly been used in social policy.

Other forms of delegated or regulated private self-regulation in the shadow of hierarchy are equally rare. While voluntary agreements at the national level abound, they have been hardly used by European business organisations to prevent EU regulation; if at all, they are found in the area of environmental and consumer protection.[45]

Private self-regulation or true governance without the state, finally, is almost impossible to find at the EU level. Non-state actors may coordinate themselves without having a mandate from or being under the supervision of supranational institutions. The EU is crowded with a multitude of non-state actors, representing both civil

[41] D. Coen and A. Héritier (eds), *Refining Regulatory Regimes in Europe: The Creation and Correction of Markets* (Cheltenham: Edward Elgar, 2006).

[42] D. Coen and M. Thatcher, 'Network Governance and Multi-level Delegation: European Networks of Regulatory Agencies' (2008) 28 *Journal of Public Policy* 49–71.

[43] Treaty Establishing the European Community, Arts 138–9.

[44] Rhodes, above n 39.

[45] Cf A. Héritier and S. Eckert, 'New Modes of Governance in the Shadow of Hierarchy: Self-Regulation by Industry in Europe' (2008) 28 *Journal of Public Policy* 113–38.

society and business. They have organised themselves at the EU level in umbrella organisations. The so-called Euro-groups have the possibility to take binding decisions for their members, eg by adopting codes of conduct, negotiating voluntary agreements, and monitoring compliance. But they seldom have embarked on collective action and, if they do, the shadow of hierarchy looms. The few EU-level voluntary agreements have been negotiated to avoid stricter EU regulation.[46] Rather than engaging in private interest government, business and civil society organisations focus on individual and collective lobbying of decision makers, both at the EU and the national level.[47] The emergence of governance without the state is further impaired by European peak associations and umbrella groups being organised around and often divided along national lines, which in turn renders consensus among its members difficult.

To conclude, governance without the state has proliferated far less in the EU than the ever-growing literature would lead us to expect. Business and civil society do play a role in EU policy making but political decisions are largely taken and implemented by inter and transgovernmental actors. Delegation and private self-regulation in and outside the shadow of hierarchy are equally rare. The dominance of state actors distinguishes European governance from both governance within and beyond the state. At the member state as well as at the international level, private actors play a much more prominent role in policy making than in the EU.[48]

Governance with the state

While the member states are still the Masters of the Treaties and dominate EU policy making at all levels, the EU does have the power of hierarchical coordination. The supranational institutions of the EC-Treaty (ECT) provide ample possibility for hierarchical coordination where supranational actors have the power to take legally binding decisions without requiring the consent of the member states. The most prominent case is the European Central Bank (ECB), which authoritatively determines EU monetary policy.[49] The presidents of the national central banks are represented in the ECB Council. However, they are not subject to any mandate by the member states.[50] Likewise, the Commission can conduct investigations into cases of suspected distortion of competition caused by member states (eg by state aid) and anti-competitive practices of private actors (eg cartel formation), impose sanctions, and take legal recourse to the European Court of Justice (ECJ).[51] The Commission can enforce competition rules set by Articles 81, 87 ECT, and a series of directives

---

[46] Ibid.

[47] D. Coen and J. Richardson (eds), *Lobbying the European Union: Institutions, Actors, and Issues* (Oxford: Oxford University Press, 2009).

[48] Cf Börzel forthcoming, above n 25.

[49] Treaty Establishing the European Community, Art 105 ECT.

[50] Ibid, Art 108.

[51] Ibid, Art 82 ECT; Art 88 ECT.

and regulations, which have been adopted by qualified majority in the Council (since the Amsterdam Treaty). In the case of public undertakings, it can also adopt legally binding regulations without the consent of the member states, if privileges of public undertakings constitute a major obstacle to the completion of the Single Market.[52]

Finally, the European Court of Justice (ECJ) can bind the member states against their will through their interpretation of European law—a power that extends beyond market-making policies. Through dynamic interpretation of the Treaties, the ECJ has expanded European regulation beyond negative integration. For instance, the ECJ empowered the EC to enact social and environmental regulations at a time when the member states had not yet bestowed the EC with the necessary competencies.[53] In a similar vein, the ECJ established the principle of state and damages liability for violations of European Law that requires the member states to provide financial compensation for damages caused by breaches of European law.[54]

In sum, the EU entails institutionalised rule structures which offer the Commission, the European Court of Justice, and the European Central Bank ample opportunities for hierarchical coordination. Yet, although the EU can legally bind the member states against their will, it lacks the coercive power to bring them into compliance. Unlike modern states, the EU does not have a legitimate monopoly of force.[55] Ultimately, the effectiveness of EU Law rests on the voluntary compliance of the member states. Member state governments can be held responsible by the Commission and the ECJ for any breaches of EU Law. And domestic courts and enforcement authorities have to execute ECJ judgments. This is particularly the case under the preliminary ruling procedures,[56] where domestic courts refer cases of conflict between national and European law to the ECJ to settle the issue. Yet member states and their enforcement authorities can openly or tacitly defy the rulings of the ECJ or the authoritative decisions of the Commission. This may entail material (eg loss of structural funds) and reputational costs. But if member states are willing to bear such costs, there is nothing the EU can do, particularly when dealing with the more powerful member states which are more likely to resist compliance with EU law.[57]

Even where the EU has exclusive hierarchical powers of decision, it must rely on member states for their enforcement. The role of the latter increases under the so-called Community Method, where the Commission holds the exclusive right of

---

[52] Ibid, Art 86, para 3.

[53] J. McCormick, *Environmental Policy in the European Union* (Basingstoke: Palgrave, 2001).

[54] P. P. Craig, 'Once More unto the Breach: The Community, the State and Damages Liability' (1997) 113 *Law Quarterly Review* 67–94.

[55] Cf J. A. Caporaso and J. Wittenbrink, 'The New Modes of Governance and Political Authority in Europe' (2006) 13 *Journal of European Public Policy* 471–80.

[56] Treaty Establishing the European Community, Art 234.

[57] T. A. Börzel et al, *Recalcitrance, Inefficiency, and Support for European Integration: Why Member States Do (Not) Comply with European Law* (CES Working Paper 148; Cambridge, Mass.: Harvard University, 2007).

legal initiative but the Council decides by qualified majority. This applies to almost all policies under the First Pillar but also to the framework decisions under the Third Pillar.[58] Since majority voting entails an element of hierarchy by binding a minority of member states against their will, the core areas of EU policy making are embedded in hierarchical structures. At the same time, the member states retain a prominent role in the policy process. While the Community Method grants the Commission and the European Parliament a significant say, EU decision making is still dominated by the Council. The Committee of Permanent Representatives, numerous Council working groups, as well as the expert committees of the Commission prepare legal proposals and execute Council decisions (comitology). While the ECJ has the power of judicial review, it is again the member states which have to implement and enforce EU law.

The role of the member states is the strongest under the Second and Third Pillars. The (European) Council usually decides by unanimity and shares the right of initiative with the Commission. The Parliament is at best consulted and the ECJ has only limited power of judicial review.[59] The areas of inter and transgovernmental cooperation, which the member states explicitly sealed against even the shadow of supranational hierarchy, largely correspond to the ideal type of interstate negotiation systems. European decisions rest on the voluntary coordination of the member states (unanimity or consent) and often do not have legally binding character (ie they constitute 'soft law'). They are prepared and accompanied by inter and transgovernmental networks, which act free from the shadow of hierarchy cast by supranational institutions. This is not only true for the Second and parts of the Third Pillar, but also for selected areas under the First Pillar (parts of social policy, macroeconomic and employment policy, research and development, culture, education, taxation), in which the EU has no or only very limited competencies and the influence of the supranational troika (Commission, Parliament, and Court) is severely restricted. Moreover, a new form of transgovernmental negotiation system or 'state-centred multi-level governance'[60] has emerged, again under the First Pillar, in which member state authorities coordinate their regulatory activities, although they are not necessarily directly controlled by their governments.

IV. TOO MUCH OR TOO LITTLE STATE?

Governance in the EU is governance with rather than without or by the state. On the one hand, the role of non-state actors is much more limited than often suggested by the literature on the EU as the prototype of network or new modes of governance. On the other hand, the EU can draw on substantial forms of hierarchical governance,

---

[58] Treaty on European Union, Art 35, para 1.

[59] Ibid, Art 35, para 6.

[60] D. Levi-Faur, 'The Governance of Competition: The Interplay of Technology, Economics, and Politics in European Union Electricity and Telecom Regimes' (1999) 19 *Journal of Public Policy* 175–207, at 201.

which cast a strong shadow of hierarchy on both negotiations and competition in the First and parts of the Third Pillar.[61] Yet, the EU lacks (the monopoly of) coercive force and must rely on member states for the enforcement of its authoritative allocation of values. While the member states have increasingly shared powers with the European Commission, the European Parliament or (trans)national regulatory authorities, they remain the central decision makers and implementers of EU policies.

Conceptualising the EU as governance with the state not only allows for a more nuanced analysis of its nature focusing on the different degrees of state involvement; it also makes the EU look less unique and facilitates comparison with other governance systems within and beyond the state. Finally, it points to some severe limitations regarding the effectiveness of EU governance. The decline of governance by the state at the national level resulted in the search for more effective solutions at the EU level, creating serious problems for the legitimacy of both the EU and the member states.[62] The lack of governance by the state at the EU level, in turn, impairs the effectiveness of EU governance in those areas where societal problems have become more prominent and the problem-solving capacity of the member states appears to be increasingly wanting.

The EU governs the largest market in the world. The various forms of governance with the state have produced a comprehensive regulatory framework that has successfully prevented and corrected market failures. Even without coercive power, compliance with EU law appears to be generally sufficient to make the Common Policies work. Member states do not always comply, and some comply better than others.[63] Yet, a polity seeking to integrate twenty-seven and more states, which are ever more diverse, may need a certain amount of non-compliance or 'institutional hypocrisy'.[64] And sooner or later all member states comply with all EU laws, even though in some cases this has taken up to eighteen years.[65]

The problem-solving capacity of the EU is not challenged by a lack of power directly to enforce its policies. Rather, it is the incapacity to adopt new policies addressing economic and social problems that concern EU citizens most. Particularly in (re)distributive policy areas, member states have not been willing to yield decision-making powers to the EU in order to counteract politically undesirable outcomes of the Single Market. At the same time, EU market integration impedes

---

[61] Cf Börzel forthcoming, above n 25.

[62] Cf F. W. Scharpf, *Governing Europe: Effective and Legitimate?* (Oxford: Oxford University Press, 1999); Scharpf in this volume.

[63] Börzel et al, above n 57.

[64] E. A. Iankova and P. J. Katzenstein, 'European Enlargement and Institutional Hypocrisy', in T. A. Börzel and R. A. Cichowski (eds), *The State of the European Union*, vol.6: *Law, Politics, and Society* (Oxford: Oxford University Press, 2003), 269–90.

[65] Börzel et al, above n 57.

member states in maintaining such functions.[66] The Single Currency largely deprives the member states of their major instruments for national macroeconomic stabilisation, while the Maastricht convergence criteria place serious constraints on state expenditures. Softer modes of governance with a strong role of the member states are unlikely to respond to this 'European problem-solving gap'.[67] Attempts to use the OMC for institutionalising member state coordination in areas such as taxation of mobile capital, employment, or social policy, where the heterogeneity and political salience of member state preferences prohibits more hierarchical forms of governance, pale in light of the redistributive effects of the EU's hierarchical powers in monetary policy on the one hand and member state competition with regard to taxes and labour costs on the other. Redistributive or normative conflicts are hard to solve without the possibility of resorting to authoritative decision making.[68] The dilemma of European governance may be that 'soft' forms appear to require a shadow of supranational hierarchy to address policy problems, which the member states refuse to make subject to 'hard' hierarchical forms of EU governance in the first place. Due to the high legitimacy requirements for imposing policies with redistributive and normative consequences, on the one hand, and the already existing legitimacy crisis of the EU, on the other, granting the EU more powers is hardly a solution to closing the problem-solving gap. The dilemma remains and is exacerbated by the current financial and economic crisis, which neither the EU (even with the new powers of the Lisbon Treaty) nor the member states have so far been able effectively to address. It remains to be seen how the loss of savings and investments, rising unemployment, and cuts in social benefits will affect the legitimacy of the state. This time, it will be hard for national policy makers to blame Brussels, which for once may emerge in the public perception as the solution rather than the problem.

V.   THE CONSTITUTIONAL CHALLENGE

The EU as a form of governance with the state closely resembles a system of cooperative federalism of which Germany is considered to be a prototype.[69] While the central level makes the laws, the constituent units are responsible for implementing them. The vast majority of competencies are 'concurrent' or 'shared'. This

---

[66] F. W. Scharpf, 'Negative and Positive Integration in the Political Economy of European Welfare States', in G. Marks et al (eds), *Governance in the European Union* (London: Sage, 1996), 15–39; M. Ferrera, 'European Integration and National Social Citizenship: Changing Boundaries' (2003) 36 *Comparative Political Studies* 611–52.

[67] F. W. Scharpf, 'The Joint-Decision Trap Revisited' (2006) 44 *Journal of Common Market Studies* 845–64, at 855.

[68] Scharpf, above n 9.

[69] Cf F. W. Scharpf, 'The Joint-Decision Trap: Lessons from German Federalism and European Integration' (1988) 66 *Public Administration* 239–78; T. A. Börzel, 'What Can Federalism Teach Us about the European Union? The German Experience' (2005) 15 *Regional and Federal Studies* 245–57.

functional division of labour requires a strong representation of the interests of the member states at the EU level, not only to ensure an effective implementation and enforcement of EU policies for which the member states are responsible but also to prevent member states from being reduced to mere 'administrative agents' of the EU. Their reduced capacity of self-determination is compensated by strong participatory rights in the process of EU decision making, mainly in the framework of the Council, which is the equivalent of a Second Chamber. The Council as the chamber of territorial representation is organised according to the *Bundesrat* (Federal Council) principle, where the member states are represented by their governments (not by directly elected representatives or members of parliament), and in relation to their population size, with smaller states being over-represented. The functional interdependence of the EU and the member state levels of government not only gives rise to 'interlocking politics' and 'joint decision making' with a high need for consensus, but also favours the emergence of a policy-making system in which policies are formulated and implemented by the administrations on both levels of government ('executive federalism'). Functional (non-territorial) interests are only weakly represented in EU decision making and cannot even rely on alternative forms of interest intermediation, such as the party system and/or sectoral associations, as we find them in Germany or Austria.

All in all, governance with the state is based on a constitutional system of the EU, where competencies are mostly shared among the EU and the member states, where territorially defined executive interests dominate over functionally defined societal interests, and where political decisions require a high degree of consensus. It has resulted in the interpenetration of supranational and national constitutional structures that have proven impossible to be disentangled. Any attempts to delineate exclusive member state jurisdictions or re-transfer European competencies to the member state level have fallen into the joint decision trap, from which they are unlikely to escape.[70] Even if the Constitutional Treaty has failed, a demise of the European Constitution as it has evolved over time has been rendered impossible by the EU-induced transmutations of the member states' Constitutions. The transfer of national sovereignty rights to the EU level has given rise to the creation of a new supranational Constitution, which does not exist as an autonomous layer but is intractably interlocked with the national Constitutions. Member states have not only created the European Constitution; they must also implement its provisions to make it work. Instead of trying to 'ring-fence' member-state responsibilities, national and European constitutional provisions should focus on properly defining the role of the member states and their institutions in EU policy making. Member states have naturally lost autonomous decision-making power in the process of European integration. Yet, some state bodies have lost more than others. While national governments have been compensated by receiving ample co-decision rights in EU

[70] Scharpf, above n 69.

policy making, the losers are the national and regional parliaments.[71] They have been weakened in their constitutional relationship with the government and the courts. If political decisions are increasingly made in Brussels rather than in Berlin, London, Paris, or Warsaw, parliaments are deprived of their legislative function and seriously constrained in holding government accountable. Moreover, the supremacy and direct effect of European law gives national courts the power to overrule national legislation that does not conform to European requirements. Finally, the delegation of executive powers to independent regulatory agencies has further undermined the possibility of controlling the execution of national and European law. Upgrading the role of national parliaments or the European Parliament in EU policy making will do little to compensate for this comprehensive loss of power. Even if the Lisbon Treaty enters into force, the constitutional challenge remains: it is for member states to redefine the balance of power between the three branches of government at the domestic level taking into account the realities of multi-level constitutionalism in the European Union.

---

[71] A. Maurer and W. Wessels (eds), *National Parliaments on their Ways to Europe: Losers or Latecomers?* (Baden-Baden: Nomos, 2001).

5

Legitimacy in the Multi-level European Polity

Fritz W. Scharpf[*]

I. LEGITIMACY

In my understanding, any discussion of legitimacy in the multi-level European polity needs to start from a functional perspective: socially shared legitimacy beliefs are able to create a sense of normative obligation that helps to ensure voluntary compliance with undesired rules or decisions of governing authority.[1] By providing justification and social support for the 'losers' consent',[2] such beliefs will reduce the need for and the cost of—controls and sanctions that would otherwise be needed to enforce compliance.[3] They should be seen, therefore, as the functional prerequisite for governments which are, at the same time, effective and liberal.

From this functional starting point, further exploration could take either an empirical turn, focusing on citizen's compliance behaviour and justifying beliefs, or a normative turn, focusing on good reasons for such beliefs. Here, I will focus on the normative discussion.

[*] This chapter has benefited greatly from discussions at EUI Florence and BIGSS Bremen and from the personal comments of Martin Höpner at MPIfG Cologne. As has been true of all my recent work, the research assistance of Ines Klughardt has again been invaluable.

[1] F. W. Scharpf, *Governing in Europe: Effective and Democratic?* (Oxford: Oxford University Press, 1999); O. Höffe, *Demokratie im Zeitalter der Globalisierung: Überarbeitete und aktualisierte Neuausgabe* (Munich: C. H. Beck, 2002), 40.

[2] C. Anderson et al, *Losers's Consent: Elections and Democratic Legitimacy* (Oxford: Oxford University Press, 2005).

[3] The need for, or functional importance of, legitimacy is a variable, rather than a constant. It rises with the severity and normative salience of the sacrifices requested, and it falls if opt-outs are allowed—eg if the waiting lists of a national health system can be avoided through access to foreign providers.

Republican and liberal legitimating discourses

Contemporary normative discourses in Western constitutional democracies are shaped by two distinct traditions of political philosophy, which may be conventionally labelled 'republican' and 'liberal'.[4] Even though individual authors may have contributed to both, the origins, premises, generative logics, and conclusions of these traditions are clearly distinguishable.

The republican tradition can be traced back to Aristotle. For Aristotle, the polity is prior to the individual and essential for the development of human capabilities.[5] What matters is that the powers of government must be employed for the common good—and the problem, under any form of government, is the uncertain 'virtuousness' of governors who might pursue their self-interest instead. The concern for the common good of the polity and its institutional preconditions had also shaped the political philosophy of republican Rome which was resurrected in the Florentine renaissance.[6] From there, one branch of the republican tradition leads through the 'neo-Roman' theorists of the short-lived English revolution to the political ideals of the American revolution,[7] and to contemporary concepts of 'communitarian' democracy.[8] The other branch leads to the radical egalitarianism of Rousseau's *Contrat Social* which shaped the political thought of the French revolution and continues to have a powerful influence on Continental theories of democratic self-government. With the classical heritage Rousseau shares the primacy of the polity and the emphasis on the common good, to which he adds the postulate of equal participation in collective choices.[9]

But then, as for Aristotle, the 'virtuousness' of the collective governors becomes a critical problem—requiring the transformation of a self-interested *volonté des tous* into a common-interest oriented *volonté générale*. This theoretical difficulty was

---

[4] R. Bellamy, *Political Constitutionalism: A Republican Defence of the Constitutionality of Democracy* (Cambridge: Cambridge University Press, 2007).

[5] Aristotle, *Politics* (*c.*335–323 BC), i. 1253a.

[6] Marcus Tullius Cicero, *De republica* (*c.*54 BC], ed K. Büchner (Stuttgart: Reclam, 1995); Niccolò Machiavelli, *The Discourses* [1531], ed B. Crick (Harmondsworth: Penguin, 1983).

[7] J. G. A. Pocock, *The Machiavellian Moment: Florentine Political Thought and the Atlantic Republican Tradition* (Princeton, NJ: Princeton University Press, 1975); Q. Skinner, *Liberty before Liberalism* (Cambridge: Cambridge University Press, 1998); R. A. Dahl, *Democracy and Its Critics* (New Haven, Conn.: Yale University Press, 1989), ch 2.

[8] H. F. Pitkin, 'Justice: In Relating Private and Public' (1981) 9 *Political Theory* 327–52; A. MacIntyre, *After Virtue* (Indiana: University of Notre Dame Press, 1984); id, *Whose Justice? Which Rationality?* (Indiana: University of Notre Dame Press, 1988); C. Pateman, *The Problem of Political Obligation: A Critique of Liberal Theory* (Berkeley: University of California Press, 1985); F. I. Michelman, 'Conceptions of Democracy in American Constitutional Argument: The Case of Pornography Regulation' (1989) 56 *Tennessee Law Review* 203–304; C. Taylor, *The Ethics of Authenticity* (Cambridge, Mass.: Harvard University Press, 1992); cf J. Habermas, *Faktizität und Geltung: Beiträge zur Diskurstheorie des Rechts und des demokratischen Rechtsstaats* (Frankfurt am Main: Suhrkamp, 1992), 324–48.

[9] Jean-Jacques Rousseau, *The Social Contract* [1762], i., ch 6; ii., chs 1 and 4.

pragmatically resolved by the invention of representative democracy, coupling the medieval representation of estates with the aspirations of democratic self-government.[10] Here, the orientation of representatives to the common good is to be ensured by the twin mechanisms of public deliberation and electoral accountability,[11] while the egalitarianism of democratic republicanism is reflected in the fundamental commitment to universal and equal suffrage.

Compared to republicanism, the 'liberal' tradition is younger, going back to the early modern period and Thomas Hobbes, rather than to Greek and Roman antiquity.[12] Here, priority is assigned to the individual, rather than to the polity; the state is justified by the need to protect individual interests; and individual self-determination replaces the value of collective self-determination. What matters, once basic security is established by the state, are strict limitations on its governing powers in order to protect the fundamental value of 'negative liberty', which—in the tradition of John Locke and Adam Smith—should be understood as the 'freedom of pursuing our own good in our own way'.[13]

Where the need for governing powers cannot be denied, individual liberty is best preserved by a rule of unanimous decisions,[14] or, in any case, by the checks and balances of multiple-veto constitutions and pluralist patterns of interest intermediation.[15] If at all possible, decisions ought to be based on the consensus of the interests affected, rather than on majority votes.

In the Continental branch of Enlightenment philosophy, by contrast, Immanuel Kant had grounded the individualist position not in self-interest, but in the moral autonomy and rationality of the individual. Being at the same time free and morally obliged to follow their own reason, they will see that their liberty is constrained by the equal freedom of all others—which means that their choices must be governed by the 'categorical imperative'.[16] But given the 'crooked timber' of human nature, the moral imperative alone does not suffice in practice to ensure the mutual compatibility of individual liberties. There is a need, therefore, for general laws that are effectively sanctioned by state authority. Such laws will approximate a state of universal liberty if they define rules to which all who are affected could agree in

---

[10] Dahl, above n 7, 28–30.

[11] J. Habermas, *Strukturwandel der Öffentlichkeit: Untersuchungen zu einer Kategorie der bürgerlichen Gesellschaft* (Neuwied: Luchterhand, 1962); J. Elster, 'Introduction', in J. Elster (ed), *Deliberative Democracy* (Cambridge: Cambridge University Press, 1998), 1–18.

[12] Thomas Hobbes, *Leviathan: Or the Matter, Form and Power of a Commonwealth Ecclesiasticall and Civil* [1651] (New York: Collier Books, 1986).

[13] I. Berlin, *Two Concepts of Liberty: An Inaugural Lecture* (Oxford: Clarendon Press, 1958), 11.

[14] J. M. Buchanan and G. Tullock, *The Calculus of Consent: Logical Foundations of Constitutional Democracy* (Ann Arbor: University of Michigan Press, 1962).

[15] R. A. Dahl, *Pluralist Democracy in the United States: Conflict and Consent* (Chicago, Ill.: Rand McNally, 1967).

[16] Immanuel Kant, *Grundlegung zur Metaphysik der Sitten* [1785] (Stuttgart: Reclam 4507, 1961).

their capacity as autonomous and rational actors.[17] As Isaiah Berlin pointed out, however, this potential-consensus test could justify a very intrusive regulatory state, especially when decisions are delegated to the 'deliberation' of politically independent agencies or courts.[18] In other words, Kantian liberalism based on the categorical imperative, just like Rousseau's republicanism based the *volonté générale*, may well be invoked to legitimate laws and policies that depart widely from the empirical preferences of self-interested citizens.

Constitutonal democracies—and the EU?

This rough sketch obviously exaggerates the differences between the dual traditions of Western political philosophy, and a fuller treatment would have to be more nuanced and differentiated. What matters here, however, is the fact that the legitimacy of Western constitutional democracies rests on normative arguments derived from *both* of these traditions. They are all liberal in the sense that governing powers are constitutionally constrained, that basic human rights are protected and that plural interests have access to the policy-making processes by which they are affected. At the same time, they all are republican in the sense that they are representative democracies where governing authority is obtained and withdrawn through regular, universal, free and equal elections, where policy choices are shaped through public debates and the competition of political parties, and where institutions that are exempt from electoral accountability will still operate in the shadow of democratic majorities or, at least, of a democratic *pouvoir constituant*. In other words, republican and liberal principles coexist, and they constrain, complement, and reinforce each other in the constitutions and political practices of all Western democracies.[19] In a sense, they are mutual antidotes against each other's characteristic perversion: republican collectivism is moderated by the protection of individual liberties, whereas libertarian egotism is constrained by the institutions of collective self-determination.

Nevertheless, the actual combinations vary, and differences matter: republican politics are facilitated in unitary states and impeded by federal constitutions; individual interests receive less judicial protection where the constitution emphasises parliamentary sovereignty; and consensus-dependent pluralism is stronger in the United States or in Switzerland than it is in the UK, New Zealand, or in France.[20] But these

---

[17] Immanuel Kant, *Metaphysik der Sitten: Einleitung in die Rechtslehre* [1797] (Hamburg: Felix Meiner, 1966); id, *Über den Gemeinspruch: Das mag in der Theorie richtig sein, taugt aber nicht für die Praxis* [1793] (Hamburg: Felix Meiner, 1992).

[18] Berlin, above n 13, 29–39; see further A. Somek, *Individualism: An Essay on the Authority of the European Union* (Oxford: Oxford University Press, 2008).

[19] Bellamy, above n 4.

[20] Looking at the 'semantics' of national normative discourses, rather than at institutions and practices, Richard Münch identifies France with republicanism and Britain with liberalism, identifying the one with French and the other one with British political discourses. In his view, however, both are manifestations of a common European commitment to 'moral universalism and ethical individualism' which drives the European transformation of national societies

differences seem to fade in importance once we turn our attention from the world of democratic nation states to the European Union (EU). If seen by itself and judged by these standards, the Union appears as the extreme case of a polity conforming to liberal principles which, at the same time, lacks practically all republican credentials.

Its liberalism is most obvious in the priority accorded to the protection of (some) individual rights and the tight constraints impeding political action: the European Court of Justice (ECJ) is more immune from political correction than the constitutional court of any democratic state. It has from early on interpreted the Treaty commitment to establish a Europe-wide market and the free movement of goods, persons, services, and capital not as a programmatic goal to be realised through political legislation, but as a set of directly enforceable individual rights that will override all laws and institutional arrangements of EU member states. In the same spirit, the principle of non-discrimination on grounds of nationality and the politically rudimentary European citizenship have been turned into individual rights of EU nationals to access the social benefits and public services of all member states.[21] At the prodding of national constitutional courts, moreover, the ECJ has also begun to protect non-economic human rights, and with the inclusion of the Charter of Basic Rights in the Constitutional Treaty the Court will be able to complete the European protection of individual rights.

At the same time, the capacity for collective political action of the European polity is impeded by extremely high consensus requirements, and the input-side of its political processes could not be more pluralist, and less majoritarian in character. The Commission itself, which has a monopoly of legislative initiatives, relies on an extended infrastructure of committees and expert groups that allow access for a wide range of organised interests. Through the Council of Ministers, moreover, whose agreement by at least a qualified-majority vote is required for all legislation, all interests that have access to the national ministries in charge will also have access to the European level. The European Parliament, finally, whose role in legislation has been considerably expanded in recent Treaty revisions, also prides itself on giving voice to interests and concerns that might possibly have been ignored in the Commission and the Council. In short, European legislation is characterised by very open and diversified access opportunities which, combined with very high consensus requirements, make it unlikely that its effect on major (organised) interests might be ignored in the process. And consensus is of course also the hallmark of the 'new modes of governance' which are employed to achieve policy coordination through 'soft law', 'benchmarking', 'deliberation', and 'institutional learning' in fields where the Union may still lack the power to legislate.[22]

(R. Münch, *Die Konstruktion der europäischen Gesellschaft: Zur Dialektik von transnationaler Integration und nationaler Desintegration* (Frankfurt am Main: Campus, 2008), ch 4).

[21] F. Wollenschläger, *Grundfreiheit ohne Markt: Die Herausbildung der Unionsbürgerschaft im unionsrechtlichen Freizügigkeitsregime* (Tübingen: Mohr Siebeck, 2007).

[22] A. Héritier, 'New Modes of Governance in Europe: Increasing Political Capacity and Policy Effectiveness?', in T. A. Börzel and R. A. Cichowski (eds), *The State of the European Union*, vol.6: *Law, Politics, and Society* (Oxford: Oxford University Press, 2003), 105–26;

To complete the liberal model on the output-side, the EU has developed considerable effectiveness as a regulatory authority. It is most powerful in the field of monetary policy, where policies of the European Central Bank (ECB) are completely immunised against political intervention. Moreover, the Commission and the Court have enjoyed similar political independence in developing a very effective competition regime not only for the private sector but also for state aids and the public-service and infrastructure functions that might distort market competition. Some of these regimes could be based directly on the Treaties, while others depended on political compromises and European legislation. Even there, however, the Commission, the Court, and standard-setting agencies have come to play such important roles in the licensing of pharmaceuticals and the regulation of product safety, food qualities, environmental standards, or workplace discrimination, that its effectiveness as a 'regulatory state' could be described as the EU's paramount legitimating achievement.[23]

But if the EU might well qualify by liberal standards, it would definitely fail by the criteria of republican democracy. On the output side, the Union's capacity to promote the common good is constrained by the extremely high consensus requirements of EU legislation. They prevent effective collective action in response to many problems that member states could not deal with nationally. The notorious inability to regulate competition over taxes on company profits and capital incomes is just one example.[24] Worse yet, these same decision rules are responsible for an extreme conservative bias of EU policy. New legislation may be based on broad consensus but, once it is adopted, it cannot be abolished or amended in response to changed circumstances or changed preferences as long as either the Commission refuses to present an initiative or a few member states object. Beyond that, rules derived from the judicial interpretation of the Treaties could only be corrected through Treaty amendments that must be adopted unanimously by all member governments and ratified by parliaments or popular referenda in all member states. In other words, once EU law is in place, the *acquis* is nearly irreversible and its correspondence with the common good becomes progressively more tenuous as time goes on.

The constraints of consensual decision making cannot be significantly relaxed as long as the peoples of twenty-seven member states lack a collective identity

---

A. Héritier and D. Lehmkuhl, 'Introduction: The Shadow of Hierarchy and New Modes of Governance' (2008) 28 *Journal of Public Policy* 1–17; B. Kohler-Koch and B. Rittberger, 'The "Governance Turn" in EU Studies' (2006) 44 *Journal of Common Market Studies* 27–49.

[23] G. Majone, 'Regulatory Legitimacy', in G. Majone (ed), *Regulating Europe* (London: Routledge, 1996), 284–301; id, 'Europe's "Democratic Deficit": The Question of Standards' (1998) 4 *European Law Journal* 5–28.

[24] S. Ganghof and P. Genschel, 'Taxation and Democracy in the EU' (2008) 15 *Journal of European Public Policy* 58–77; S. Ganghof and P. Genschel, 'Deregulierte Steuerpolitik: Körperschaftsteuerwettbewerb und Einkommensbesteuerung in Europa' in M. Höpner und A. Schäfer (eds), *Die politische Ökonomie der europäischen Integration* (Frankfurt am Main: Campus, 2008), 311–34.

that could legitimate Europe-wide majority rule. And even if citizens were to develop a sense of common solidarity and a stronger attachment to the European polity than to their own nation state (perhaps in response to external challenges from America, Russia, or China), they would presently lack all the societal and institutional prerequisites of input-oriented democracy: no Europe-wide media of communication and political debates, no Europe-wide political parties, no Europe-wide party competition focused on highly salient European policy choices, and no politically accountable European government that must anticipate and respond to the egalitarian control of Europe-wide election returns. There is no theoretical reason to think that these deficits should be written in stone. But at present, input-oriented republican legitimacy cannot be claimed for the Union.

While these stylised diagnoses may be somewhat overdrawn, they suggest a prima facie plausible interpretation of current disputes over the existence of a 'European democratic deficit'. Authors and political actors starting from a 'liberal' framework of normative political theory will find it easy to attest to the democratic legitimacy of the EU by pointing to its protection of individual rights, to its pluralist openness to policy inputs, its consensual decision rules, and the effectiveness of its regulatory policies.[25] By contrast, authors and political actors viewing the EU from a 'republican' perspective will point to deficiencies on the output side, where the concern for individual rights and the responsiveness to organised interests are accompanied by a systemic neglect of redistributive policy goals. Their more salient criticism is, however, directed at the glaring democratic deficits on the input side, emphasising the lack of a common public space, the lack of Europe-wide political debates, party competition, and political accountability.[26] If some of these authors nevertheless assume that these deficiencies might eventually be overcome through institutional reforms and the mobilisation strategies of European parties, they seem to underestimate the disruptive potential of political mobilisation and confrontation in an institutional framework which, in the absence of a strong collective identity, would still require consensual decision making.[27]

---

[25] A. Moravcsik, *The Choice for Europe: Social Purpose and State Power from Messina to Maastricht* (Ithaca, NY: Cornell University Press, 1998).

[26] M. T. Greven, 'Can the European Union Finally Become a Democracy?', in M. T. Greven and L. W. Pauly (eds), *Democracy beyond the State? The European Dilemma and the Emerging Global Order* (Lanham: Rowman & Littlefield, 2000), 35–62; C. Harlow, *Accountability in the European Union* (Oxford: Oxford University Press, 2002); A. Follesdal and S. Hix, 'Why There Is a Democratic Deficit in the EU: A Response to Majone and Moravcsik' (2006) 44 *Journal of Common Market Studies* 533–62; S. Hix, *What's Wrong with the European Union and How to Fix It* (Cambridge: Polity, 2008).

[27] S. Bartolini, *Restructuring Europe: Centre Formation, System Building, and Political Restructuring between the Nation State and the European Union* (Oxford: Oxford University Press, 2005); id, *Taking 'Constitutionalism' and 'Legitimacy' Seriously* (MS Florence: Robert Schuman Centre for Advanced Study. European University Institute, 2008).

II. LEGITIMACY IN MULTI-LEVEL POLITIES

In any case, however, the EU in its present shape is so far from meeting the republican criteria of democratic legitimacy that it cannot benefit from the coexistence and mutual reinforcement of liberal and republican principles that supports the legitimacy of constitutional democracies at the national level.[28] But does this matter if it is acknowledged that the EU is not a free-standing, single-level polity? In the two-level constellation of the European polity, the member states are indeed expected to conform to the full range of liberal as well as republican criteria of legitimacy. It seems reasonable to ask, therefore, how this constellation should be treated in normative discussions about the legitimacy of the European polity.

For an answer, it is useful to compare the compliance and legitimating relationships between citizens and governments in different institutional constellations. In a unitary state, these relationships are congruent: compliance is demanded by the central government through its administrative agencies, and the legitimacy of these requests is established through national public discourses and the accountability of the central government to the national electorate. Congruence can also be achieved in two-level polities if their institutional architecture conforms to the model of 'dual federalism'. There, each level of government has its own domain of autonomous legislative authority, its own implementation structures, and its own base of electoral accountability.

Matters are more complicated, however, in a 'unitary federal state' like Germany where most legislative powers are exercised nationally, whereas national legislation is implemented by the *Länder*. Hence *Land* authorities are expected to comply with federal mandates, and citizens are expected to comply with the rules enforced by the *Land* authorities, regardless of their national or local origin. In the unitary political culture of the German two-level polity, however, this two-step compliance relationship does not create problems of democratic accountability. Public attention and public debates are almost exclusively focused on the politics and the policy choices at the national level. *Länder* elections, which may affect party-political majorities at the national level (in the *Bundesrat*), are generally and justifiably considered as second-order national elections where parties fight about national issues and voters express their approval or disapproval of the national government's performance.[29] In other words, while the compliance relationship runs between citizens and their respective *Länder* authorities, the dominant legitimacy relationship in Germany runs between citizens and the national government, which is held accountable for public policies that affect the citizen.

---

[28] U. K. Preuss, 'National, Supranational and International Solidarity', in K. Bayertz (ed), *Solidarity: Philosophical Studies in Contemporary Culture 5* (Dordrecht: Kluwer, 1999), 281–92.

[29] S. Burkhart, *Blockierte Politik: Ursachen und Folgen von 'Divided Government' in Deutschland* (Frankfurt am Main: Campus, 2008).

   The two-level polity comprising the EU and its member states shares some important structural characteristics with German federalism,[30] but in the context of a discussion about political legitimacy the differences appear to be much more important.
Compared to Germany, the Union is far more dependent on its member states: European legislation must be transposed through national legislatures; European law must
be implemented through the administrative agencies and courts of the member states;
and European revenue depends almost entirely on national contributions. As a consequence, compliance is even more a two-step process than is true in Germany.

   From the perspective of citizens, compliance is exclusively demanded by national
administrative agencies, tax authorities, and courts. And except where the Commission may directly prosecute the violation of competition rules, even business firms
are never directly confronted with the EU as a governing authority. By the same
token, the compliance that matters from the perspective of the Union is the willingness and ability of its member governments to ensure the implementation of
European law. This is the compliance which the Commission keeps monitoring, and
which is also the subject of a growing body of compliance research.[31]

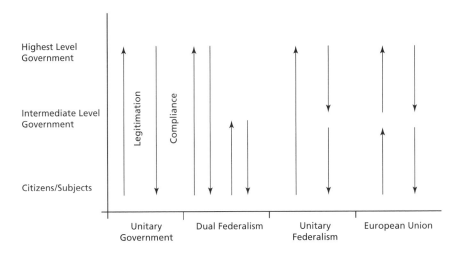

Figure 5.1

Compliance and legitimation in multi-level governments.

[30] F. W. Scharpf, 'The Joint Decision Trap: Lessons from German Federalism and European
Integration' (1988) 66 *Public Administration* 239–78.

[31] G. Falkner et al, *Complying with Europe: EU Harmonisation and Soft Law in the Member
States* (Cambridge: Cambridge University Press, 2005); M. Zürn and C. Joerges (eds), *Law and
Governance in Postnational Europe: Compliance beyond the Nation-State* (Cambridge: Cambridge
University Press, 2005); T. A. Börzel et al, *Recalcitrance, Inefficiency, and Support for European
Integration: Why Member States Do (Not) Comply with European Law* (CES Working Paper 148;
Cambridge, Mass.: Harvard University, 2007).

As in Germany, therefore, we have a two-step compliance relationship—between citizens and their respective national governments, and between these and the EU. In contrast to Germany, however, we also have a two-step legitimating relationship in the European polity. Whereas in German federalism, citizens address their demands and their electoral responses to the higher (national) level of government, the higher level of the European polity is beyond the horizon of citizen's expectations and political demands, it is not the target of public debates and party competition, and it is not vulnerable to electoral sanctions.[32] As far as citizens are concerned, they are only connected to the lower (member-state) level of government through a legitimating feedback loop. And since voters are not obliged to be fair and, in any case, could not know the origin of the rules with which they are asked to comply, 'the politics of blame avoidance'[33] is not a useful option for member governments. They must in fact carry the full burden of political accountability for their exercise of governing authority, regardless of how much European law may have contributed to it.

In the two-level European polity, therefore, the EU must be seen and legitimated not as a government of citizens, but as a government of governments. What matters foremost is the willingness and ability of member states to implement EU law and to assume political responsibility for doing so. It seems fully appropriate, therefore, that compliance research focuses exclusively on the relationship between the EU and its member states. But if that is so, then it is not obvious that normative discussions of EU legitimacy should treat the Union as if it were a free-standing polity, and that normative discussions of EU legitimacy should employ monistic concepts that ignore the two-step relationship and focus almost exclusively on the presence or absence of a 'democratic deficit' in the relation between the EU and its citizens or subjects. Instead, we need to discuss the legitimating arguments that justify the compliance of member states with EU mandates, and the conditions that allow member states to legitimate this compliance in relation to their own citizens.

III. LEGITIMATING MEMBER STATE COMPLIANCE

From the perspective of member governments, membership in the EU is fully justified by its contribution to peace and democracy on the European continent, while the record appears more ambivalent with regard to the economic promises of integration. In any case, the attraction of membership continues to exercise its pull in the near abroad, and secession does not seem to be on the agenda of any of the old and newer member states. But just as the fact that most citizens will not emigrate is no sufficient indicator of the democratic legitimacy of a nation state, the holistic assessment of the benefits of membership will not, by itself, establish the legitimacy of all Union mandates. As is true in democratic nation states, what matters are more specific characteristics of the policy-making institutions and processes that generate

---

[32] P. Mair, 'Popular Democracy and the European Union Polity', in D. Curtin and A. Wille (eds), *Meaning and Practice of Accountability in the EU Multi-Level Context* (Connex Report Series No 07; Mannheim: University of Mannheim, 2008), 19–62.

[33] R. Kent Weaver, 'The Politics of Blame Avoidance' (1986) 6 *Journal of Public Policy* 371–98.

the mandates with which member governments are expected to comply. Here, I find it useful to distinguish between two fundamentally differing modes of EU policy making, for which I use the labels 'political' and 'non-political'.[34]

Political modes are those in which member governments have a voice—most directly in Treaty negotiations and in those policy areas where EU legislation still requires unanimous agreement. But even where legislation by the 'Community Method' depends on an initiative by the Commission and the agreement of the European Parliament, the requirement of qualified majorities in the Council and the consensus-enhancing procedures of the Council ensure member governments of a significant voice in the process. This is not so in the non-political modes of EU policy making. Member states, or the European Parliament, for that matter, have no voice when the ECB determines the course of monetary policy, when the Commission decides to prosecute certain practices of EU member states as Treaty violations, and when the ECJ uses its powers of interpretation to shape the substance of primary and secondary European law. Since the effects of policies so adopted may exceed the importance of many acts of EU legislation, their legitimacy needs to be explicitly discussed as well.

Political modes of policy making

From the perspective of member governments, the high consensus requirements of EU legislation seem to ensure its input legitimacy. Policies are adopted with their agreement, and even where Council votes are taken by qualified majority, consensus-seeking practices are so effective, that politically salient national interests that are vigorously defended by the respective governments are rarely overruled. But that does not mean that EU legislation is without problems from the perspective of member governments.

The most obvious problem is that high consensus requirements will often[35] prevent majorities of member states from achieving 'European solutions' to problems which, in their view should and could be resolved at the European level.

---

[34] F. W. Scharpf, 'Notes toward a Theory of Multilevel Governing in Europe' (2001) 24 *Scandinavian Political Studies* 1–26.

[35] Often, but not always. There are indeed policy areas where EU legislation appears more 'progressive' and 'perfectionist' than one should expect in light of the political preferences of the median member state—for instance the fields of consumer protection, work safety, or environmental policy. One reason may be the strong commitment to the success of EU initiatives of 'Europhile' national representatives in the Council Secretariat and in COREPER: see J. Lewis, 'The Janus Face of Brussels: Socialization and Everyday Decision Making in the European Union' (2005) 59 *International Organization* 937–71. But at least a contributing cause may also be the relative weakness of cross-sectional policy coordination within the Commission and in the Council. This may allow policy specialists whose aspirations are frustrated in interministerial bargaining at home to pursue these in intergovernmental consensus within their specialised Council. Thus blockades and compromises on the lowest common denominator should be primarily expected where intergovernmental conflicts occur within the same specialised policy area—as seems to be true for tax harmonisation, industrial relations, or social policy.

From their perspective, therefore, the output legitimacy of European legislation remains systematically constrained. Nevertheless, where this is a first attempt at European regulation, failure to agree on common rules leaves member governments free to cope with the problem as best as they can at the national level. A potentially much more difficult problem arises, however, once a European rule is in place. Its 'supremacy' will not only displace all existing national law that is inconsistent with it, but it will also 'occupy the field' and pre-empt future attempts to deal with the same matter through national legislation.

At the same time, moreover, the existing European rule is now protected against changes by exactly the same high consensus requirements that had impeded its earlier adoption. So even if the policy does not work, or if circumstances or the political preferences of most member governments have changed significantly, it will remain in force and cannot be reformed as long as it is still supported by either the Commission (without whose initiative no amendments are possible) or by a small blocking minority in the Council.[36] In other words, European legislation is much less reversible than national legislation which may be adopted, amended, and revoked by the same simple majorities.[37] As a consequence, the presumption that existing legislation continues to be supported by a political consensus is less plausible for the EU—and the potential discrepancy is bound to increase over time.

Non-political policy making

The presumption of consensus is, of course, even more attenuated for the non-political modes of EU policy making in which member states have no voice. For the monetary policy choices of the ECB, an unconditional preference for price stability over all other goals of economic policy was stipulated in the Maastricht Treaty (Article 105 ECT). And even if governments might prefer a more flexible mandate today, they could not adopt it over the objections of even a single member state. The same is true of the Court's power to interpret European law (Article 220 ECT). If the interpretation is based on provisions of the European Treaties, reversals by unanimous Treaty amendments are practically impossible, and they are extremely difficult for the 'secondary law' of European regulations and directives.

---

[36] In fact, resistance to reform may be stronger than resistance to the initial adoption of a policy—which may benefit from a widely shared interest in having some 'European solution' to pressing national problems. Once this interest is satisfied, later reforms may be resisted by the beneficiaries of the status-quo rule. The problem must be particularly acute for the new member states which are bound by an *aquis* in whose adoption they had no voice, which may not fit their conditions, and which cannot be modified to accommodate their interests and preferences.

[37] Even more than two decades ago, Cappelletti et al spoke of the 'acute danger of legal obsolescence' arising from 'the combination of binding instruments and irreversible Community competence coupled with the increasingly tortuous Community decision-making process'. It did not become attenuated over time. See M. Cappelletti, M. Seccombe, and J. H. H. Weiler (eds), *Integration through Law: Europe and the American Federal Experience* (Berlin: DeGruyter, 1985), 40.

If the difficulty of reversing or amending EU law creates an asymmetry between the defenders of the status quo and the promoters of change, what matters here is that it also creates an asymmetry in the principal–agent relationship between those who are politically legitimated to formulate European law and those who have a mandate to apply it. Since application always requires some interpretation, the agents necessarily have some power to shape the content of the rules under which they operate. And the domain of that power will expand if legislators are unable to correct interpretations that deviate from the legislative intent.[38] Given the immense obstacles to amending the European Treaties and secondary European law, the potential scope for judicial legislation is wider in the EU than it is in all constitutional democracies at the national level. But should this wider scope of judicial review give rise to problems of legitimacy? If the question is considered at all, a negative answer is generally based on one of two arguments, neither of which seems fully convincing.

The first sees the Court in a role that was institutionalised by member states to serve their rational self-interest. They agreed to give to the Commission the power to prosecute, and to the Court the power to decide on, alleged violations of their obligations under the Treaties—and (like the ECB) Commission and Court are doing exactly what they are supposed to do, even if individual governments may not like the decision in a particular case that affects them individually.[39] The basic argument is analytical and game-theoretical. It presumes that Treaty commitments of member governments should be modelled as solutions to a (symmetric) N-person Prisoners' Dilemma—ie a constellation where all will benefit from cooperation, but all are tempted to free ride, in which case the cooperative arrangement would unravel and all would be worse off. Under these conditions, it was rational for all governments to create agencies beyond their direct political control, and to invest these with the authority to monitor and sanction violations of their commitments.

Empirically, this argument is surely overgeneralised. The assumption that EU law reflects constellations of a symmetrical Prisoners' Dilemma may be plausible for free-trade rules, but the jurisdiction of the Court extends to a wide range of policy areas that cannot be so characterised. Moreover, even within its empirical domain, the argument is theoretically overextended. The Dilemma model provides justification for creating politically independent *enforcement* agencies that will monitor compliance and may prosecute and sanction free riders. But it provides no analytical or normative support for taking the *rule-making* function

[38] G. Tsebelis, *Veto Players: How Political Institutions Work* (Princeton, NJ: Princeton University Press, 2002).

[39] G. Garret, 'International Cooperation and Institutional Choice: The European Community's Internal Market' (1992) 46 *International Organization* 533–60; id, 'The Politics of Legal Integration in the European Union' (1995) 49 *International Organization* 171–81.

out of the hands of politically accountable principals.[40] Not much is gained, moreover, if the Dilemma argument is complemented by an 'incomplete-contracts' extension.[41]

It suggests that in a contract situation, rational actors, realising that they could not foresee and regulate all future eventualities, and appreciating the high transactions costs of continuous renegotiation, would agree on having future disputes over the interpretation of their contract settled by a neutral agent. In game-theoretic terms, this argument presupposes an underlying interest constellation resembling the 'Battle of the Sexes', where all parties prefer agreement over non-agreement but disagree over the choice among specific solutions.[42] But while the argument may support a strong role of the Commission as an 'honest broker' in the process of European political legislation, it does not support judicial legislation.

For an explanation, assume two sets of member states, one with status-quo institutions resembling 'liberal market economies' and political preference for a liberal European regime, and the other one with the status-quo institutions of a 'coordinated market economy' and preferences for regulated capitalism at the European level.[43] In political legislation, it might be possible to find a compromise that both sides prefer over their respective status-quo solutions. If not, the different national regimes would remain in place. If the Court is allowed to define the European rule, however, it must do so in a specific case that challenges and may invalidate the existing law of a particular member state without its consent. In doing so, however, the Court could not create a new European regime to replace national solutions; it can only remove existing national impediments to the free movement of goods, services, capital and persons, to the freedom of establishment, to undistorted competition, and to the principle of non-discrimination. In other words: for structural reasons (which are quite independent of any 'neoliberal' preferences of the judges), judicial legislation must have an asymmetric impact on our two sets of member states: by itself, it can only impose liberalising and deregulatory policies. Under conditions of complete information, therefore, member states with coordinated market economies and concomitant political preferences would not be persuaded by an incomplete-contracts argument and would not accept rule making by judicial legislation.

---

[40] Similar empirical and theoretical objections apply to efficiency-based arguments trying to exempt the European 'regulatory state' from the need for political legitimation (Majone, above n 23). They apply at best to a narrow subset of European policy areas. And even there, efficiency arguments presuppose value judgments about ends and means, and efficiency-oriented decisions generate distributional consequences that require political legitimation (Follesdal and Hix 2006, above n 26; Hix 2008, above n 26).

[41] E. Maskin and J. Tirole, 'Unforeseen Contingencies and Incomplete Contracts' (1999) 66 *Review of Economic Studies* 83–114.

[42] F. W. Scharpf, *Games Real Actors Play: Actor-Centered Institutionalism in Policy Research* (Boulder, Col.: Westview, 1997), ch 6.

[43] P. A. Hall and D. Soskice (eds), *Varieties of Capitalism: The Institutional Foundations of Comparative Advantage* (Oxford: Oxford University Press, 2001).

In the actual history of European integration, however, that choice was not available. Since the 'Luxembourg Compromise' had reinforced the unanimity rule in the Council, the greater diversity of national interests after the original Six had been joined by the UK, Denmark, and Ireland had almost stopped the progress of integration through political legislation. In particular, attempts at harmonising national trade regulations had bogged down in interminable bargaining rounds. Hence the Court was widely applauded when its *Dassonville*[44] and *Cassis*[45] decisions began to remove national non-tariff barriers by giving direct effect to Treaty-based economic liberties. In effect, 'good Europeans' everywhere came to welcome 'Integration Though Law'[46] as an effective substitute for the perceived erosion of the 'political will' of member states.

Paradoxically, however, the immediate effect was a new stimulus to political integration. The *Cassis* decision had confronted all member states with the threat of having their own regulations displaced by a rule of 'mutual recognition'—a threat which, whenever the Commission so chose, could be made real through Treaty infringement prosecutions.[47] With this change of the 'default condition', agreement on political harmonisation became considerably more attractive. Thus member states responded positively to Jacques Delors's Single Market initiative and agreed to adopt the Single European Act which introduced qualified-majority voting in the Council for the harmonisation of rules affecting the functioning of the internal market (Article 95 ECT). And since *Cassis* had reduced the bargaining power of high-regulation countries, the new legislation also had a liberalising and deregulatory tendency.

In the 1980s, it is true, that effect did indeed correspond to the political preferences of a majority of 'liberal' governments in the Council.[48] But it is not explained by these preferences. And it was not reversed when, in the second half of the 1990s there was a preponderance of left-of-centre governments in the EU. Instead, the overall pattern is shaped by an institutional constellation in which political legislation must be negotiated in the shadow of judicial decisions which, for structural reasons, have a liberalising and deregulatory impact. In other words, the empowerment of judicial legislation in the European polity cannot be justified by game-theoretic or contract-theoretic arguments that try to show that it would, or ought to be, chosen as an efficiency-increasing solution by all self-interested member states or their governments.

---

[44] Case 8/74 *Procureur du Roi v Benoit and Gustave Dassonville* [1974] ECR 837.

[45] Case 120/78 *Rewe-Zentral AG v Bundesmonopolverwaltung für Branntwein* [1979] ECR 649.

[46] This is the common title of the series of volumes produced by the famous 'European Legal Integration Project' of the EUI Law Department. It should be noted, however, that the editors of the series were very much aware of the normative and pragmatic ambivalences implied by the divergence of legal and political integration: see Cappelletti et al, above n 37.

[47] S. K. Schmidt, 'Mutual Recognition as a New Mode of Governance' (2007) 14 *Journal of European Public Policy* 667–81; K. Nicolaïdis and S. K. Schmidt, 'Mutual Recognition "on Trial": The Long Road to Services Liberalization' (2007) 14 *Journal of European Public Policy* 717–34.

[48] Moravcsik, above n 25.

For most governments, of course, justifications derived from normative rational-choice theory are not of crucial relevance. What did and does matter much more for them is the socially shared expectation that they should operate as 'a government of laws and not of men', that courts should have the authority 'to say what the law is', and that respect for the rule of law obliges them to respect and obey the decisions of the ECJ.[49] By itself, of course, this syllogism would not define the proper domains of judicial and political legislation.[50] It is true that judge-made law, disciplined by its internal juristic logic and by the running commentary of the legal profession, continues to play a very important and legitimate role in common-law as well as in civil-law countries. But in constitutional democracies, it is developed in the shadow of democratically legitimated legislation which could (but generally will not) correct it by simple-majority vote. Since ECJ jurisprudence cannot be politically corrected, the fact that member states have, by and large, acquiesced when decisions were going against them, cannot be invoked as an indirect legitimation of judicial legislation.

The more pertinent question is therefore whether the legitimacy of ECJ jurisdiction could be equated with that of national constitutional courts. They may indeed override parliamentary legislation—and for that reason, the legitimacy of judicial review continues to be considered problematic in polities with a strong democratic tradition.[51] But even if these fundamental doubts are set aside for the moment, the status of ECJ jurisprudence cannot be equated with that of judicial review under national constitutions. First, as Stefano Bartolini noted, it would have to ignore the fact that national constitutions are generally limited to rules that organise the institutions of government and protect civil liberties and human rights.[52] By contrast, the European Treaties, as they are interpreted by the ECJ, include a wide range of detailed provisions which in constitutional democracies are matters for legislative determination, rather than constitutional interpretation. As a consequence, the politically unconstrained powers of the ECJ reach so much further than the powers of judicial review under any national constitution. Even more important, however, is a second difference.

The judicial review exercised by national constitutional courts is embedded in national political cultures with taken-for-granted normative and cognitive understandings and shared discourses about appropriate policy choices.[53] In public debates, the courts are important, but by no means the only, interpreters of common value orientations.

---

[49] K. Alter, *Establishing the Supremacy of European Law* (Oxford: Oxford University Press, 2001).

[50] C. Möllers, *Die drei Gewalten: Legitimation der Gewaltengliederung in Verfassungsstaat, Europäischer Integration und Internationalisierung* (Göttingen: Velbrück Wissenschaft, 2008).

[51] A. Bickel, *The Least Dangerous Branch: The Supreme Court at the Bar of Politics* (Indianapolis, Ind.: Bobbs-Merrill, 1962); L. D. Kramer, *The People Themselves: Popular Constitutionalism and Judicial Review* (Oxford: Oxford University Press, 2004); Bellamy, above n 4.

[52] Bartolini (2008), above n 27.

[53] J. G. March and J. P. Olsen, *Rediscovering Institutions: The Organizational Basis of Institutions* (New York: Free Press, 1989).

They must assume that the commitment to the common values of the polity is shared by all branches of the national government, and that all are oath-bound to uphold the constitution. They will thus approach legislation in a sprit of judicial self-restraint, and with a presumption of its constitutionality. And if they must nevertheless intervene against the majorities of the day, the legitimacy of their intervention depends on their capacity to express 'the sober second thought of the Community'.[54]

From the perspective of member states, these preconditions of judicial self-restraint, which at the same time limit and legitimate judicial review, are lacking in their relationship to the ECJ. Regardless of what may be true in its relationship to the Commission and the European Parliament, there cannot be such shared orientations between the Court and the governments, legislatures, and publics of the Union's twenty-seven extremely heterogeneous member states, and there is certainly no presumption of Treaty conformity when the Court is dealing with national legislation. Instead, from the Court's perspective, European integration is a mission to be realised against the inertia or recalcitrance of member states; and European law is not the expression of shared values but an instrument to discipline, and transform national policies, institutions, and practices.

So where has this discussion led us? There is of course no question of the formal legality of the Court's jurisdiction. Article 220 ECT has clearly empowered it to apply and interpret European law. Lawyers may dispute some of its interpretations, but they will not judge them *ultra vires*.[55] Given the sweeping generality of some Treaty provisions and the intentional ambiguities in secondary law, it would in any case be extremely difficult for the Court to follow the 'original intent' of the masters of the Treaties or of the multiple authors of legislative compromises. But as Europeans have had to learn through bitter experience, formal legality does not necessarily equate with legitimacy.[56] It suffices for ensuring acquiescence with the everyday constraints and demands imposed by governing authorities in fundamentally legitimate polities. But when highly salient interests and normative preferences are violated, positive legitimating arguments are needed to stabilise the routines of voluntary compliance.

In the relationship between member states and the EU, the Roman-law maxims of *pacta sunt servanda* and *volenti non fit injuria* will have considerable weight. Their governments or their predecessors have participated in creating present-day EU institutions, including the authorisation of policy making in the non-political decision modes; and governments of the newer member states have knowingly joined the

---

[54] Bickel, above n 51, 26; L. Fisher, *Constitutional Dialogues: Interpretation as Political Process* (Princeton, NJ: Princeton, University Press, 1988); M. Höreth, *Die Selbstautorisierung des Agenten: Der Europäische Gerichtshof im Vergleich zum U.S. Supreme Court* (Baden-Baden: Nomos, 2008).

[55] The most obvious characteristic of ECJ jurisprudence is its extreme form of teleological interpretation (*effet util*). But this tendency is shared by modern national jurisprudence as well: G. Lübbe-Wolff, 'Expropriation der Jurisprudenz?', in C. Engel and W. Schön (eds), *Das Proprium der Rechtswissenschaft* (Tübingen: Mohr Siebeck, 2007), 282–92.

[56] C. Joerges and N. Singh Ghaleigh (eds), *Darker Legacies of Law in Europe: The Shadow of National Socialism and Fascism over Europe and its Legal Traditions* (Oxford: Hart, 2003).

previously established institutions and the accumulated *acquis*. But these obligations are limited by the third Roman maxim of *ultra posse nemo obligatur*. And as I suggested above, the capacity of member states to comply with EU law reaches its limits when doing so would undermine their own legitimacy in relation to their national constituencies. In the following sections, I will first explore the general conditions of this legitimating relationship, and I will then turn to a series of recent decisions where the jurisdiction of the ECJ seems to pushing against the limits of legitimate compliance.

IV. THE NEED FOR JUSTIFICATION

Since the law of the Union must be implemented by its member states, it is the legitimacy of the member state that must ensure citizen compliance and citizen support. As conceptualised above, it is based on 'liberal' as well as 'republican' normative foundations. By and large, however, the EU law generated through judicial legislation is unlikely to challenge the specifically liberal principles of national constitutions.[57] But what may indeed be at stake is the 'republican' legitimacy of national governments.

Democratic republicanism requires not merely the formal existence of general elections and representative parliaments, but it presumes that the mechanisms of electoral accountability may make a difference for public policy. At a minimum, this (input-oriented) requirement implies that governments will be responsive to citizen interests and preferences, and that changing governments may have an effect on policies that are strongly opposed by popular majorities. At the same time, however, governments are under a 'republican' (and output-oriented) obligation to use the powers of government for the common good of the polity. In the normative traditions of constitutional democracies, both of these obligations are of equal and fundamental importance. But their implications may conflict when public-interest oriented policies are unpopular while popular policies may endanger the public interest. Under these conditions, normative political theory from Aristotle to Edmund Burke did accord priority to the public interest, whereas even theorists of democracy who reject the paternalistic or technocratic implications of

---

[57] It is true that the protection of human rights was in issue when the German constitutional court initially considered the possibility that it might have to review the constitutionality of EU law in its *Solange* decisions—BverfGE 37, 271 (29.05.1974), BverfGE 73, 339 (22.10.1986). In the meantime, the ECJ responded and this issue has been laid to rest: J. H. H. Weiler and N. J. S. Lockhart, 'Taking Rights Seriously: The European Court and Its Fundamental Rights Jurisprudence' (1995) 32 *Common Market Law Review* 51–94 (Pt I), 579–627 (Pt II). The rights to collective industrial action that are involved in the *Viking* and *Laval* cases discussed below could, in my view, not be classified as an implication of 'liberal' constitutional principles.

output-oriented arguments[58] will rarely defend radical populism as a normatively acceptable alternative.[59]

Instead, modern democratic theory focuses on the interactions between governors and the governed. Responsible governments must pursue the common good, but its substantive understanding, and the policies serving its attainment, should arise from deliberative interactions in the shared public space of the polity.[60] More specifically, Vivien Schmidt focuses on the role of policy-oriented 'communicative discourses' in which governors must explain and justify the unpopular policies which they consider necessary and normatively appropriate.[61] The more these policies violate highly salient interests or deviate from the strongly held normative preferences of their constituency, the more urgent is the need for justification showing how the measures in question will serve the values of the polity under present circumstances.

If these communicative discourses succeed in persuading the constituency, input-oriented policy legitimacy is maintained. If they fail to persuade, governments are at risk. In general, of course, electoral accountability is neither a precisely targeted nor a very sensitive mechanism of popular control. Voters only have a single ballot to express their pleasure or displeasure over a multitude of policy choices, assorted scandals and the personality traits of leading candidates; and even if public protest was concentrated on a single issue yesterday, it may have disappeared from public attention by the next election.[62] But if a policy does violate highly salient interests or deeply held normative convictions of the constituency, a government that sticks to its guns but fails to convince may indeed go down in defeat.[63] If that happens, the

---

[58] Greven, above n 26; Bartolini (2005), above n 27; Hix 2008, above n 26.

[59] Y. Mény and Y. Surel (eds), *Democracies and the Populist Challenge* (Houndmills: Palgrave Macmillan, 2002).

[60] Habermas, above nn 11, 8; J. Habermas, 'Hat die Demokratie noch eine epistemische Dimension? Empirische Forschung und normative Theorie', in J. Habermas, *Ach Europa: Kleine politische Schriften XI* (Frankfurt am Main: Suhrkamp, 2008), 138–91; J. S. Dryzek, *Deliberative Democracy and Beyond: Liberals, Critics, Contestations* (Oxford: Oxford University Press, 2000); Greven above n 26; C. de Vreese and H. Schmitt (eds), *A European Public Sphere: How much of it do we have and how much do we need?* (Connex Report Series No 02; Mannheim: University of Mannheim, 2007).

[61] V. A. Schmidt, 'The European Union: Democratic Legitimacy in a Regional State' (2004) 42 *Journal of Common Market Studies* 975–99; ead, *Democracy in Europe: The EU and National Politics* (Oxford: Oxford University Press, 2006).

[62] In real-world democracies, political responsiveness may nevertheless be quite high: In Germany, national governments are tested in 16 *Land* elections during the four-year term of the national parliament; in all competitive democracies, opposition parties will try their best to refresh voters' memories before the next election; and in any case, governments cannot know in advance which issue will ultimately be decisive for which voters. By the 'rule of anticipated reactions' they will therefore try to respond to all potential grievances if they can (Scharpf, above n 42, 183–8).

[63] This was true when the Dutch government reformed disability pensions in the early 1990s: A. Hemerijck, B. Unger, and J. Visser, 'How Small Countries Negotiate

government will not have established the input legitimacy of these policies. But it will have reaffirmed the institutional legitimacy of the system of responsible and democratically accountable government.

The opposite is true, however, if policies that violate politically salient interests and normative convictions in national polities are not, and cannot be explained and justified in communicative discourses. When that happens, the legitimacy of constitutional democracies will be undermined and may ultimately be destroyed. This is the critical risk if governments are required to implement European law that has been created without the involvement of politically accountable actors by institutionally autonomous judicial legislation.

That is not meant to say that judge-made European law that violates politically salient interests or deeply held normative convictions in member-state polities could never be justified as being necessary and appropriate. But it suggests that justification is more demanding here than it is in the case of political legislation in which governments had a voice and for which they therefore should be able to provide good reasons. In principle, there could be two types of justification.

The first would appeal to 'enlightened' national self-interest. It would try to show how, all things considered, the country will benefit more from the policy or rule in question than from its absence. In essence, these are arguments that would facilitate agreement in a political bargaining process—and they would justify compliance with European rules that are in fact providing effective solutions under conditions which, in game-theoretic terms, resemble Pure Coordination, Assurance, Battle of the Sexes, or (symmetric) Prisoners' Dilemma constellations.[64] But what if the constellation is characterised by asymmetric conflicts—so that the rule that is imposed by non-political European authority cannot be justified in terms of the enlightened self-interest of the member state in question? Analytically, one might then try to justify uncompensated national sacrifices by reference to the collective self-interest of the Union as a whole. However, depending on the salience of the sacrifice requested, this justification would presuppose a collective European identity that is strong enough to override concerns of national self-interest. Unfortunately, however, that is a precondition which not even the most enthusiastic 'Europeans' would claim to see presently fulfilled in the Union of twenty-seven member states.[65]

Change: Twenty-Five Years of Policy Adjustment in Austria, the Netherlands, and Belgium', in F. W. Scharpf and V. A. Schmidt (eds), *Welfare and Work in the Open Economy, Vol.II: Diverse Responses to Common Challenges* (Oxford: Oxford University Press, 2000), 175–263, at 220–4. It was again true in Germany when the Schröder government pursued its 'Agenda 2010' reforms in spite of mass protests and rapidly declining popular support: C. Egle and R. Zohlhöfer (eds), *Ende des rot-grünen Projekts: Eine Bilanz der Regierung Schröder 2002–2005* (Wiesbaden: VS Verlag, 2007).

[64] Scharpf, above n 42, ch 6.

[65] J. Pollak, 'Ist eine europäische Identität möglich? Warum wir lernen müssen, Zwiebeln zu lieben', in C. Joerges, M. Mahlmann, and U. K. Preuß (eds), *'Schmerzliche Erfahrungen der Vergangenheit' und der Prozess der Konstitutionalisierung Europas* (Wiesbaden: VS Verlag, 2008), 63–80.

But that does not mean that asymmetric national sacrifices could never be justified in national discourses. The most powerful of such justifications is, of course, the achievement of European integration itself. The outcome has not been, and may never be, the creation of a 'United States of Europe' modelled after successful federal nation states.[66] But integration has been able to establish peace and cooperation among European nations after centuries of internecine warfare, and to secure democracy and respect for human rights on a continent that has brought forth the most pernicious regimes in human history. These outcomes could not have been attained by the bloody-minded pursuit of national self-interest. Being part of the European community of nations presupposes member states whose institutions and policies are compatible with the basic requirements of communality, and whose preferences are modified by a normative commitment to the 'inclusion of the other'.[67] The preservation of these achievements may indeed justify constraints on national autonomy even where these may conflict with politically salient interests and preferences in member polities. Hence European rules protecting the preconditions of communality, regardless of whether they are formulated in political or non-political processes, may be justified on substantive grounds—and if that is so, they also can and should be defended by member governments even against strong domestic opposition.

V. IS THE COURT PUSHING AGAINST THE LIMITS OF JUSTIFIABILITY?

Given the equally valid legitimation arguments supporting democratic self-determination at the national level and the normative claims of European communality, however, a convincing justification must assess the relative weight at stake in the specific case. The greater the political and normative salience of the national institutions and policy legacies that are being challenged, the greater must be the normative and practical significance of the countervailing European concerns. For many decades, however, the need to develop explicit criteria for that normative balance did not arise. Most issues of European law never did catch the attention of national publics, and the Court itself seems to have taken care to develop its doctrines in a long series of decisions where the substantive outcomes at stake were of very low political salience or downright trivial. Thus it was hard to get politically excited about the *Cassis* decision which told Germany that it could not exclude a French liqueur on the ground that its alcohol content was *too low*—but which, in doing so, also introduced the crucial doctrines of mutual recognition and home-country control.

---

[66] K. Nicolaidis and R. Howse (eds), *The Federal Vision: Legitimacy and Levels of Governance in the United States and the European Union* (Oxford: Oxford University Press, 2001).

[67] J. Habermas, *Die Einbeziehung des Anderen: Studien zur politischen Theories* (Frankfurt am Main: Suhrkamp, 1996); J. H. H. Weiler, 'To Be a European Citizen: Eros and Civilization', in his *The Constitution of Europe* (Cambridge: Cambridge University Press, 1999), 324–57.

That is why earlier warnings of the implications of ECJ jurisprudence for the viability of national social systems[68] could be dismissed as unrealistic scares.[69] But now, as the legal principles seem firmly established in its case law and accepted by national courts, the European Court and the Commission seem ready to face more serious political conflicts. I will briefly mention only a few recent decisions that illustrate this more intrusive and potentially more damaging judicial strategy.

The first case has nothing to do with the neoliberal preferences which are often ascribed to the Court and the Commission. Austria, where university education is free and accessible to all graduates of a gymnasium saw its medical faculties over-crowded by applicants from Germany whose grades were not good enough to qualify under the German *numerus-clausus* regime. In defence, Austria had adopted a rule under which applicants from abroad had to show that they would also be eligible to study medicine in their home country. The Commission initiated a Treaty violation procedure, and the Court found that the Austrian rule was violating students' rights to free movement and non-discrimination under Article 12 ECT.[70] As an immediate result of the decision, more than 60 per cent of applicants at some Austrian medical faculties came from Germany.

The second series of recent decisions was indeed about the priority of economic liberties over social rights guaranteed by member-state constitutions. In *Viking*,[71] a Finnish shipping company operating from Helsinki had decided to reflag its ferry as an Estonian vessel. The Finnish union threatened to strike, the company sued for an injunction, and the case was referred to the ECJ which defined the strike as an interference with the company's freedom of establishment. In the *Laval* case,[72] a Latvian company building a school in Sweden refused to negotiate about wages at the minimum level defined by Swedish collective bargaining agreements. The ECJ defined the Swedish union's industrial action as violation of the company's freedom of service delivery that was not covered by a narrow reading of the Posted Workers' Directive.[73]

If *Viking* and *Laval* were directed against the constitutionally protected rights of Finnish and Swedish unions to pursue collective interests through industrial action, the *Rüffert*[74] and *Luxembourg*[75] cases established the priority of free service delivery over national wage legislation. *Rüffert* disallowed a statute of Lower Saxony that required providers in public procurement to pay locally applicable collective-bargaining wages,

---

[68] eg Scharpf, above n 1.

[69] A. Moravcsik and A. Sangiovanni, 'On Democracy and "Public Interest" in the European Integration', in R. Mayntz and W. Streeck (eds), *Die Reformierbarkeit der Demokratie: Innovationen und Blockaden* (Frankfurt am Main: Campus, 2003), 122–50.

[70] Case C-147/03 *Commission v Republic of Austria* [2005] ECR I-5969.

[71] Case C-438/05 *ITWF and Finnish Seamen's Union v Viking Line ABP* [2007] ECR I-10779.

[72] Case C-341/05 *Laval un Partneri Ltd v Svenska* [2007] ECR I-11767.

[73] Dir 96/71/EC.

[74] Case C-346/06 *Rüffert v Land Niedersachsen* [2008] ECR I-1989.

[75] Case C-319/06 *Commission v Luxembourg* [2008] ECR I-4323.

whereas Luxembourg had transposed the Posted Workers' Directive in a statute requiring all providers to observe local labour law including the automatic adjustment of wages to the rate of inflation. In both cases, the Court defined the Directive as setting maximum, rather than minimum standards, with the consequence that local legislation exceeding these was held to violate the freedom of service delivery. At the same time, the freedom of establishment is being used to hollow out the capacity of member states to shape the rules of corporate governance in their economies in accordance with national institutional traditions and political preferences.[76] In other cases the Court has drastically reduced the capacity of member governments to protect their revenue systems against tax avoidance that is facilitated by decisions protecting the freedoms of capital movement and of service delivery.[77] Here, as in the line of decisions enforcing the access of EU citizens to public services and social transfers in other member states,[78] the Court gives priority to the subjective rights to free movement and non-discrimination without regard to reciprocal obligations to contribute to the resources of the polity.

VI. THE LIBERAL UNDERMINING OF REPUBLICAN LEGITIMACY

In these decisions and others, the Court has obviously intervened against important and politically salient laws, institutions, and practices of individual member states. But why should it be impossible to justify these interventions in national communicative discourses? The root of the problem is a basic asymmetry in how the Court defines the balance between the legitimate concerns of member-state autonomy and the legitimate requirements of European community.[79] It has its origin in the very first decision postulating the direct effect of European law in *Van Gend en Loos* (1963).[80] In order to establish this doctrine, the Court had to interpret the obligation of a member state to maintain existing tariffs as the subjective right of a company against the state. Combined with its nearly simultaneous assertion of the supremacy of European

---

[76] See, eg Case C-212/97 *Centros Ltd v Erhvervs-og Selskabsstyrelsen* [1999] ECR I-1459; Case C-112/05 *Commission v Federal Republic of Germany* [2007] ECR I-8995.

[77] Ganghof and Genschel, 'Steuerpolitik', above n 24.

[78] M. Ferrera, *The Boundaries of Welfare: European Integration and the New Spatial Politics of Social Protection* (Oxford: Oxford University Press, 2005); D. Martinsen, 'The Europeanization of Welfare: The Domestic Impact of Intra-European Social Security' (2005) 43 *Journal of Common Market Studies* 1027–54; D. Martinsen and K. Vrangbaek, 'The Europeanization of Health Care Governance: Implementing the Market Imperatives of Europe' (2008) 86 *Public Administration* 169–84.

[79] As Weiler explained in a different context, the issue is not, or at least not initially, a conflict over the location of a *Kompetenz-Kompetenz* in the multi-level European polity, but a deep concern about the political consequences following from the asymmetric logic of the Court's jurisdiction: J. H. H. Weiler, 'The Autonomy of the Community Legal Order: Through a Looking Glass', in his *The Constitution of Europe* (Cambridge: Cambridge University Press, 1999), 286–323.

[80] Case 26/62 *van Gend en Loos v Netherlands Inland Revenue Administration* [1963] ECR 1.

law,[81] this construction has permitted the Court to define and expand subjective rights against member states, and thus to shift the balance between the rights and obligations of citizens or subjects that had been established in national polities.

Since the commitments in the original Treaty were primarily intended to achieve economic integration, their transformation into 'economic liberties' does account for the strongly 'market-liberal' effects of the Court's jurisprudence. It should be noted, however, that where the primary or secondary European law provided a handle for the definition of non-economic subjective rights, the Court has been similarly ready to intervene against national impediments to their exercise. This has long been true for decisions enforcing and extending the equality of men and women in the workplace under Article 141 ECT;[82] and it is now also true of the extension of rights to the free movement of persons outside of the labour market, of rights of non-discrimination on accounts of nationality, and of the generalisation of (non-political) citizenship rights. This has been hailed by some as a fundamental reversal of the Court's market-liberal bias,[83] whereas it is in fact only the application of its negative-integration and liberalising logic to fields that have newly become accessible to the Courts jurisdiction.

In the framework developed by the ECJ, the European concerns that might justifiably override democratically legitimated national institutions and policy legacies are defined as subjective rights of individuals and firms, rather than as substantive requirements on which the viability of the European community of nations, or the internal market, for that matter, would depend. Given the simultaneous assertion of the supremacy doctrine, this definition has the effect of transforming the hierarchical relation between European and national law into a hierarchical relationship between liberal and republican constitutional principles.[84] Subjective rights derived from (the interpretation of) European law may, in principle, override all countervailing national objectives, regardless of their salience as manifestations of democratic self-determination.

Given the impossibility of political correction, the Court was and is of course free to extend the reach of European rights. In the field of free trade, for instance, the Treaty forbids quantitative restrictions and 'measures having equivalent effect' (Article 28 ECT). Originally that had been understood to exclude the discriminatory treatment of imports. In the early 1970s, however, that understanding was replaced by the famous *Dassonville* formula, according to which 'all trading rules enacted by member states

---

[81]   Case 6/64 *Costa v ENEL* [1964] ECR 585.

[82]   R. A. Cichowski, 'Women's Rights, the European Court, and Supranational Constitutionalism' (2004) 38 *Law & Society Review* 489–512.

[83]   J. A. Caporaso, *The European Union: Dilemmas of Regional Integration* (Boulder, Col.: Westview, 2000); J. A. Caporaso and S. Tarrow, 'Polanyi in Brussels: European Institutions and the Embedding of Markets in Society', paper presented at the APSA 2008 annual meeting, Boston, Mass., 28 August 2008.

[84]   Münch has described the legal order created by the jurisdiction of the ECJ as being 'made for competitive economic actors. It is more appropriate for the market citizen of liberalism than for the political citizen of republicanism or for the social citizen of welfare states in the social democratic or conservative sense' (R. Münch, 'Constructing a European Society by Jurisdiction' (2008) 14 *European Law Journal* 519–41, at 540).

which are capable of hindering, directly or indirectly, actually or potentially, intra-community trade are to be considered as measures having an effect equivalent to quantitative restrictions'.[85] In other words, instead of effective discrimination, a merely hypothetical impediment to free trade, free capital movement, free service delivery, or free establishment would now be enough to strike down a national rule.

It is true that after *Dassonville*, the *Cassis* decision also began to systematise the somewhat haphazard public-order exceptions (eg in Articles 30, 39/3, 46/1, 55, or 58/1b ECT) through which the Treaty had tried to limit the obligations to liberalise national economies. In most areas, therefore, the Court does now allow for the possibility that the exercise of European liberties could be limited by (some) countervailing national concerns.[86] But if this has the appearance of a balancing test, the balance is highly asymmetrical—which manifests itself in three dimensions.

First, some national concerns of major importance are simply defined as irrelevant to begin with. Of greatest practical importance among these is the consistent refusal to consider national fiscal concerns as a potential limit on the exercise of European liberties. Thus in the Austrian case mentioned earlier, the effect which the free movement and non-discrimination of German students would have on the budgetary constraints of Austrian medical education is entirely ignored. The same is true in cases where the free movement of persons is invoked to allow the access of migrants to national social transfers,[87] or where the freedom of service provision requires national health (insurance) systems to pay for services consumed abroad.[88] Moreover, revenue concerns are declared irrelevant when national rules against tax avoidance are treated as violations of free capital movement.[89]

By treating the fiscal implications of its decisions as irrelevant, the Court is destroying the link between the rights and duties of membership in the polity which is reflected in centrality of parliamentary taxing and spending powers in all constitutional democracies.[90] In a republican perspective, German students and their taxpaying parents may have good reasons to protest against the spending priorities of their own governments, but that would not give them a legitimate claim against taxpayers in Austria. The same would be true of other tax-financed services, of social transfers

---

[85] *Dassonville*, above n 44.

[86] U. Haltern, *Europarecht: Dogmatik im Kontext* (Tübingen: Mohr Siebeck, 2nd edn, 2007), 742–55.

[87] See, eg Case C-10/90 *Masgio v Bundesknappschaft* [1991] ECR I-1119; Joined cases C-245/94 and C-312/94 *Hoever* and *Zachow v Land* [1996] ECR I-4895; Case C-131/96 *Romero v Land* [1997] ECR I-3659; Case C-160/96 *Molenaar v Allgemeine* [1998] ECR I-843; Case C-85/96 *Sala v Bayern* [1998] ECR I-2691.

[88] See, eg Case C-120/95 *Decker v Caisse de maladie* [1998] ECR I-1831; Case C-158/96 *Kohll v Union des caisse de maladie* [1998] ECR I-1931; Case C-157/99 *Geraets-Smits* and *Peerbooms* [2001] ECR I-5473; Case C-385/99 *Müller-Fauré* and *Van Riet* [2003] ECR I-4509 (Martinsen, above n 5; Martinsen, above n 78.)

[89] Ganghof and Genschel, 'Steuerpolitik', above n 24.

[90] Ganghof and Genschel, 'Taxation', above n 24.

or of public health systems, and of compulsory health insurance systems in which total contributions must finance an adequate capacity on the supply side.[91] Similarly, firms and individuals availing themselves of the public infrastructure and public services in one country would be under a republican obligation to contribute to the tax price of their maintenance.

By replacing the reciprocal link between entitlements and contributions with the assertion of unilateral individual rights, the Court may seem generous. But its generosity ignores the club-good character of most of the benefits and services provided by the solidaristic nation state. Allowing the easy exit of contributors and the easy entry of non-contributors must undermine the viability of these clubs. If the logic of these decisions will shape national responses, the most likely outcome will not be universal generosity but private insurance, private education, and gated communities for those who can afford them, and eroding public benefits, public services, and public infrastructure for those who cannot pay for private solutions (including the no-longer discriminated migrant students, workers, and their families).

Second, even where national public-interest objections, or nationally protected collective rights, are in principle considered as potential limits on the exercise of European rights, the Court's treatment is highly asymmetrical. Whereas European liberties, no matter how trivial their violation may be in the specific case, are accorded full value, all countervailing arguments are discounted by a substantive and procedural 'proportionality' test.[92] In this, the Court will first evaluate (by its own lights) the normative acceptability of the specific purpose that is allegedly served by a national measure. And even if the purpose is accepted in principle, the government must show that, first, the measure in question would in fact be effective in serving the stated purpose and, second, that this purpose could not also have been served by other measures that would be less restrictive on the exercise of European liberties.[93] For all of these conditions, the burden of proof is on the member state defending a particular impediment to the exercise of European liberties and, as Dorte Martinsen shows, the procedural requirements for establishing (scientific) proof can be tightened to an extent that will ensure a negative outcome for the member state.[94]

For an illustration, take the decision striking down the *Volkswagen* statute[95] which had defined 20 per cent of all shares (instead of the usual 25 per cent) as a block-

---

[91] This is not meant to deny that the 'inclusion of the other' may imply an obligation to provide non-contributory benefits in many constellations. If this obligation were asymmetrically subordinated to fiscal concerns, the trade-off would indeed need to be corrected through judicial intervention. But that balancing question cannot be addressed if fiscal considerations are treated as being by definition irrelevant.

[92] Case 261/81 *Rau v De Smedt PvBA* [1982] ECR 3961 [12].

[93] Haltern, above n 86, 751–7.

[94] D. Martinsen, 'Conflict and Conflict Management in the Cross-border Provision of Healthcare Services' (2009) 32 *West European Politics* 792–809.

[95] *Volkswagen*, above n 76. The discussion quoted is at [55].

ing minority. In the Court's view, this rule created a potential deterrent to direct investments from other member states,[96] while evidence showing that VW stock was in fact widely traded internationally and that the share of direct foreign investments was as high as in comparable companies was declared irrelevant. In other words, the existence of an impediment to the free movement of capital is treated as an incontrovertible presumption.[97]

Or take the Austrian case, where the Court did at least entertain the idea that the danger of overcrowding in Austrian universities might be a valid national concern. But the idea was quickly dismissed with the suggestion that this problem could be averted through non-discriminatory entry exams.[98] The fact that Austria may have needed to give priority to Austrian students in order to train a sufficient number of medical practitioners for its own healthcare system remained completely outside the range of permissible arguments. In the asymmetrical jurisprudence of the Court, in other words, European rights are substantively and procedurally privileged and will generally prevail over even very important and politically salient national concerns.

A third problem arises from the discrepancy between the uniformity of European law and the diversity of national republican institutions. The Treaty-based economic liberties are of course defined at the European level and without regard to national differences. The same is true where the Court recognises other subjective rights at the European level—which may increase in number and variety if the Lisbon Treaty comes into force.[99] And where countervailing national concerns are considered at all, these are also defined in uniform and (highly restrictive) terms by the Court. For an example, take the decision in the *Laval* case, where the Court would have accepted minimum wages to be set by state legislation, but disallowed the delegation to collective-bargaining agreements. In doing so, it ignored the fact that minimum-wage legislation, while common in many EU member states, was totally unacceptable in 'neo-corporatist' Sweden, where wage determination since the 1930s has been left entirely to highly organised unions and employers' associations.[100] In short, the Court's regime of Treaty-based rights and of potentially acceptable national exceptions makes no allowance whatever for the fact that uniform European law has an impact on national institutions and policy legacies that differ widely from one

---

[96] The Court conceded that private shareholders might set the blocking minority at 20 per cent of all shares, but insisted that a democratically accountable legislature could not do so.

[97] Since under the *Dassonville* formula a *potential* impediment is sufficient to constitute a violation of free-movement rights, it is indeed difficult to see what kind of evidence could disprove the assertion.

[98] *Austria*, above n at [61].

[99] As the *Laval* decision made clear, however, such rights (including the freedoms of expression, assembly, and the protection of human dignity) can be exercised only within the tight constraints of the proportionality test whenever they might impede the economic liberties rooted in the Treaty (*Laval*, above n 72, at [94]).

[100] P.-A. Edin and R. Topel, 'Wage Policy and Restructuring: The Swedish Labor Market since 1960', in R. B. Freeman, R. Topel, and B. Swedenborg (eds), *The Welfare State in Transition: Reforming the Swedish Model* (Chicago, Ill.: University of Chicago Press, 1997), 155–201.

member state to another. Such differences exist not only in the field of industrial relations, but also in corporate governance, public services, public infrastructure, media policy, social policy, pension policy, healthcare, vocational and academic education, or public infrastructure, and so on. Present solutions differ because they have been shaped by country-specific historical cleavages and by difficult compromises between conservative, progressive, and liberal political forces—which is why attempted changes tend to have very high political salience everywhere.

Political resistance to change is likely to be strongest where institutions and policies have a direct impact on the lives of citizens—which is most obvious for welfare state transfers and services, industrial relations, employment conditions, education, or healthcare. In many instances, existing policies have attained the status of a 'social contract' whose commitments support the legitimacy of the national polity. That is not meant to suggest that such normatively charged institutions and policy legacies should or could be immune to change. In fact, their continuing viability under external and internal pressures is often quite uncertain.[101] But if the legitimacy of the national polity is to be preserved, such changes must be defended and justified in national communicative discourses—by governments who must be ready to face the consequences of their electoral accountability.

In fact, the text of the Treaty does recognise the need to respect the autonomy of member-state political processes in precisely these policy areas. In Maastricht and Amsterdam, European competences have been explicitly denied in policy areas of high normative salience at the national level. Thus Article 137/5 ECT stipulates that European competencies in the field of social affairs 'shall not apply to pay, the right of association, the right to strike or the right to impose lockouts'. Similarly, European measures in the field of employment 'shall not include harmonisation of the laws and regulations of Member States' (Article 129/2 ECT), and exactly the same formula is repeated for education (Article 149/4 ECT), for vocational education (Article 150/4), and for culture (Article 151/5), while Article 152/5 ECT provides that 'Community action ... shall fully respect the responsibilities of the Member States for the organisation and delivery of health services and medical care'. In other areas, the Treaty has for similar reasons maintained the requirement of unanimous decisions in the Council.

In the Court's legal framework, however, these prohibitions could at best[102] impede *political legislation* at the European level. But they are considered irrelevant for *judicial legislation* where it is protecting Treaty-based liberties.[103] That is why the

---

[101] F. W. Scharpf and V. A. Schmidt (eds), *Welfare and Work in the Open Economy* (Oxford: Oxford University Press, 2000), 2 vols.

[102] If the Commission should find that the *difference* between national rules (provided that they individually have passed the proportionality test) interferes with the internal market or constitutes a distortion of competition, a harmonising directive could still be introduced under Arts 95 and 96/2 ECT: see Haltern, above n 86, 740–1.

[103] The typical formula is that, yes, member states retain the right to shape their own social security and healthcare systems. But in doing so, they must of course observe Community law. See, eg *Kohll*, above n 88, at [16], [19–20]. This illustrates the fundamental significance of the Court's initial dogmatic choice: by treating the Treaty commitments to creating a

cases cited could and did indeed regulate strikes in Finland and Sweden, and they did abolish national pay regulations in Germany and Luxembourg or national regulations of university admissions in Austria as well as national regulations of health services and medical care in Luxembourg and the Netherlands.

In short, even unanimous amendments to the Treaties, formally ratified in all member states, could not protect the autonomy of national political processes against judicial intervention. In the absence of a political mandate, and ignoring explicit Treaty provisions that were intended to limit the reach of European law, the Court is now intervening in areas that are of crucial importance for the maintenance of democratic legitimacy in EU member states.

VII. NEEDED: A POLITICAL BALANCE OF COMMUNITY AND AUTONOMY

From a pragmatic perspective, this appears dangerous: national welfare states are under immense pressure to cope with and adjust to external and internal changes.[104] But this adjustment must be achieved through legitimated political action. The Court can only destroy existing national solutions, but it cannot itself create 'Social Europe'. At the same time, political action at the European level is impeded by the prohibitions stipulated in the Maastricht and Amsterdam Treaties, and if these were lifted, by high consensus barriers and the politically salient diversity of existing national solutions. In short, European law as defined by the Court is undermining national solutions without being able to provide remedies at the European level. The practical effect must be a reduction of the overall problem-solving capacity of the multi-level European polity.

From a normative perspective, what matters is that the Court's interventions are based on a self-created framework of substantive and procedural European law that has no place for a proper assessment of the national concerns that are at stake, and in which the flimsiest impediment to the exercise of European liberties may override even extremely salient national policy legacies and institutions. Within this highly asymmetrical juristic framework a normatively persuasive balance between the essential requirements of European communality and the equally essential respect for national autonomy and diversity cannot even be articulated. By the same token, the legal syllogisms supporting these judicial interventions could not

---

common market characterised by the free movement of goods etc, not only as a source of legislative competencies, but as a guarantee of individual rights, the Court eliminated the *legal* possibility of defining areas of national competence that cannot be reached by European law. As is true in national federal constitutions, nationally defined and enforced individual rights are a powerful centralising force which may reach any and all substantive fields. While legislative powers may be limited through constitutional amendments, the judicial protection against impediments to the exercise of individual rights knows no legal limits. If limits are considered desirable, therefore, they can only be political.

[104] Scharpf and Schmidt, above n 101.

possibly persuade opponents in communicative discourses between member-state governments and their constituents. In short, the politically unsupported extension of judge-made European law in areas of high political salience within member-state polities is undermining the legitimacy bases of the multi-level European polity.

But this cannot be a plea for unconstrained member-state autonomy or a relocation of the *Kompetenz-Kompetenz* to the national level.[105] The result might indeed be an escalation of protectionist and beggar-my-neighbour policies that could well disrupt the Union. It should be realised, after all, that *Viking* and *Laval* did obviously involve a distributive conflict between high-wage and low-wage member states whose fair resolution would have raised difficult normative issues—and the same may also be true of the *Rüffert* and *Luxembourg* cases.[106] There are, therefore, good theoretical reasons for some kind of European review of national measures impeding free movement among member states. But the review would need to allow for a fair consideration of all concerns involved—which the jurisdiction of the ECJ does not. Its self-referential legal framework prevents any consideration of the normative tension between solidarity achieved, with great effort, at the national level and a moral commitment to the 'inclusion of the other' in a European context.

But which institution would be better qualified to assess the balance between politically legitimate, and divergent, national concerns on the one hand, and the equally legitimate constraints that national polities must accept as members of a European community of states? In my view, the European institution that would be uniquely qualified to strike a fair balance is the European Council.[107] From the perspective of individual member states, its decision would be a judgment of peers who are aware of the potential domestic repercussions which may be caused by the obligation to implement European law, and who must realise that they might soon find themselves in the same spot. At the same time, however, these peers would also

---

[105] Weiler, above n 67.

[106] But we should remain realistic: the transnational redistributive benefits (for workers from low-wage countries) that may follow from these judgments are likely to be dwarfed by intranational redistributive damages, as wages of national workers are pushed downwards if protective legislation and collective agreements are being disabled.

[107] Weiler, above n 67, 322, called for a 'Constitutional Council' composed of sitting members of national constitutional courts to decide issues of competence; and a similar proposal was recently promoted by Roman Herzog, former president of the German constitutional court and of the European convention that produced the Charter of basic rights (R. Herzog and L. Gerken, 'Stoppt den Europäischen Gerichtshof' in *Frankfurter Allgemeine Zeitung,* 8 September 2008, p 8). In my view, being a judicial body that is bound by its own precedents and obliged to generalise its decision rules, this Council would also tend to define uniform standards that could not accommodate the legitimate diversity among member-state institutions and practices. What is needed is the disciplined 'adhocery' of a political judgment that understands that it may be necessary to allow, for the time being, national parliaments and courts to have the last word on abortion in Ireland, alcohol in Sweden, and drugs in the Netherlands, even if that should interfere with European liberties protected elsewhere (Paulette Kurzer, *Markets and Moral Regulation: Cultural Changes in the European Union* (Cambridge: Cambridge University Press, 2001)).

be fully aware of the dangers of protectionist free-riding, of beggar-my-neighbour policies and of discriminatory practices that would violate solidaristic obligations. Moreover, and most importantly, in their role as 'masters of the Treaties', the members of the European Council would be best placed to determine whether and where the Court, in its interpretation of primary and secondary European law has so far exceeded the legislative intent that a political correction appears necessary.

Even if the basic logic of this suggestion should be accepted, however, its adoption by a unanimous Treaty amendment seems most unlikely. But there is a scenario that might change these probabilities. Remember what I said about the fundamental dependence of the EU and its legal system on the voluntary compliance of its member states, and about the lack of control of political actors over the expansion of judicial legislation. And now imagine that the governments of some member states, say Austria or Sweden or Germany, would openly declare their non-compliance with specific judgments that they consider to be *ultra vires*. Without more, such a declaration would surely trigger a constitutional crisis. There is of course a lot of incomplete compliance and tacit non-compliance among EU member states, but a declaration of open non-compliance would strike at the foundations of the European legal system. That is why governments would, and indeed should, hesitate to trigger this 'nuclear option'. But what if the declaration was presented as a reasoned appeal to the political judgment of the European Council and coupled with the promise that a (majority) vote affirming the ECJ decision would be obeyed? This would separate the protest against the ECJ from the charge of disloyalty to the Union.

Whether the Council would accept the role thrust upon it by such a declaration is of course highly uncertain. If it did, however, the Union would finally have a forum[108] and procedures[109] in which the basic tension between the equally legitimate concerns of community and autonomy could be fairly resolved.[110] Similarly welcome would be the probable effects on the jurisprudence of the Court itself. Faced with the possibility of political reversal in the Council, it could be expected to pay more systematic attention to the relative weight of national concerns that might justify minor impediments to the exercise of the Treaty-based liberties. If that were the case, European law, even in the absence of 'republican' input legitimacy, would cease to be characterised by the single-minded pursuit of rampant 'individualism'.[111]

[108] In order to ensure procedural viability, the Council would need to relay on the preparatory work of a permanent committee that would hear and evaluate the relevant claims and arguments. But the final decision would have to remain with the heads of governments.

[109] In my view, the affirmation of the ECJ judgment should need only a simple majority in the Council.

[110] Once introduced, the same rules might also be used to allow 'conditional opt-outs' from the pre-emptive effect of the legislative *acquis*. This would ease the problems caused by the near-irreversibility of existing secondary law, and the possibility of later opt-outs could also facilitate political agreement on new legislation. But these extensions go beyond the present argument and their discussion would exceed the limits of this article.

[111] Somek, above n 18.

Constitutionalism and Representation

European Parliamentarism in the Treaty of Lisbon

Sonja Puntscher Riekmann

I. INTRODUCTION

Modern constitutionalism is bound to representation.[1] This claim holds true for the *pouvoir constituant* as much as for the *pouvoir constitué*. Even if driven by 'constitutional moments',[2] constitutions are not brought about—let alone written—by the people in a collective effort. But they do have to be accepted by the people to be legitimate and functional. Such acceptance may come through popular elections of constitutional assemblies or conventions and by referenda on the outcome of these assemblies' deliberations and negotiations. At the heart of any democratic institutional setting lies the parliament that is normally entitled to change the fundamental law according to specific rules that may or may not give again a voice to the people.

Since the eighteenth century, constitutionalism has relied on the people (generally identified with the nation) to legitimate the political order created by representative bodies that in turn must demonstrate that their product 'bears the imprint of the people'.[3] If the product is rejected, that demonstration has failed and the relation between representatives and represented is flawed. This was the situation in the European Union (EU), where the constitutional process had come to a halt after its rejection in three national referenda.[4] The European constitutional process is, however, peculiar in that changes to the fundamental law are to be ratified not by supermajorities as in the member states, but by unanimity. We may thus question the real meaning of the rejection by one or two, if all others have ratified. European constitutionalism

---

[1] For the discussion about premodern and modern constitutionalism, see D. Grimm, *Die Zukunft der Verfassung* (Frankfurt am Main: Suhrkamp, 2nd edn, 1994), 31 et seq and 101 et seq.

[2] B. Ackerman, *We the People I: Foundations* (Cambridge, Mass.: Belknap Press, 1991).

[3] A. Somek, 'The Owl of Minerva: Constitutional Discourse before its Conclusion' (2008) 71 *Modern Law Review* 473.

[4] I subsume the two negative referenda on the Treaty establishing a Constitution for Europe in France and the Netherlands together with the Irish referendum rejecting the Treaty of Lisbon, the latter being the continuation of the former and thus pertaining to the same constitutional process.

is said to be unique or in any case different from constitutional processes of the nation states, whereas a number of political actors and academic scholars continue to deny even the plausibility of an EU-related constitutionalism. Indeed, the very idea of constitutionalism beyond the nation state is contested.

Taking up the general theme of this volume, I discuss the question about the possible demise or transmutation of constitutionalism due to the fading of politics into the twilight of transnationalism from the specific perspective of the EU. Two premisses will guide my arguments. The *first* premiss is that the process of European integration is not simply to be described in terms of globalisation and global governance. The pooling of sovereignty at the European level was strategically meant to remove the very sting of national sovereignty which is considered to be one cause of the past political, economic, and cultural disasters in Europe.[5] By birth and subsequent setting the transnational order of the EU is of a different kind to other international regimes. Conceived as a novel form of transnational cooperation with the explicit aim of preserving peace on a torn continent, the Union is based on a mix of intergovernmental and supranational institutions geared towards 'an ever closer community/union' whose legal order came to supersede and effectively transform national legal orders by the principles of supremacy and direct effect.[6] From its inception, the new construct bore federative elements, whereas intergovernmentalism slowly but steadily became mitigated by the principles of loyalty and solidarity as well as by decision making allowing for qualified majority voting.[7] The European Commission, the Court of Justice, and the Parliament (in particular after its first direct election in 1979) have at different stages and at a different pace countervailed and undermined the role of member states as the sole 'arbiters of the treaties'. This phenomenon is to be distinguished from international regimes and institutions evolving from global socio-economic activities, although today the two realities may overlap and mutually reinforce each other.[8]

---

[5] Judgments about the degree of success of this aim differ considerably: Milward's thesis that in reality national sovereignty was rescued through European integration marking one extreme and Leonard's projection about the bright future of the Union in the twenty-first century the other. See A. S. Milward et al (eds), *The Frontier of National Sovereignty: History and Theory 1945–1992* (London: Routledge, 1994), 1–32; M. Leonard, *Why Europe will run the 21st Century* (London: Fourth Estate, 2005).

[6] See M. Eilstrup-Sangiovanni and D. Verdier, 'European Integration as a Solution to War' (2005) 11 *European Journal of International Relations* 99–135; P. Gerbet, *La Construction de l'Europe* (Paris: Imprimerie Nationale, 1983); T. Judt, *Post-War: A History of Europe since 1945* (London: Heinemann, 2005).

[7] Even if the mode of decision by consensus prevails up to this very day (see F. Hayes-Renshaw and H. Wallace, *The Council of Ministers* (Basingstoke: Houndmills, 2006, 154)), the possibility of qualified majority voting has changed the game in particular after the last two rounds of enlargement.

[8] On the juncture between European integration and globalisation, see H.-P. Kriesi et al, 'Globalization and the Transformation of the National Political Space: Six European Countries Compared' (2006) 45 *European Journal of Political Research* 921–56.

As a *second* premiss I hold that the European polity making does indeed require constitutionalisation. The controversy on the question about whether the Union should or should not have a constitution or whether it already has one is an instance for an unequalled level of fusion of nation states into a novel polity, even if definitions of that polity remain contested. The transfer of the constitutional concept onto the supranational level can be interpreted as an example of constitutional transmutation rather than of demise. Without prejudging the quality of this transfer, it is notable that it has been accompanied by the appearance of a considerable quantity of scholarly work on the European constitutional process.[9]

This chapter is written in the light of progress, and in the shadow of failure: in the light of a decade-long debate on a European constitution within and without European institutions,[10] in the European Parliament (launched by Spinelli), in two Conventions as well as in a number of Intergovernmental Conferences (IGCs), and in the shadow of the rejection of their outcome. The Treaty Establishing a Constitution for Europe failed in the French and Dutch referenda of 2005 and so did the attempt to save the substance of the Constitutional Treaty in the Treaty of Lisbon rejected by the Irish referendum in 2008. Although all references to the classical constitutional aspects, in particular the very term 'constitution', had been shed, the Treaty of Lisbon could not gain the acceptance of the Irish people. The parties advocating 'No' won the battle, however spurious their arguments.

The thesis guiding my argument is that negative referenda in France, the Netherlands, and Ireland revealed a deep cleft between representatives and represented: even if parliaments had voted favourably, the people did not follow suit. Apparently, the involvement of European and national parliamentarians in the work of the Conventions had hardly added legitimacy to the process of constitutionalisation, whereas in some member states the instances of rejection had negative repercussions on the parliamentary ratification. In Austria, for instance, the social-democratic chancellor, under the influence of the Irish rejection of the Treaty of Lisbon, went so far as to declare that the already concluded ratification by the parliament was mistaken and promised to submit any further Treaty revision to a

---

[9] See, among others, J. H. H. Weiler, *The Constitution of Europe: Do the New Clothes have an Emperor?* (Cambridge: Cambridge University Press 1998); K. Laenerts and P. van Nuffel, *Constitutional Law of the European Union*, ed R. Bray (London: Sweet & Maxwell, 1999); A. von Bogdandy, 'Constitutional Principles', in A. von Bogdandy and J. Bast (eds), *Principles of European Constitutional Law* (Oxford: Hart, 2006), 1–52; A. von Bogdandy, 'A Disputed Idea Becomes Law: Remarks on the European Democracy as a Legal Principle', in B. Kohler-Koch and B. Rittberger (eds), *Debating the Democratic Legitimacy of the European Union* (Lanham: Rowman & Littlefield, 2006), 33–44; A. Peters, *Elemente einer Theorie der Verfassung Europas* (Berlin: Duncker & Humblot, 2001); S. Puntscher Riekmann and W. Wessels, *The Making of a European Constitution: Dynamics and Limits of the Convention Experience* (Wiesbaden: VS-Verlag, 2006), 35–67. See also the Jean Monnet Working Paper Series 'Altneuland': The EU Constitution in a Constitutional Perspective (New York: NYU School of Law, 2004 et seq).

[10] W. Loth, *Entwürfe einer europäischen Verfassung: Eine historische Bilanz* (Bonn: Europa Union Verlag, 2002).

national referendum, whereas the Czech President hailed the Irish rejection as 'a triumph of freedom'. The different reasons provoking the popular rejection of the Constitutional Treaty and the Treaty of Lisbon notwithstanding, ratification points to a classical dilemma of any constitutional process, namely, that that the legitimacy of the *few* writing a constitution for *all* is open to question.

Constitutional processes are driven by unexpected dynamics and may produce unintended results. In the case of the EU, neither Convention was elected by the people but installed by governments, even though the second Convention was given a very broad list of tasks to tackle. The Declaration of Laeken in 2001, while broaching the idea of a constitution, envisaged it only as a long-term goal. Moreover, despite two-thirds of European citizens approving of a 'European Constitution' in principle,[11] citizens were hardly aware of the concrete constitutional struggles within the Convention. We may not share the verdict about the 'accidental constitution',[12] but we must acknowledge that, although the Convention's majority was composed of directly elected European and national members of parliaments, it did not succeed in communicating the constitutional preferences that were represented and negotiated to the general public. Similar allegations could of course be made to most constitution-making bodies since the eighteenth century, but time and again we are taught that the historical examples associated with the nation state cannot serve as a yardstick for the EU.[13] Even if there are good arguments against the categorical ruling out of historical comparison,[14] important questions are raised. Does the actual problem really lie in the often-cited lack of a European public sphere or the lack of the Convention's legitimacy? What is at stake, given the fact that the Convention had been installed by the European Council, whose legitimacy is not (at least not overtly) put into question, whereas the final text was approved by the Intergovernmental Conference according to Article 48 TEU and thus unanimously?

The problem of European constitution-making seems to lie first and foremost in the existence of colliding political arenas and thus of colliding forms of representation. The European Council in its role of constituent power has created the Convention and endowed it with the interim power to prepare a new text for treaty revision after it had itself failed to produce satisfactory results in past IGCs. However, once it became obvious that the Convention was prone to transcend its mandate, member states again claimed the driver's seat. The idea of enhancing the legitimacy of the constitutional process by giving some of the power to parliamentarians foundered

---

[11] *Standard Eurobarometer 66* (2006) <http://ec.europa.eu/public_opinion/archives/eb/eb66/eb66_highlights_en.pdf>.

[12] P. Norman, *The Accidental Constitution: The Story of the European Convention* (Brussels: EuroComment 2003).

[13] Somek, above n 3, 487.

[14] S. Puntscher Riekmann, *Die kommissarische Neuordnung Europas: Das Dispositiv der Integration* (Vienna: Springer, 1998). Here I elaborate on the question of tackling integration in a historical comparative perspective.

on the fear of national governments of losing control. During the referenda govern-ments half-heartedly advocated the Constitutional Treaty which they themselves had manipulated, whereas the Convention no longer existed to defend its results. In this twilight zone created by member states' governments, the protest of discon-tent organised by euro-sceptic movements on both the left and right of the political spectrum flourished.

In the EU, however, there is another inconsistency to be tackled: the Union is based on international treaties which have repeatedly been accepted, by the Euro-pean Court of Justice (ECJ) as well as by academic scholars, as her 'constitutional charter'.[15] The contracting parties, so it may be argued, have allowed for a process of integration by stealth, thereby creating a novel supranational polity incrementally and developing a 'veiled constitution'.[16] In this vein, it might be said that the Conven-tion of 2002–3 did not crown a 'revolution' with a constitution, but tore off the veil by revising the treaties and finally by calling them by their proper name. After the product had been rejected, however, constitutionalism was discovered to be the real culprit, and governments turned again to hide the constitution behind the veil.[17]

This masque of European constitutionalism seems to be a tactical response to the general citizens' feeling of unease and uncertainty stemming from the tectonic shifts in the political order of their nation states due to European integration. European citizens today are haunted by questions such as: Who are we? What is Europe and what is the nation state? Where is the place of 'the political'? Where is the centre and where the periphery? Who represents whom or what? Who gets what and why? Who is to be trusted? How can I verify and judge political action? These are questions raised by members of many political communities, but they become all the more salient if the old communities are merged into a new one. For over two centuries, one answer of paramount importance has been given by constitutionalism: the device that defines norms, institutions, and procedures, taming and thus 'constituting' power in the new

---

[15] With regard to the ECJ, see Case 294/83 *Les Verts v European Parliament* [1986] ECR 1339. As a more recent instance of the constitutional ECJ discourse, see AG Poiares Maduro's opinion of 23 January 2008 on an alleged fundamental rights breach by the Council and the Commission where he states that in the *Van Gend en Loos* ruling the Court 'considered that the Treaty has established a "new legal order", beholden to but distinct from the existing legal order of public international law. In other words, the Treaty has created a municipal legal order of transnational dimensions, of which it forms the "basic constitutional charter".' And thus, the AG continues, the Court 'seeks, first and foremost, to preserve the constitu-tional framework created by the Treaty' (Joined cases C-402/05 P and C-415/05 P *Kodi and Al Barakaat IF v Council of the EU and Commission of the European Communities* [2008] ECR I-6351).

[16] Wiener writes about the 'invisible constitution', see Antje Wiener, *Evolving Norms of Constitutionalism in Europe: From 'Treaty Language' to 'Constitution' in Altneuland: The EU Constitution in a Constitutional Perspective*, Jean Monnet Working Paper 5/04 (New York: NYU School of Law, 2004), 26.

[17] Council of the European Union, *Presidency Conclusions* 21–22 June 2007, Annex I, 15: 'The constitutional concept, which consisted in repealing all existing Treaties and replacing them by a single text called "Constitution", is abandoned.'

polity.[18] The question today is whether constitutionalism is still capable of delivering the answer, especially with respect to a Union which has continuously been growing in size and depth and whose sub-units are still said to be the epitome of difference.

This chapter aims, *firstly*, at challenging the nexus between constitutionalism and nationhood, arguing that like the nation states, which are also the outcome of integration processes merging regions into states, the EU must accommodate difference and that until now she does so by veiling constitutionalism. It will, *secondly*, argue that the current problems of the Union resulting from the rejection of treaty revisions stem from the citizens' lack of trust in organs of supranational and national representation and that this wont is fuelled by the colliding systems of representation simultaneously based on supranationalism and on intergovernmentalism. It will also, *thirdly*, discuss the citizens' ambivalences regarding their trust in European institutions as they surface in public opinion polls, and interpret them as a misfit of expectations and results of European politics. *Fourthly*, and by way of conclusion, I will discuss the democratic potential offered by the Treaty of Lisbon to bridge the gap between representatives and represented through a combination of enhanced parliamentarism and citizens' involvement. Despite all the shortcomings and paradoxes created by the IGC, the 'Treaty of Parliaments',[19] I argue that it would indeed mark a significant turn in European constitutionalism.

II. ACCOMMODATING DIFFERENCE AND CONSTITUTING POWER

The EU is first and foremost a construction to accommodate difference by a set of institutions combining intergovernmentalism and supranationalism and ultimately fusing the two principles to the extent that today the term 'intergovernmental supranationalism'[20] is perfectly justified. The Union is not a copy of the national states; it emulates some of their institutions, while others are new inventions. However, all its institutions and procedures serve the purpose of facilitating and promoting cooperation for the purposes of preventing war between the Union's members and fostering their socio-economic success. Their task is to identify shared problems and to negotiate European solutions according to the competencies delegated to the Union by primary law. After the defeat of the European Defence Community in 1954, creating a single market became the guiding idea of integration, with the four freedoms and competition law as its linchpin. As expected, the idea was always jeopardised by the reality of diverging national and subnational interests. In spite of

[18] See Grimm, above n 1, 37.

[19] E. Brok and M. Selmayr, 'Der "Vertrag der Parlamente" als Gefahr für die Demokratie? Zu den offensichtlich unbegründeten Verfassungsklagen gegen den Vertrag von Lissabon' (2008) 3 *Integration*, 217–34.

[20] P. Ludlow, *The Leadership in an Enlarged European Union: The European Council, the Presidency and the Commission* (Brussels: EuroComment, 2005).

the many difficulties and fallbacks stemming therefrom, in the course of six decades a considerable quantity of power was shifted onto the European level.

Thus, from the Coal and Steel Community to this very day, the Union has come a long way on the path to closer Union. Despite the exclusion of the use of force and identity building measures, this process is not completely dissimilar to the one leading regions into nation states.[21] At its core lies the construction of a new legal order to foster community building by giving all citizens the same rights of movement and exercise of socio-economic activities, although the term of European citizenship were enshrined in primary law only by the Treaty of Maastricht.[22] And whereas nation states were successful in constructing the homogeneity of their peoples through cultural and coercive devices, the Union cannot avail itself of such instruments. Nevetheless, in most nation states, homogeneity is less than perfect; nor does homogeneity of culture and language preclude political or socio-economic differences. As shown by a number of EU member states the capacity to accommodate difference is continuously put to the test: recently, resolutions of conflicts between majority and minority populations or between centre and periphery in the UK, France, Italy, and Spain have been brought about by constitutional (re)arrangements and the devolution of power. Moreover, redistribution of wealth between regions or groups of citizens is, if to different degrees, a permanent issue of contention in all member states.

Turning to the issue in question in this volume, something other than the dichotomy of heterogeneity and homogeneity is of equal importance: this is the issue of the legitimate use of Community instruments in matters of the distribution of power and the redistribution of wealth. Even if we accept Majone's definition of the Union as a 'regulatory state' rather than a redistributive one, we must conclude that the creation and imposition of regulations is an act of power. So much so that Majone finds the term 'state' appropriate for the Union as well.[23] By way of European governance today, some 500 million citizens are subjected to supranational rule in order to accommodate differences of all kinds.

Here lies the very simple reason why it was only a matter of time before constitutionalism entered the stage of European politics. Constitutionalism is, first and foremost, a device that seeks to tame power by constituting it. It concerns the creation of a system of checks and balances, of power sharing and control, of the differentiation of 'state' functions, of creating mechanisms to avoid deadlocks (eg by calling in the electorate as ultimate arbiter), and of the peaceful adjustment of the fundamental law. Last but not least, it concerns the creation of individual rights and

---

[21] Puntscher Riekmann, above n 14.

[22] TEU Arts 17–20; see P. Craig and G. de Búrca, *EU Law: Text, Cases and Materials* (Oxford: Oxford University Press, 3rd edn, 2003), 706–11.

[23] G. Majone, 'The Rise of the Regulatory State' (1994) 17/3 *West European Politics* 1–41. See also S. Puntscher Riekmann, 'The State of Europe: Towards a Theory of European Integration. From Grand Theories to Metaphorical Description and Back', in S. Puntscher Riekmann, M. Mokre, and M. Latzer (eds), *The State of Europe* (Frankfurt am Main: Campus, 2004), 9–31.

liberties protected against encroachment by any or all power holders.[24] Why should these fundamental functions of constitutionalism not apply to the power wielded by the Union? If its rule is to be democratic, its power has, by the same token, to be limited and 'constituted'.

But time and again the Union's capacity to accommodate differences has been challenged by the argument of size and boundaries.[25] Although the Union's boundaries coincide with those of her outer members, enlargement from six founding to twenty-seven member states in 2007 seems to create a feeling of boundlessness. Moreover, and in spite of the rule that only European states are entitled to apply for membership, we cannot shun the problem of defining Europe's limits. The continent is indeed an 'Asian peninsula'.[26] The debate on Turkish membership has only highlighted the issue. Yet, the question of size can hardly be settled by abstract reasoning. How big or small a political community can be in order to guarantee democratic rule is open to interpretation. EU enlargement has been driven by (geo)political as much as economical considerations, and it has also depended on contingencies of historical development such as the transformation of authoritarian regimes and the fall of the iron curtain. The constitutional debate was also provoked by enlargement, in that an institutional set-up that had been created for six could hardly be said to work equally well for twenty-seven members.[27] This is not to frivolously downplay the extraordinary situation the Union is facing after the last rounds of enlargement; issues of governability and compliance with supranational rules and regulations are indeed one of a kind.

Still, as the current financial crisis has demonstrated, the unity of the many is less a matter of lofty identity debates than of sheer necessity. The turmoil of global financial markets is a 'state of emergency' compelling even anti-Europeans to acknowledge the usefulness of the Union. In the end utilitarianism has always been a stronger driving force of integration than the evocation of a common culture.[28] It is difficult though to imagine that common action in the current financial crisis could have been easily orchestrated without the long-standing practice of cooperation in many other policy fields. And yet, bearing in mind the general topic of this volume, the argument has to be qualified in two respects. Firstly, the example of the European reaction to the financial crisis is not to be misinterpreted in a neo-functionalist

---

[24] K. Loewenstein, *Political Power and the Governmental Process* (Chicago, Ill.: University of Chicago Press, 2nd edn, 1965), 127.

[25] Somek, above n 3, 487.

[26] P. Valéry, 'La Crise de l'Esprit', in his *Oeuvres*, ed J. Hytier (Paris: Gallimard, 1957), i. 988–1014.

[27] The debate on size had incidentally haunted also the American founding fathers challenged by the Anti-Federalists on similar grounds: see Alexander Hamilton, James Madison, and John Jay, *The Federalist* (London: Dent & Tuttle, 1992); *The Debate on the Constitution: Federalist and Antifederalist Speeches, Articles, and Letters during the Struggle over Ratification* (Washington, DC: The Library of America, 1993), 2 vols.

[28] The importance of national economic preferences was forcefully demonstrated by A. Moravcsik, *The Choice for Europe: Social Purpose and State Power from Messina to Maastricht* (London: UCL, 1999).

perspective: it does not per se allow for any conclusions about constitutional issues, since all actions were taken by heads of governments or states in a largely intergovernmental approach. Secondly, states of emergency may embolden the European executives to reaffirm themselves as arbiters of the treaties rather than to strengthen other institutions such as the Commission or the European Parliament or national parliaments. The future will show whether this development exacerbates the system of colliding arenas of representation, or even displaces the axis of power toward strong executives and thus further undermines the constitutional and democratic progress reached by the Treaty of Lisbon. It may, however, enhance the citizens' uncertainties about whom they are to trust and thus their swaying loyalties.

III. REPRESENTATION AND TRUST: THE RIVEN SOUL OF EUROPEAN CITIZENS

Although an old political concept, representation has become of paramount importance in modern democracy. Hence, constitutionalism to a significant extent concerns the definition of representative organs, their norms, competencies, and decision-making procedures. Leaving aside the complexities of the politico-philosophical debate on the issue,[29] I will focus on one crucial aspect of this: the link between representation and trust. The represented must trust that their representatives somehow act on their behalf; representation is thus associated with responsibility. As a sub-function of legitimate representation, responsibility concerns the public justification of decisions and the bearing of the consequences of public assessment.[30] Responsibility entails sanctions, in legal, political, and social terms. While legal sanctions for wrongdoing can be clearly spelled out, political and social sanctions are more difficult to grasp.[31] Because power is delegated to representatives for a given

---

[29] See E. Voegelin, *Die Neue Wissenschaft der Politik* (Munich: Alber, 4th edn, 1991); H. Pitkin, *The Concept of Political Representation* (Berkeley: University of California Press, 1967); J. Pollak, *Repräsentation ohne Demokratie: Kollidierende Systeme der Repräsentation in der Europäischen Union* (Vienna: Springer 2007).

[30] The legitimacy of a democratic system to a degree, yet not exclusively, depends on the well-functioning of procedures of control. Besides elections one core element of modern constitutionalism is the creation of checks and balances in the organisation of power. From Montesquieu's famous dictum 'le pouvoir arrête le pouvoir' to the *Federalist Papers* stressing at length the problem of political actors being prone to the abuse of power and of how to prevent them from actually abusing it, authors have laid the foundations of a theoretical discourse on legitimacy and responsibility which remain valid until this very day.

[31] Today, responsibility and accountability have almost become synonyms. Accountability in particular has become the magic word of modern political discourse. It is suggested that as long as decision makers are accountable, things will work out well. However, this term is far from being clear. Accountability is generally understood as reporting of one institution to another. The notion is per se devoid of consequences. See S. Puntscher Riekmann, 'In Search of Lost Norms: Is Accountability the Solution to the Legitimacy Problems of the European Union?' (2007) 13 *Comparative European Politics* 121–37.

period of time and generally with a broad mandate, representatives must account for what they have done during that period, how they have fulfilled their duties, and whether they have met expectations. Representative democracy has to reckon with the human fabric made of two seemingly contradictory, but actually complementary attitudes, namely trust and distrust. By electing them, we entrust candidates with the power to rule. But that trust is never absolute. And even if we trust, we wish to verify. Consequently, we establish mechanisms for 'operationalising' control, with elections being of paramount importance.

How are these preconditions of legitimate rule met in the EU? By way of generalisation, it may be said that procedures of responsibility and the channels of control are impaired. This judgment results not only from a scrutiny of the peculiar institutional set-up of the Union. Not exactly replicating the classical triad derived from nation-state structures, European institutions are dominated by the Council as an organ exercising legislative and executive functions at the same time without being under the control of the Parliament; national parliaments, by contrast, may in theory control their executives even when acting at the European level, but not with respect to the Council as a collective organ. The Commission is responsible to the Council, as well as to the Parliament. All three organs are controlled by the ECJ, but only if a lawsuit is filed either by one of the other organs, by members states, or by individual citizens.[32] The predominance of the Council (and the European Council) stems of course from the initial construction of the Union as a semi-international regime. Despite Monnet's dream of the Council being eventually transformed into a second chamber, this has not yet occurred and will not occur in the foreseeable future. The members of the Council, though, claim to be as (if not more) representative of their national citizens as the European Parliament.

The clash between two forms of representation and thus of legitimation constitutes the core conflict: it is a dispute about directly and indirectly legitimated representation. The issues though are complex. The directly elected representatives in the European Parliament struggle against citizens' ignorance of their work as well as against the image of emerging from 'second order elections', demonstrated by the reduced interest of national parties or media in European election campaigns and ever lower turnouts.[33] On the other hand, the indirectly elected members of government, by veiling their role at the European level, enjoy considerable 'permissive consensus' with respect to day-to-day politics. National executives have successfully sold the idea of 'Brussels' as an autonomous source

---

[32] Financial correctness is checked by the Court of Auditors and OLAF, whereas the Treaty of Maastricht created the European Ombudsman empowered to receive individuals' complaints concerning instances of maladministration by one of the organs with the exception of the ECJ and the Court of First Instance. However, the latter institutions are not representative organs strictly speaking.

[33] J. Gaffney (ed), *Political Parties and the European Union* (London: Routledge, 1996); S. Puntscher Riekmann 'Autriche' [with R. Picker], in Y. Deloye (ed), *Dictionnaire des élections européennes: collection études politiques* (Paris: Economica, 2005), 38–43.

of power identified with the Commission and, though less so, with the ECJ impinging upon national orders, whereas they tend to present themselves to their domestic audiences as 'warriors of national interests'. If successful, they claim all the credit; if they fail they may scapegoat Brussels. Such behaviour is well known from national federations, but it works particularly well within the opaque structure of the Union.

Another difficulty to be considered in this context is the growing loss of power by national parliaments due to European integration. Although this is not the case to the same degree in all member states, the dominance of the Council and the European Council also have repercussions for national relations between the legislative and executive branches of power. European politics is the privilege of the executives, which have a lead over the legislatures in terms of knowledge and resources. Owing to these advantages, executives succeed in projecting themselves as efficient decision makers also in the eyes of the public and this feeds into a general, if ambivalent, fascination with decision making trumping deliberation.[34] In the Union, moreover, a considerable part of political deliberations also takes place in the plethora of committees and working groups of the Commission as well as of the Council, and this adds to the picture of European politics as the realm of fused bureaucracies.[35] The flourishing of European agencies created at the European level to carry out such diverse tasks as the administration of fisheries, medicines, or external borders has added yet another layer of decision making.

The purpose of this rough sketch of the European institutional web is to demonstrate the difficulties Union citizens encounter when they are to judge by whom and how they are represented, how they may gather information about the issues at stake, and whom they may hold responsible for the decisions taken. Interestingly though, citizens appear quite ambivalent when the question of trust in institutions is posed to them in surveys, such as those conducted by Eurobarometer. They claim to trust parliaments more than executives and they give greater credit to supranational than to national institutions, parliaments, and governments alike.[36] Thus, with all cautions against opinion polls taken into account, we might propose some working hypotheses to be tested by further in-depth studies. European citizens recognise

[34] See, eg H. C. Mansfield, Jr, *Taming the Prince: The Ambivalence of Modern Executive Power* (Baltimore Md.: Johns Hopkins University Press, 1993).

[35] See M. Bach, 'Eine leise Revolution durch Verwaltungsverfahren: Bürokratische Organisationsprozesse in der Europäischen Gemeinschaft' (1992) 21 *Zeitschrift für Soziologie* 16–30; W. Wessels, 'Staat und (westeuropäische) Integration: Die Fusionsthese', in M. Kreile (ed), *Die Integration Europas,* special issue, (1992) 23 *Politische Vierteljahresschrift* 36–61. S. Puntscher Riekmann, 'Die Meister und ihr Instrument: Institutionenkonflikte und Legitimitätsprobleme in der Europäischen Union', in M. Bach (ed), *Europäische Integration,* special issue, (2000) 4 *Kölner Zeitschrift für Soziologie und Sozialpsychologie* 131–50.

[36] *Standard Eurobarometer 69* and 70 (2008) <http://ec.europa.eu/public_opinion/archives/eb/eb69/eb69_en.htm>, <http://ec.europa.eu/public_opinion/archives/eb/eb70/eb70_en.htm>.

and accept that, owing to European integration, inter-institutional power relations have deeply changed. Coming to terms with the new reality, they are willing to trust European institutions; but they also wish to have a voice in regards to the decisions stemming therefrom. They are, however, confined to their national settings in which they are continuously confronted with a paradoxical discourse: political actors whose vote and office seeking depends on national elections simultaneously advocate the sustainability of national sovereignty and the need (if not irreversibility) of European integration, whereas anti-European parties live and thrive on the exploitation of that paradox. The paradox—thus my last hypothesis—is not to be resolved without offering constitutional answers to the classical questions already outlined.

IV. CONSTITUTING SUPRANATIONAL POWER

If in times of transnational politics constitutionalism were on its way to demise then democracy too is doomed to disappear. Hence, if democracy is to survive, the exclusive nexus between constitutionalism and the nation state must be reconsidered. As mentioned, I will not dwell on the conditions created by global regimes; I limit myself to an analysis of the EU that until now could offer the best option for recasting democracy at the supranational level. Owing to the degree of integration and democratic institution building, it is not by accident that the Union has already developed a number of constitutional principles and has embarked on a more fundamental constitutional debate. Indeed, as von Bogdandy argues, 'the Union's and the Member States' constitutions confront the same central problem: the phenomenon of public power as the heart of every constitutional order'.[37]

Even if the difference between the Union and the member states is marked by the degree of political unity, and even though the Union's exercise of power does not stem from the will of a single sovereign but rather from the common action of various actors, constitutionalism has gradually entered European legal thinking. Was this to be expected? I deem the answer is yes. If the problem we are discussing here concerns power, and if power has to be defined and tamed, then constitutionalism seems the right answer; this because for more than two centuries constitutionalism has been one important line of European political and legal thinking. In the vein of historical institutionalist theory, we are also confronted with a phenomenon of path dependence demonstrated by the fact that, from the outset, constitutional discourse accompanied European unification.[38] Thus the conclusions drawn by a group of French constitutional scholars in 1998 should not come as a surprise: 'L'identité de l'Europe sera constitutionelle ou elle ne sera pas.'[39]

The importance of this statement is underlined by the evolution of the European constitutional history: despite incomplete polity building, the Union has already developed a number of constitutional principles largely based on judicial and scholarly

[37] Bogdandy, 'Constitutional Principles', above n 9, 10.

[38] Loth, above n 10.

[39] *Le Monde*, 5 May 1998, p 17.

work and which were codified in Article 6 EU of the Treaty of Amsterdam.[40] Even if these principles are often hazy with regard to their content and are ambiguous in their relations, von Bogdandy's argument that '[t]he development of a European doctrine of principles may channel and perhaps rationalise political and social conflicts, treating them as conflicts of principles which can be resolved according to the rules of legal rationality'[41] is convincing. What are these principles, and how do they relate to the topic at hand? The main principles as spelled out in Article 6 EU are liberty, democracy, and respect for human rights and fundamental freedoms and the rule of law. The Treaty of Lisbon in Article 2 EU adds some more, when it postulates: 'The Union is founded on the values of respect for human dignity, freedom, democracy, equality, the rule of law and respect for human rights, including the rights of persons belonging to minorities. These values are common to the Member States in a society in which pluralism, non-discrimination, tolerance, justice, solidarity and equality between women and men prevail.'

For the purpose of this argument, the most important principle is democracy, though this must, of course, be discussed in relationship with the others. Democracy is a form of rule entailing a specific organisation of power that draws its legitimacy from the citizens. Giving preference to the term 'citizens' rather than to the notion of 'people' is not only to avoid the sterile debate about the Union lacking a people: it is consistent with the opening article of the Constitutional Treaty, which states that the Constitution establishing the Union reflects 'the will of the citizens and the States of Europe'.[42] Moreover, as a corollary of the principle of liberty as the first to be mentioned in Article 6 EU (Treaty of Amsterdam), the term 'citizen' is much more appropriate to modern Europe. Liberty is a principle constituting the individual citizen and not the people, and the same holds true for the principles of the respect of human rights and fundamental freedoms that were subsequently enshrined in the Charter of Fundamental Rights solemnly declared at the European Council of Nice 2000 and now part of the Treaty of Lisbon. These principles relate to the provisions establishing the Citizenship of the Union (Articles 20–4 EC Treaty of Lisbon). Further, the Provisions on Democratic Principles (Articles 9–12 EU Treaty of Lisbon) do not mention the people, but citizens as addressees of rights; these provisions introduce the Citizens' Initiative (Article 11, para 4) as a new element of participative democracy to be organised transnationally and thus transcending the concept of people when stating that 'one million citizens who are nationals of a significant number of Member States' are entitled to pursue such initiative.

What is most of interest here, however, is that the principle of liberty constituting the individual citizen has to be put in relation to the principle of democracy which is *expressis verbis* qualified in terms of representation: 'The functioning of the Union shall be founded on representative democracy' (Article 10, para 1 EU), whereby 'citizens are directly represented in the European Parliament' (para 2). Indeed, the

---

[40] Bogdandy, 'Constitutional Principles', above n 9, 6 (n 15).

[41] Ibid.

[42] Treaty Establishing a Constitution for Europe 2006, Art I, 1.

Treaty of Lisbon aims to significantly enhance parliamentarism at the European and at the national level, whereas the upgrading of parliaments is in itself the result of a 'revolution' of the parliamentarian majority in the Constitutional Convention against the dominance of governments. Due to the transfer of relevant provisions to the Treaty of Lisbon, the latter may appropriately be called 'The Treaty of Parliaments'.[43] What these provisions will mean in practice is considered in the concluding section.

Parliaments decentred

The institutional centrepiece of modern democracy is the parliament, its absence being considered the most obvious instance of the lack of democracy. Interestingly, from its inception intergovernmental cooperation in European institutions went hand in hand with the establishment of an assembly whose members quickly called it a Parliament and whose powers were gradually expanded, including direct election and co-legislative competencies. But the European Parliament does not engender a European government; it does not rest on a fully-fledged trans-European party system, and neither does it elicit turnouts comparable to national elections. At the same time, national parliaments have witnessed their downgrading, due to the rising power of national as well as supranational executives, courts and (semi)-independent agencies. Thus, the centrepiece of democracy appears decentred and often devaluated to the role of rubber-stamping its government's initiatives.

This general assessment varies from member state to member state, with some parliaments being more self-assertive than others, some even regaining importance. Parliaments may be decentred but they are not dead. Although battered, they remain an important part of any constitution for several reasons: in modern democracy, parliaments symbolise the place of 'the political' defined as a principle based on the recognition of difference and hence on the agonism and antagonism of societal interests; they visualise the representation of interests; they legitimise legislation as a result of deliberation and accommodation of difference; parliamentary elections lead to the formation of governments (with the notable exception of presidential systems such as the USA or the special supranational system of the EU), whereby the executive power is to be balanced and controlled by parliamentary power; and, most importantly, members of parliaments are responsible to the electorate. The scoundrels may be thrown out in a peaceful way, without jeopardising the whole system of governance.

However, parliamentarism has fallen prey to discontent due to two contradicting arguments: one advocating output-legitimacy and the other input-legitimacy.[44] Since the emergence of the democratic deficit discourse in the 1990s, both arguments have also come to dominate the debate on European democracy. The first argument stresses the need for good and efficient governance by experts, whereas the second

---

[43] Brok and Selmayr, above n 19.

[44] On this issue, see F. W. Scharpf, *Governing in Europe: Effective and Democratic?* (Oxford: Oxford University Press, 2004).

points to the need for greater input by opening channels for direct participation. Moreover, advocacy for good governance is enhanced by advocacy for deliberative democracy ensured by expert argumentation. Deliberative democracy is said to be an alternative to adversary, economic, or aggregative models of democracy because it operates under strict criteria of truth and justice and in a context of free and open discourse in which decisions are justified towards the affected parties. Yet, are these criteria not pertinent to parliamentarism as well, at least in its ideal form? That the ideal is time and again perverted has its reason in the crude fact that deliberation is only one part of the coin, the other one being constituted by the power plays of all interested parties. Thus, the critical question to be posed to the advocates of deliberative democracy is how they incorporate interests and powers into their model. Expert committees are not interest-free zones, and if experts have no stakes in the issue, they remain agents whose principals most certainly have. Since there is no such thing as depoliticised politics, we cannot rid ourselves of the question of who nominates experts, how experts are to be held accountable for their advice, and how, if need be, the eventual scoundrel is to be thrown out. Herein lies the role of parliaments, who should have a voice in the nomination of experts, and to whom the latter should be accountable.

Yet, parliaments also face the challenge of advocates of participatory democracy. In the wake of transnational politics dominated by executives and administrations, which increasingly escape parliamentary control, social movements hardly call for the empowerment of their parliaments, but rather for direct participation. In the EU as a polity in the making, direct participation has engendered ambivalent elite positions due to the repeated negative votes in referenda on Treaty revisions and membership. Elites who fear the dismantling of the whole process of integration that for decades had been pushed forward by stealth tend to abhor plebiscites. As a matter of fact, referenda on Treaty revision are about approval or rejection of a rather complex text negotiated behind the closed doors of IGCs. Proposals of amendment are impossible. For executives having negotiated the reform generally in difficult processes of accommodating the most diverse national interests, acceptance has become synonymous with good 'Europeanness', whereas rejection is labelled as old-fashioned nationalism. When confronted with such denial, pro-European political and academic actors almost by reflex resort to the interpretation that the Union is far too complex and has therefore to be conducted by enlightened elites. This stance, however, was time and again only to provoke even greater support for the advocates of direct participation. Astonishing as it may be, the Constitutional Convention has responded to this claim by inventing the Citizens' Initiative, also maintained by the Treaty of Lisbon.

Parliaments recentred

The *Treaty of Lisbon* contains novel provisions which are to enhance European democracy by paying tribute to both representative and participatory democracy. In line with the declaration that the EU is based on representative democracy, the further extension of the powers of the European Parliament, which will become the true co-legislator of the Council, is perhaps less astounding. The upgrading of national parliaments and the Citizens' Initiative, however, are important additional steps that are needed to bolster the Union's commitment to democracy.

According to calculations by legal scholars, the Treaty of Lisbon upgrades the European Parliament as co-legislator in 95 per cent of all cases by subjecting them to ordinary legislative procedure.[45] Thus, co-legislation will apply to the common agricultural policy (Article 43, para 2 TFEU[46]), energy policy (Article 194, para 2 TFEU), the use of the euro (Article 133 TFEU), trade policy (Article 207, para 2 TFEU), and most notably in matters of judicial and police cooperation, where not only the European but also the national parliaments are given a voice (Articles 82, para 2; 83, para 1; 85, para 1; 88, paras 2 and 69 TFEU). Moreover the distinction between legal acts, non-legal acts, delegated acts, and implementation acts (Articles 289–91 TFEU) could finally create a hierarchy of norms which eventually will become decisive in cases of norms collision. Giving the European Parliament's equal rights regarding decisions on the EU budget, the distinction between obligatory and non-obligatory expenditures being abolished (Article 314 TFEU), is of paramount importance. And so too are the provisions regarding the Parliament's role in Foreign and Security Policy: first, the High Representative for Foreign and Security Policy as a member and vice-president of the Commission is also responsible to the European Parliament (Article 18 TEU[47]), whose clout will also gain by the nomination of the Commission's president according to the results of European elections (Article 17, para 7 TEU). Last but not least, the European Parliament's consent is required for most of the international treaties (Article 218, para 6 TFEU).

In terms of democracy, the promotion of national parliaments may appear more surprising, yet it is simply the concession of governments to the long debated principle of subsidiarity. Interestingly, national parliaments (Article 12 TEU) appear in the Treaty of Lisbon even before the European Parliament (Articles 13 and 14 TEU). National parliaments are to be informed by the Commission about new initiatives directly and without interference of governments (Article 5, para 3 TEU). This will significantly reduce the advantages the latter have enjoyed in the past. Each parliament will be endowed with the right to voice concern about a possible infringement of the principle of subsidiarity (Article 7, para 1, Protocol on Subsidiarity and Proportionality). If such concern is shared by a third of other national parliaments the Commission is compelled to review its proposal. If the issue at stake regards justice and home affairs a quarter of votes will suffice (Article 7, para 2). The opinion of the Commission will then be presented to the European Parliament and the Council together with those of national parliaments. They will also be given the right to bring a case of infringement of subsidiarity before the ECJ (Article 8). National parliaments will, moreover, have a voice regarding Treaty revisions (Article 48, para 7 TEU), new memberships

[45]   Brok and Selmayr, above n 19, 228.

[46]   Consolidated Version of the Treaty on the Functioning of the European Union (TFEU), Official Journal C115, 9 May 2008.

[47]   Ibid.

(Article 49, para 2 TEU), and financial resources of the Union (Article 311, para 3 TFEU), and most notably the so-called 'flexibility clause' (Article 352 TFEU).

By enshrining the principle of multi-level parliamentarism in the Constitutional Treaty and subsequently in the Treaty of Lisbon, the founders have not only taken an important symbolic step but have also opened new channels for concrete action and influence of national parliaments. Whether and how these channels will be used remains to be seen. In particular, as practice implies parliamentary multilateralism in order to be effective, parliaments have to find allies to force the Commission to review a legislative proposal they characterise as transgressing the red line of subsidiarity. For such initiatives to succeed a transnational political culture has still to be developed. In that respect, the inter-parliamentary cooperation spelled out in Protocol No 1 on the role of national parliaments in the Union has to find effective forms of information exchange and of negotiating common positions in order to be heard at the supranational level.

At last, the new provisions on direct participation are to create a new democratic culture in the Union that is also a novelty to some member states. However, the Citizens' Initiative implementation procedures have still to be worked out, as the Treaty just tells us that 'not less than one million citizens who are nationals of a significant number of Member States may take the initiative of inviting the European Commission, within the framework of its powers, to submit any appropriate proposal on matters where citizens consider that a legal act of the Union is required for the purpose of implementing the Treaties' (Article 11, para 4). Derided by most eurosceptics, it could, if taken seriously, initiate popular mobilisation and thus promote the formation of a European public sphere.

VII. CONCLUSIONS: EUROPEAN CONSTITUTIONALISM AS A TOOL TO BRING CITIZENS BACK IN?

Has then the story of European constitutional debate been a success in terms of representative as well as participatory democracy? Does it allow for an optimistic perspective on the future integration process? There are no clear-cut answers. Even after the second referendum in Ireland positively concluded in October 2009, the affirmative ruling of the German Constitutional Court and the subsequent legislative charges by the German Bundestag as well as the assert of Poland and the Czech Republic, a cautionary approach is appropriate. This chapter, though, has aimed at investigating the problems that led to the constitutional debate as well as the solutions worked out by two Conventions and the subsequent IGC.

Parliamentarisation appears to be one strategy chosen by European political elites to court their disgruntled electorates who may also voice their concern directly by the instrument of the Citizens' Initiative. Whereas the empowerment of the European Parliament is in line with the past logic of constitutional change, the new role of national parliaments opens new channels of power to be exploited by national actors that until now, regardless of some exceptions, had merely been onlookers. While this shift to more intensive parliamentary activity may be qualified positively in democratic terms, it may also be viewed more sceptically in terms of further deepening and widening of the Union. In particular, little can be said on how national parliaments will cope with the public shift 'from permissive consensus to constraining dissensus',[48] and how they will at the same time maintain a positive role in the construction of Union.

But some of the problems, at least, are not to be shunned. *First*, the new powers given to national parliaments will only become real if they are capable of opening a new chapter in their history and if they allow for new experiments of transnational cooperation going beyond the niceties of COSAC. *Second*, with regard to further integration, national parliaments must not only think in terms of subsidiarity red lines, and thus invoke national or subnational interests as being sacrosanct; they must also consider their role in terms of giving a contribution to the unification process. The danger of subsiding to populisms of all shades obviously looms large. In this respect, cooperation with their counterparts in the European Parliament is of utmost importance. Last but not least, they have to cope with the fact that today complex issues are discussed and prepared for decision in different fora than their own committees, independent agencies being one case in point. Consequently, in order to be themselves able to take their own responsibilities seriously, parliaments at all levels must envisage how such agencies are to be controlled and held accountable. In order to re-establish appropriate systems of checks and balances, parliaments also need, to a degree, to distance themselves from governments. If parliaments yield all power to the executives, they make themselves superfluous. European constitutionalism as enshrined in the Treaty of Lisbon could create the instruments to open a new game in the history of integration.

---

[48] L. Hooghe and G. Marks, 'A Postfunctionalist Theory of European Integration: From Permissive Consensus to Constraining Dissensus' (2008) 39 *British Journal of Political Science* 1–23.

PART III

CONSTITUTIONALISM WITHOUT DEMOCRACY?

7

More Law, Less Democracy?
Democracy and Transnational Constitutionalism

Petra Dobner

I. INTRODUCTION

Constitutionalism has an impressive past as a means of framing and taming the political, guiding legislation and uniting societies in tacit consensus. This success has powered the worldwide conviction that the political has either to be organised constitutionally or will fail the demands of democracy if not modernity. But while the process of national constitutionalisation is still going on, we are simultaneously, confronted with the decline of state-centred constitutionalism as an effective way of fully subordinating political power to constitutional law. The main reason for this increasing inability of the state's constitution to fulfil its tasks is the changing quality of statehood itself. The transformation of statehood shatters the former unity of territory, power, and people, and challenges the constitution's ability comprehensively to encompass the political entity of the state.

One answer to this problem has been to extend the concept of constitutionalism to the global arena and to promote the idea of a global constitutionalisation. The constitution's journey from a state-centred concept to a transnational project has opened new perspectives, not only in theory but also by the practical achievement of subjecting the exercise of public authority to higher law. Recent trends towards the transnationalisation, privatisation, and sectoralisation of public policy have, during the last decade, captured the attention of constitutional scholars and are leading to the promotion of new ideas about how to theorise the emerging world of globalised law, which extend from positions that defend the state's indispensability to visions of a truly new global constitutionalism beyond the state.

But this transfer of constitutional thinking from the state to the postnational constellation does not come about without losses. One blind spot is remarkable: throughout the debate, there exists general perplexity about how to meet the normative demand of a democratic legitimation for legal arrangements in the globalised world. Since the idea of global democracy remains an unfinished project both theoretically as well as practically, this does not come as a surprise. But the lack of democratically legitimised legal arrangements still renders the project of global constitutionalisation not only incomplete but also dangerous.

The future democratic quality of law is also called into question by a third development. In recent years, the promotion of democracy has tended to be substituted by the promotion of the rule of law. As the American Bar Association puts it, there is a growing belief 'that rule of law promotion is the most effective long-term antidote to the pressing problems facing the world community today, including poverty, economic stagnation, and conflict'.[1] While there can be no doubt that the rule of law forms a necessary part of democratic governance, it is doubtful that its external promotion can of itself foster democratic governance. The rule of law as such is not necessarily democratic, and was not in the beginning of its installation in Western societies.[2] In order to fulfil democratic needs, the rule of law has itself to be democratised. The question therefore remains whether and how the promotion of the rule of law can be turned into a precondition for democratic self-government.

There is, then, a growing drift between law and democracy. Surprisingly, this has so far stirred little commotion among legal scholars. Pragmatic answers prevail, and the urgent question of democratic legitimacy is put aside or postponed. There is, to be sure, no ready-made solution to the question of how the normative call for democratic legitimacy is to be reconciled with the political and legal evolution of global rule. Yet concealing the vacancy is no remedy either: it merely shrouds the fact that it has remained indispensable for any legitimate exercise of power to be based upon the consent of the governed and that this major achievement of modernity is seriously threatened by the process of globalisation in general as well as by the globalisation of law in particular.

The practical effects of the dissolution of law and democracy and the normative desirability of promoting democratised law will in this chapter be examined in four steps. The first section recalls the mutual constituency of state, democracy, and constitution, identifies the major drivers for processes of deconstitutionalisation, and interprets them as indicators of a loosening relationship between democratic legitimacy and constitutional law within the state. The second shows how and why the move towards global law does not compensate for the losses in democratic legitimacy, and instead adds to it. The third section presents and evaluates the most salient normative approaches in the neo-Kantian tradition, which claim to present an answer to the open question of the democratic legitimacy of global law. Finally, the last section takes a deflated outlook on the prospects of a fully legitimised rule of law in the globalised world.

---

[1] American Bar Association, 'Promoting the Rule of Law', <http://www.abanet.org/rol/> (accessed 25 June 2009).

[2] E.-W. Böckenförde, 'Entstehung und Wandel des Rechtsstaatsbegriffs', in his *Recht, Staat, Freiheit: Studien zur Rechtsphilosophie, Staatstheorie und Verfassungsgeschichte* (Frankfurt am Main: Suhrkamp, 1991), 143–69, at 148.

II. STATE, DEMOCRACY, AND CONSTITUTION

For classical constitutional thought, the state and its constitution are mutually constituent and dependent. It is the state's material and geographical existence which necessitates constitutions. Without the state's will to act constitutionally, and without the state's ability to preserve and defend the viability and validity of the constitution, it would be merely a piece of paper. For the democratic state at least, the reverse is also true, namely that the state depends on the constitution, for there has thus far been no other means of regulating in a binding manner both the democratic practices and the legitimation of rule in secular societies.

In order to serve as an institution which guarantees democratic governance, the constitution must be conceptualised as a specific form of legal regulation. In this perspective, the particularities of constitutional regulation can be determined by three key characteristics. Compared to their predecessors in the form of contracts with rulers, constitutions not only limit the ruler's exercise of power but also *legitimise* such exercise; their coverage of matters is not individualised but *universal*; and they bind not only some people in a given territory but *all people*.[3] A democratic constitution then, in contrast to other kinds of regulation, is a set of norms which a community has agreed upon, which at least in principle is applicable to all important matters of this community, and which is equally valid and mandatory for all members of this community.

Thus understood, constitutions can be considered to be the ingenious answer to the demands of secular societies to be free and bound to rules at the same time, by forming a mutual contract—one individual with every other—in which the security and freedom of the individual are preserved by putting the 'natural rights' of everyone in the hands of the elected few. Constitutions are hence a functional solution to a problem which could only evolve historically and culturally. In response to the problem of how to preserve freedom and security in societies which had discovered what Lefort calls the 'empty place of power', constitutions have filled this place with their own production of legitimate rule.

With the constitution being a set of norms given by a state, for a state, and which is valid within a state, it is coextensive with the state. The constitutional order ends at the borders of a state, with both of them, states and constitutions, having to give way to other states, people, and constitutions at these borders. As the normative counterpart of the state, a constitution must address all of the state's components, ie the territory, power, and people. The unity of these elements in the state also has to be represented in the institutional design of the constitution, which, to be the order of the totality of the state, is a territorial order, a power order, and social order in one.

Crucial to this picture of statehood and the modern constitution is the idea of *congruence*: in a given territory, but not beyond, the state and only the state is legitimised to rule over the people, who, by their consent, agree to be ruled under the

---

[3] D. Grimm, *Deutsche Verfassungsgeschichte 1776–1866* (Frankfurt am Main: Suhrkamp, 1988), 12.

laws of the constitution. On considering the major transformations of the political, however, one finds that all of the classical elements of statehood are changing. In sum, it is this congruence of territory, power, and people—which is reflected in the constitution as a territorial, power, and social order—that is dissolving, thus changing the conditions of constitutional rule.[4]

The principle of territoriality is most decisive for the modern state. It relies on the acceptance of territorial borders as the material limit to the exercise of power. Prepared for in the 1555 peace treaty of Augsburg and resolved in the 1648 peace treaty of Osnabrück and Münster, the overlapping power claims based on personal loyalties were replaced by a system of defined territorial borders. Modern states 'explicitly claim, and are based on, particular geographic territories, as distinct from merely occupying geographic space which is true of all social organizations. ... Territory is typically continuous and totally enclosed by a clearly demarcated and defended boundary'.[5] Altogether, the system of modern territorial states organises geographical space by a system of 'territorially disjoint, mutually exclusive, functionally similar, sovereign states'.[6]

The territorial foundation of the state is an issue which was taken for granted as soon as it was established. The political philosophers of the period in which the shift from personal to territorial systems took place easily incorporated the geographic border into their theories.[7] Despite its revolutionary effects on the structures of legitimation, the extension of power, the general self-understanding of states, the organisation of the international system, the concept of security, and the formation of a people, territoriality has only become a major issue of political and scientific concern in the last few years.

This concern follows from the fact that the territorial basis is fading due to changes both *in* and *of* space. Changes *in space* take place where territory formerly controlled by the state's authorities now is ruled by various competing actors, among which the state is but one. Changes in space reorganise the relation between geographic space, its users and/or usage, and its organising forces. A similar degree of attention devoted to changes *in* space has been paid to changes *of space* and/or our perception of space. The sense of territoriality in general is being questioned by the growing importance of non-geographic spaces such as the virtual space of digitality. Without taking the position that geography no longer matters, the geographically organised state is still losing control of the growing virtual space, a fact which also undermines its authority in

[4] P. Dobner, *Konstitutionalismus als Politikform: Zu den Effekten staatlicher Transformation auf die Verfassung als Institution* (Baden-Baden: Nomos, 2002).

[5] J. Anderson, 'Nationalism and Geography', in J. Anderson (ed), *The Rise of the Modern State* (Atlantic Highlands, NJ: Humanities Press, 1986), 115–42, at 117.

[6] J. G. Ruggie, 'Territoriality and Beyond: Problematizing Modernity in International Relations' (1993) 47 *International Organziation* 139–74, at 151.

[7] Thomas Hobbes, *Leviathan oder Stoff, Form und Gewalt eines Kirchlichen und Bürgerlichen Staates*, ed I. Fetscher (Frankfurt am Main: Suhrkamp, 1984), 173; Jean Bodin, *Über den Staat* (Stuttgart: Reclam, 1976), 11; John Locke, *Two Treatises of Government* [1689], ed P. Laslett (Cambridge: Cambridge University Press, 1963), 343, 92.

geographic territories. Virtual space challenges the notion of *locus*; it raises the question of whether it can make sense to speak of space and place anymore, and if so, how, if territorial fixation is abandoned. With a restructuring of the geopolitical landscape on the one hand, and a redefinition of space in general on the other, the state enters into a new competition over the control of space and territory. Being territorially fixed, and having a concept of agency and power adjusted to geographic space understood in terms of unquestionable property, the state is 'territorially left behind' vis-à-vis other actors engaging in territorial fluidity.[8] Once an unquestioned and reliable structure of the political, territory is today marked by an increasing number of contingencies.

Among the terms used to describe political modernity, 'sovereignty' occupies an outstanding position: ever since it was transplanted from its original theological background to political reasoning, it has served as a focal point of political action and self-understanding.[9] The continuity in the use of the term, though, can easily betray the fact that 'sovereignty' has undergone a severe change of meaning (from *Fürsten-souveränität* to *Volkssouveränität*), so modern usage of the term is not only different from but in some respects even contradicts the original intentions of its inventor. When in the sixteenth century Jean Bodin first applied the idea of sovereignty to the political context, his main concern was to pacify a multitude of competing powers by the means of centralisation and hierarchy, and to put an end to religious and civil war. Following the philosophical reasoning about sovereignty up to the *Federalist Papers* and the constitution of the USA, the concept of sovereignty has been successively enriched and partly redirected. Whereas Bodin basically argued for the *centralisation* of power, Hobbes claimed the *rationality* of absolute power, and although his intentions were different, he opened rather than closed the door to a *democratic share* of this power. This door was swung open wide by Locke, who argued that there is no remedy to the uncertainties of the state of nature so long as power is held by an absolute monarch, who 'commanding a multitude, has the Liberty to be Judge in his own Case, and may do to all his Subjects whatever he pleases, without the least liberty to any one to question or controle those who Execute his Pleasure'.[10] Locke therefore claims that government has to be resigned to the public, for 'there and only there is a Political, or Civil Society'.[11] Following this line on to the *Federalists* as the ones to finally constitutionalise sovereignty, one should not neglect the contribution made by Paine in *Common Sense*, who promoted a mass democratic acceptance of the right to self-government.[12]

---

[8] W.-D. Narr and A. Schubert, *Weltökonomie: Die Misere der Politik* (Frankfurt am Main: Suhrkamp, 1994), 28.

[9] For the early history of sovereignty cf H. Quaritsch, *Souveränität: Entstehung und Entwicklung des Begriffs in Frankreich und Deutschland Vom 13. Jahrhundert bis 1806* (Berlin: Duncker & Humblot, 1986).

[10] Locke, above n 7, 316.

[11] Ibid 368.

[12] Thomas Paine, *Rights of Man and Common Sense* (New York: Everyman, 1994).

Ever since the first constitution of modern times, sovereignty has shown a two-sided face: it claims the centralisation of power in the state *and* binds it to democratic consent. The concept of democratically exercised sovereignty (*Volkssouveränität*) now links two questions about power: the question as to the objects and extent of power, and locating them within the state; and the question of the formal responsibility for the exercise of this power by situating it ultimately with the people.

The concept of sovereignty for a long time has had its critics. During the early decades of the twentieth century, Harold Laski questioned whether sovereignty was but a hiding place for the issue of power and if there was any more legitimation to locating it in the state than in the individual wills of the people.[13] At the same time, Hans Kelsen argued that sovereignty is incompatible with international law (*Völkerrecht*), with his preferences being clearly in favour of the latter.[14] This early theoretical reasoning for a critical view on the concept of state sovereignty has recently gained renewed support as a result of the state acquiring the status of *primus inter pares*—as a national actor within the 'corporate state', and as an international actor within the structures of global politics.

Taking up the differentiation of the objects and extent of power as one side of sovereignty and the democratic responsibility as the other, the changes in sovereignty can now be evaluated in two steps. First, we see an exodus of objects of power out of the state, in the sense that an increasing number of basic issues such as environmental matters, trade relations, legal affairs, and also legal sanctions and tax matters are no longer either adequately or completely covered by one state. And second, this also leads to a decrease in the number of democratic options for controlling the ways in which this power is exercised, for these options have been till now located only in the state. Although these two processes are linked, they can be differentiated analytically and should be valued differently. Assessing the loss of the state's supremacy is purely a matter of measuring the output efficiency of decision-making processes, and this assessment should be based on empirical studies rather than political convictions. But political convictions quite rightly have their place in evaluating the loss of democratic control accompanying this process.

Political theory insists that the legitimation of the constitutional order must be based directly or indirectly on the consent of the people. Ever since Rousseau's formulation of the social contract, the problem has been how consent can be formed if the people have free and different wills. One answer has prevailed, namely the assumption of homogeneity on the basis of traditional, cultural, or ethnic bonds, which either legitimates excluding the dissenters as irrelevant 'others', or which ideally includes the dissenting minority into the community by

[13] H. Laski, 'Die Souveränität des Staates', in H. Kurz (ed), *Volkssouveränität und Staatssouveränität* (Darmstadt: Wissenschaftliche Buchgesellschaft, 1970), 90–108.

[14] H. Kelsen, 'Der Wandel des Souveränitätsbegriffs', in H. Kurz (ed), *Volkssouveränität und Staatssouveränität* (Darmstadt: Wissenschaftliche Buchgesellschaft, 1970), 164–78; H. Kelsen, *Das Problem der Souveränität und die Theorie des Völkerrechts: Beitrag zu einer Reinen Rechtslehre* (Aalen: Scientia, 1981).

assuming that sooner or later it will be part of a majority again. The construction of homogeneity can come about aggressively as in the version of Carl Schmitt,[15] or be seen as a constitutional goal as expressed by Otto Kirchheimer,[16] or simply be presented as a normatively necessary precondition for success in the general deliberation as maintained by Jürgen Habermas.[17] Without denying important differences between these theories, one significant concurrence of these arguments must be stated: there is no other way of constructing legitimate rule under secular and democratic conditions than by assuming the ability to achieve consent on the basis of shared views and values.[18] Ever since they were introduced into constitutional theory, homogeneity and consent have been theoretical constructions as opposed to realistic descriptions. Nevertheless, we seem to have reached a period in which these fictions have become less convincing, especially if we take seriously the sociological observations of a growing self-reflexivity, individualisation, differentiation, and transnational migration. These social changes challenge the political fiction of a 'closed society',[19] a fiction which lies at the foundation of democratic theory and the democratic practices in most countries.

Territorial contingency, the diffusion of power, and social plurality together alter the conditions under which the supremacy of democratic constitutionalism within the state was established. The exercise of public authority within the state can no longer be considered to be under the full control of constitutional law. Insofar as the constitution is understood as the legal realisation of the social compact of a people, these changes also imply that democratic control by means of constitutional law gives way to an exercise of political power beyond constitutional norms, or to put it differently: that the linkage between law and democracy is loosened. Globalising law is one remedy to put the exercise of public authority, which has escaped the nation state, anew under legal regulations. But while the establishment of transnational law undoubtedly can produce norms for matters beyond the state, it fails to meet the criteria for democratic legitimacy of legal arrangements.

---

[15] C. Schmitt, 'Legalität und Legitimität', in his *Verfassungsrechtliche Aufsätze aus den Jahren 1924–1954* (Berlin: Duncker & Humblot, 3rd edn, 1985), 263–350, at 235.

[16] O. Kirchheimer, 'Weimar—was dann?', in his *Politik und Verfassung* (Frankfurt am Main: Suhrkamp, 1981), 9–56, at 17–18.

[17] J. Habermas, *Faktizität und Geltung: Beiträge zur Diskurstheorie des Rechts und des demokratischen Rechtsstaates* (Frankfurt am Main: Suhrkamp, 1994).

[18] A noteworthy exception to this rule is the idea of *nichtüberzeugter Verständigung* ('unconvinced understanding') in N. Luhmann, *Beobachtungen der Moderne* (Opladen: Westdeutscher Verlag, 1992), 202 (unfortunately Luhmann used the term once only, and failed to provide further explication).

[19] S. Benhabib, 'Democracy and Identity: Dilemmas of Citizenship in Contemporary Europe', in M. T. Greven (ed), *Demokratie—Eine Kultur des Westens? 20. Wissenschaftlicher Kongreß der Deutschen Vereinigung für Politische Wissenschaft* (Opladen: Leske und Budrich, 1998), 225–48, at 237.

III. THE DEMOCRATIC BLIND SPOT IN TRANSNATIONAL
CONSTITUTIONALISM

'Transnational constitutionalism' is here understood in an encompassing sense as a common denominator for various attempts to extend the project of global law beyond the traditional frame of public international law. It therefore extends beyond the type of law which only concerns relations between sovereign states and intergovernmental organisations.[20] This younger debate observes and conceptualises a global law which addresses or affects citizens directly and which is not restricted to law between states but between different social, economic, or political entities within and outside of states. Independent of whether or not the term 'constitutionalism' is used to coin those projects by the authors themselves and irrespective of the general difficulties in applying the term of constitution to global law,[21] these approaches share the idea that the global arena itself is a legislative sphere in which binding regulations are produced which overrun the constitutional autarky of every single state and which therefore can claim constitutional quality themselves.

From the perspective of political science, the main task for global public law in this newer sense is to regain regulatory control over the exercise of legal or political power. From a democratic standpoint this necessarily involves a full democratic legitimacy for the production process of this law, its application, and its control. The problem is that this demand can no longer be fulfilled by means of a legitimacy chain (in which the people as members of sovereign states are viewed as authors and addressees of the law), when either the coverage of global law leaves the paths of interstate conventions or when the production of global law is a task for expert conventions or private committees which are not representatives of the affected civil societies. In either case the legitimacy chain is disrupted, thus leaving open the question of consent. None of these conditions is denied to be empirically correct: there is a widespread agreement that the emerging global law is a conglomerate of rules and regulations which exceed the sphere of human rights, which can overrun national constitutions (and not only within the EU), that compliance is enforced by means of either juridical or economic sanctions, and that the production of these rules has become a matter for hybrid actors, including not only states or intergovernmental organisations, but also private, economic, and civil actors of all kinds. The new global law therefore is confronted with a structural lack of democratic legitimacy which can be stated in two respects: by general substantiation and by empirical observations of new concepts of transnational law.

The democratic foundation of constitutional law and vice versa its ability to found democratic governance within the state is closely linked to the different aspects which have been outlined in the first section: first, that the rule of constitutional law must be limited to a distinct territorial-personal unit and cannot claim

---

[20] The term therefore covers concepts such as international constitutional law, global constitutionalism, societal constitutionalism, and global administrative law.

[21] Cf Grimm, Preuss, Loughlin, and Wahl in this volume.

validity beyond this unit; and, secondly, that it must address a specific political entity within this unit which is responsible for the exercise of public authority, ie government. Transnationalisation and privatisation of public authority challenge these basic preconditions of the state's constitution: a clear distinction between inside and outside as well as a distinct separation of public and private.[22] Following Grimm in this basic argument about the inapplicability of constitutional thinking beyond the state, the argument can be extended to liberal democracy in general: not only constitutional thinking, but liberal democracy itself is dependent on a constricted political entity. In political theory this condition is conceptualised as a social compact between a given people. The limitation of this people is crucial for the idea of a social compact, for only the seclusion of a political entity allows for those who are ruled to consent to the ones who rule them. Practically the compliance with this compact depends on the development of a specific organisation which exercises governmental power, because the separation between a social and a political sphere is a precondition for the constitutional subjection of the exercise of political authority. All in all, the diffusion between governmental and private actors, the dissolution of clearly demarcated political entities into the transnational sphere, and the blending of private and public actors in the exercise of political authority, which altogether characterise the transnational constellation, diminish the options for democratic control over the exercise of political authority, and neither can these open questions be answered, nor are they answered in the conceptions of transnational constitutionalism. Those which so far are available fall short of explaining how exactly global regulations can be legitimised by the consent of the people who are affected.

How then is this problem addressed in conceptions of global law? The range of answers is wide. Many scholars simply leave the question of legitimacy aside, while those who do address the problem either (1) consider it to be a transitional phenomenon, (2) continue to rely on the legitimacy chain, or (3) deny that there is any problem at all. These stances are sketched in turn.

Representative of the first response is Christian Tomuschat, who maintains that

> no group of countries is opposed in principle to the recognition of human rights as an important element of the international legal order, almost no group rejects democracy as a guiding principle for the internal systems of governance of States. Given this rapprochement towards the emergence of a true international community, objections to general principles of law are progressively losing the weight which they carried 25 years ago.[23]

[22] D. Grimm, 'Die Verfassung im Prozess der Entstaatlichung', in M. Brenner, P. M. Huber, and M. Möstl (eds), *Der Staat des Grundgesetzes—Kontinuität und Wandel: Festschrift für Peter Badura* (Tübingen: Mohr Siebeck, 2004), 145–67. See also Grimm in this volume.

[23] C. Tomuschat, *International Law: Ensuring the Survival of Mankind on the Eve of a New Century, General Course on Public International Law*, 281 Recueil des Cours (The Hague et al: Nijhoff, 1999), at 339.

While it may be true that the international community shares a set of normative values, including human rights and democracy, it remains questionable whether a basic agreement can count as a substitute for direct involvement, co-determination, and control of general principles of law. Critically viewed, Tomuschat's argument is paradoxical: if we all agree to be democrats, we do not have to be democratic anymore. The basis of his argument is a substitution of practices with beliefs. Instead of *acting* democratically we agree upon the principle. While a shared belief in democracy (if it were true) should not be underestimated, it still cannot serve as a substitute for a practical democratic legitimation of global principles.

Armin von Bogdandy and colleagues clearly see the problem. They state that we are in the 'difficult situation whereby international institutions exercise public authority which might be perceived as illegitimate, but nevertheless as legal—for lack of appropriate legal standards. Consequently, the discourse on legality is out of sync with the discourse on legitimacy'.[24] For them, and I agree, the newer attempts to make up for the legitimacy deficit by looking at 'accountability' and 'participation' do not suffice, since 'there is hardly any shared understanding about their material content. Presently, these concepts do not provide accepted standards to determine legality, but are not much more than *partes pro toto* for the concept of legitimacy.'[25]

Representing the second approach, Bogdandy et al address the question of legitimacy of global law through their own 'public law approach'. They start by approving some findings of the global governance concept. They note that

> the global governance concept recognizes the importance of international institutions, but highlights the relevance of actors and instruments which are of a private or hybrid nature, as well as of individuals—governance is not only an affair of public actors. Second, global governance marks the emergence of an increased recourse to informality: many institutions, procedures and instruments escape the grasp of established legal concepts. Third, thinking in terms of global governance means shifting weight from actors to structures and procedures. Last but not least, as is obvious from the use of the term 'global' rather than 'international,' global governance emphasizes the multi-level character of governance activities: it tends to overcome the division between international, supranational and national phenomena.[26]

They criticise, however, the fact that the concept of global governance 'is mainly understood as an essentially technocratic process following a little questioned dogma

[24] A. von Bogdandy, P. Dann, and M. Goldmann, 'Developing the Publicness of Public International Law: Towards a Legal Framework for Global Governance Activities' (2008) 9 *German Law Journal* 1375–400, at 1389.

[25] Ibid.

[26] Ibid 1378.

of efficiency'[27] and seek in their own approach for a 'response ... to such claims of illegitimacy from a public law perspective'.[28]

The public law perspective is defined by the dual function of public law: in the liberal and democratic tradition public authority may only be exercised if it is based on public law (constitutive function) and is controlled and limited by it (limiting function).[29] On this basis the answer to the legitimacy of public authority is provided in three steps. First, the authors want to look at those activities only which 'amount to an exercise of unilateral, i.e. public authority'.[30] They argue, that the global governance perspective is insufficient in singling out these unilateral acts, since 'global governance flattens the difference between public and private, as well as between formal and informal ones' and, moreover, rather concentrates on processes than on single acts.[31] Second, a workable concept of public authority is therefore needed. The authors define '*authority* as the legal capacity to *determine* others and to reduce their freedom, i.e. to unilaterally shape their legal or factual situation' and differentiate between binding and conditioning acts of this authority.[32] The third and final step defines the 'publicness' and internationality of public authority. This is understood as follows:

> We consider as international public authority any authority exercised on the basis of a competence instituted by a common international act of public authorities, mostly states, to further a goal which they define, and are authorised to define, as a public interest. The 'publicness' of an exercise of authority, as well as its international character, therefore depends on its *legal basis*. The institutions under consideration in this project hence exercise authority attributed to them by political collectives on the basis of binding or non-binding international acts.[33]

Although the authors concede that these institutions only have limited resources of democratic legitimacy, since those are 'largely state-mediated',[34] nevertheless the gap between the exercise of public authority and its democratic founding may be closed via their connection to the legitimacy chains rooted in their 'constituent polities'.[35] But is the problem really solved? I have my doubts. The global governance perspective clearly informs us about the fact that public authority defined as the 'legal capacity to determine others and to reduce their freedom' is indeed exercised by a

[27] Ibid 1379.

[28] Ibid 1380.

[29] Ibid.

[30] Ibid.

[31] Ibid 1381.

[32] Ibid 1381–2.

[33] Ibid 1382.

[34] Ibid 1400.

[35] Ibid.

multitude of actors, private and public, formally and informally. Starting from the empirically informed observation that the exercise of public authority is no longer limited to those who are public by means of their *formation*, but by the *effects* they have on the global public, the authors return to an idea of publicness in the first sense only. The broad global governance perspective is narrowed by the normative decision to count only those acts as an exercise of public authority which are exercised by states or intergovernmental organisations and which have a 'legal basis' for their operations. For those actors the legitimacy is quite unquestionable, since they are representatives of given polities. The severe problem of legitimising the exercise of public authorities by *other* actors, which are active in the production of global law—a fact which is by no means denied by the authors themselves—remains unaddressed.

Illustrative of the third response is the work of Erika de Wet. De Wet states that 'many critics regard the value system developing under the influence of international institutions and tribunals as an illegitimate, super-imposed normative system that takes place beyond any form of democratic control or accountability'.[36] In addition to the arguments which have been accentuated here, the general criticism addresses the lack of democratic accountability for the elite groups of national officials, the questionable legitimacy of non-governmental organisations of the emerging Global Public Policy Networks. De Wet reports that 'the impact of this illegitimacy becomes even more palpable when the law of the international organization is enforced directly in the domestic legal order without the national parliament's imprimatur, especially where a Member State is outvoted in the international organization that produced the directly applicable decision'.[37] Correct though her account of the criticism is, her conclusion is questionable: 'It is submitted that the flaw in these arguments lies in their *mythologizing* of national democratic governance as a model for international governance.'[38] It would be more correct to state that the flaw of the arguments lies not in the mythology of national democratic governance but in the fact that the democratic legitimacy of governance is an inalienable right and therefore must be transferred to the global arena—and that otherwise, if this is not possible, the globalisation of law must be criticised. But at this point de Wet turns the argument round by questioning whether democracy really equates with legitimacy.

Her first argument is based on the diversity of democracies. Surely, democracy can 'mean many different things, including popular democracy, representative democracy, or pluralist democracy, to name but a few'.[39] But the fact that there are different organisational forms of democracies does not challenge the basic fact that all of them must base their governmental system on the consent of the people.

[36] E. de Wet, 'The International Constitutional Order' (2006) 55 *International and Comparative Law Quarterly* 51–76, at 71.

[37] Ibid 72.

[38] Ibid.

[39] Ibid.

In her second argument de Wet challenges the nature of democratic theory. She states:

> [I]t has not yet been convincingly explained why the concept of democracy would in and of itself be determinative for the legitimacy of any form of governance. Even in well established democracies, the legitimacy of the decision-making process has been undermined by the fact that national democracies tend to exclude many who are affected by their policies, simply because they are not part of the *demos* as understood in a particular ethno-cultural sense. However, it is questionable whether such ethno-cultural definitions of *demos* are compatible with the founding principles of constitutional democracies which aim at full representation and participation of all affected by the decision-making process. It thus becomes questionable whether the substance of the national democratic legislative decision-making process would necessarily reflect the actual wishes of the majority of those affected by it.[40]

What is this referring to? Modern concepts of citizenship have gone far beyond the inclusion of an 'ethno-cultural demos', and overcome the *ius sanguinis* principle of citizenship (which itself was never the dominant modern principle of citizenship). The argument that the 'substance' of the decision-making process does not reflect the wishes of the majority of the affected refers back to a long tradition of anti-democratic rhetoric, but a tradition that also has been widely rejected. Direct democracies do tend to represent the empirical will better than representative democracies but they tend to do so on the basis of the subjection of the minority; representative democracies, by contrast, possess a greater propensity to forge compromises.[41] By definition a compromise is something that nobody would have voted for if there had not been others with diverging ideas. Moreover, governments and parliaments also have the function of articulating and translating the popular will into viable policies. The argument that democracies produce decisions that do not reflect the 'actual will' is a merely populist one.

De Wet continues, thirdly, that

> even in instances where groups are officially represented in the governmental decision-making process, the legitimacy of the process suffers from the lack of the de facto access of many of these groups to the public debate leading up to the governmental decision-making process; as well as the lack of transparency of the decision-making process itself; and the (perceived) lack of independence and expertise of the decision-makers in question.[42]

---

[40] Ibid 73.

[41] E. Fraenkel, 'Die repräsentative und plebiszitäre Komponente im demokratischen Verfassungsstaat', in his *Deutschland und die westlichen Demokratien* (Frankfurt am Main: Suhrkamp, 1991), 153–203.

[42] De Wet, above n 36, at 73.

This argument also must be rejected: modern democracies contain an abundance of experts and expert-commissions,[43] interest groups, and non-governmental participators of all kinds which offer a wide array of formal and informal modes of participation, including membership of political parties, the right to elect and to be elected, and thus be part of the political decision-making process. Also the idea that parliamentarians and members of governments lack 'independence and expertise' repeats long-standing prejudices against parliamentarian democracies which have been rebutted in practically every serious scientific piece which has been produced on this subject.[44]

The main aim of de Wet's argument is to call into question the legitimacy of domestic democracy in order to evade the issue of democratic legitimacy of global politics and law: if domestic democracy cannot provide for legitimacy, why then should international policy- and law-making ever strive for it? In her own words:

> However, if one accepts that democracy does not necessarily result in legitimate decision-making either, it becomes plausible to ask whether the international legitimacy deficit can be overcome through other measures than democratic decision-making. These would include but not be limited to measures aimed at a more accessible and transparent decision-making process. Viewed in this light, it is inappropriate to dismiss the possibility of legitimate post-national decision-making out of hand.[45]

But what if one does not agree that democracy does not result in legitimacy? Or rather: what if one is convinced that democracy is the only means to reach full legitimacy?

IV. KANT AND HIS SUCCESSORS: DEMOCRATISING TRANSNATIONAL CONSTITUTIONALISM?

The normative argument for a democratic legitimation of law is most clearly expressed in the Kantian project of outlining the necessary preconditions for eternal peace. According to these, constitutional law is crucial for putting into reality the principles of moral philosophy. Following Hobbes's idea that men are by nature in a state of war, Kant sees the only remedy in establishing a rule of law to which everybody consents. Since a state of peace will not simply evolve, it must be established by means of law.

---

[43] S. Siefken, *Expertenkommissionen im Politischen Prozess: Eine Bilanz zur Rot-Grünen Bundesregierung 1998–2005* (Wiesbaden: VS Verlag für Sozialwissenschaften, 2007).

[44] S. S. Schuettemeyer, *Fraktionen im Deutschen Bundestag 1949–1997: Empirische Befunde und Theoretische Folgerungen* (Opladen: Westdeutscher Verlag, 1998). W. Patzelt, 'Politikverdrossenheit, populäres Parlamentsverständnis und die Aufgaben der politischen Bildung', in *Aus Politik und Zeitgeschichte (APuZ)*, B7/8-1999, 31–8.

[45] De Wet, above n 36, at 73–4.

Starting from a conflict theory, Kant sees the need to establish three elements of a global legal order aimed at solving possible clashes. Conflict can occur between people of one state, between states, and in the relation between individuals and states. In symmetry with the possible sources of conflict three different elements of a global legal order have to be established in order to make peace possible:

> All men, who have a mutual influence over one another, ought to have a civil constitution. Now every legitimate constitution, considered in respect of the persons who are the object of it, is I. either conformable to the civil right, and is limited to the people (*jus civitatis*). II. Or to the rights of nations, and regulates the relations of nations among each other (*jus gentium*). III. Or to the cosmopolitical right, as far as men, or states, are considered as influencing one another, in quality of constituent parts of the great state of the human race (*jus cosmopoliticum*). This division is not arbitrary; but necessary in respect of the idea of a perpetual peace.[46]

According to these considerations 'the civil constitution of every state ought to be republican'.[47] A republican constitution results from the idea of a social compact, 'without which one cannot conceive of a right over a people',[48] and is defined as a constitutional order which respects the liberty of men, enables the equal subjection of all to the law, and is based on equality of all members of a state. Legal and exterior liberty therefore, is not 'the faculty of doing whatever one wishes to do, provided it injures not another. It consists in rendering obedience to those laws alone to which I have been able to give my assent'.[49] Earlier in this essay Kant had already argued that a state is not 'like the soil upon which it is situate, a patrimony. It consists of a society of men, over whom the state alone has a right to command and dispose'.[50] Although Kant goes beyond Rousseau in stating that representatives can exercise the task of finding the right decisions, he does not leave any doubt that the state *is* society, and that therefore the state's right 'to command and dispose' must ultimately be rested on self-government. Normatively, there is no doubt that the right to self-government is closely linked to the right to legislate, which can be traced back to the people's

---

[46] Immanuel Kant, *Project for a Perpetual Peace: A Philosophical Essay. Translated from the German* (London: Vernor & Hood, 1796), at 13.

[47] Ibid 13.

[48] Ibid 4.

[49] Ibid 14.

[50] Ibid 3. The thought that it is society alone which can make the rules to which it shall obey is expressed even more clearly in the German version, where Kant clearly states the identity of state and society: 'Der Staat ist nämlich nicht (wie etwa der Boden, auf dem er seinen Sitz hat, eine Habe (patrimonium). Er ist eine Gesellschaft von Menschen, über die niemand anders als er selbst, zu gebieten und zu disponieren hat' (Immanuel Kant, 'Zum Ewigen Frieden: Ein Philosophischer Entwurf', in W. Weischedel (ed), *Immanuel Kant: Schriften zur Anthropologie, Geschichtsphilosophie, Politik und Pädagogik I, Werkausgabe Band XI* (Frankfurt am Main: Suhrkamp, 1795/1993), 191–251, at 197).

own consent, and that both rights are indispensable for the establishment of, if not perpetual, at least temporary peace.

Kant's vision for eternal peace based on the consent of the people can be summarised as a multi-level system, in which a domestic republican constitution is complemented by an international public law, which regulates the relation between states, and a global layer of universal human rights. His insistence on the right of legal self-determination and his attempt to connect this thought with the vision of peaceful international order has inspired a discussion about the modernity and applicability of his thoughts for the post-national constellation. Two different readings of Kant prevail: one reading is recommendatory, in the sense that it seeks to adopt Kant's proposal as a guideline for the establishment of the international order. The second reading is more factual, claiming that Kant's ideas are already materialising in the existing order. I will argue, however, that Kant's premises prohibit thinking about the democratic legitimacy of law in continuity with his scheme.

Representative of the recommendatory line is Ernst-Ulrich Petersmann. For Petersmann, 'Kant was the first political thinker who developed a comprehensive theory of national and international constitutionalism based on the insight that the problem of establishing a perfect civil constitution is subordinate to the problem of a law-governed external relationship with other states and cannot be solved unless the latter is solved'.[51] Petersmann therefore asks if 'modern international law and the UN Charter offer such a constitutional framework for cosmopolitan cooperation and perpetual peace among legally free and equal citizens'.[52] While his account on the constitutional quality of the UN remains sceptical, since 'lasting peace cannot be effectively secured by power-oriented organizations like the UN',[53] Petersmann is more optimistic about the WTO and European constitutional law. With the latter being an 'interlocking layered system of national and international guarantees of human rights, democracy, and rule of law which can be directly invoked and enforced by European citizens',[54] it shows, according to Petersmann, that 'this constitutional insight—that cosmopolitan international guarantees of freedom, non-discrimination, and rule of law can strengthen and extend corresponding national legal guarantees of citizens also within their own countries vis-à-vis their own government—goes far beyond Kant's draft treaty for perpetual peace'.[55] European constitutional law and its underlying Kantian theory therefore could—or, rather, should—inspire a reform process of the UN. For Petersmann the Kantian project has not yet become reality, but it nevertheless instructs us on how to proceed. In his view, the UN Charter 'needs to be supplemented by a new UN constitution focusing

---

[51] E.-U. Petersmann, 'How to Constitutionalize International Law and Foreign Policy for the Benefit of Civil Society?' (1998) 20 *Michigan Journal of International Law* 1–30, at 7.

[52] Ibid 12.

[53] Ibid 14.

[54] Ibid 16–17.

[55] Ibid 17.

on effective protection of fundamental rights and constitutional democracies as preconditions for lasting peace'.[56]

Jürgen Habermas is the most prominent author of those who comply with the second line of approach to the Kantian outline of an international constitutional order. In his essay 'Does the Constitutionalization of International Law Still Have a Chance?', he argues that Kant's proposal should be read as a model for a multi-level system, and not be misunderstood as a model for a *Weltrepublik*.[57] Therefore national constitutions and a constitutionalised world order do not have to be of the same kind: while national constitutions must be republican in the sense of adopting democratic self-government, it suffices for the international order to lay down the cosmopolitan principles of universal human rights. But 'liberal constitutions beyond the state, if they are to be anything more than a hegemonic legal façade, must remain tied at least indirectly to the processes of legitimacy within constitutional *states*'.[58] While Habermas sees that the realisation of the Kantian vision is challenged by other projects, especially the neoliberal design of a denationalised *Weltgesellschaft*, the post-Marxist scenario of a decentred empire, and the anti-Kantian project of *Großraumordnungen* in the tradition of Carl Schmitt's thinking,[59] he nevertheless finds some evidence that the Kantian project is emerging. He finds the basis for this optimism mainly in the UN Charter and several newer features of the UN: in contrast to the League of Nations, which basically concentrated on the prevention of war, the UN Charter lays down and enforces human rights. This is underlined by the right of the UN Commission on Human Rights (UNCHR) to influence national governments as well as by the right of everyone for petition to the UNCHR. Although this right has so far not been used extensively, it nevertheless documents the recognition of individual citizens as direct subjects of global public law (*Völkerrecht*).[60] Secondly, the renunciation of force is now supported by Articles 42 and 43 of the UN Charter which enlarge the possibilities for the engagement of the Security Council in general, by for example extending its rights to intervene in intrastate conflicts. Thirdly, the UN is an inclusive organisation and not, as with the League of Nations, an avant-garde of liberal democracies.[61] All in all, Habermas concludes, the International Community sees itself committed to the enforcement of those constitutional principles, which so far have only been realised by nation states only, on a global scale.[62]

Two hundred years ago, the world was different. This is more than a banal statement when it comes to the question of the applicability of philosophical ideas which have been produced against the background of a completely different world. For

---

[56] Ibid 30.

[57] J. Habermas, 'Does the Constitutionalization of International Law Still Have a Chance?', in his *The Divided West* (Cambridge: Polity, 2006), 115–93.

[58] Ibid 140.

[59] Ibid 185–6.

[60] Ibid 162.

[61] Ibid 163.

[62] Ibid 160.

Habermas it is evident that there are some prejudices in Kant's thinking which derive from his contemporary biases: Kant is neither fully aware of the implications of cultural differences nor of the force of nationalism, and he shares the 'humanist' idea of the superiority of the European civilisation.[63] Habermas is nevertheless convinced that the 'provinciality of our historical consciousness vis-à-vis the future is not an objection to the universalistic program of Kantian moral and legal philosophy'.[64] I dare to doubt that.

Kant's argument for a republican constitution as the legal foundation of every state lies at the heart of his whole project of eternal peace. It is based on two premisses: first, that since men are all equal they have the *right* to obey those laws only which they themselves have agreed to; and secondly that since men are potentially hostile to each other in the state of nature they have the *duty* to subject themselves to common laws. The right of self-determination is thus coupled with the necessity of self-protection, which in cases of doubt can turn against *others'* right of self-determination. Since a man or a nation in the state of nature 'deprives me of that security, and attacks me, without being an aggressor, by the mere circumstance of living contiguous to me, in a state of anarchy and without laws; menaced perpetually by him with hostilities, against which I have no protection, I have a right to compel him, either, to associate with me under the dominion of common laws, or to quit my neighbourhood'.[65] The right of self-determination is obviously unevenly distributed around the globe. What does that mean under the circumstances of a 'global neighbourhood'? It cannot be interpreted other than the right of those who have united under republican constitutions to compel those who have a different idea about which laws they want to obey or to 'disappear'. This, of course, leads off the track from 'eternal peace' and has little to do with a *universalistic* right to self-governance.

To put it differently, Kant's belief in the republican constitution is *not* a universalistic truth beyond all cultural differences; it is the expression of the belief in the superiority of the European civilisation and the fruits of the enlightenment as the *only* remedy for hostility among people. Notwithstanding the fact that there is a certain tension between the 'right to one's own right' and the duty to interpret this right in the canalised way of republicanism, let us assume that this is a correct assumption. What does that imply for the conception of the multi-level system of the international order? One conclusion is that the second and third layer, the *ius gentium* and the *ius cosmopoliticum*, must include provisions for cases in which states which have not—by self-determination—agreed upon a republican constitution must have these imposed upon them by the world community. This is not far from reality, especially not far from the rule of law promotion, be it merely politically suggested or militarily imposed. But is it compatible with Kant's plea for a legal autonomy at home, peaceful cooperation among states, and the cosmopolitan duty of hospitality? It

[63] Ibid 145–6.
[64] Ibid 146.
[65] Kant, above n 46, 13.

certainly contradicts Kant's fifth preliminary article: 'No state shall by force interfere with either the constitution or government of another state.'[66] A second conclusion is that Kant's reasoning does not provide answers for *all* the moral problems which are posed by a globalised, multi-centric, multi-ethnic, and multi-religious world.

Kant may not have been aware of the idea of nationalism, but he certainly perceived the world as ultimately constituted by states: the autonomous state, an independent polity, is the backbone of his whole account. But common wisdom and empirical evidence show that states have been relativised in their capacity to be the only and autonomous political actors on the global scene; in many cases, they may not even be the most important ones any longer with respect to the formation of the international order. What consequences does this have for the applicability of Kantian thought on today's problems? Habermas repeats the claim that the legitimacy for any transnational constitution must be derived from democratic nation states; but what if nation states are simply not the central actors in this construction? The idea of a legitimacy chain cannot then be applied, and the problem of how the evolution of globalised law can be democratically legitimised remains unsolved.

Kant not only believed in 'democratic peace' but also in the evolution of peace on the basis of free trade:

> It is the spirit of commerce that sooner or later takes hold of every nation and it is incompatible with law: the power of money being that which of all others gives the greatest spring to states, they find themselves obliged to labour at the noble work of peace, though without any moral view; and instantly seek to stifle, by mediations, war, in whatever part it may break out, as if for this purpose they had contracted a perpetual alliance; great associations in a war are naturally rare, and less frequently still successful.[67]

This peaceful picture of the merits of commerce will hardly be subscribed to by those nations which since the 1980s have been forced into the 'free' trade system by the structural adjustment programmes of the World Bank. It may be the 'power of money' which is here at work, but not only since the privatisation of world politics and the involvement of economic actors has it become possible that the 'power of the law' becomes subservient to the 'power of money'.[68] The idea that economic commerce is an independent sphere, which encourages states to 'labour at the noble work of peace', is so far away from the hard competition on and for markets that not only Karl Marx but also free-traders like Adam Smith would shake their heads about such naivety. Moreover, Kant's belief that free trade evolves outside of law prevents us from relating his position to the attempt to understand the promotion of legal arrangements for the benefit of commercial interests. But regulations for the 'free'

---

[66] Ibid 2.

[67] Ibid 42.

[68] K. Polanyi, *The Great Transformation: Politische und ökonomische Ursprünge von Gesellschaften und Wirtschaftssystemen* (Frankfurt am Main: Suhrkamp, 1976).

market are among the most prominent examples for the evolution of global law, whether they be praised like the '*lex mercatoria*' or disliked by many, such as aspects of patent law.

Finally, Kant and his successors seem to agree that the global arena is sufficiently legally organised if it guarantees human rights. Without denying the importance of human rights, one cannot ignore the fact that global law extends far beyond human rights: the debate on global law is concerned with trade law, social law, global private law, patent law, financial law, and administrative law to name but a few. These all have an impact on domestic and international, as well as global, subjects and polities, determine their policies, and challenge their 'legal autonomy'. Limiting the quest for global law to human rights, and finding that those have already been laid down more or less satisfactorily and that therefore the project of global democracy is within grasp fails to account for the fact that there *is* a darker side of global regulations which affect the political, economic, social, and personal lives on earth—independent of and beyond our consent. This is the hard case for the search for means of legitimation, and every failure to find these means (or stop the production of this law) will ultimately deepen the gap between democracy and law. If philosophy still seeks to keep abreast of contemporary developments, it cannot ignore real world developments, which are far removed from the well-organised ideal world of citizens living peaceably and hospitably in independent (republican) states.

V. OUTLOOK

The account of our achievements in legitimising law—and the exercise of public authority on the global scheme—must remain pessimistic. On the domestic scene, changes of statehood induce a process of deconstitutionalisation which also includes a loss of our 'right to our own right'. On the global level, the production of law is undertaken in many fields, and those who observe and promote this production either do not care about its democratic control or they are unable to provide satisfactory answers to how it could be legitimised. This pessimistic outlook may easily arouse the question whether I am exaggerating in one of two (or both) directions. Do I take the quest for democratic legitimacy too seriously? And am I too critical about the prospects for the democratic legitimacy of global law?

The normative argument that human equality *must* be interpreted as the right to decide upon one's own government is hard to refute. Article 21 of the Universal Declaration of Human Rights recognises that

> [e]veryone has the right to take part in the government of his country, directly or through freely chosen representatives. The will of the people shall be the basis of the authority of government; this shall be expressed in periodic and genuine elections which shall be by universal and equal suffrage and shall be held by secret vote or by equivalent free voting procedures.[69]

---

[69] Universal Declaration of Human Rights, 10 December 1948, A/RES/217A(III).

Who, but the citizens themselves, should—in a secular world—have the right to tell them where to go, what to approve of, what to spend their money on, and what kind of government they want to have? If this is a universalistic moral imperative, then there is no exception, neither for Western Europe, nor for Papua New Guinea. The right of self-determination cannot be abandoned or bent without giving up on the essential basis of modernity: the equality of mankind as the normative starting point for all our reasoning about social, political, and individual life.

Further, can it really be denied that we are moving away from the realisation of this ideal rather than drawing nearer? Is the 'world system' bringing us closer to self-determination, or does it present itself as an inevitable force which we have to accept and subject ourselves to? The latter seems closer to the truth of the matter. But it is not the 'world system' as such—after all, this is still a man-made world, with interests and biases, and with the general propensity to present those interests as common ones. Whom does the disregarding of democratic legitimacy serve? Who profits when democracy is abandoned? And how can we go on promoting democracy as the basis of 'eternal peace' when we are about to forget about its merits and indispensability in the heart of its invention? This neglect of democracy does not come as a natural force; it is a consequence of a shift in attention and valuation from legitimacy to efficiency, from political to legal constitutionalism,[70] from democracy to legal technocracy. So, at what point have we arrived? Back at the very beginning of thinking about the legitimate production of global law.

---

[70] See Loughlin in this volume.

8

On Constitutional Membership

Marcus Llanque

I. INTRODUCTION

The allegiance that moderns feel towards the democratic nation state is now being placed in question by the claims of postnationalism, supranationalism, and cosmopolitanism. But what does affiliation to the democratic nation state actually mean? Although the term used to mark this affiliation is commonly that of 'citizen', modern constitutions tend to neglect the concept: they often employ the term to point out a distinction between people and citizens, but rarely define what citizenship entails. Constitutions only hint at the role of the citizen, and the entire picture is revealed only through a mosaic consisting of legislative acts and executive orders as well as constitutional laws. The task must be to draw a more complete picture of what constitutional democracies have in mind when they refer to individual actors as 'citizens'. The underlying idea of this chapter is that the model of citizenship applied by modern constitutions has emerged from the republican tradition of political thinking, and this can best be described as the constitutional membership model.

II. THE PEOPLE, CITIZENS, NATIONALITY

One role of modern constitutions is to identify the actors who are entitled to play a part in the political process. Modern constitutions lay down different types of political actors. First, there are institutional actors, whether individuals, such as the head of state, or collective entities, like the government or the judiciary. Establishing these institutional actors is usually the major concern of constitutions. Such types of actor possess artificial personality. Without the constitution they would not make much sense: they are defined by the constitution and integrated into the political system created by the constitution. In reality, political systems may have actor types of their own, such as political parties which often are not mentioned in constitutions, even though they are invariably recognised by constitutional law and practice.

Besides institutional actors, modern constitutions also refer to non-institutional individual actors. These form collective bodies, commonly called the 'people' or the 'nation'. 'The people' is a concept which extends from the entire population of a given territory to the idea of a collective body that consists of certain characteristic features different to other comparable groups. Because constitutions refer both to the people as well as citizens, the two terms would appear to be connected. This is not strictly accurate, however, since the people includes children and other parts of the population who are not accorded specific rights and duties and it also includes individuals who have lost some of their civil rights and duties due to their mental condition (being declared legally incapable) or to their behaviour (such as criminals disenfranchised due to the severity of their deeds). The citizenry or demos, then, consists only of a section of the people.[1] Furthermore, the people may even include individuals who are not present, such as those who are already dead or who are expected to live in the future.

Use of the term 'the people' therefore carries with it certain ambiguities of meaning, and similar semantic difficulties have arisen as a result of confusion between the terms nationality and citizenship.[2] In order to avoid these problems, I propose to use the term 'constitutional membership' to denote the citizen as the individual actor in modern democratic constitutional states.[3] The term has previously been deployed by Aleinikoff to describe all persons who are under the jurisdiction of the US Constitution, including aliens as well as citizens.[4] But here the term is used to emphasise the membership aspect of citizenship. This membership aspect needs to be borne in mind in all discussions about the connection between constitutionalism and democracy, not least because constitutionalism tends to incorporate a membership approach to citizenship, whereas democracy often regards all individuals as belonging to the demos or nation.

The term 'constitutional membership', then, is intended here to refer to the provisions a constitutional state makes for the purpose of defining what is expected of citizens in terms of behaviour and actions, rights and duties. This citizen is a member of the citizenry, the principal political group within a population. To speak of membership stresses the functional aspect of those individual actors who are expected to operate the constitution's idea of the political system. The term underlines the difference to any approach which defines the citizen in a more substantive

[1] D. Colas, *Citoyennetè et nationalité* (Paris: Gallimard, 2004), 11: 'The demos is just "une fraction de population".'

[2] On the different meanings of citizenship contrasting it with subjecthood and nationality, see D. Gosewinkel, 'Citizenship, Subjecthood, and Nationality: Concepts of Belonging in the Age of Modern Nation States', in K. Eder and B. Giesen (eds), *European Citizenship: Between National Legacies and Postnational Projects* (Oxford: Oxford University Press, 2001), 17–35. On different paths that lead to the idea citizenship, see M. R. Somers, *Genealogies of Citizenship: Markets, Statelessness, and the Right to Have Rights* (Cambridge: Cambridge University Press, 2008).

[3] For a similar perspective on citizenship, see M. Koessler, ' "Subject", "citizenship", "national", and "permanent allegiance" ' (1946) 56 *Yale Law Journal* 58–76, at 61: 'the possession … of the highest or at least of a certain higher category of political rights and (or) duties, established by the nation's or state's constitution.'

[4] T. A. Aleinikoff, *Semblances of Sovereignty: The Constitution, the State, and American Citizenship* (Cambridge, Mass.: Harvard University Press, 2002), 172.

way, in which individuals are believed to be citizens because of their characteristics as forming part of a collective body like a nation or of the people defined in terms of history, collective experience, language, ethnicity, or even race. In this substantive definition, the individual *belongs* to something, rather than simply being a *member* of something. And this leads to a debate on aspects of identity building or identity politics, which focuses on how individuals acquire a specific identity that provides them with the competence to be a citizen of a political system and to show allegiance to that system.[5]

A similar discourse has also arisen with respect to immigration policy, in which some authors assume that nationality and citizenship are interchangeable terms.[6] Nationality makes sense only as a term designating the belonging of an individual to a state, which belonging must be recognised by all other states. Citizenship, by contrast, designates the relationship of an individual to that state and to their status within the citizenry. That is, nationality deals with belonging to collective bodies such as the nation or the people. It treats the individual as a part of that collective body, a body which is identifiable by attributes and characteristics that are not changeable by constitutional provisions. Nationality generally refers to cultural, territorial, historical, linguistic, and often ethnic attributes.

The belonging aspect of citizenship is not meaningless. The community one belongs to is no fictitious trick of ideology. It may be the result of an intergenerational effort to develop and maintain a political system, including its cultural, historical, linguistic, and ideological heritage.[7] In one sense, even constitutional membership is the result of a specific political culture. The cultural aspect of membership consists of the intentional disregard of attributes of belonging for the sake of the institutional approach to citizenship understood not in terms of belonging to communities but as membership of associations.

---

[5] V. Broch-Due (ed), *Violence and Belonging: The Quest for Identity in Post-Colonial Africa* (London: Routledge, 2005); J. DeBernardi, *Rites of Belonging: Memory, Modernity, and Identity in a Malaysian Chinese Community* (Stanford, Calif.: Stanford University Press, 2004); A. Harneit-Sievers, *Constructions of Belonging: Igbo Communities and the Nigerian State in the 20th Century* (Rochester: University of Rochester Press, 2006); N. Yuval-Davis (ed), *The Situated Politics of Belonging* (London: Sage, 2007). Cf T. A. Aleinikoff and D. Klusmeyer (eds), *From Migrants to Citizens: Membership in a Changing World* (Washington, DC: Carnegie Endowment, 2000).

[6] U. K. Preuß, 'Probleme eines Konzepts europäischer Staatsbürgerschaft', in H. Kleger (ed), *Transnationale Staatsbürgerschaft* (Frankfurt am Main: Campus, 1997), 249–70, at 251; R. Rubio-Marin, *Immigration as a Democratic Challenge: Citizenship and Inclusion in Germany and the US* (Cambridge: Cambridge University Press, 2000), 19. The terms nationality and citizenship are perhaps so often confused precisely because they are so closely connected (A. M. Boll, *Multiple Nationality and International Law* (Leiden: Nijhoff, 2007), 57–8). On separating the terms nationality and citizenship from each other, see Koessler, above n 3.

[7] K. L. Karst, *Belonging to America: Equal Citizenship and the Constitution* (New Haven, Conn.: Yale University Press, 1989); Aleinikoff, above n 4, 178.

A great deal of confusion that characterises these debates on citizenship and nationality concerns the status of the concept of the citizen: is it a relationship in which individuals are members of something in which they act, or does it refer to individuals as parts of something? If we talk about members of nation states or members of specific democracies, we should refer to them as associations and consider citizenship along the lines of membership. The constitution provides the framework of the association and it defines how and when a person becomes a citizen acting in the name of and as part of the citizenry. If we talk of individuals as belonging to the people or to a nation characterised by specific attributes and if we think of these individuals as part of the people or the nation by sharing these attributes acquired through socialisation or identification, then we should refer to them not as citizens but as nationals.

III. THEORIES OF CITIZENSHIP WITHOUT THE CONSTITUTION

If constitutions refer to their individual actors as citizens it seems appropriate also to apply the general discourse on citizenship in law, philosophy, and social sciences to the constitutional setting. Most of the debate on citizenship does not discuss the meaning of the citizen in terms of a constitution.[8] The constitution is considered as something citizens should have faith in,[9] or as something they should feel patriotic about.[10] But what constitutions actually say about the role of citizens is largely neglected. In such debates, the constitution is taken to be a synonym for liberalism. But without having a theory of citizenship and without identifying the institutional context of citizenship, such conceptions of citizenship may well come close to wishful thinking. There is a variety of answers to the question of what a citizen should be, starting with the citizen who calculates his interests in a most rational way and ending with the one who, because he identifies himself with the political community, is dedicated to the common good without considering his immediate personal benefit. One might even write lists of attributes of a good citizen, which may include showing solidarity, obeying the laws, not evading taxes, forming one's own opinions, and being self-critical.[11]

In any case, the concept of citizenship is linked to the framework in which the citizen is placed. This framework can be philosophical in a sense that higher norms like

[8] Cf the typology given by Thomas in which constitutional provisions as such have no part (E. Thomas, 'Who Belongs? Competing Conceptions of Political Membership' (2002) 5 *European Journal of Social Theory* 323–49).

[9] S. Levinson, *Constitutional Faith* (Princeton, NJ: Princeton University Press, 1988).

[10] On the concept of 'constitutional patriotism' as an alternative to national patriotism, see J.-W. Müller, *Constitutional Patriotism* (Princeton, NJ: Princeton University Press, 2009).

[11] B. Denters, O. Gabriel, and M. Toscal, 'Norms of Good Citizenship', in J. W. van Deth, J. R. Montero, and A. Westholm (eds), *Citizenship and Involvement in European Democracies: A Comparative Analysis* (London: Routledge, 2007), 88–108, at 95.

justice or the philosophical concept of human rights give the concept of citizenship its significance. Some prominent theorists like Michael Walzer discuss citizenship in terms of *membership* understood *as a public good* that can be distributed.[12] This brings the concept of distributive justice into the picture. But more often theorists who look at citizenship through the lens of justice do this in a universalistic way. Globally orientated thinkers in particular regard the idea of universal justice as a complementary concept to a universalistic world, each being justified in the same way. Being universalistic they are of more importance than particular or cultural approaches to justice.

Since the cosmopolitan approach does not take into account membership aspects of citizenship, it can easily argue for an *all-inclusive citizenship*. Insofar as cosmopolitanism is mainly a normative approach, any unequal treatment of human beings is seen as normatively unacceptable and unjust.[13] In addition, cosmopolitans consider it unacceptable to refuse human beings the share of recognition connected with their citizenship as a relationship between equal individuals.[14] For many authors the treatment of *foreigners*, especially *immigrants* as residents, denizens, or citizens is the test case for future concepts of citizenship in terms of transnational democracy.[15] The cosmopolitan approach *separates citizenship from the nation state* and identifies universal mankind as the relevant community to which all individuals belong.

Authors who seek to justify restrictions on granting citizenship to permanent residents often invoke the language of faith and allegiance.[16] These are expectations based on an intense relationship of the citizen to the state and this intensity of relationship exists only with respect to citizens who dedicate themselves to the political community, such as office holders, whether holding a permanent position or elected for a specific period of time. Such office holders must show dedication so long as they perform activities on behalf of the citizenry. New citizens are supposed

[12] M. Walzer, 'The Distribution of Membership', in P. Brown and H. Shue (eds), *Boundaries: National Autonomy and its Limits* (New York: Rowman & Littlefield, 1981), 1–36. Cf R. van der Veen, 'The Adjudicating Citizen: Equal Membership in Walzer's Theory of Justice' (1999) 29 *British Journal of Sociology* 225–58.

[13] S. Benhabib, 'Citizens, Residents and Aliens in a Changing World: Political Membership in the Global Era', in U. Hedetoft and M. Hjort (eds), *The Postnational Self: Belonging and Identity* (Minneapolis: University of Minnesota Press, 2002), 85–119; R. Rubio-Marin, above n 6.

[14] L. Bosniak, 'Denationalizing Citizenship', in T. A. Aleinikoff and D. Klusmeyer (eds), *Citizenship Today: Global Perspectives and Practices* (Washington, DC: Carnegie Endowment, 2001), 237–52; L. Bosniak, *The Citizen and the Alien: Dilemmas of Contemporary Membership* (Princeton, NJ: Princeton University Press, 2006).

[15] B. Honig, *Democracy and Foreigner* (Princeton, NJ: Princeton University Press, 2001).

[16] N. J. Pickus, *True Faith and Allegiance: Immigration and American Civic Nationalism* (Princeton, NJ: Princeton University Press, 2005).

to take an oath of allegiance to the constitution,[17] which would appear to invoke the constitution as the institutional background to citizenship. But in this case the constitution is referred to more as a symbol than a system of laws which frames a model of citizens. If faith and allegiance are supposed to be the major attributes of citizens, should not naturally born citizens who inherit their citizen status from their parents be deprived of it once they prove to lack the degree of loyalty and allegiance expected of new citizens? That is, if a complete picture is to be drawn, not only the ways of acquiring citizenship but also the ways of being deprived of it should be discussed. This rarely happens.[18]

There exist a number of more complex models which divide citizenship into active and passive parts.[19] The active part of citizenship includes the right to act 'behind the law', which means having one's share in all powers, legislative as well as judicative and executive. In this model, citizenship is not only a bundle of rights but incorporates an entire programme including rights, civic consciousness, allegiance to the state and to one's fellow citizens, and to the capacity and right to participate as a full and equal member within the polity.[20]

IV. MEMBERSHIP AND BELONGING

Another way of looking at citizenship as categorically distinct from the normative approach is to understand constitutional citizenship in terms of membership. The membership approach regards citizenship as a special relationship between individuals which are treated as members of the political system seen as an association. Social as well as political associations have statutes making the structure of their organisations explicit. The roles individuals play in those associations are defined by their statutes.

Membership is not exclusively a constitutional concept. Collective bodies such as churches, political parties, voluntary associations, and states all have statutes, some of them called constitutions, which not only define their purposes and their organisational features, but also provide a concept of membership in terms of rights and duties, expectations and entitlements. There is no 'natural' or abstract concept of citizenship which can determine the grounds and limits of a citizen's role without having regard to its place in the institutional setting of

---

[17] S. Levinson, 'Constituting Communities through Words that Bind: Reflections on Loyality Oaths' (1986) 84 *Michigan Law Review* 1440–70.

[18] T. A. Aleinikoff, 'Theories of Loss of Citizenship' (1986) 84 *Michigan Law Review* 1471–503.

[19] B. Turner, 'A Theory of Citizenship' (1990) 24 *Sociologia* 189–217; P. Riesenberg, *Citizenship in the Western Tradition: From Plato to Rousseau* (Chapel Hill, NC: University of North Carolina Press, 1992).

[20] R. Bellamy, 'The Making of Modern Citizenship', in R. Bellamy, D. Castiglione, and E. Santoro (eds), *Lineages of European Citizenship: Rights, Belonging and Participation in Eleven Nation-States* (Houndmills: Palgrave, 2004), 1–21, at 6–7.

a constitution. In a way, political reality shows that all citizenship is 'tailored'.[21] That is, it is modelled after the necessities of a given political system and it changes in accordance with these necessities. The association defines what individuals are expected to do to be citizens. Membership is a relationship of individuals who form associations,[22] whereas belonging is related to individuals who live in communities.

Individuals act not only on behalf of themselves but also in groups. The individuals' relation to groups may be the major motivation for their activities. The contents as well as the limits of individual rights may be defined or at least influenced by the interpretation which is common in the group to which the individual is related. So the relationship individuals have to each other in the framework of a certain group and in the light of the values individuals share becomes a vital factor in the reality of individuals.

Individuals can belong to many different communities, of which the nation is just one among others. Individuals belong to mankind as well as to religious communities, neighbourhoods, voluntary associations formed as parts of greater populations, and such like. Belonging to many different groups may cause some problems for individual identity. In a way communities compete with each other for the commitment of individuals. No society is neatly divided between groups. The plurality of groups causes conflicts of divided and overlapping loyalties among individuals. Political communities owe their emergence to the effort to create a certain level of cooperation to solve conflicts arising from group plurality and the different demands on their loyalty.

To live in a world of divided and overlapping loyalties is not an entirely modern phenomenon; it was a common feature of political communities in ancient times, which competed with familial, gentile, and all sorts of client communities. Republics and states also competed with churches and other social powers. The genuinely political solution has always been to make it clear that, in the case of conflicting loyalties, citizens owe their prior loyalty to the political system. The question is whether political systems should be treated as communities and therefore individuals as belonging to them or whether they should be organised as membership associations treating individuals as members.

Dual citizenship offers a clue to the general problem of understanding citizenship in terms of membership.[23] For many authors dual citizenship is no longer seen as a

---

[21] C. R. Miller, *Taylored Citizenship: State Institutions and Subjectivity* (Westport, Conn.: Praeger, 2002).

[22] On membership as an associational feature among very different social and political organisations and communities, see N. L. Rosenblum, *Membership and Morals: The Personal Uses of Pluralism in America* (Princeton, NJ: Princeton University Press, 1998).

[23] P. H. Schuck, 'Plural Citizenships', in R. Hansen and P. Weil (eds), *Dual Nationality, Social Rights, and Federal Citizenship in the U.S. and Europe: The Reinvention of Citizenship* (New York: Berghahn Books, 2002), 61–99.

major challenge for the concept of citizenship.[24] But many authors who conceptualise the nation state as a political community instead of an association have difficulties with dual citizenship. They want to restrict multiple citizenship and raise doubts whether dual citizenship—seen as the first step to a postnational citizenship—may be able to tie human beings to a political order the same way it did in the era of national citizenship.[25] If we think of citizenship as a matter of belonging and self-identification, and if we think that active citizenship concerns value systems and loyalties supported by feelings and beliefs, we are approaching a highly problematic terrain. States may then manipulate the self-images of their citizens by means of propaganda and mass communication.

If individuals are not expected to identify themselves with the political system any longer, it does not follow that the state to which they are attached becomes meaningless. In associations, all members have certain expectations of one other, they owe each other specific attention and consideration. How should a member of an association regard the fact that another member wants to also be a member of the competing association? Is it tolerable to be a member of all political parties competing for votes in the political process? Does it matter what kind of membership is at stake? Are there differences between ordinary members and office holders on the representative level of that association? It may be possible to vote in two or three countries without getting involved in conflicts of loyalty. The task of balancing these different demands is mainly up to the individual himself; it is mainly a problem of ethics and practicability. But if one becomes a member of parliament of one country it would be a major concern for the citizenry if it was not evident to which country the individual is committed. The more a citizen is obliged to act in the name of the people, the more he can be expected to focus on the association in question, being faithful to the constitution and respecting his allegiance not only passively but actively.

The clearer the duties are defined, the more transparent the process of definition is, and the more it is open to the citizens themselves to adjust the rights and duties of citizenship, then the easier it becomes to appeal to these duties not only to call themselves citizens but also to act as citizens regardless of their individual motivation. So citizenship in political associations is a model in which individual rights and duties are balanced. Constitutional membership makes these rights and duties explicit.

---

[24] K. Rubinstein and D. Adler, 'International Citizenship: The Future of Nationality in a Globalized World' (2000) 7 *Indiana Journal of Global Legal Studies* 519–48; T. Faist (ed), *Dual Citizenship in Europe: From Nationhood to Societal Integration* (Aldershot: Palgrave Macmillan, 2007); A. M. Boll, *Multiple Nationality and International Law* (Leiden: Nijhoff, 2007).

[25] D. Miller, 'Bounded Citizenship' in K. Hutchings and R. Dannreuther (eds), *Cosmopolitan Citizenship* (Basingstoke: Macmillan, 1999), 61-80; D. Miller, *Citizenship and National Identity* (Cambridge: Polity Press, 2000); N. J. Pickus, *True Faith and Allegiance: Immigration and American Civic Nationalism* (Princeton, NJ: Princeton University Press, 2005).

V. THE DUTIES AND RIGHTS OF CITIZENSHIP

The liberal approach to citizenship tends to overlook the aspect of duties.[26] The efforts constitutions make to bring citizenship into a balance between rights and duties are somewhat obscured by liberalism. The liberal political language is a language of rights, not of duties. One of the reasons for this can be traced back to the seminal approach of T. H. Marshall, which even today gives the citizenship debate its structure. In his essay of 1950, 'Citizenship and Social Classes', he focused on the rights aspect of citizenship, or rather on the evolution of rights.[27] Marshall's influence on the sociological debate cannot be overestimated. But, unnoticed by many of his commentators,[28] Marshall was also convinced of the importance of the duties of citizenship, declaring that 'if citizenship is invoked in the defence of rights, the corresponding duties of citizenship cannot be ignored'.[29] Marshall insisted on the importance of loyalty to the state and went so far as to suggest that the role of propaganda in achieving that goal should not be ignored. But he was not overly optimistic that this aim could be realised. In his view, the role of duty in the practice of citizenship in general is limited by the fact that 'the national community is too large and remote to command this kind of loyalty and to make it a continual driving force'.[30] This statement shows that Marshall thought of citizenship in its relation to communities rather than to associations and that he looked at duties as something corresponding to right.

Modernity is often attributed to the language of rights. But the language of duties is still present in modern constitutions.[31] Many constitutions mention duties of citizens to defend their country, to undertake jury duty, or define the right to vote as a duty (compulsory voting). Some duties are so basic that many constitutions fail even to mention them. But this does not mean they do not exist as a matter of constitutional law. The most basic duty, for example, is the duty to obey the law including those laws an individual may personally not know or think of as unconstitutional. Another general duty is to pay taxes. The interesting aspect of both these duties is that they are binding not only on nominal citizens but non-citizens as well. The active duties are reserved for citizens only.

---

[26] For a modern discussion of duties in terms of a rights philosophy, see J. Waldron, 'Special Ties and Natural Duties' (1993) 22 *Philosophy and Public Affairs* 3–30. For a natural rights approach see K. Greenawalt, 'The Duty to Obey the Law' (1985–6) 84 *Michigan Law Review* 2–62.

[27] T. H. Marshall, *Citizenship and Social Classes: Alfred-Marshall-Lecture 1949* (Cambridge: Cambridge University Press, 1950).

[28] J. M. Barbalet, *Citizenship: Rights, Struggle and Class Inequality* (Minneapolis: University of Minnesota Press, 1988), 82.

[29] Marshall, above n 27, 112.

[30] Ibid 119.

[31] For a comparison of constitutions with regard to the concept of duty, see H. van Maarseveen and G. van der Tang, *Written Constitutions: A Computerized Comparative Study* (Dobbs Ferry, NY: Oceana Publications, 1978), 121–4.

Liberal authors seem to have both in mind when they speak of the 'rights and duties' of citizens. The leading metaphor here is the coin of which rights and duties form its two sides. The metaphor suggests a complementary relation between rights and duties which justifies the focus on the rights side alone. In fact liberalism tends to ignore the categorial difference that exists between both concepts.

It is a short but nevertheless wrong step to leap from universal rights to universal duties. Rights are politically senseless without individuals possessing duties corresponding to these rights. Duties are burdensome and oblige individuals to do something that may not be in their personal interest.[32] Duties exist between citizens and they are designed in a reciprocal fashion.[33] These aspects of the concept of duty are best grasped by republican political theory; here citizenship is seen as a set of obligations more than of rights, as an office more than a status.[34]

By understanding citizenship as some kind of actorship which is required for running a political system we shift the focus on citizenship from the bundle of rights that individuals can claim against the state to a role of citizenship defined by a number of rights and duties including behaviour and actions. Some of these duties are implicit while others are explicitly mentioned in constitutions and are required by law to the extent that the state may force the individual to fulfil his duties as a citizen. To understand this shift it is essential that not only the liberal tradition with its language of rights, but also the republican tradition with its language of duties, maintains an adequate description of citizenship.

VI. REPUBLICAN CONSTITUTIONALISM

Citizenship has a long history.[35] A major part of it had been discussed in a discourse we today call republican. It is in republican discourse that the duty aspect of citizenship is most clearly developed. It is no coincidence that constitutionalism emerged from the republican city states in early modern times, and that within republican

---

[32] H. Shue, 'Mediating Duties' (1988) 98 *Ethics* 687–704, at 689: 'We have no reason to believe … that everyone has burdensome duties toward everyone else even if everyone else has meaningful rights.'

[33] R. E. Goodin, 'What is so Special about our Fellow Countrymen?' (1988) 98 *Ethics* 663–86, at 674: 'When we say that compatriots may have their income taxed, their trucks commandeered, or their liberties curtailed by conscription, that is surely to say little more than that people may be required to do what is required in order to meet their special duties toward their fellow citizens—duties born of their fellow citizens' similar sacrifices to benefit them.'

[34] R. Bauböck, 'Changing the Boundaries of Citizenship: The Inclusion of Immigrants in Democratic Polities', in R. Bauböck (ed), *From Aliens to Citizens: Redefining the Status of Immigrants in Europe* (Aldershot: Avebury, 1994), 199–232, at 213–14; A. Oldfield, *Citizenship and Community: Civic Republicanism and the Modern World* (London: Routledge, 1990); H. van Gunsteren, *A Theory of Citizenship: Organizing Plurality in Contemporary Democracies* (Boulder, Col.: Westview Press, 1998).

[35] J. G. A. Pocock, 'The Ideal of Citizenship since Classical Times', in R. Beiner (ed), *Theorizing Citizenship* (Albany: State University of New York Press, 1995), 29–52; D. Heater,

discourse the concept of the citizen was discussed primarily in terms of duties owed to the republic. While the genealogy of constitutionalism is complex, its republican roots are well known,[36] though not everybody is aware of it.[37] Republicanism aims at founding a 'constitutional authority',[38] a legitimate power to regulate and control the affairs of its citizens according to the constitution.

The idea of the constitution had always been at the centre of the republican discourse. The constitution was used to describe analytically the structure of a political system. To speak of the constitution of the Roman Republic or the constitution of Venice or the constitution of England thus meant the whole political system, no matter whether this system was defined by law or by custom, whether by the hierarchy of offices or the religion of the people, as long as it had the most decisive impact on the political reality.

The founders of what we now call the constitutional state referred to the constitution of Venice and England without arguing that the written constitution marked the major difference between the older and the newly established political systems. To them written constitutions simply made explicit what was often implicitly found in the older political systems, and which at the end of the eighteenth century were still used as examples of the constitutional state. Since then the narrower meaning of the constitution, understood as the singular document which codifies the constitutional law, started its career.

Republicanism did not promote the concept of the constitution for its own sake, but with respect to the individuals and their capability to bear the burden of free self-government. Is man created for being a citizen, or does this attribute belong only to a small elite? The classical republican concept that addressed this point was the concept of virtue.[39] Two major approaches within the republican discourse that connect individual virtue and the political constitution can be discerned. The first assumes that in order to establish and maintain a proper constitution, individuals must already be virtuous. Consequently, only exceptional personalities are able to realise this action, and Machiavelli and Rousseau discussed this type of personality in relation to such historical personalities as Lycurgus or Moses. The second approach considers virtue

Citizenship: The Civic ideal in World History, Politics, and Education (Manchester: Manchester University Press, 3rd edn, 2004).

[36] J.-E. Lane, *Constitutions and Political Theory* (Manchester: Manchester University Press, 1996), 31–2; M. van Gelderen and Q. Skinner, *Republicanism and Constitutionalism in Early Modern Europe, Vol. 1: Republicanism: A Shared European Heritage* (Cambridge: Cambridge University Press, 2002); N. Buttle, 'Republican Constitutionalism: A Roman Ideal' (2001) 9 *Journal of Political Philosophy* 331–49.

[37] S. Gordon, *Controlling the State: Constitutionalism from Ancient Athens to Today* (Cambridge, Mass.: Harvard University Press, 1999).

[38] P. Pettit, *Republicanism: A Theory of Freedom and Government* (Oxford: Oxford University Press, 1997), 67.

[39] For the theory and history of republicanism see I. Honohan, *Civic Republicanism* (London: Routledge, 2002); I. Honohan and J. Jennings (eds), *Republicanism in Theory and Practice* (London: Routledge, 2006).

to be a consequence of the effect that institutions have on individuals: moral excellence was promoted by institutional arrangements.[40] Here the concept of virtue is embedded within the institutional setting and not beyond it.[41] Individuals become virtuous by following the procedures and respecting the contents of the constitution. Respect for the constitution is a necessary habit, a political culture secured by such auxiliary aspects of political life as education and ceremonies. What each approach shares in common, however, is the underlying idea that men need to go through a process of transformation to become a citizen. Citizenship is the expression of the full meaning of being a person, the individual who lives the model of *vita activa*, achieved by living under a jurisdiction of self-government.[42]

The concept of duty forms a major component of the *vita activa* model. The concept of duty derives from the Roman *officium*, which is not identical with the modern, more institutional idea of office. The catalytic work was Cicero's *De officiis*, one of the most studied books up to the founding of the constitutional state at the end of the eighteenth century.[43] Office means the whole complex of duties a person owes to others, starting with friends and relatives and reaching to the entire citizenry and the obligations laid down by law. Republican thinking does not treat citizenship as a relationship between individuals and the state but between citizens among each other. In a strict sense, all entitlements of individuals to participate in the running of a republic relate more to duties than rights. Even the right to vote can be understood as a duty everyone owes his fellow citizens to start the political process of the republic by electing individuals into offices. This does not mean necessarily that voting rights should be made compulsory, as is the case in countries such as Belgium and Greece today. But it does mean that political participation cannot entirely be discussed only in terms of personal rights.

The notion of actors fulfilling their duties is part of the broader concept of the republican 'rule of law' principle, classically defined by James Harrington.[44] In the

---

[40] J. T. Kloppenberg, *The Virtues of Liberalism* (Oxford: Oxford University Press, 1998), 8–9.

[41] Especially D. Höchli, 'Zur politischen Sprache Giannottis', in Donato Giannotti, *Die Republik Florenz* [1534], trans A. Riklin (Munich: Fink, 1997), 76–116, at 91–6.

[42] W. Vogl, *Aktion und Kontemplation in der Antike: Die geschichtliche Entwicklung der praktischen und theoretischen Lebensauffassung bis Origines* (Frankfurt am Main: Lang, 2002); J. Kraye, 'Moral Philosophy', in C. B. Schmitt and Q. Skinner (eds), *The Cambridge History of Renaissance Philosophy* (Cambridge: Cambridge University Press, 1988), 303–86, at 334–8.

[43] M. Llanque, 'Die politische Rezeptionsgeschichte von Cicero', in E. Richter and R. Voigt (eds), *Res Publica und Demokratie: Die Bedeutung von Cicero für das heutige Staatsverständnis* (Baden-Baden: Nomos, 2007), 223–42.

[44] James Harrington, *Oceana*, ed J. G. A. Pocock (Cambridge: Cambridge University Press, 1992), 8–9: 'government (to define it *de jure*, or according to ancient prudence) is an art whereby a civil society of men is instituted and preserved upon the foundation of common right or interest; or, to follow Aristotle and Livy, it is the empire of laws, and not of men.' Harrington refers to Aristotle (*Politics,* iii. chs 6 and 11), Livy (*Histories,* ii. ch 1, pt 1) as well as Machiavelli (*Discorsi,* preliminary of ii.). See further, L. Baccelli, 'Machiavelli, the Republican Tradition, and the Rule of Law', in P. Costa and

republican discourse this principle differs from the liberal one. In full it reads 'rule of laws and not of men' and aims at avoiding arbitrary power. It is the law which should define the individual's role in running the republic and not their personal wish, or their belonging to a community. Harrington had a major influence on the development of republican discourse, especially in shaping the language which was used by the authors of the *Federalist Papers* and other framers of the US Constitution.[45] As Article 30 of the constitution of Massachusetts in 1780 shows, the constitutions of the American colonies also imitated that language,[46] and modern constitutional adjudication also began by referring to the same principle.[47]

The weakness of republican discourse was that it tended to oscillate between these two concepts of virtue: virtue as a certain constitution of the character, and virtue understood as the product of the institutional setting (or what we nowadays call the modern constitution). By focusing only on virtue as the character of the individual, some parts of republicanism supported the emergence of a more totalitarian approach which integrated individuals into the political system whether they liked it or not. Because most individuals are not virtuous in themselves before the political transformation, their personal will is without significance. Individuals are only able to judge their real interests and preferences once they have become integrated into the republic as citizens. And then they will have no other will than that of the republic. This is Rousseau's paradox of republicanism. Thus, the republican idea could turn into the kind of educational dictatorship Robespierre promoted and many socialists had in mind when they thought that emancipation could be seen as the logical result of a sometimes violent process of transformation of men into the citizens of the socialist society.

As a result, liberalism emerged as a kind of counter-ideology to the republican concept of virtue and to some extent absorbed the institutional branch of republicanism. This institutional branch of the republican discourse takes individuals as they are: with all their faults and limits in their energy to behave like full citizens, in need of support by a proper institutional setting to pass many temptations to act corruptly and not virtuously, especially those who hold offices and have special

D. Zolo (eds), *The Rule of Law: History, Theory, and Criticism* (Dordrecht: Springer, 2007), 387–420.

[45] J. G. A. Pocock, *The Machiavellian Moment: Florentine Political Thought and the Atlantic Republican Tradition* (Princeton, NJ: Princeton University Press, 1975). The 'definition of republic is an empire of laws and not of men' ((John Adams) Novanglus, Boston Gazette, 6 March 1775 in: *The Papers of John Adams*, ii. 314, John Adams, 'Thoughts on Government', January 1776 in *Works of John Adams*, vi. 415).

[46] 'In the government of this commonwealth, the legislative department shall never exercise the executive and judicial powers, or either of them: the executive shall never exercise the legislative and judicial powers, or either of them: the judicial shall never exercise the legislative and executive powers, or either of them: to the end it may be a government of laws and not of men' (Massachusetts Constitution Art 30).

[47] *Marbury v Madison* (1803) 1 Cranch, at 137: 'The government of the United States has been emphatically termed a government of laws and not of men.'

powers which help to promote their particular interest at the cost of the common good of the citizenry. The common good is expressed in constitutionalism by adding general norms and values like basic rights to the organisational part of the constitution.

This institutional branch of republicanism provides the background for constitutionalism and aims at the regulation and moderation of political power by organising it, mostly in terms of balance: balancing political and social powers, interests of the entire population and individual interests, balancing the collective and the individual will, responsibility for actions and discretion, all branches of political power, and last but not least balancing rights and duties. Thus understood, constitutionalism rose not as a consequence of democracy but with republican political systems. This fact has important consequences for the understanding of the concept of the citizen.

In terms of the genealogy of the modern democracy,[48] the ideas of constitutionalism and democracy are believed to be symbiotically connected. Modern democracies started as constitutional states at the end of the eighteenth century. The people on both sides of the Atlantic took power and immediately framed their newly gained power through constitutional texts. But a closer look reveals that republics rather than democracies had initiated the modern life of the constitutional state. Republics are not the same as democracies: not every naturally born individual living under the legislation of the republic's laws was considered to be a citizen of the republic. The tension between the constitution and democracy is mirrored in the competition between different political actors in a constitutional democracy: on the one side we have representatives who act in the name of, and on behalf of, the people and, on the other, guardians of the constitution who act in the name of, and on behalf of, the constitution.[49]

The modern constitutional state started as a republic and then turned into a democracy, gradually and sometimes convulsively forced by wars and civil wars, in this way including more and more parts of the regular population into the people. Constitutionalism and democracy differ not only in their genealogy, but also with respect to their purposes. The autonomy as well as the freedom of decision making of a collective body is bound by the constitution, a binding which is legitimate because it is intended autonomously. Democracy is the dynamic element in constitutional democracies, whereas the constitution is the static element. Some

---

[48] For the genealogy of the term, see M. Llanque, *Politische Ideengeschichte: Ein Gewebe politischer Diskurse* (Munich: Oldenbourg-Verlag, 2008); id, 'Das genealogische Verhältnis der konstitutionellen Demokratie zur kosmopolitischen Menschenrechtsidee', in A. Brodocz, M. Llanque, and G. Schaal (eds), *Bedrohungen der Demokratie* (Wiesbaden: Verlag für Sozialwissenschaft, 2008), 311–33.

[49] M. Tushnet, *Taking the Constitution away from the Courts* (Princeton, NJ: Princeton University Press, 1999); R. Hirschl, *Towards Juristocracy: The Origins and Consequences of the New Constitutionalism* (Cambridge, Mass.: Harvard University Press, 2004); R. Bellamy, *Political Constitutionalism: A Republican Defence of the Constitutionality of Democracy* (Cambridge: Cambridge University Press, 2007).

actors act on behalf and in the name of the people, others in the name and on behalf of the constitution. The constitution may be the result of the people's will and often needs the approval of the people to come into force. But once established, the constitution stands above the will of the people unless it is changed by the people or swept away in a revolutionary process. So constitutionalism and democracy are not identical, and they sometimes operate against each other.

As already mentioned, the republican roots of constitutionalism differ from those of liberalism. The language of liberalism is the language of rights whereas republicanism prefers the languages of duties. Rights focus on an individual's protection from interferences by others. Duties are closely linked to the cooperation evoked by the aims and necessities of the association formed by citizens. Constitutional membership means that the grounds, reasons, and limits of membership of the political association are defined by law and can therefore be adapted to changing historical circumstances and different institutional demands.

In most constitutional systems not every citizen is entitled to all roles of constitutional membership. Voting is the most fundamental activity of citizens and has the lowest level of preconditions, such as age and mental capacity. But others, such as jury duty, demand additional years of experience, and sometimes an oath is required. These are formal requirements to grant the knowledge necessary to fulfil the citizen's duties as a citizen on the jury bench. Exams and taking an oath are required for civil service. And office holding, the most prestigious role a citizen can play, encounters further restrictions, especially through the need to find the support of fellow citizens who elect the candidate into office. There is, in short, no unitarian model of citizenship; rather, there are different levels and grades of citizenship with which a citizen *de nomine* is confronted while striving for full citizenship.

Some duties apply to all residents, such as obeying the law and paying taxes, so they may be regarded as constitutional members without being nationals. Membership in the citizenry can start long before individuals acquire full citizen status. Often naturalisation laws require a certain time period of residency as the major prerequisite for applying for naturalisation. This is not only necessary for getting acquainted with the particularities of a people, its political culture, and political communication, but is also a test for readiness to obey the law, one fundamental duty of all citizens. If we expect citizens to act as members of the political association instead of individuals belonging to a community we may consider all permanent residents to be potential candidates for citizenship; it would not be contrary to the idea of constitutional membership to make that clear and combine it with certain rights and duties. The right to vote on the communal level for all European Union members in any state of their residence is such a kind of membership right without having full citizenship at all. Even naturally born descendants from citizens are supposed to grow into the role of a citizen. Some countries make it possible to deprive citizens of their political participation rights in cases of severe violation of the laws. Others make residence a prerequisite even for born citizens to exercise their voting rights.

Republicanism as the greater intellectual background for the emergence of constitutionalism and the concept of the citizen enables us to get a more complete picture of what citizenship means in terms of modern constitutional democracies. The republican perspective provides a sense of the conditions and opportunities of constitutional membership seen as a flexible balance of rights and duties.

VII. THE FUTURE OF CONSTITUTIONAL MEMBERSHIP

The major advantage of the constitutional membership approach to citizenship is that it is open to more complex political systems than the classical unitarian nation state with its sovereignty claims.

A more globalised world makes cosmopolitan prospects more plausible. The question is whether belonging to the world can be balanced with the requirements of membership in the world political association once it comes to conflicts with other political entities like nations, regions, transnational communities of regional composition, and so on. It is not 'belonging to the world'[50] that matters, but how we construct membership in a world association. A future constitution of the world must take membership into account. It cannot simply focus on the belonging scheme in which every human being is considered to be a citizen of one world. That approach is not complex enough to deal with the political problems at stake.

There is a theory of federal citizenship which leans on membership rather than belonging, and therefore offers more possibilities of devising a complex citizenship with different levels of activities.[51] If identity is considered to be necessary for federal citizenship, then federal systems would appear to be unable to establish a full sense of citizenship; the mostly artificial character of federal systems would prevent any attitude of belonging to it. But if we shift the focus to membership, we are able to concentrate on matters of functionality and levels of citizenship, including more or less intensity required for individual actors.

Constitutional membership can thus serve as a means for clarifying the ongoing struggle to understand citizenship in times of transcending the nation-state paradigm. It is one thing to try to overcome the traditional nation state to clear the path for a more cosmopolitan approach. But in the course of doing so cosmopolitan and democratic discussions should not forget that citizenship is a relationship between individuals and the political system as well as between individuals among each other. Even if the nation state vanishes the problem of citizenship will not.

The task is to define constitutional membership of a future polity which is able to balance national as well as transnational, supranational, postnational, or cosmopolitan claims of allegiance and loyalty. The potential conflicts involved here cannot be

---

[50] S. L. Croucher, *Globalization and Belonging: The Politics of Identity in a Changing World* (Lanham, Md.: Rowman & Littlefield, 2004), 185–96.

[51] P. H. Schuck, 'Citizenship in Federal Systems' (2000) 48 *The American Journal of Comparative Law* 195–228. Regarding the special case of the European Union see A. Follesdal, 'Union Citizenship: Unpacking the Beast of Burden' (2001) 20 *Law and Philosophy* 313–43 and C. Schönberger, *Unionsbürger: Europas föderales Bürgerrecht in vergleichender Perspektive* (Tübingen: Mohr, 2005).

solved by mere declarations of which identity individuals should consider to take on as world citizens. There must be a way of determining how to solve such conflicts as members of a world association. Across their diverse and plural belonging to different communities a world constitutional membership should give all individuals the scheme to react as citizens to conflicts which arise from difficulties of maintaining loyalty to different communities at the same time. The model of constitutional democracy on the level of nation states is not an obstacle to that development. It can be an example for it, but only if we define constitutional democracy not in terms of national belonging but in terms of constitutional membership, an artificial institutional setting in which citizens are enabled to act independently from their belonging to communities including the nation.

If we acknowledge that in genealogy as well as in principle, the idea of constitutionalism is not identical with the idea of democracy and the nation state, and that constitutional membership is always rooted in the republican discourse in which the citizen is defined by a system of duties, then we can find in constitutional membership a model for a more complex and advanced political system, which in the end may be of world scale. This world constitution will not replace the constitutional democracy: it adds another level of citizenship to the already existing ones, starting with the communal association and perhaps ending with the stratum which acknowledges the fact that all men are residents of the world, wherever they live.

9

Constitutionalism and Democracy in the World Society

Hauke Brunkhorst

I. CONSTITUTIONAL REVOLUTION

The democratic revolutions of the eighteenth century demonstrate an impressive process of social and institutional learning, which has regularly led to the inclusion of formerly excluded persons, groups, classes, sexes, races, countries, and regions. In the words of Rawls: 'The same equality of the Declaration of Independence which Lincoln invoked to condemn slavery can be invoked to condemn the inequality and oppression of women.'[1] The experience of a successful learning process of social inclusion can be, and has been, extended to incorporate formerly silenced voices of Western societies as well as the oppressed voices of non-Western cultures. But normative learning does not tell the whole story. In many cases (and, in some perspectives, in all cases) the expansion of social inclusion was acquired at the price of new exclusion, or of new forms of latent or manifest oppression. The history of Western civilisation and Western democracy is not only a Rawlsian success story of expansion through the inclusion of the other. It is at the same time a Foucaultian or Anghien story of expansion through imperialism, a story from the 'heart of darkness'.[2] Since the first European division of the world in the Treaty of Tordesillas of 1494 between Spain and Portugal, imperialism vanished and reappeared in constantly changing fashion, and with constantly changing labels—some of which in fact were even anti-imperialist.[3] Even the present state of inclusion of the other within an emerging cosmopolitan civil society sometimes appears to be nothing more than the expression of a highly exclusive 'class consciousness of frequent travellers'.[4]

---

[1] J. Rawls, *Political Liberalism* (New York: Columbia, 1993), xxix.

[2] Joseph Conrad, *Heart of Darkness* (New York: Norton, 2005).

[3] A. Anghie, *Imperialism, Sovereignty and the Making of International Law* (Cambridge, Mass.: Harvard University Press, 2004).

[4] C. Calhoun, 'The Class Consciousness of Frequent Travelers' (2002) *South Atlantic Quarterly* 869–97.

But the reproduction of social structures of class rule and relations of domination, exclusion, and silencing does not change the normative facticity that resides in the fact that all modern democratic constitutions since the eighteenth century rely on the universal legal principles of the inclusion of all human beings and the exclusion of inequality.[5] The normative meaning of these two principles becomes manifest when communicative power appears as the (albeit deeply ambivalent) 'power of revenge', which was awakened in Seattle and in Genoa with the cry: 'You are G8, we are 6,000,000,000.'[6] Constitutional law textbooks are not only talk: they are what Hegel called 'objective spirit', and they 'can strike back'.[7]

If there is anything specifically characteristic of what Berman calls the 'Western legal tradition', it is the dialectical dual structure of law. It is, on the one hand, the immunity system of society, a medium of repression and a means to stabilise expectations. But, on the other hand, law is able to change the world and seek to establish the *civitas Dei* on earth. Expressed in more secular terms, law is a medium of emancipation, which is why Kant and Hegel even identified law with egalitarian freedom and defined law as the 'existence of freedom' (*Dasein der Freiheit*).[8] The Declaration of Independence is a medium of emancipation which declares that 'all men are created equal' and claims, against the King of Great Britain, open access for all emigrants. But the Declaration is also a document of bloody oppression that legalises the genocide of the aboriginal population of America—not only the king, but also his supposed allies, 'the merciless Indian Savages', were declared to be public enemies of 'civilized nations'.

Specifically characteristic of Western constitutional law is its ability to reconcile these deep tensions between the two faces of repression and emancipation by legal institutions which coordinate conflicting powers and enable the always risky and fragile 'productivity of the antinomy'.[9] Harold Berman terms this a 'dialectical reconciliation of opposites',[10] but we could also add that it is a dialectical (and procedural) reconciliation of lasting opposites, of lasting conflicts, differences,

---

[5] T. H. Marshall, *Citizenship and Social Class* (London: Pluto Press, 1992); R. Stichweh, *Die Weltgesellschaft* (Frankfurt am Main: Suhrkamp, 2000), at 52.

[6] M. Byers, 'Woken up in Seattle', *London Review of Books*, 6 January 2000, 16–17.

[7] Friedrich Müller, *Wer ist das Volk? Eine Grundfrage der Demokratie: Elemente einer Verfassungstheorie VI* (Berlin: Duncker & Humblot, 1997), 54.

[8] Immanuel Kant, *Metaphysik der Sitten, Rechtslehre, Werke VII* (Frankfurt am Main: Suhrkamp, 1974), at 345, 434, 464; Georg Wilhelm Friedrich Hegel, *Grundlinien der Philosophie des Rechts § 4, Werke 7* (Frankfurt am Main: Suhrkamp, 1970), at 46; id, *Philosophie des Rechts Vorlesung 1819/20* (Frankfurt am Main: Suhrkamp, 1983), at 52; Karl Marx, 'Verhandlungen des 6. Rheinischen Landtags: Debatten über das Holzdiebstahlsgesetz (Oktober 1842)' in *Marx-Engels Werke 1* (Berlin: Dietz, 1972), 109–47, at 58.

[9] T. Kesselring, *Die Produktivität der Antinomie* (Frankfurt am Main: Suhrkamp, 1984).

[10] H. J. Berman, *Law and Revolution II: The Impact of the Protestant Reformation on the Western Legal Tradition* (Cambridge, Mass.: Harvard University Press, 2006), 5–6.

and contradictions.[11] The point is that the Western legal tradition emerged from the terror and fanaticism of a series of great and successful legal revolutions since the papal revolution of the eleventh and twelfth centuries.[12] But the constitutional regimes which were the final outcome of all great and successful European Revolutions established legal conditions for a much less violent struggle *for* equal rights *within* the claim of right.

The constitutional spirit of the revolutions of the eighteenth century became objective for the first time within the borders of the modern nation state. This state always had many faces: the Arendtian face of *violence*, the Habermasian face of *administrative power*, the Foucaultian face of *surveillance and punishment*, the faces of imperialism, colonialism, war-on-terror, and so on.[13] However, the nation state, once it became democratised, possessed not only the *administrative power of oppression and control*, but at the same time the *administrative power to exclude inequality* with respect to individual rights, political participation, and equal access to social welfare and opportunities.[14] Only the modern nation state has not only the normative *idea*, but also the administrative *power* to achieve that. From the very beginning this formed the core of the Enlightenment ideal. Up to the present all advances in the reluctant *inclusion of the other*, and so also all advances of cosmopolitanism, are to a greater or lesser degree advances that have been accomplished by the modern nation state. National constitutional regimes have solved the three basic conflicts of the modern capitalist and functionally differentiated society. Stated in general historical terms, which leave a number of empirical questions open, we can say that the formation and democratic development of the nation state has provided a series of solutions that are constitutive of modern societies.

---

[11] *Law of collision* or '*Kollisionsrecht*' is deeply rooted in Western constitutional law: see A. Fischer-Lescano and G. Teubner, 'Regime-Collisions: The Vain Search for Legal Unity in the Fragmentation of Global Law' (2004) 25 *Michigan Journal of International Law* 999–1045. Chantal Mouffe refers to this as a transformation from *antagonism to agonism*, but ignores the constitutive role of constitutional law in this process (C. Mouffe, *On the Political* (London: Routledge, 2005)).

[12] Berman, above n 11.

[13] This is a complex argument and needs some explanation. So, Arendt opposes power and violence (in German: *Gewalt*) and argues that law is concerned with power not violence or force. But this makes no sense because there is no power which is not backed by force as its 'symbiotic mechanism'. Therefore Habermas, who has taken up Arendt's concept of power, likened it not to force or violence but to *administrative power*, now calling Arendt's concept of power *communicative power*. Communicative power in particular is backed by revolutionary violence which Habermas calls the power (violence) of revenge (in German: *rächende Gewalt*). Arendt seeks explicitly to separate power from force and violence but implicitly refers to a power which is backed by revolutionary violence simply because her paradigm case of *power* is revolution, and she never argues for something like resistance without violence. See H. Arendt, *On Revolution* (Harmondsworth: Penguin, 1973); J. Habermas, *The Theory of Communicative Action*, i. (London: Heinemann, 1984).

[14] Marshall, above n 5; Stichweh, above n 5.

First, the nation state has solved the motivational *crisis of religious civil war* sparked by the Protestant Revolutions of the sixteenth and seventeenth centuries; this has been achieved through the constitutional reconciliation of lasting conflicts between religious, agnostic, and anti-religious belief systems.[15] This was the result of a two-step development, accomplished in a manner that was both functionally and normatively universal. On the one hand, the functional effect of the formation of a territorial system of states transformed the uncontrolled explosion of religious freedom into a controlled chain reaction that kept the productive forces of religious fundamentalism alive and its destructive forces (to some degree) under control.[16] This was initially the repressive effect of the confessionalisation of the territorial state.[17] On the other hand, the long and reluctant process of democratisation of the nation state replaced repressive confessionalisation by emancipatory legislation which ultimately led to the implementation of the equal freedom *of* religion and the equal freedom *from* religious and other belief systems.[18]

Second, the emerging nation state also solved the legitimacy and constitutional crisis of the public sphere, of public law, and public power, which marked the old European *Ancien Regime* and culminated in the constitutional revolutions of the eighteenth and nineteenth centuries. Constitutions have transformed antagonistic class struggles into agonistic political struggles between political parties, unions, and entrepreneurs, civic associations, etc.[19] In the more successful processes of Western history, bloody constitutional revolutions turned into permanent and legal revolutions.[20] Once again, the effect was twofold. It led, on the one hand, to a functional transformation of the destructive and oppressive potential of a highly specialised politics of power accumulation for its own sake into a more or less controlled explosion

---

[15] On the distinction of different types of crises (motivational, legitimisation, etc), see J. Habermas, *Legitimation Crisis* (Boston, Mass.: Beacon Press, 1975).

[16] Max Weber, *Die protestantische Ethik und der Geist des Kapitalismus* [1905], in his *Gesammelte Aufsätze zur Religionssoziologie*, i. (Tübingen: Mohr, 1920), 1–206.

[17] W. Reinhard, *Geschichte der Staatsgewalt* (Munich: Beck, 1999); H. Schilling, *Die neue Zeit* (Berlin: Siedler, 1999); H. Dreier, 'Kanonistik und Konfessionalisierung: Marksteine auf dem Weg zum Staat', in G. Siebeck (ed), *Artibus ingenius: Beiträge zu Theologie, Philosophie, Jurisprudenz und Ökonomik* (Tübingen: Mohr Siebeck, 2001), 133–69; M. Stolleis, ' "Konfessionalisierung" oder "Säkularisierung" bei der Entstehung des frühmodernen Staates' (1993) 20 *Ius Commune XX* 1–23, at 7; W. Reinhard and H. Schilling (eds), *Die katholische Konfessionalisierung: Wissenschaftliches Symposion der Gesellschaft zur Herausgabe des Corpus Catholicorum und des Vereins für Reformationsgeschichte* (Münster: Aschendorff, 1995); H. Schilling, *Die Neue Zeit: Vom Christenheitseuropa zum Europa der Staaten. 1250 bis 1750* (Berlin: Siedler, 1999).

[18] T. Parsons, *The System of Modern Societies* (Englewood Cliffs, NJ: Prentice Hall, 1972).

[19] For the distinction between *antagonism* and *agonism*, see Mouffe, above n 11.

[20] See J. Habermas, 'Ist der Herzschlag der Revolution zum Stillstand gekommen? Volkssouveränität als Verfahren; ein normativer Begriff der Öffentlichkeit?' in his *Die Ideen von 1789 in der deutschen Rezeption* (Frankfurt am Main: Suhrkamp, 1989), 7–36.

of all the productive forces of administrative power.[21] This, in turn, was accompanied by democratic emancipatory legislation, which finally brought about the implementation of the freedom *of* public power together with the freedom *from* public power.

Third, the nation state also solved the social class conflicts in the social revolutions of the nineteenth and twentieth centuries. It accomplished this through the emergence of a regulatory social welfare state, which transformed the elitist bourgeois parliamentarianism of the nineteenth century into egalitarian mass democracy. The social class struggle was institutionalised,[22] and the violent social revolution became a legally organised 'educational revolution'.[23] In this respect, it was the great functional advance of social democracy to keep most of the productive forces and to get rid to some degree of the destructive forces of the exploding free markets of money, real estate, and labour.[24] It achieved this by overcoming the fundamentalist bourgeois dualism of private and public law.[25] In the first decades of social welfare regimes, this was more or less the merit of administrative law and bureaucratic rule in a regime of low-intensity democracy.[26] The ongoing democratic rights revolution which was directed against low-intensity democracy finally led to the implementation of the freedom *of* markets together with the freedom *from* markets. This transformed the system of individual rights based on the freedom of property into a comprehensive system of welfare and anti-discrimination norms.[27]

Despite this, however, the impressive normative and functional advances of the Western democratic nation state were obtained at the price of the cosmopolitan claims of the French Revolution. These claims were integral to the Enlightenment, the intellectual basis and the source of the directing ideas of the law of the constitutional revolutions in the late eighteenth and early nineteenth centuries. For a long time, they were at best soft law but expressed in important legal documents (even if without legal force) like the American Declaration of Independence and the French Declaration

---

[21] In this respect three very different approaches (one historical, one power-theoretical, and the third from system theory) are in agreement. See A. Lüdtke, 'Genesis und Durchsetzung des modernen Staates' (1980) 20 *Archiv für Sozialgeschichte* 470–91; M. Foucault, *Discipline and Punish: The Birth of the Prison* (Harmondsworth: Penguin, 1979); N. Luhmann, 'Verfassung als evolutionäre Errungenschaft' (1990) 9 *Rechtshistorisches Journal* 176–220.

[22] D. Hoss, *Der institutionalisierte Klassenkampf* (Frankfurt: EVA, 1972).

[23] Parsons, above n 18.

[24] K. Polanyi, *The Great Transformation: Politische und ökonomische Ursprünge von Gesellschaften und Wirtschaftssystemen* (Frankfurt: Suhrkamp, 1997).

[25] H. Kelsen, *Das Problem der Souveränität und die Theorie des Völkerrechts* [1920] (Aalen: Scientia, 1981); id, *Reine Rechtslehre* [1934] (Vienna: Verlag Österreich, 1967); id, *Demokratie und Sozialismus: Ausgewählte Aufsätze* (Darmstadt: Wissenschaftliche Buchgesellschaft, 1967).

[26] S. Marks, *The Riddle of all Constitutions* (Oxford: Oxford University Press, 2000).

[27] Cf Berman, above n 10, 16 et seq; id, *Justice in the USSR* (Cambridge, Mass.: Harvard University Press, 1963); Alexander Somek, *Das europäische Sozialmodell: Die Kompatibilitätsthese* (Berlin: e-man, 2008).

of Rights. Once it came to concretise them in ordinary legislation, the universality inherent in the spirit of the equal rights of citizens vanished and was combined with an unequal status of the others—women, workers, non-Europeans. Yet this did not mean that they were forgotten; on the contrary, as Kant had rightly observed, they stayed alive and their communicative power grew in the course of history until they were implemented by binding decisions at least partially, but step by step.

II. THE EMERGENCE OF WORLD SOCIETY

Until 1945, the modern nation state was the state of the regional societies of Europe, America, and Japan. The rest of the world was either under the imperial control of these states or kept outside the system of nation states. Until the mid-twentieth century, the 'exclusion of inequality' meant equality for the citizens of the state and inequality for those who did not belong to the regional system of states. There was not even any serious demand for a global exclusion of inequality.

When Kant proposed the 'cosmopolitan condition' of linking nations together on the grounds that in modern times 'a violation of rights in one part of the world is felt everywhere',[28] his notion of *world* (concerning the political world in contrast to the *globe*, which for Kant was only a transcendental scheme) was more or less reduced to Europe and the European system of states. Also Hegel's claim of the 'infinite importance' that 'a human being counts as such because he is a human being, not because he is a Jew, Catholic, Protestant, German, Italian, etc.'[29] is relativised by his reductionist understanding of the legal meaning of human rights as applicable to male citizens, biblical religions, and European nations only. He also explicitly limits human rights to national civil law (of the *bürgerliche Gesellschaft* and its *lex mercatoria*), and this law loses its validity when confronted with the essential concerns of the executive administration of the state and its particular relations of power (*besondere Gewaltverhältnisse, justizfreie Hoheitsakte*). Hegel therefore condemns any 'cosmopolitanism' that is opposed to the concrete ethical practices (*Sittlichkeit*) of the state.

Some decades later, when Johann Caspar Bluntschli declared the implementation of a 'humane world order' (*menschliche Weltordnung*) to be the main end of international law, he neither saw any contradiction between this noble aim and his (and his colleagues') identification of the modern state with a male dominated civilisation[30] nor with his at least latently racist thesis that all law is Aryan.[31] The liberal cosmopolitanism of the 'men of 1873' who founded the Institut de Droit International and invented

---

[28]   Immanuel Kant, 'Toward Perpetual Peace', in his *Practical Philosophy*, ed M. Gregor (Cambridge: Cambridge University Press, 1996).

[29]   Georg Wilhelm Friedrich Hegel, *Grundlinien*, above n 8.

[30]   Johann Caspar Bluntschli: '*Der Staat ist der Mann*': cited in M. Koskenniemi, *The Gentle Civilizer of Nations: The Rise and Fall of Internataionl Law 1870–1960* (Cambridge: Cambridge University Press, 2001), at 80.

[31]   Ibid 77.

a cosmopolitan international law was completely Eurocentric, relying on the basic distinction between (Christian) *civilised nations* and *barbarian people*.[32] The generous tolerance of the men of 1873 was paternalistic and repressive from its very beginning. Hence, it is no surprise that the liberal cosmopolitan humanists who wanted to found a humane world order soon became apologists of imperialism, defending King Leopold's private-measures state (*Maßnahmestaat*) in the 'heart of darkness' by drawing a distinction between *club members* on the one side and *outlaws* on the other.[33] Following this line of argument, Article 35 of the Berlin Conference on the future of Africa (1884–5) offers 'jurisdiction' for the civilised nations of Europe and 'authority' for those in the heart of darkness.[34] The global world order during the nineteenth and early twentieth centuries was a universal *Doppelstaat* (dual state).[35] Guantanamo has a long history.

Since 1945, however, colonialism and classical imperialism have vanished,[36] and Euro-centrism has become decentred.[37] Western rationalism, functional differentiation, legal formalism, and moral universalism are no longer specifically Western phenomena. The deep structural and conceptual change that this decentring of Euro-centrism has brought about is not yet sufficiently understood. For good or ill, everybody today must conduct his or her life under the more or less brutal conditions of the selective and disciplinary machinery of markets, schools, kindergartens, universities, lifelong learning, traffic rules, and 'total institutions' such as jails, hospitals, or military barracks.

At the same time, state sovereignty was equalised as the state went global. The last square metre of the globe became state territory (at least legally[38]), and even the moon became an object of international treaties between states.[39] Together with

[32] N. Bermann, 'Bosnien, Spanien und das Völkerrecht: Zwischen "Allianz" und "Lokalisierung"' in H. Brunkhorst (ed), *Einmischung erwünscht? Menschenrechte und bewaffnete Intervention* (Frankfurt: Fischer, 1998), 117–40; Anghie, above n 3.

[33] Koskenniemi, above n 30, at 80, 168–9.

[34] Ibid 126.

[35] E. Fraenkel, *Der Doppelstaat* [1941], in his *Gesammelte Schriften,* ii. ed A. von Brünneck (Baden-Baden: Nomos, 1999).

[36] M. Hardt and A. Negri, *Empire* (Cambridge, Mass.: Harvard University Press, 2001); A. Fischer-Lescano and G. Teubner, *Regime-Kollisionen* (Frankfurt: Suhrkamp, 2005); S. Buckel, *Subjektivierung und Kohäsion: Zur Rekonstruktion einer materialistischen Theorie des Rechts* (Weilerswist: Velbrück Wissenschaft, 2007); B. S. Chimni, 'International Institutions Today: An Imperial Global State in the Making' (2004) 15 *European Journal of International Law*, 1–37.

[37] H. Brunkhorst, *Solidarity: From Civic Friendship to a Global Legal Community* (Cambridge, Mass.: MIT Press, 2005).

[38] S. Oeter, 'Prekäre Staatlichkeit und die Grenzen internationaler Verrechtlichung' in R. Kreide and A. Niederberger (eds), *Verrechtlichung transnationaler Politik: Nationale Demokratien im Kontext globaler Politik* (Frankfurt am Main: Campus, 2008), 90–114.

[39] P. Dobner, *Konstitutionalismus als Politikform: Zu den Effekten Staatlicher Transformation auf die Verfassung als Institution* (Baden-Baden: Nomos, 2002).

the globalisation of the modern constitutional nation state, therefore, all functional subsystems, which from the sixteenth century until 1945 were bound to state power and to the international order of the regional societies of Europe, America, and Japan, became global systems.

Sociologists rightly and successfully have criticised the 'methodological nationalism' of their own discipline,[40] and have started to replace the pluralism of national societies by the singular concept of a 'global social system' or a 'world society' which includes all communications,[41] which is normatively integrated,[42] and which has transformed all political, legal, economic, cultural, functional, and geopolitical differences into internal differences of the one and only world society. These differences now depend entirely on the fundamental societal structure of the world society and its cultural constituents.[43]

Whereas the function of the basic structure primarily is selective and constraining, the function of the superstructure of the global secular culture (or the background of global knowledge, the global *Lebenswelt*) is shaping and constituting for the behaviour and the subjectivity of everybody everywhere on the globe. Everybody, whether they want it or not, is shaped by the individualism and rationality of a single global culture which includes human rights culture as well as the culture of individualised suicide bombing.[44] All cultural differences are now of the same society and of individualised persons who have to organise and reorganise, construct and reconstruct their ego and their personal and collective identity lifelong, and in order to do that they rely only on the (weak or strong) means of their own autonomy. Sartre was right: everybody now is *condemned to be free*. Yet as 'free men' we are not looking with Sartre into the abyss of nothingness, but are acting against a dense and common background of relatively abstract, highly general and formal, thoroughly secular, nevertheless substantial global knowledge that is implicit in the global social life-world. This is so simply because traditional identity formations no longer and nowhere are available without a permanently growing and changing variety of

---

[40] U. Beck, *Macht und Gegenmacht im globalen Zeitalter* (Frankfurt am Main: Suhrkamp, 2002).

[41] N. Luhmann, 'Die Weltgesellschaft' (1971) 57 *Archiv für Rechts- und Sozialphilosophie* 1–34; id, *Die Gesellschaft der Gesellschaft* (Frankfurt am Main: Suhrkamp, 1997), at 145 et seq.

[42] T. Parsons, 'Order and Community in the International Social System', in J. N. Rosenau (ed), *International Politics and Foreign Policy* (Glencoe, Ill.: The Free Press, 1961), 120–9; R. Stichweh, 'Der Zusammenhalt der Weltgesellschaft: Nicht-normative Integrationstheorien in der Soziologie', in J. Becker et al (eds), *Transnationale Solidarität: Chancen und Grenzen* (Frankfurt am Main: Campus, 2004), 236–45.

[43] J. W. Meyer, 'World Society and the Nation-State' (1997) 103 *American Journal of Sociology* 144–81; id, *Weltkultur: Wie die Westlichen Prinzipien die Welt Durchdringen* (Frankfurt: Suhrkamp, 2005).

[44] R. Rorty, 'Human Rights, Rationality, and Sentimentality' in S. Shute and S. L. Hurley (eds), *On Human Rights, Oxford Amnesty Lectures* (New York: Basic Books, 1993), 111–20; O. Roy, *Der islamistische Weg nach Westen: Globalisierung, Entwurzelung und Radikalisierung* (Munich: Pantheon, 2006).

alternative offers, in Teheran as well as in New York, in the Alps of Switzerland as well as in the mountain regions of Afghanistan, Pakistan, or Tibet.[45]

These developments are now reflected more and more by the scientific superstructure, not only in social sciences but also in history and philosophy. For over twenty years we have been observing a strong turn in history from national to European and world history; in philosophy Kant's essay on perpetual peace is suddenly no longer a marginal subject. Even jurists have now started to develop Hans Kelsen's insight from the 1920s that there is no dualist gap between national and international law, but only a continuum.[46] In the last decade, there has been a mushrooming of national–international hybrids and new branches of legal disciplines such as transnational administrative law.

III. THE AGE OF EXTREMES?

The twentieth century strikingly has been called an 'age of extremes',[47] and every attempt to bridge the abyss that separates these extremes would be an 'extorted reconciliation'.[48] This century was the catastrophe that has incurably 'damaged life'.[49] But it was also the century of a great legal revolution which transformed not only law but society as a whole: a revolution that triggered experimental-communicative productivity in new social and cultural practices, political and legal institutions, and scientific and philosophical discourse.

If we call the twentieth century the totalitarian century, then this is at the same time right *and* wrong. After disastrous revolutionary and counterrevolutionary worldwide wars, after battles for material and battles of attrition, bombing wars and civil wars, pogroms, genocides, concentration and death camps, national uprisings, racist excesses, terrorism and counter-terrorism, the destruction and founding of states and fascist, socialist and—not to forget—democratic grand experiments—totalitarianism was not the winner, but the loser. In particular, the World Wars were fought by their winners not only for national interest alone, but also for democracy, global peace, and human rights.

---

[45] Parsons, above n 18; Parsons and G. M. Platt, *Die amerikanische Universität* (Frankfurt am Main: Suhrkamp, 1990); R. Döbert, J. Habermas, and G. Nunner-Winkler (eds), *Entwicklung des Ichs* (Königstein: Anton Hain, 1980).

[46] H. Brunkhorst, 'Kritik am Dualismus des internationalen Recht—Hans Kelsen und die Völkerrechtsrevolution des 20. Jahrhunderts' in Kreide and Niederberger (eds), above n 38, 30–63.

[47] E. Hobsbawm, *The Age of Extremes: The Short Twentieth Century, 1914–1991* (London: Michael Joseph, 1994).

[48] T. W. Adorno, 'Erpreßte Versöhnung', in his *Noten zur Literatur* (Frankfurt am Main: Suhrkamp, 1974), 251–80.

[49] T. W. Adorno, *Minima Moralia: Reflexionen aus dem beschädigten Leben* (Frankfurt am Main: Suhrkamp, 1951).

The twentieth century was not only the century of state-organised mass terror (which could not, on this scale, have been organised any other way than by state).[50] It was also the century of ground-shaking normative progress, through which democracy was universalised and constitutional law transformed into global constitutionalism, national human rights into global civil rights, constitutional state sovereignty into democratic sovereignty, and the bourgeois state into a social welfare state. Between Europeans and non-Europeans there has existed for hundreds of years the formal and legal unequal distribution of rights: jurisdiction for us, authority for the others.[51] Now, for the first time in history, rights are formally equal. Admittedly, the massive human-rights violations, social exclusion and outrageous, unequal treatment of entire world regions have not disappeared. But human-rights violations, lawlessness, and political and social disparity are now for the first time considered to be our common problem—a problem that concerns every single actor in this global society. Only now are there serious and legally binding claims to the global (and not any longer just national) exclusion of inequality.

The global law and the human rights culture of the late twentieth century was not only the result of the negative insight from 1945 that Auschwitz and war should never again happen. It was also the positive result of a great and successful legal revolution, which began at the end of the First World War with the American intervention in the war in 1917, and was fought for progressive, new, and supposedly more inclusive rights, and more and expanded individual and political freedom.[52] In 1917 President Wilson forced the reluctant Western allies to claim revolutionary war objectives, and from this moment the war (and later the Second World War, again as a result of American intervention) was fought, not only for self-preservation and national interest, but also for global democracy and peace: 'To make the world safe for democracy.' The leader of the Russian Revolution and the religious Marxist (Lenin) and the Calvinist–Kantian American President who believed in the social gospel and God's personal mandate (Wilson), both recognised the First World War—from very different perspectives—as the beginning of a global revolution and as a revolutionary war against war.

Lenin and Wilson were both fierce opponents of the then still powerful monarchies and the existing pluralism of monarchist and democratic, imperialistic, federate, and nationalistic constitutional regimes. This negative objective was achieved first: constitutional monarchy—reinvented in every new, great revolution since the pontifical revolution of the twelfth century—was so thoroughly abolished that hardly anyone remembers it today.[53]

---

[50] Reinhard, above n 17.

[51] Concluding protocol of the Berlin Conference on West Africa in 1884–5, Art 35.

[52] H. Brunkhorst, 'Die Globale Rechtsrevolution: Von der Evolution der Verfassungsrevolution zur Revolution der Verfassungsevolution?', in R. Christensen and B. Pieroth (eds), *Rechtstheorie in rechtspraktischer Absicht: Freundesgabe zum 70. Geburtstag von Friedrich Müller* (Berlin: Dunker & Humblot, 2008), 9–34.

[53] 'Der alte Offizier konnte es bis zum letzten Augenblick ... nicht für möglich halten, dass ein vielhundertjähriges Reich einfach vom Schauplatz der Geschichte verschwinden könne'

While Wilson wanted to transform international law according to Kant's plan and unite the nations in a great federation of democratic nations,[54] Lenin was trying to revolutionise social conditions and build up a socialist and Soviet world empire. According to Kelsen, the Treaty of Versailles and the concomitant founding of the League of Nations were events as revolutionary as the Russian Revolution.[55] While the success of the October Revolution made the drastic reform of property law in an entire world region possible and subsumed the legal system under socio-political and socio-pedagogical goals, the Treaty of Versailles and the 'Covenant of the League of Nations [supplanted] the *ius publicum europaeum*'.[56]

Russia and America—the two sides of this revolutionary pincer movement that laid siege to Europe and put pressure on its centre—were brothers hostile to each other from the beginning, but who had to respond to each other in a mutually beneficial manner. The West felt compelled to turn the attack on property law and the powerful, global, and social-revolutionary impulse of the Russian Revolution into a 'peaceful revolution', and thus opened a way towards socialism that conformed to constitutionality.

At the end of the Second World War, the Soviet Union had to get on board with international politics, found the United Nations *together* with the United States, their European allies and some representatives of the then emerging later so-called Third World. From this time on, the Soviet Union was in the web of international law and human rights. Up until the Conference on Security and Cooperation (CSCE) they had to sign human rights declarations that helped to make it implode in the end.[57] The radical changes in the twentieth century led to variants of the same legal reforms—pre-constitutional and pseudo-democratic in the East, democratic–constitutional in the West.[58] These radical changes repealed the bourgeois centring of equality rights around property and turned these rights into a comprehensive system of anti-discrimination norms.[59] Franklin D. Roosevelt's famous 'Second Bill of Rights' from January 1944 was

---

(H. Kelsen, *Veröffentlichte Schriften 1905-1910 und Selbstzeugnisse*, ed M. Jestaedt (Tübingen: Mohr Siebeck, 2006), at 51).

[54] G. Beestermöller, *Die Völkerbundidee: Leistungsfähigkeit und Grenzen der Kriegsächtung durch Staatensolidarität* (Stuttgart: Kohlhammer, 1995); O. Eberl, *Demokratie und Frieden: Kants Friedensschrift in den Kontroversen über die Gestaltung globaler Ordnung* (Baden-Baden: Nomos, 2008).

[55] H. Kelsen, *Das Problem der Souveränität und die Theorie des Völkerrechts* [1920] (Aalen: Scientia, 1981); A. Verdross, *Die Verfassung der Völkerrechtsgemeinschaft* (Vienna: Springer, 1926).

[56] O. Eberl, *Demokratie und Frieden: Kants Friedensschrift in den Kontroversen der Gegenwart* (Baden-Baden: Nomos 2008).

[57] This, of course, was accompanied by other developments, in particular the much better working functional differentiation in Western democracies and their higher reflexive capacity to observe themselves together with the particular blindness of the socialist countries to produce adequate knowledge of their own society.

[58] Cf Berman, above n 10, 16–17.

[59] C. Sunstein, *After the Rights Revolution: Reconceiving the Regulatory State* (Cambridge, Mass.: Harvard University Press, 1993).

the beginning of a 'rights revolution' whose waves of anti-discrimination legislation continued into the 1970s and 1980s, extending rights of equality to other spheres. In his address to Congress, Roosevelt declared the existing 'inalienable political rights' of the constitution to be valid but insufficient for dealing with a complex society. Rather, he stated, we need to ensure 'equality in the pursuit of happiness' within this society through social rights. Although mentioning 'free speech', 'free press', 'free worship', 'trial by jury', and 'freedom from unreasonable searches and seizure', he did not refer at all to property rights, an absence that is the most significant aspect of the text.

The revolutionary reforms further changed the legislation from conditional to final programming,[60] developed a comprehensive administrative planning law (tried and tested in the World Wars),[61] and introduced a new system of regulative family, socialisation, and conduct law. To adopt Luhmann's phrase, one could call it 'alteration of persons' law' (*Personenänderungsrecht*); Berman, by contrast, speaks of 'parental law' and of a 'nurturing' or 'educational role of law'; and with Foucault one could speak of the law of discourse police and bio-power.[62]

The legal revolution ended in 1945 with the constitution of the United Nations in San Francisco. A new system of basic human rights norms, coupled with a completely new system of inter, trans, and supranational institutions was created during the short period from 1941 to 1951. This system in fact included international welfarism, which was invented before the great triumph of national welfare states.[63]

International law has changed deeply since the revolutionary founding of the United Nations. It has witnessed a turn from a law of coexisting states to a law of cooperation,[64] the founding of the European Union, the Human Rights Treaties from the 1960s, the Vienna Convention on the Law of the Treaties, and the emergence of international *ius cogens*, etc. The old rule of equal sovereignty of states became 'sovereign equality' *under* international law (Article 2, para 1 UN Charter);

---

[60] D. Grimm (ed), *Wachsende Staatsaufgaben: Sinkende Steuerungsfähigkeit des Rechts* (Baden-Baden: Nomos, 1990); D. Grimm, 'Der Wandel der Staatsaufgaben und die Krise des Rechtsstaats', in his *Die Zukunft der Verfassung* (Frankfurt am Main: Suhrkamp, 1991), 159–75; N. Luhmann, *Politische Theorie im Wohlfahrtsstaat* (Munich: Olzog, 1981); F. Neumann, 'Der Funktionswandel des Gesetzes im Recht der bürgerlichen Gesellschaft' (1937) 6 *Zeitschrift für Sozialforschung* 542–96.

[61] W. Seagle, *Weltgeschichte des Rechts: Eine Einführung in die Probleme und Erscheinungsformen des Rechts* (Munich: Beck, 1951); H. Maurer, *Allgemeines Verwaltungsrecht* (Munich: Beck, 17th edn, 2009).

[62] Luhmann, above n 60; Berman, *Justice in the U.S.S.R.*, above n 27, especially 277–8. Concerning the beginning in the 1930s see C. Joerges and N. Singh Ghaleigh (eds), *Darker Legacies of Law in Europe: The Shadow of National Socialism and Fascism over Europe and its Legal Traditions* (Oxford: Hart, 2003).

[63] L. Leisering, 'Gibt es einen Weltwohlfahrtsstaat?', in M. Albert and R. Stichweh (eds), *Weltstaat und Weltstaatlichkeit* (Wiesbaden: VS-Verlag, 2007), 185–205.

[64] J. Bast, 'Das Demokratiedefizit fragmentierter Internationalisierung', in H. Brunkhorst (ed), *Demokratie in der Weltgesellschaft, Soziale Welt Sonderband 18* (Baden-Baden: Nomos 2009), 185–93.

individual human beings (in the good and in the bad) became subject to International Law; democracy became an emerging right or a legal principle that can also be enforced against sovereign states; and the right to have rights, whose absence Arendt lamented in the 1940s, is now a legal norm that binds the international community.[65] All these legal rules are regularly broken. However, this is not a specific feature of international law; and it happens with national law as well, which to a considerable degree is also soft, symbolic, or dead law. What is new today is that international and cosmopolitan equal rights have become binding legal norms, and as such they have to be taken seriously. There is no longer any space for any action outside the law or outside the legal system.[66] Every single action of every kind of actor, individuals, states, and organisations is either legal or illegal—*tertium non datur*. In consequence, the difference in principle between national and international law has vanished, a point that Hans Kelsen, Alfred Verdross, Georges Scelle, and other cosmopolitan international lawyers were already claiming during the First World War.

IV. GLOBAL LAW?

As with other things in a highly accelerated and complex modern society,[67] this international (and national) legal and revolutionary progress is deeply ambivalent and fragile. The basic legal principles of the global inclusion of the other and the exclusion of inequality coexists with global functional systems, global actors, and global values which are emerging with great rapidity, and which tear themselves from the constitutional bonds of the nation state. This is a double-edged process that has caused a new dialectic of Enlightenment. The most dramatic effect of this formation of the global society is the decline of the nation state's ability effectively to abolish inequalities, even within the highly privileged world of the Organisation for Economic Co-operation and Development. This has three significant consequences.

First, we can observe in the economic system the complete transformation of the 'state-embedded markets of regional late capitalism' into the 'market-embedded states of global turbo-capitalism'.[68] The negative effect of economic globalisation on rights is that the freedom *of* markets explodes globally, and again at the cost of the freedom *from* the negative externalities of disembedded markets, and it is combined with heavy,

---

[65] For a more comprehensive overview see Brunkhorst, above n 52.

[66] M. Byers, 'Preemptive Self-Defense: Hegemony, Equality and Strategies of Legal Change' (2003) 2 *The Journal of Political Philosophy* 171–90, at 189.

[67] Hartmut Rosa, 'The Universal Underneath the Multiple: Social Acceleration as the Key to Understanding Modernity', in S. Costa et al (eds), *The Plurality of Modernity: Decentering Sociology* (Munich: Hampp, 2006), 22–42.

[68] W. Streeck, 'Sectoral Specialization: Politics and the Nation State in a Global Economy', paper presented to the 37th World Congress of the International Institute of Sociology, Stockholm 2005. As we now can see, the talk about late capitalism was not wrong but should be restricted to state embedded capitalism, and state embedded capitalism indeed is over. But what then came was not socialism but global disembedded capitalism which seems to be as far from the state embedded capitalism of the old days as from socialism.

sometimes warlike competition, in particular about the oil and energy resources of the earth, and now even combined with a global economic crisis: *there will be blood.*[69]

Surprisingly, in questions regarding the *religious sphere of values* we can make a similar observation and identify similar consequences. Global society makes the proposition that what is true for the capitalist economy is equally true for the autonomous development of the religious sphere of values. In consequence, we are now confronted with the transformation of the state embedded religions of Western regional society into the religion embedded states of the global society.[70] Since the 1970s, religious communities have crossed borders and have been able to escape from state control. Again, the negative effect of this on our rights is that the freedom *of* religions explodes whereas the freedom *from* religion comes under pressure. At the same time the fragmented legal and administrative means of states, inter, trans, and supranational organisations seems not to be sufficient to get the unleashed destructive potential of religious fundamentalism under control: *there will be blood.*

Last but not least, the internally fragmented executive branches of the state have decoupled themselves from the state-based separation, coordination, and unification of powers under the democratic rule of law, and they too have gone global.[71] The more they are decoupled from national control and judicial review, the more they are coordinated and associated on regional and global levels, where they constitute a group of loosely connected transnational executive bodies. Postnational governance without (democratic) government is performed at one and the same time through a partly formal and egalitarian rule of law, through an elitist *rule through law*, and through an informal bypassing of (constitutional) law and the demos by means of a

---

[69] One-sided but in this point striking is the neo-Pashukanian analysis of international law by C. Mieville, *Between Equal Rights: A Marxist Theory of International Law* (London: Haymarket, 2005).

[70] H. Brunkhorst, 'Democratic Solidarity under Pressure of Global Forces: Religion, Capitalism and Public Power' (2008) 17 *distinktion: Scandinavian Journal of Social Theory* 167–88.

[71] On transnational administrative law, during the last few years a whole industry of research emerged: see C. Tietje, 'Die Staatsrechtslehre und die Veränderung ihres Gegenstandes' (2003) 17 *Deutsches Verwaltungsblatt* 1081–164; C. Möllers, 'Transnationale Behördenkooperation' (2005) 65 *Zeitschrift für ausländisches öffentliches Recht und Völkerrecht (ZaöRV)* 351–89; Krisch and Somek in this volume; C. Möllers, A. Voßkuhle, and C. Walter (eds), *Internationalisierung des Verwaltungsrecht: Eine Analyse anhand von Referenzgebieten* (Tübingen: Mohr Siebeck, 2007); A. Fischer-Lescano, 'Transnationales Verwaltungsecht' (2008) 8 *Juristen-Zeitung* 373–83. On the globalisation of executive power: K.-D. Wolf, *Die neue Staatsräson: Zwischenstaatliche Kooperation als Demokratieproblem der Weltgesellschaft* (Baden-Baden: Nomos, 2000); P. Dobner, 'Did the State Fail? Zur Transnationalisierung und Privatisierung der öffentlichen Daseinsvorsorge: Die Reform der globalen Trinkwasserpolitik', in K.-D. Wolf (ed), *Staat und Gesellschaft: Fähig zur Reform? Der 23. wissenschaftliche Kongress der Deutschen Vereinigung für Politikwissenschaft* (Baden-Baden: Nomos, 2007), 247–61; G. Lübbe-Wolf, 'Die Internationalisierung der Politik und der Machtverlust der Parlamente', in H. Brunkhorst (ed), *Demokratie in der Weltgesellschaft*, above n 64, 127–42.

new regime of soft law. This law has so far no normatively binding force. Empirically, however, it has a strong compulsory effect.[72] It therefore resembles the old Roman *senatus consultum*, which had no legally binding force, but which every official was well advised to follow.[73] As a result, the new globalised executive power seems to be undergoing the same transformation as markets and religious belief systems, and it is thus transformed from *state embedded power* to *power embedded states*. This leads to a new privileging of the globally more flexible second branch of power vis-à-vis the first and third one, which jeopardises the achievements of the modern constitutional state.[74] The effect of this is an accelerating process of an original accumulation of global power beyond national and representative government.

The three great transformations of the world society have turned the democratically elected and legally organised political power within the nation state into the power of a transnational politico-economic–professional ruling class—including high ranked journalists and media stars who function as a bypass system, which are implemented to remove the core of political decision making from any spontaneous formation of communicative power through an untamed and anarchic public sphere. It seems now as if, in a new transformation of the public sphere, the Habermasian and Petersian filters, supposed to transform public opinion into political decision making,[75] are working the other way round, and are closing the doors on public opinion. White-Paper-Democracy is the outcome.[76] The new transnational ruling class hardly relies any longer on egalitarian will formation. This class is (like the *national* bourgeoisie of the nineteenth century) highly heterogeneous and characterised by multiple conflicts of interest. Yet it has a certain number of common class interests: for instance, it seeks to increase its room for manoeuvre by withdrawing itself from democratic control and, as a comfortable side-effect of this, it aims to preserve and increase its enormously enlarged, individual, and collective opportunities for private profit generation.[77] This is the new cosmopolitism of the few.[78] Instead of global democratic government we are now approaching some kind of directorial global Bonapartist governance: that is, soft Bonapartist governance for *us* of the North-West, and hard Bonapartist governance for *them* of the South-East, the failed and outlaw states and regions of the globe:[79] *there will be blood.*

---

[72] J. von Bernstorf, 'Procedures of Decision-Making and the Role of Law in International Organizations' (draft paper MPI, Heidelberg, 2008), 22; Möllers, 'Transnationale Behördenkooperation', above n 71.

[73] U. Wesel, *Geschichte des Rechts* (Munich: Beck, 1997), 163.

[74] Wolf, *Die neue Staatsräson*, above n 71.

[75] B. Peters, *Öffentlichkeit* (Frankurt: Suhrkamp, 2008).

[76] European Commission, 'European Governance: A White Paper', COM(2001) 428 final of 25 July 2001, OJ C287/2001, <http://ec.europa.eu/governance/white_paper/index_en.htm>.

[77] Wolf, *Die neue Staatsräson*, above n 71.

[78] Calhoun, above n 4.

[79] Anghie, above n 3.

The deep division of the contemporary world into two classes of people—those with good passports and those with bad ones[80]—is mirrored by the constitutional structure of the world society. Today, there already exists a certain kind of global constitutionalism, which is one of the lasting results of the revolutionary change that began in the 1940s, and observed already by Talcott Parsons in 1960, a sociologist who was never under suspicion of being an idealist.[81] However, existing global constitutions are far from being democratic.[82] All postnational constitutional regimes are characterised by a disproportion between legal declarations of egalitarian rights and democracy and its legal implementation by the international constitutional law of checks and balances.[83] Hence, the legal revolution of the twentieth century was successful, but it was unfinished. The one or many global constitutions are in bad shape, based on a constitutional compromise that mirrors the hegemonic power structure and the new relations of domination in the world society.[84]

Scientific and technical expertise has again become an ideology[85] which obscures the social fact that 'most regulatory decisions involve normative assumptions and

---

[80] Calhoun, above n 4.

[81] Parsons, above n 42, at 126.

[82] For the thesis that the UN Charter is the one and only constitution of the global legal and political order, see B. Fassbender, 'The United Nations Charter as Constitution of the International Community' (1998) *Columbia Journal of Transnational Law* 529–619; A. von Bogdandy, *Europäisches Verfassungsrecht: Theoretische und dogmatische Grundzüge* (Berlin: Springer, 2003); id, 'Constitutionalism in International Law' (2006) 47 *Harvard International Law Journal* 223–42; M. Albert and R. Stichweh, *Weltstaat und Weltstaatlichkeit* (Wiesbaden: VS, 2007); H. Brunkhorst, 'Globalising Democracy without a State: Weak Public, Strong Public, Global Constitutionalism' (2002) 31 *Millennium: Journal of International Studies* 675–90; id, 'Demokratie in der globalen Rechtsgenossenschaft' (2005) *Zeitschrift für Soziologie: Sonderheft Weltgesellschaft*, 330–48. For the thesis of constitutional pluralism, see G. Teubner, 'Globale Zivilverfassungen' (2003) 63 *ZaöRV* 1–28.

[83] For the original version of this thesis see Brunkhorst, above n 82.

[84] 'The treaties and the law-making are increasingly comprehensive, and the courts and dispute-settlement bodies are increasingly judicially organized and operatively effective. They are however still different than the similar forms of nation-state organized institutions in a number of ways. The treaties and the law-making are comprehensive, but fragmented and asymmetrical. Each treaty dealing with one set of problems or purposes—without the abilities of seeing the different types of problems in relation to each other. The organizations are not democratic in relation to citizens. They are generally based on states as members and many of them are dominated by internal secretariats and experts. They are set up as top-down tools for dealing with separate issues and areas of problems. They are dominated by different elites' (I. J. Sand, 'A Sociological Critique of the Possibilities of Applying Legitimacy in Global and International Law', paper presented at Onati School for Sociology of Law, Onati, Spain, 2008).

[85] H. Marcuse, 'On Science and Phenomenology', in *Boston Studies in Philosophy of Science*, ii. (New York: Proceedings of the Boston Colloquium for the Philosophy of Science, 1965), 279–91; J. Habermas, *Technik und Wissenschaft als 'Ideologie'* (Frankfurt am Main: Suhrkamp, 1968).

trigger redistributive outcomes that cannot be reduced to seemingly objective scientific inquiries; each time someone wins and someone loses'.[86] Hence, what seems to be necessary and out of reach in the present situation of pre-democratic global constitutionalism is a Kantian *Reform nach Prinzipien* (Kant),[87] or 'radical reformism' (Habermas), or a new 'democratic experimentalism' (Dewey) that operates on the same level as the power of the emerging transnational ruling class: that is, beyond representative government and national government.[88]

V. REFORM NACH PRINZIPIEN

What could radical reformism or *Reform nach Prinzipien* mean today? I don't know. But before posing the hard questions of constitutional change and institutional design which often fail because conceptually they fail to recognise the level of complexity of modern society, we should start again with concepts and principles, and that means with a critique of *dualism* and *representation* in legal and political theory.

Dualistic and representational thinking has already been deconstructed completely by the revolutionary philosophy (and scientific praxis) of the twentieth century, in particular by philosophers like John Dewey, Ernst Cassirer (after his symbolic turn), early Heidegger, late Wittgenstein, or W. V. O. Quine.[89] Yet, representational thinking that is deeply based on dualism still prevails in political and legal theory. In particular, in international law and international relations dualism covers a broad mainstream of opposing paradigms. From international relations realism to critical legal studies, from German *Staatsrecht* to critical theory, from liberalism to neo-conservatism, the state-centred dualism is tacitly accepted—that is, the dualism between *Staatenbund* and *Bundesstaat*, international law and national law, constitution and treaty, public law and private contract, state and society, politics (or '*the* political') and law, law-making and law-application, sovereign and subject, people and representatives, (action-free) legislative will formation and (weak-willed) executive action, legitimacy and legality, heterogeneous population and (relatively) homogeneous people, *pouvoir constituant* and *pouvoir constitué,* etc. All these dualisms prevent us from constructing European and global democracy adequately and, finally, to join the *civitas maxima*.

Yet, what Dewey and the pragmatists did with classical idealistic and metaphysical dualisms in philosophy, Kelsen and his students did with the dualisms in political, legal, and constitutional theory. They have replaced each of them by a *continuum*.

---

[86] Bernstorf, above n 72, at 8.

[87] C. Langer, *Reform nach Prinzipien: Untersuchung zur politischen Theorie Immanuel Kants* (Stuttgart: Klett-Cotta, 1986).

[88] Marks, above n 26, at 2–3.

[89] A paradigmatic account is: R. Rorty, *Philosophy and the Mirror of Nature* (Princeton, NJ: Princeton University Press, 1980). For recent developments see R. Brandom, *Making It Explicit: Reasoning, Representing & Discursive Commitment* (Cambridge, Mass.: Harvard University Press, 1994); J. Habermas, *Wahrheit und Rechtfertigung* (Frankfurt am Main: Suhrkamp, 1997).

Kelsen's and Merkl's paradigm case was the legal hierarchy of steps (*Stufenbau des Rechts*).[90] The doctrine of *Stufenbau* transforms the dualisms of legislative will and executive performance, of political generation and professional application of legal norms, of general law and specific judgment, and last but not least of international and national law into a *continuum of concretisation*.[91] Hence, if all levels on the continuum of legal norm concretisation are politically created, then the principle of democracy is fulfilled only if those who are affected by these norms are included fairly and equally on all levels of their creation.

Moreover, if we follow Jochen von Bernstorff one step further than Kelsen and drop the transcendental foundation of a legal hierarchy and the *Grundnorm*,[92] then we are left with an enlarging or contracting circle of legal and political communication which has no beginning and no end *outside* positive law *and* democratic will formation.[93] Only then could democracy replace the last (highly transcendentalised and formalised) remains of the old-European *legal hierarchy* and *natural law* that is higher than democratic legitimisation, and that means getting rid of the last inherited burden of dualism which 'weighs heavily like a nightmare on our brains' (Marx). We should no longer read Kelsen's theory primarily as a scientific theory of pure legal doctrine, but as a practically orientated theory which anticipates the global legal revolution of the twentieth century. It should also be read as a hopeful message—an attempt to change our worldview and vocabulary to fits a praxis that emancipates us from ideological blindness and helps us to get rid of the old international law of 'sorry comforters' (Kant).

Post-representation, democratic institutions should be designed to enable the expression of political and individual self-determination in a great variety of different governmental bodies at all levels, and through a variety of procedures of egalitarian will formation: participatory, deliberative, representative, or direct. Although Kelsen is sometimes read as a strong defender of representational democracy and parliamentary supremacy, this reading is wrong because Kelsen, like Dewey, made a powerful criticism of representation and replaced it with the idea of a continuum of different practical methods to express political opinions and make egalitarian

---

[90] A. Merkl, *Allgemeines Verwaltungsrecht* (Vienna: Springer, 1927), 160, 169; id, 'Prolegomena zu einer Theorie des rechtlichen Stufenbaus', in H. Klecatsky, R. Marcic, and H. Schambeck (eds), *Adolf Merkl und die Wiener rechtstheoretische Schule* (Vienna: Europa Verlag, 1968), 252–94.

[91] J. von Bernstorff, 'Kelsen und das Völkerrecht', in H. Brunkhorst and R. Voigt (eds), *Rechts-Staat: Staat, internationale Gemeinschaft und Völkerrecht bei Hans Kelsen* (Baden-Baden: Nomos, 2008), 167–90, at 181.

[92] J. von Bernstorff, *Der Glaube an das universale Recht: zur Völkerrechtstheorie Hans Kelsens und seiner Schüler* (Baden-Baden: Nomos, 2001).

[93] This comes close to Habermas's normatively strong or Luhmann's normatively neutralised idea of circulations of communication without a subject (*subjektlose Kommunikationskreiläufe*). J. Habermas, *Faktizität und Geltung* (Frankfurt am Main: Suhrkamp, 1992); N. Luhmann, *Legitimation durch Verfahren* (Frankfurt am Main: Suhrkamp, 1983); in conjunction with M. Neves, *Zwischen Themis und Leviathan* (Baden-Baden: Nomos, 2000).

decisions.[94] Radical criticism of representational democracy is not directed at parliamentary democracy. It leads, first, to a reinterpretation of parliamentary democracy as one (possible[95]) part of a comprehensive procedural method of egalitarian will formation, deliberation, and decision making,[96] and, second, to a relativisation of parliamentary legislation. Parliaments can no longer be interpreted as the highest organs of the state, or as the one and only true representative of the general will of the people, or as the expression of the essential, higher, or refined will of the better self of the people (the one that fits better to the ideas of intellectuals), or as the representation of the *Gemeinwohl* or commonwealth (whatever that is). Although parliaments may be the best method of achieving democratic will formation in a given historical situation, this is contingent.

To conclude: the double criticism of dualism and representation has far-reaching implications for theories of democracy and constitutional design which are Kelsenian but go far beyond Kelsen's advocacy of parliamentary democracy:

1. If all levels of the continuum of legal norm concretisation are politically created, then the principle of democracy is only fulfilled if those who are affected by these norms are included fairly and equally on all levels of their creation (local, national, regional, and global) and in all institutions (political, economic, social, and cultural levels; hence, the whole Parsonian AGIL-schema is open for democratisation[97] as far as it does not destroy either private or public autonomy[98]).

2. The different institutions (public and private) and procedures of legislation, administration, and jurisdiction are all in equal distance to the people, and no institution or procedure is taken to represent the people as a whole: 'No branch of power is closer to the people than the other. All are in equal distance. It is meaningless to take one organ of democratic order and confront it as the *representative* organ to all others. There exists no democratic priority (or supremacy) of the legislative branch.'[99] Instead of one substantial sovereign democracy, the regime must express itself in '*subjektlosen Kommunikationskreisläufen*' (circulations of communication without a subject).[100]

---

[94] H. Kelsen, *Vom Wert der Demokratie* [1920] (Aalen: Scientia, 1981); id, *Allgemeine Staatslehre* [1925] (Vienna: Österreichische Staatsdruckerei, 1993); id, *Reine Rechtslehre* [1934] (Vienna: Österreichische Staatsdruckerei, 1967).

[95] Nothing is necessary in a democratic legal regime except the normative idea of equal freedom: Kant, above n 8, 345; I. Maus, *Zur Aufklärung der Demokratietheorie* (Frankfurt am Main: Suhrkamp, 1992); Brunkhorst, *Solidarity*, above n 37, 67–77; C. Möllers, *Demokratie: Zumutungen und Versprechen* (Berlin: Wagenbach, 2008), 13–14, 16.

[96] Kelsen, *Demokratie*, above n 94.

[97] C. Möllers, *Staat als Argument* (Munich: Beck, 2001), 423.

[98] Maus, above n. 95; Habermas, *Faktizität und Geltung*, above n 93.

[99] C. Möllers, 'Expressive vs. repräsentative Demokratie', in R. Kreide and A. Niederberger (eds), above n 38, 160–82.

[100] Habermas, *Faktizität und Geltung*, above n 93, at 170, 492–3.

3. Whereas the concept of the higher legitimacy of a ruling subject (the king, or the state as *Staatswillenssubjekt*) is as fundamental for power limiting constitutionalism as it was for medieval regimes of 'the king's two bodies',[101] democratic and power founding constitutionalism replaces legitimacy completely by a legally organised procedure of egalitarian and inclusive legitimisation.[102] The procedures of legitimisation become nothing other than the products of democratic legislation; legitimisation is therefore circular in the sense of an open, socially inclusive hermeneutic circle or loop of *legitimisation without legitimacy*.[103]

4. Democracy is not, as the young Marx once wrote, the 'solved riddle of all constitutions' but, as Susan Marks has objected, the 'unsolved riddle of all constitutions'.[104] Hence, a constitution that is democratic has to keep the riddle open. It belongs to the necessary modern meaning of democracy that the 'meaning' of 'democratic self-rule and equity' never can be 'reduced to any particular set of institutions and practices'.[105] Without the normative surplus of democratic meaning which always already transcends any set of legal procedures of democratic legitimisation, the people as the 'subject' of democracy would no longer be a self-determined group of citizens, or a self-determined group of 'all men'[106] who are affected by a given set of binding decisions.

[101] E. H. Kantorowicz, *The King's Two Bodies* (Princeton, NJ: Princeton University Press, 1957).

[102] Habermas, *Faktizität und Geltung*, above n 93; C. Möllers, *Gewaltengliederung: Legitimation und Dogmatik im internationalen Rechtsvergleich* (Tübingen: Mohr, 2005).

[103] Democratic legitimisation is inclusive because it is governed by the one and only constitutional principle of democracy, and that is the principle of self-legislation or autonomy. This principle is socially inclusive because it presupposes that a procedure of legitimisation that is democratic has to include everybody who is concerned by legislation and jurisdiction. Consequently, all exceptions (eg babies) have to be justified publicly and need compensation through human rights: cf Müller, above n 7; Brunkhorst, *Solidarity*, above n 37, ch 3; Marks, above n 26.

[104] Marks, above n 26.

[105] Ibid 103, 149.

[106] 'All men' can mean many different things, eg all men in a bus, all men on German territory, all men with US passports (which is far less than all US citizens), all men on the globe, all men in the universe, all men who are French citizens, all men who are addressed by a certain legal norm. Democracy and democratic legitimisation is only concerned with the last two meanings, and the possible tension between them.

PART IV

CONSTITUTIONAL LAW AND PUBLIC INTERNATIONAL LAW

10

The Best of Times and the Worst of Times

Between Constitutional Triumphalism and Nostalgia

Mattias Kumm

I. CONSTITUTIONALISM BETWEEN TRIUMPHALISM AND NOSTALGIA

The idea of a 'postnational constellation' conjures up a world in which globalisation, privatisation, and individualisation have changed the basic configuration of the legal and political world. The state has become disaggregated as regulatory authority has shifted towards transnational governance structures and devolved to subnational public authorities or private actors. There are a number of questions one might ask about these changes. Have they strengthened human rights and have they furthered peace, justice, and prosperity within and across societies? Or have they created new inequities and new dangers? The literature on these questions, either generally, or addressing specific policy issues, is endless. This chapter will leave all of them aside. The focus here is the more limited question of how these changes can best be described and assessed in constitutional terms. Specifically the question is: How are these changes affecting the tradition of modern constitutionalism?

The constitutional literature addressing this issue can be roughly divided into two camps. According to the first—call them constitutional triumphalists—we are witnessing the triumph and radical expansion of constitutionalism. Not only has liberal democracy spread considerably after the end of the Cold War, but international legal practices have also gone through a process of constitutionalisation.[1] More generally, during the last decade the idea of constitutionalism beyond the state has gained considerable ground, and it is no longer unconventional to refer to the EU or the UN in constitutional terms. According to the second camp—call them constitutionally concerned—we are witnessing a threat to and perhaps even the demise of

---

[1] See, eg J. Dunoff and J. Trachtman (eds), *Ruling the World: Constitutionalism, International Law and Global Governance* (Cambridge: Cambridge University Press, 2009); N. Tsagourias (ed), *Transnational Constitutionalism* (Cambridge: Cambridge University Press, 2007); J. H. H. Weiler and M. Wind (eds), *European Constitutionalism beyond the State* (Cambridge: Cambridge University Press, 2003).

constitutionalism. Since the end of the Cold War the capacity of national constitutions to serve as a framework for the self-governing practices of a national community has been significantly eroded. Constitutionalism is either in its twilight years: part of an era that has gone by (the nostalgic key, characteristic of European scholars)[2] or something that needs to be regained and protected (the more assertive tone associated with 'revisionist' scholars writing on the law of foreign affairs in the US).

An obvious way to resolve this dispute in favour of the first position is to suggest that constitutionalism is alive and well, and has simply transformed itself to address new challenges.[3] Some degree of national constitutional self-government might have been lost, but that loss is only the result of the emergence of, at least in principle, desirable constitutionalised forms of transnational governance that compensate for the deficiencies of domestic constitutionalism.[4] In the end, a position along these lines is, in my view, correct. But, as will become clear, that position is not as obvious or easy to adopt as many of those embracing the idea of constitutionalism beyond the state might believe. There are deep commitments, connected to ways of imagining the legal and political world and tied to conceptual structures that have played a central role in the tradition of modern constitutionalism, with which the idea of constitutionalism beyond the state is in tension. If it is plausible to talk of constitutionalism beyond the state, it can only be because some of these basic conceptual structures and the legal and political world that is imagined through them turn out to have been inappropriate and misguided. The stakes in this debate, then, are high. And the attempt to come to a facile resolution should be avoided. The point of this chapter is not primarily to resolve the issue, but to develop a deeper understanding of what is at stake. To the constitutional triumphalists it sounds a note of

---

[2]   2 See A. Somek, *Individualism: A Theory of Constitutional Authority* (Oxford: Oxford University Press, 2008), ch 8 and D. Grimm, 'The Constitution in the Process of Denationalization' (2005) 12 *Constellations* 447–65.

[3]   On the domestic level the most visible sign of this transformation in terms of constitutional provisions and doctrine concerns the shifts that have taken place in the field of the constitutional law of foreign relations. Here the big picture questions are broken down into more specific issues. Is it constitutionally permissible for a state to sign and ratify treaties that establish institutions that have some degree of regulatory authority? If so, are there any limits to the kind of regulatory authority these institutions may have related to sovereignty or national self-government? What is the constitutionally required procedure for such treaties to be ratified? What status do the regulation and decisions of such institutions have as a matter of domestic law and to what extent are they directly effective or self-executing? Many of the old constitutional settlements with regard to these questions have come under pressure as a result of new exigencies, making the constitutional law of foreign affairs one of the most dynamic areas of contemporary constitutional law in many jurisdictions.

[4]   A. Peters, 'Compensatory Constitutionalism: The Function and Potential of International Norms and Structures' (2006) 19 *Leiden Journal of International Law* 579–610; E. de Wet, 'The International Constitutional Order' (2006) 55 *International & Comparative Law Quarterly* 51–76. See also M. Kumm, 'The Cosmopolitain Turn in Constitutionalism: On the Relationship between Constitutionalism in and beyond the State', in Dunoff and Trachtman (eds), above n 1, 258–324.

caution: be aware of the historical depth and conceptual structure of the world that is left behind and the radical rethinking of the constitutional tradition—a genuine paradigm shift—that will have to come with it. That kind of constitutional transformation is only plausible in conjunction with a genuine revolution in the way law and politics are understood, a revolution no less deep conceptually than that brought about by the emergence of the Westphalian order. To the constitutional nostalgists it offers a challenge: it is not enough to simply repeat the old certainties with a sense of superiority, imagining constitutional triumphalists as Settembrinièsque, whiggish fools who rush in where wise men fear to tread. Those old certainties are themselves open to serious questioning and critical analysis and need to be assessed in light of an alternative constitutional paradigm that might just turn out to be persuasive.

Ultimately this chapter not only serves the function of providing a deeper understanding of the nature of the dispute between triumphalists and nostalgists, even though that is its primary purpose. It also takes a position and develops an argument defending that position, even if here that argument can only be provided in a rudimentary form.

My argument is that the nostalgist's position is connected to a particular and ultimately unconvincing paradigm of constitutionalism that might be called *democratic statism*. Democratic statism conceptually connects the core commitments of the modern constitutional revolutions with the tradition of statehood and sovereignty. It exhibits a positivist and nationalist deep structure that emphasises some of the core ideas underlying the French and American revolutions, but underplays others. The triumphalist position, on the other hand, is compatible with a conception of constitutionalism—call it the *practice conception of constitutionalism*—that attempts to liberate constitutionalism from the statist paradigm and the biases to which it is connected. States become one institutional context for constitutionalism—certainly a very important one—along with others. Ultimate constitutional authority is not located in a particular institution (eg a constitutional court), a particular text (the Constitution), or a source ('We the People' as *pouvoir constituant*). Instead, claims to constitutional authority are made whenever a law makes a claim to authority that is not derived from a legal source. To put this another way: constitutional authority is claimed whenever law makes a claim to authority that is not plausibly legitimated by reference to the procedure that was used to enact it. It is possible to conceive of a world in which only national constitutions fulfil this requirement. But as a matter of contemporary practice not only national constitutions, but also the UN Charter, the EU's Constitutional Charter, and the European Convention on Human Rights (ECHR) make such claims to authority.

There is, accordingly, a plurality of constitutional sources, potentially giving rise to constitutional conflict. When different constitutional claims collide, they must be assessed in light of the constitutional principles that support them, by whatever institution is called upon to address constitutional conflicts. There is no one institution that is the final arbiter of constitutional claims. Constitutional conflicts get resolved by reference to underlying constitutional principles that determine which claims to constitutional authority have more weight under which circumstances. It follows that both with regard to constitutional sources and to institutional actors constitutionalism has a pluralist structure.[5] The coherence and unity of constitutional practice is neither guaranteed by the cohesion of a *pouvoir constituant*, a written text, or a final arbiter as the guardian of the constitution, but by a mutually deferential and engaging constitutional practice held together by common principles.

The following argument is divided into two main parts: the first provides an analysis and critique of democratic statism (II), the second describes the core structural features of the practice conception of constitutionalism (III), and is followed by a brief conclusion that suggests that democratic statists are today what scholars of the German *Reichspublizistik* were in the late eighteenth and early nineteenth centuries (IV).

II.　THE STRUCTURE OF CONSTITUTIONAL NOSTALGIA:
DEMOCRATIC STATISM

The core structural features of democratic statism can be reduced to three basic propositions: constitutional law, paradigmatically codifed in the form of a written constitution, establishes the supreme law of a sovereign state; the authority of the Constitution is based on the idea that it can be fairly attributed to 'We the People' as the constituent power; and this constituent power is tied to the existence of a genuine political community that is the prerequisite for meaningful democratic politics.

On the proper domain of constitutionalism

Those who think of constitutionalism in terms of democratic statism have reasons to be sceptical about 'constitutionalism beyond the state'. Too many of the core features of constitutionalism are absent in settings beyond the state; it is generally not sociologically plausible to posit the existence of a constituent power beyond the state. Beyond the state there is only law based on treaties signed and ratified by states. And to the extent that these treaties establish institutions, these are not institutions that establish democratic processes that are embedded in a genuine political community.

True, there are some structural features of international law that bear some resemblance to features associated with domestic constitutional law. In part these are formal: there are elements of a hierarchy of norms in international law. They range from *jus cogens* norms to Article 103 of the UN Charter, establishing the

---

[5] Among the authors first developing the idea of constitutional pluralism along these lines are N. Walker, 'The Idea of Constitutional Pluralism' (2002) 65 *Modern Law Review* 317–59; M. Maduro, 'Contrapunctual Law: European Constitutional Pluralism in Action', in N. Walker (ed), *Sovereignty in Transition* (Oxford: Hart, 2003), 502–37; and M. Kumm, 'Who is the Final Arbiter of Constitutionality in Europe?' (1999) 36 *Common Market Law Review* 261–386. For a more recent discussion, see M. Avbelj and J. Komarek (eds), *Four Visions of Constitutional Pluralism*, EUI Working Paper 2008/21.

priority of the UN Charter over other norms of international law. In part they are functional: there are multilateral treaties that serve as regime-specific constitutional charters for institutionally complex transnational governance practices. And in part they are substantive: human rights obligations have long pierced the veil of sovereignty that kept the relationship between the state and its citizens from the purview of international law. The individual has long emerged as a subject of rights and obligations under international law. There are international human rights courts established by treaties that authorise individuals to vindicate their rights before international courts. International law even criminalises certain types of particularly serious human rights violations.

True also, is that these features are more characteristic of modern constitutional systems than of international law conceived as the law among states. But without the core features of democratic statism—a constituent power establishing an ultimate authority that enables democratic politics—constitutionalism beyond the state is at best a pale analogy to constitutionalism properly so called. If it is to be referred to as constitutionalism at all, it is constitutionalism with a small *c*, wheras constitutionalism within the context of the state is constitutionalism with a big *C*. Only constitutionalism with a big *C* is concerned with the establishment of an ultimate authority linked to a genuine constituent power and genuine democratic politics. To the extent that transnational legal and political practices are increasingly delinked from requirements of specific state consent, and to the extent such international legal obligations increasingly limit and constrain the meaningful exercise of constitutional self-government within the context of the state, that is not an expansion of constitutionalism, but a symptom of its demise. The language of constitutionalism beyond the state should not be used to cover up that fact. Small *c* constitutionalism is in tension with big *C* constitutionalism.

This, as far as I see, is the core structure of the argument that underlies the idea of the 'twilight of constitutionalism' and scepticism about constitutionalism beyond the state. Even though the claim that small *c* constitutionalism is at odds with big *C* constitutionalism is correct, that is not a reason to abstain from the language of constitutionalism to describe and assess legal and political practices beyond the state. Instead the premises are problematic. The very distinction between small *c* and big *C* constitutionalism, I will argue, is based on a mistake. The idea of an ultimate constitutional authority linked to one constituent power is misguided. And as important as electoral processes organised on the national level are, they are only one type of procedure among others to create legitimate law, necessary and appropriate in many contexts but less appropriate in others, particularly when the legitimate interests of outsiders are affected in relevant ways.

Before I engage in the argument in greater depth a caveat is in order: nothing I say in the following suggests that the transformations of international law and the restrictions on national self-government are without costs. The core argument is not even that, notwithstanding these costs, the overall evolution of these practices is desirable because of greater benefits. This is not an exercise of apologetics. It is an exercise of legal criticism; legal criticism, furthermore, with a conceptual focus. It criticises those who make claims about the limits of constitutionalism in a way that tends to *delegitimise* transnational legal practices by suggesting that these are reflective of a 'demise of constitutionalism'. It is not the case that international lawyers have inappropriately co-opted constitutional language to legitimise a dubious project of transnational integration. If the argument here is correct, it is national lawyers who inappropriately delegitimise transnational legal and political practices by failing to acknowledge their constitutional status and the claims to legitimate authority that come with it. Once the jeremiad of 'constitutionalism lost' is dropped, there might well be good reasons on political grounds to criticise specific features of transnationalisation. Furthermore, specific features of those practices might raise important concerns that constitutional analysis might help clarify and assess. What is not constitutionally plausible is to delegitimise wholesale transnational practices, not plausibly linked to state consent, that restrict national constitutional practice by suggesting that it undermines constitutionalism. In that sense the argument here rehearses a classical argument against a conceptually focused jurisprudence: that it hides moral and political choices behind implausible conceptual arguments.

The voluntarist and positivist structure of democratic statism

The conceptual structure of democratic statism reflects a particular interpretation of constitutionalism. Constitutional law, ideally codified in the form of a written constitution, is conceived as posited law. That posited constitutional law is then imagined as establishing the supreme law of the land. It constitutes, authorises, and constrains all public authority. Where does the authority of the Constitution come from? On what grounds does it assume the status of supreme law of the land?

There appears to be a deceptively simple answer to the question of the Constitution's legal authority. A lawyer might simply point to the *convention* in his jurisdiction, that the Constitution is, as a matter of fact, *accepted* as the supreme law of the land. To the extent that is the case, a court trying to establish what the law is might in many contexts not need to know anything more. But even though it is clearly true that conventions matter for establishing what the law is, there are all kinds of ways in which that answer is insufficient.[6] All of these ways have something to do with the fact that law, unlike the claims made by a highway robber demanding that money be handed over at the point of a gun, *makes a claim to legitimate authority.*[7]

An appeal to convention is first of all insufficient from the point of view of citizens subject to the constitution. One of the core features of the modern constitutional tradition is that law's claim to legitimate authority has to be justifiable to those to whom it is addressed. Addressees of the law are imagined not as dominated by their superiors or paternalistically taken charge of by well-meaning elites, or socialised

---

[6] For a sophisticated defence of legal conventionalism that acknowledges its limits, see A. Marmor, 'Legal Conventionalism', in J. Coleman (ed), *Hart's Postscript* (Oxford: Oxford University Press, 2001), 192–217.

[7] See J. Raz, 'The Claims of Law', in his *The Authority of Law* (Oxford: Clarendon Press 1979), ch 2 and J. Raz, 'Authority, Law and Morality', in his *Ethics in the Public Domain* (Oxford: Clarendon Press 1994), ch 10.

into a tradition of sacred origin that has existed since time immemorial. They are imagined as subjects who participate in the law-generation process as free and equal citizens, to whom any laws have to be justifiable. Simply pointing to convention would not be sufficient from the perspective of educating citizens, especially when those citizens raise the all-important question why they should accept the constitution as supreme law of the land.

But pointing to conventions would not be sufficient from a more narrow legal perspective either. On the one hand, a convention might come under pressure, so that it becomes insufficient simply to point to well-established facts to resolve questions of authority. The authority of the Constitution as the supreme law of the land might become subject to dispute, as it has, for example, in Europe, where the European Court of Justice (ECJ) has made the claim that courts of member states should set aside domestic constitutional law when it conflicts with the EU Law. Whether or not the claim to primacy of this kind is warranted and should be accepted by national courts needs to be engaged. It cannot simply be ignored by constitutional courts. Once conventions become unsettled and subject to dispute, there is nothing to do but to point to the best justifications underlying them to see whether they are convincing in light of competing claims. But the grounds for the Constitution's claim to legitimate authority are not only relevant for resolving competing claims of primacy; those grounds are also relevant for the interpretation of the Constitution. Many of the constitutional provisions—for example those relating to the status of international law—are open to interpretation. When faced with difficult interpretative questions the court would do well to interpret the Constitution in such a way that would be compatible with its claim to legitimate authority. A purposive interpretation of constitutional provisions would therefore have to be informed by the underlying account of what makes the Constitution's claim to legitimate authority plausible. Certainly no conception of constitutional scholarship worth its mettle would exclude from its ambit the grounds for a constitution's claim to legitimate authority.

For the most part, constitutional scholarship—not surprisingly—does provide such an answer, as do some national courts. Indeed, democratic statist courts and scholars point to the idea of 'We the People' as a validating source for the Constitution as positive law. Clearly, there is something plausible about that answer. 'We the People willed it' is a more plausible answer to the question where the Constitution derives its authority from than, for example, 'because the king, by the grace of God, willed it so' or 'because time immemorial has sanctioned it'. But the idea of We the People as the source of law willing into existence a constitution nonetheless remains obscure and implausible.[8]

---

[8] For a series of essays on the role that the idea of constituent power plays in different constitutional traditions, see M. Loughlin and N. Walker (eds), *The Paradox of Constitutionalism: Constituent Power and Constitutional Form* (Oxford: Oxford University Press, 2007). The purported paradox of constitutionalism lies in the paradoxical fact that 'the People' who are imagined as willing into existence the constitution come into existence only by virtue of the constitution.

To the extent the act of willing is imagined to take place at the time the Constitution enters into force, it is not plausible for one of two reasons. In some constitutional jurisdictions there was simply no procedure underlying its coming into force that could plausibly be interpreted as the will of We the People. Think, for example, of the German Constitution, both when it was first enacted and in the context of reunification. After the Second World War, German public authorities in the western parts of a divided country were pressurised by the Western allied occupying forces to work out a Basic Law in order to consolidate western Germany's position in the emerging Western alliance and to pre-empt Soviet manoeuvring ultimately aimed at anchoring a unified Germany in the Soviet sphere of influence. The document eventually produced by the Constitutional Convention was subject to approval by the allied powers and was ultimately ratified by state parliaments. And after the Cold War, when reunification occurred, it took the form of a Treaty, by which East Germany acceded to West Germany. It would appear highly contrived to locate the authority of the German constitution in an original constitutive act either 1949 or 1990. The most prominent context in which We the People made an appearance in the jurisprudence of the Federal Constitutional Court was in the context of the nationally recalcitrant *Maastricht* and *Lisbon* decisions.[9]

Even when the Constitution has been established following a procedure that could more plausibly be interpreted as articulating a popular will, as was the case in the US Constitution,[10] it is still puzzling why that procedure, used more than 220 years ago, should have any significant legitimating force for establishing authority over those it seeks to bind today.[11] How can the dead hand of the past legitimately exercise control over the living? Jefferson himself suggested that only the new adoption of a constitution every generation could solve the 'dead hand of the past' problem.

What follows from this is not that there is anything illegitimate about either the German or US Constitution. What follows is that, if the German and US Constitutions are to be rightly regarded as legitimately establishing the highest national law, it must be in virtue of features that are largely disconnected from the original circumstances of its ratification. *There is no procedure that in and of itself is either necessary or sufficient to establish the legitimate authority of a constitution.*[12]

---

[9] See C. Möllers, 'We are (afraid of) the People: Constitutent Power in German Constitutionalism', in Loughlin and Walker (eds), above n 8, ch 5.

[10] The issue is further complicated, of course, by the original exclusion of blacks, women, and unpropertied males as well as native Americans.

[11] For an attempt to deal with this problem head on, see J. Rubenfeld, *Freedom and Time: A Theory of Constitutional Self-Government* (New Haven, Conn.: Yale University Press, 2001).

[12] The view that legitimate constitutional authority does not depend in any strong sense on the procedure originally used to enact it, is not new for legal theorists. For an overview, see L. Alexander (ed), *Constitutionalism: Philosophical Foundations* (Cambridge: Cambridge University Press, 1998), 1. See further, J. Raz, 'On the Authority and Interpretation of the Constitution: Some Preliminaries', ibid, at 152–93. That does not mean that the procedure is irrelevant. A Europe-wide referendum would, if successful, no doubt provide the EU with

That alone is an important insight. It suggests, for example, that it is a mistake to presume that the constitutional status of the EU's primary law or the UN Charter can be resolved by simply focusing on how they came about. The fact that EU Law and UN Law is written into treaties that require ratification by states following national constitutional requirements does not resolve the question of their status as constitutions or define the scope and limits of their authority. The idea of a Constitutional Treaty is not a contradiction in terms. After all, few would claim that the fact that East Germany acceded to the West German Constitution by way of a treaty undermines the authority of the German Constitution for people who were citizens of East Germany.

But if the legitimate authority of a constitution is not linked to the procedure that was used to enact it in a strong way, what is it that grounds constitutional authority? Even if the constitutive act of volition by We the People cannot be located in the original constitution-giving act, perhaps it might be located in some other way. It might be imagined at work in particular moments in constitutional history,[13] or as a permanent force in the background, *pace* Renan, upholding the Constitution's legitimate authority in an imagined *plébiscite de tous les jours*.[14,15] What holds all these theories together is their voluntarist structure and the fact that an entity that qualifies as We the People does the willing. Ultimately the *will* of the people, however its manifestation might be imagined, is constitutive of legitimate constitutional authority.

As a voluntarist conception of constitutionalism, democratic statism does plausibly reflect *some* central ideas of constitutionalism. The idea that ultimate authority is grounded in a collective will reflects the idea that all positive law, even the highest law, is made by human beings and is susceptible to critique and total revision. It also suggests that those who are to be bound by the Constitution participate in its enactment in some way and should be able to recognise it as theirs. The very idea of We the People as the constituent power suggests that citizens collectively

---

additional constitutional legitimacy. But its success or failure as legitimate constitutional authority ultimately depends on other criteria.

[13] Bruce Ackerman, for example, insists that in the US We the People as a constituent power has been active not only in the eigthteenth century at the time of the founding, but also in the nineteenth century in the context of the civil war and its aftermath and in the twentieth century surrounding the debates and constitutional battles concerning the New Deal: see B. Ackerman, *We the People: Foundations* (New Haven, Conn.: Yale University Press, 1991).

[14] Note how the structure of the theories about the relationship between the Constitution's legitimate authority and the *pouvoir constituant* mirrors theological positions relating to God's relationship to the world. God can be imagined as present only at the time of creation (God as the watchmaker), he can be imagined as intervening every once in a while (through miracles), or he can be imagined as an ever-present force (occasionalism).

[15] The idea that the Constitution is upheld by We the People in the daily recognition of the laws that it generates comes close to a straighforwardly conventionalist understanding of constitutions in Hartian terms: the Constitution is the supreme law of the land if and to the extent it is recognised as such by public authorities and those subject to the laws generally recognise and obey the laws that are generated under the Constitution.

remain empowered to abolish and substitute the Constitution with one they deem more fitting. The empowering effect of this idea could be seen in the demonstration in East Germany leading up to the fall of the Berlin Wall: the demonstrators encountering the armed forces of the established authorities of the East German Communist regime held up placards and chanted 'We are the People'. This was a menacing reminder to the public authorities that all legally established power derives from them and that the people acting collectively can claim the authority to abolish established authorities if and when they deem fit.

But there are central elements of constitutionalism that democratic statism as a voluntarist conception de-emphasises and assigns only a contingent role. Neither the idea of democracy, nor the idea of respect for human rights is conceptually hardwired into democratic statism's conception of constitutional authority. If We the People willed into being a constitution that declares that the Sharia, as interpreted by learned theologians sitting on the highest court,[16] is part of the supreme law of the land, then nothing in democratic statist's conception of constitutional authority would suggest they could not do that. The label of constitutional law would still be applied to the result and its authority, from a legal point of view, would remain untouched, even if that result was deeply at odds with the core commitments of the modern tradition of constitutionalism. Democratic statists might, of course, insist on the importance of democracy and human rights as a political matter, they might even endorse constitutional provisions that immunise commitments to human rights and democracy against ordinary constitutional amendment. But that does not change the fact that primacy is given to the idea that We the People as the constituent power can establish just about anything as the supreme law of the land. The voluntarist and positivist elements are the necessary ingredients for the construction of constitutional authority. Democratic institutions and human rights are comparatively contingent, even when they are regarded as desirable. Democratic statists would not hesitate to describe any constitutions plausibly willed into being by a *pouvoir constituant* as constitutions properly so called, even as they deny such a status to institutions established by treaties beyond the state. As we shall see later, the practice conception of constitutionalism does the inverse.

The nationalist deep structure of democratic statism

Perhaps the most obvious and disturbing feature of democratic statism is its relationship to international law. It simply assumes that the Constitution of the sovereign state establishes the supreme law of the land. How can it do so plausibly, when the national constitution imposes constraints on the enforcement, say, of EU Law or of UN Law?

One answer is, of course, that the authority of the national constitution can paradigmatically be traced back to an act of We the People. But that is not much of a

---

[16] See Art 2 Iraqi Constitution: 'Islam … is a fundamental source of legislation. … No law that contradicts established provisions of Islam may be established.' Art 79 determines that judges on the Federal Supreme Court include experts in Islamic Jurisprudence.

convincing answer. Why should We the People on the national level have the authority to trump what 'We the United Nations' have determind to be legally required? Another answer is that UN Law ultimately derives its authority from the consent of states. It is based, after all, on a treaty signed and ratified by all states. But that too is not convincing. Why should the treaty-making and ratification process not be a way for the political community of the 'United Nations' to act as a constituent power by way of state representatives? After all, some national constitutions come about by ratification of state parliaments of state ratification conventions. As was established above, there is no prescribed procedure by which a constituent power can be identified. So the argument shifts again, this time to sociology: the claim is that there is no genuine political community on the global or European level, whereas there is one on the national level. A genuine political community, a nation properly so called, the kind of community that makes genuine democratic self-government involving majoritarian decision making possible, exists on the level of the state, but not on the level of the European community and certainly not on the level of the global community. Democratic statism, then, has a nationalist deep structure that the language of democratic self-government only barely covers up: supreme legal authority is derived from the nation.

Of course the nationalist structure of democratic statism does serve one important constitutional value, even if it undermines others. Democracy properly so called, involving at least some meaningful form of electoral accountability, does depend on presuppositions that are not easily replicated in settings beyond the state. What exactly those presuppositions are and whether they plausibly exist on the level of the European Union (EU) might be an open question,[17] but there can be little doubt that on the level of the UN meaningful electoral politics cannot be institutionalised. Clearly the existence or non-existence of genuine electoral accountability needs to be a central element in any account of constitutional authority that is plausible, even though I will argue below that questions of constitutional authority cannot be reduced to democracy. But note that within democratic statism the function of the idea of a genuine political community is to establish where the ultimate source of authority in the form of We the People is located. The voluntarist conception of We the People, however, does *not* require that a people decides to constitutionalise genuine democracy. The content of constitutional norms is contingent. Democratic statism, then, does not insist on a strong and unqualified connection between genuine democracy and constitutional authority. The mere sociological possibility of genuine democracy, assumed to exist within the right kind of political community, is sufficient for the purpose of establishing contitutional authority. The deep structural commitment is to the genuinely political community, not democracy.

That does not mean that democratic statists are nationalists. Whether a particular constitution is nationalist or cosmopolitan depends on the specific content of the Constitution. Democratic statism is an account of constitutional authority that *does*

---

[17] D. Grimm, 'Does Europe Need a Constitution?' (1995) 1 *European Law Journal* 282–302; J. Habermas, 'A Response to Dieter Grimm' (1995) 1 *European Law Journal* 303–12.

not say anything about the content of constitutional norms that define the terms of engagement with the international community. Democratic statism is perfectly compatible with the idea of an open constitution that authorises deep participation in and engagement with transnational institutional practices. *But nothing in its conception of constitutional authority requires it.* Whether and to what extent the constitution is open or closed to transnational engagement is reconstructed as a political choice reflected in concrete constitutional provisions or interpretations of these provisions. Like the decision on the form of government and the respect for human rights, the nature of the relationship to the larger international community is a contingent choice left for the constitutional legislator to decide. The only thing that is *not* contingent is the fact *that the national constitution decides* how that relationship is to be conceived.[18] On the level of deep structure democratic statism is not only voluntarist/positivist, but nationalist.

III. THE PRACTICE CONCEPTION OF CONSTITUTIONALISM

What might constitutionalism be, once it is not imagined within a democratic statist framework but nonetheless remains committed to the French and American revolutionary tradition?

What is constitutionalism?

The following is an attempt to spell out—not to argue for, but simply to state clearly and thus make explicit—some assumptions about the core elements of modern constitutionalism. These assumptions define *the common ground* between democratic statism and the practice conception of constitutionalism. It is that common ground which makes it possible to recognise both democratic statism and the practice conception as paradigms of constitutionalism properly so called. Conversely, conceptions of constitutionalism that do not share these assumptions do not qualify as constitutional in the modern tradition. Both the democratic statist and the practice conception of constitutionalism can be understood as constitutional paradigms that try to develop a coherent conceptual framework that integrates and interprets these elements and their relationship to one another in different ways.

At the heart of modern constitutionalism—the tradition of constitutionalism associated with the American and French Revolutions[19]—is the idea that the exercise of legitimate public authority is not unlimited and requires a certain kind of

---

[18] Even when a nation decides that its Constitution should never ever be used as a ground not to enforce international law, the ground for the authority of international law as a matter of domestic law would still be the result of a choice by the national constitutional legislator.

[19] I am not interested, for the purpose of this argument, either in the tradition of comparative constitutionalism as a study of different forms of political organisation that goes back to Aristotle's *Politics*, or in accounts of Roman Republicanism that reach their late high point with Cicero's writing in *De respublica, De legibus,* and *De officiis.*

justification. Legitimate public authority is circumscribed and has to justify itself before a *higher law*. In order to be legitimate, all exercise of public authority has to be derived from and shown to be compatible with that higher law.

That higher law is not simply a version of ancient or medieval natural law. With the advent of modern constitutionalism the foundations of law and politcs have shifted. The higher law of constitutionalism is not imagined to be inscribed into the structure of the cosmos and accessible to those who reason rightly about God, nature, and the salvation of the soul. The higher law of constitutionalism insists on the emancipation of law and politics from theology and comprehensive world-views. That new higher law insists that all posited law must be conceiveable by those whom it addresses as *the result of a deliberate collective choice of free and equal individuals.*

There are three connected ideas. First, law is conceived to be the result of *a deliberate choice.*[20] It is a human artefact, not the result of an authoritative imposition by a higher being or the legal imprint of a blind historical process that simply has to be accepted as given. That law is conceived as the result of a deliberate choice also means that it is susceptible to *reasoned* criticism and change. Second, the deliberate choice embodied in the law must be *reasonably attributable to those whom it addresses*. To be plausible, such attribution requires appropriate procedural mechanisms for participation as well as outcomes that reflect equal respect and concern for all those addressed. Third, the subject matter of that choice concerns the legal and political relationships between *persons conceived as free and equal*. It is not directly concerned with the salvation of the soul of those *sharing a faith*, nor is it imagined as partaking in a world-historic struggle addressed to members of a particular *class*, and nor is it directly concerned with the flourishing of members of a particular group, defined by *ethnicity*. Of course the idea of freedom and equality itself *presents a perspective* from which questions of respect for someone's faith, the unequal social and economic status of individuals, or their sense of belonging to a particular ethnic group can be addressed as a political or legal—even constitutional—issue. But that perspective is defined by the idea that individuals are free and equal as addressees and constructive authors of the laws. The domain of law and politics is irreducible and distinctive, as is the kind of justification appropriate for acts of public authorities.[21]

When these basic ideas are translated into constitutional requirements, they give rise to three types of constitutional norms. Constitutional norms address questions relating to: basic institutions and their respective powers; procedures that allow for the appropriate forms of participation and deliberation; and norms—which

---

[20] See James Madison, Alexander Hamilton, and John Jay, *The Federalist Papers* [1788], ed I. Kramnick (London: Penguin, 1987), No 1 (Hamilton): 'It seems to have been reserved to the people of this country, whether societies of men are capable or not, of establishing good government by reflection and choice, or whether they are forever destined to, for their political constitutions on accident and force.'

[21] The core elements of constitutionalist thought can be found in the second paragraph of the 1776 Declaration of Independence and the first six articles of the French Declaration of the Rights of Man and Citizen of 1789.

generally take the form of rights—for assessing whether outcomes are justifiable to those burdened by them as free and equal.

These general features of constitutionalism are elaborated and given a particular shape by different conceptions of constitutionalism. The structural features of democratic statism have already been examined; the structural features of the practice conception will now be described.

What is a constitution?

In order to get a handle on the basic structural features of the practice conception of constitutionalism it is helpful to ask basic questions anew. What is a constitution? Is EU primary law constitutional law properly so called? Is the ECHR? Is the UN Charter? If so, in virtue of what are they constitutional norms properly so called? Clearly these laws fulfil some formal and functional criteria of constitutions. They establish higher law that organises an institutional practice, and it is not enough to deny these laws constitutional status simply by pointing to the procedure that was used to establish them. As the discussion above illustrates, there are no necessary or sufficient procedural conditions for the establishment of constitutional authority. The idea of a treaty with constitutional authority is not a contradiction in terms, because constitutions can be established by just about any legal or political procedure. True, if a state enters into such a treaty, then the domestic constitution generally provides the resources to determine the status of treaties as a matter of domestic law. But the claim relating to *these treaties* is that the rules that usually apply to treaties as a source of law do not apply to EU law. The authority of these laws, so the claim goes, is not derivable from the procedure used to enact it. *This, in a negative form, is the defining characteristic of a constitutional law: that the law makes a claim to authority that is not exclusively source based; derivative, but original.* But if constitutional authority is not derived from another legal source and not derived from We the People as a constituent power, what is it derived from?

Constitutional authority is in part directly derived from the constitutional principles it claims to instantiate and give concrete shape to. Without states signing and ratifying the treaty it would obviously have not come about. But now that it has come into existence, its authority is not derived simply by the fact that it came about by way of a treaty-making process. The practice conception of constitutionalism connects the underlying ideas of constitutionalism more directly and deeply with constitutional practice, without mediation by the voluntarist/positivist, nationalist/statist conceptual framework that is central to democratic statism. The normative presuppositions of constitutionalism are translated directly into a set of basic formal, jurisdictional, procedural, and substantive legal principles that are conceived as underlying existing legal and political practices and in light of which that practice can be reconstructed and assessed.[22] A treaty can claim original constitutional authority if it directly

---

[22] These principles were first described in M. Kumm, 'The Legitimacy of International Law: A Constitutionalist Framework of Analysis' (2004) 15 *European Journal of International Law* 907–31.

instantiates in the institutions, procedures, and substantive norms it establishes the principles of constitutionalism.

In Article 6 TEU the EU claims to be based on the principles of the rule of law, human rights, and democracy, as well as respect for national identities. Even though the EU is not a state and even if there is no such thing as a European people that governs itself within the framework established by the European constitution, the EU still has a constitution. Constitutional law properly so called extends beyond the nation and beyond the state. The EU's constitution and the constitutions of member states are all constitutions in that they claim authority derived at least in part directly from the constitutional principles they embody and help realise. *A constitution speaks directly in the name of those over whom it claims authority. National constitutions speak in the name of We the People, and the EU constitution speaks in the name of European citizens and member states.* And the latter does so with a promise to respect, protect, and promote the realisation of the constitutional principles of human rights, democracy, and the rule of law, while respecting national identities.

The structure of constitutional pluralism

The fact that a treaty is a constitution does not mean that it establishes the supreme law of the land. It means merely that its authority cannot be determined with reference to the procedure used to enact it. Instead the scope of its authority depends on the extent to which a constitution actually fulfils its promise to instantiate and help realise constitutional principles. In case of conflict with other constitutional claims a comparative assessment needs to establish which of the competing claims to authority is more plausible under the circumstances. To illustrate what that means it might be useful to offer a simplified sketch of the German Constitutional Court's response to the ECJ's claim that EU law requires national constitutional law to be set aside.

The German Constitution, until the early 1990s,[23] contained no specific provisions addressing European integration, though the Preamble mentioned Germany's commitment to strive for peace in a united Europe. The Constitution did authorise Germany to enter into treaties establishing international institutions.[24] And it contained general provisions giving international treaties the same status as domestic statutes.[25] Yet the ECJ had claimed that EU law was to be regarded as the supreme law of the land and required member states' courts to set aside any national law, even national constitutional law, if it conflicted with requirements of EU law.[26] How was the Federal Constitutional Court (FCC) to respond? Was the ECJ's claim really plausible? Had member states established a new supreme law of the land by

---

[23] In the context of the ratification of the Maastricht Treaty Art 23 the Basic Law was amended to address questions of European integration.

[24] See Art 24 Basic Law.

[25] This is the dominant interpretation of Art 59 II Basic Law.

[26] See ECJ Case 6/64 *Costa v ENEL* [1964] ECR 585; ECJ Case 106/77 *Simmenthal SpA* [1978] ECR 629.

signing and ratifying a set of treaties the core objective of which was to establish a common market? On the other hand, was it plausible to claim that the EU Treaties, which established institutions that had been endowed with significant legislative authority, and played a significant role to secure peace and prosperity in war ravaged Europe, should be treated like any other treaty? Was it really adequate to apply the general rule applicable to treaties according to which an ordinary statute enacted after the Treaty was ratified would trump it? If the FCC accepted the basic ideas underlying democratic statism and its idea of constitutional self-government, that is probably the conclusion the Court would have reached. If, on the other hand, the FCC accepted EU Law as legitimate constitutional authority on the grounds that it was necessary to secure the rule of law to enable the effective and uniform enforcement of EU Law, it would follow the ECJ. But the FCC chose neither of these options. It embraced an intermediate solution. That intermediate solution illustrates the connection between the practice conception of constitutionalism and the complex set of doctrines that national courts have in fact developed for assessing the ECJ's claims concerning the supremacy of EU Law.

First the FCC accepted without much ado that EU law trumps ordinary statutes, even statutes enacted later in time, because of the importance of securing an effective and uniformly enforced European legal order.[27] The principle of ensuring the effective and uniform enforcement of EU law—expanding the rule of law beyond the nation state—was a central reason for the Court to recognise the authority of EU law over national statutes.

Yet, contrary to the position of the ECJ, the Court recognised that that principle was insufficient to justify the supremacy of EU law over all national law. The principle of legality matters, but it is not all that matters. The *second* issue before the Court was whether it should subject EU Law to national constitutional rights scrutiny. Could a resident in Germany rely on German constitutional rights against EU law? Could the protection of national residents against rights violations guaranteed in the national constitution be sacrificed on the altar of European integration? Like other questions concerning the relationship between EU law and national law, the German Constitution provided no specific guidance on that question. In *Solange I*[28] the FCC balanced the need to secure the fundamental rights of residents against the needs of effective and uniform enforcement of EU law and established a flexible approach: for so long as the EU did not provide for a protection of fundamental rights that is the equivalent to the protection provided on the national level, the Court would subject EU Law to national constitutional scrutiny. At a later point, the Court determined that the ECJ had significantly developed its review of EU legislation and held that the standard applied by the ECJ was essentially equivalent to the protection provided by the FCC's interpretation of the German Constitution.[29] For so long as that remained the case, the FCC would not exercise its jurisdiction to review EU law on national

[27]   BVerfGE 22, 293 (1967) and BVerfGE 31, 145 (1971).

[28]   BVerfGE 37, 271 (1974).

[29]   BVerfGE 73, 339 (1986).

constitutional grounds. Because the ECJ through its own jurisprudence provided the structural guarantees that fundamental rights violations by EU institutions would generally be prevented, it conditionally accepted the authority of EU law. To put it another way: structural deficits in the protection of fundamental rights on the European level provided the reason for the FCC to originally insist that it should not accept the authority of EU law, insofar as constitutional rights claims were in play. When those specific concerns were effectively addressed by the ECJ, the authority of EU law extended also over national constitutional rights guarantees and the FCC as their interpreter. The authority of EU law, then, was in part a function of the substantive and procedural fundamental rights protections available to citizens as a matter of EU law against acts of the EU.

But this is not yet the whole story. There are two residual lines of resistance drawn by national courts to the wholesale acceptance of the authority of EU law. The drawing of these lines is justified by reference to the principle of democracy and the absence of meaningful democratic politics and a meaningful European identity on the European level.

In its *Maastricht* decision,[30] the FCC determined that it had jurisdiction to review whether or not legislative acts by the EU were enacted *ultra vires*. If such legislation were enacted *ultra vires*,[31] it would not be applicable in Germany. As a matter of EU law it is, of course, up to the ECJ to determine as the ultimate arbiter of EU Law whether or not acts of the EU are within the competencies established by Treaties.[32] But the ECJ had adopted an extremely expansive approach to the interpretation of the EU's competencies, raising the charge that it allowed for Treaty amendments under the auspices of Treaty interpretation. Under these circumstances the FCC believed it appropriate for it to play a subsidiary role as the enforcer of limitations on EU competencies of last resort. In this decision, arguments from democracy played a central role. Democracy in Europe remains underdeveloped, with electoral politics playing a marginal role. The national domain remained the primary locus of democratic politics. Under those circumstances, ensuring that EU institutions would remain within the competencies established in the Treaties is of paramount importance. Whatever EU institutions decide can no longer be decided by directly electorally accountable national actors.

This points to a final line of resistance, not as yet explicitly endorsed by the FCC, but visible in the jurisprudence of other courts. When a national constitution contains a specific rule containing a concrete national commitment—say a commitment to free secondary education,[33] or a restriction to national citizens of the right to vote in municipal elections,[34] or a categorical prohibition of extradition of citizens

---

[30]　BVerfGE 89, 155 (1993).

[31]　This position was restated in the FCC's more recent decision on the Treaty of Lisbon, BVerfG, 2BvE 2/08, 30 June 2009.

[32]　See Art 230 ECT.

[33]　Belgian Constitutional Court, European Schools, Arbitragehof, Arrest No 12/94, BS 1994, 6137–46.

[34]　Spanish Constitutional Court, Municipal Electoral Rights, (1994) 3 CLR 101.

to another country[35]—these commitments will not generally be set aside by national courts. Instead, national courts will insist that the constitution is amended to ensure compliance with EU law. This line of cases also reflects an understanding that the realm of the national remains the primary locus of democratic politics. For so long as that remains the case, a commitment to democracy is interpreted by some member states courts to preclude setting aside national constitutional commitments as they are reflected in these concrete and specific rules. It is then up to the constitutional legislature to initiate the necessary constitutional amendments.

This stylised and schematic account illustrates the operation of a conception of legitimate constitutional authority: one that puts the principles of constitutionalism themselves front and centre.[36] The principle of legality and its extension beyond the nation state has an important role to play to support the authority of EU law, but concerns relating to democracy and human rights may provide countervailing reasons for limiting the authority of EU law in certain circumstances. Furthermore the constitutional principles that govern the relationship between national and EU law do not themselves derive their authority from either the national constitution or EU law. The relative authority of EU and national constitutions is a question to be determined by striking the appropriate balance between the competing principles of constitutionalism in a concrete context.

The Treaties establishing the European Union are the EU's constitution, the ECHR is part of the body of European constitutional law and the UN Charter is the constitution of a global community. They derive their authority not exclusively from the treaty-making procedure that was necessary to enact them, but the constitutional principles they embody, even if that does not mean that they effectively establish the supreme law of the land. Furthermore, even if EU law does not, without further qualifications, establish the supreme law of the land, this does not imply that the constitutions of member states establish an ultimate legal authority. European integration has transformed the nature of national constitutional authority, and not just the substance of national constitutional commitments. The authority of competing constitutional norms in any particular context is assessed in light of constitutional principles. Straightforward hierarchical rules— national constitutional supremacy or European constitutional supremacy—have been replaced by a complex form of principled interface-management. Common principles of constitutionalism, and not an ultimate rule either of national or European or UN constitutional supremacy, provide the ultimate norms for guiding European constitutional practices.

---

[35] Polish Constitutional Court, Judgment of 27 April 2005, P 1/05, English Summary available at <http://www.trybunal.gov.pl>.

[36] For a more fully developed account, see M. Kumm, 'The Jurisprudence of Constitutional Conflict: Constitutional Supremacy before and after the Constitutional Treaty' (2005) 11 *European Law Journal* 262–307.

IV. CONCLUSION: DEMOCRATIC STATISM AS *REICHSPUBLIZISTIK*

This chapter offers an account of the basic structural features of two competing paradigms of constitutionalism: democratic statism and the practice conception of constitutionalism. Its core purpose is to provide a deeper understanding of two very different perspectives on constitutionalism at the beginning of the twenty-first century, one inclined to mourn the twilight of constitutionalism, the other to celebrate its new dawn. It suggests that those proclaiming its new dawn might have the better case on their side, but if they have, it means that the way law and politics is imagined has to go through the kind of basic, tectonic shift that the emergence of statist thinking brought about in the sixteenth and seventeenth centuries. These different paradigms do not reflect fleeting fashions. They relate to basic conceptual structures that provide different interpretations of the constitutional heritage of the eighteenth century.

In the long run, something like the practice conception of constitutionalism might well have history on its side, as constitutional practice evolves in a way that increasingly makes apparent the lack of explanatory or normative plausibility of democratic statism. But it is unlikely that democratic statism will either in this generation or even the next lose its credibility as a serious paradigm for the study of constitutional law. In 1667, only a few years after Hobbes published *Leviathan*, Pufendorf declared the Reich—the Holy Roman Empire of German Nations—to be like a monster (*monstrum simile*).[37] After the Thirty Years War and the Peace of Westphalia, it no longer seemed possible, as Carl Schmitt was later to comment,[38] for legal thinkers to think about law and politics in any conceptual framework but that of the state. But of course that is not true. Radical and deep changes relating to the imagination of the legal and political world do not generally replace traditional ways of thinking that quickly. In Germany the learned legal literature on the moribund Reich—the *Reichspublizistik*—continued to flourish until the turn of the nineteenth century, when the Reich was finally formally dissolved.[39] The future of democratic statism in the twenty-first century might well be like the eigthteenth century past of the *Reichspublizistik*. Learned scholars of subtlety and sophistication will continue to describe and assess a world of public law using a legal framework whose hold on the world is increasingly tenuous and whose normative justification is dubious. Given the fact that states are unlikely to collectively dissolve themselves, and given that grand political projects for a world made new are nowhere on the horizon, constitutional nostalgia in Europe and constitutional revisionism in the US might well turn out to be with us for some time.

---

[37] Samuel von Pufendorf, *De imperii romani: de statu imperii germanici liber unus* (Geneva, 1667).

[38] C. Schmitt, 'Corollarien', in his *Der Begriff des Politischen* (Berlin: Dunckler Humblot, 1933).

[39] M. Stolleis, *Geschichte des Öffentlichen Rechts in Deutschland* (Munich: Beck, 1992), ii. 48–57.

❦ 11 ❦

In Defence of 'Constitution'

Rainer Wahl[*]

I. INTRODUCTION

For over 200 years, 'constitution' has been a key concept of political–juridical thinking. Its widespread transposition to the European and international level today might therefore be assumed to trigger fundamental thinking about the justification of this terminological and conceptual analogy. A successful transplantation could provide both levels—European and international—with a reinvigorated experience of how the concept of the constitution became so successful in nation states. But an inflationary and substantively inaccurate transfer from the level of the state to levels beyond the state might only offer an illusory solution, one that acts as a barrier against devising more adequate conceptual solutions. The title of this chapter anticipates its hypothesis: that the concept of the constitution is not strengthened but weakened when the terms 'constitution', 'constitutionalism', and 'constitutionalisation' are transferred without thought to the international level.

The term 'constitution' is placed in quotation marks in the title for a reason. What needs to be defended is not existing constitutions, but the linguistic and conceptual use of the term. The core of the controversy does not concern conceptual issues. Terms such as 'constitution' are linguistic usages which can be altered. But when a term is well established, it may prove inexpedient or even misleading to adopt a substantially different use of it. In the context of usage of the term 'constitution', the claim being made by those extending it beyond the state level is that the essence of the existing term applies with equal effect to the new usage, and this extension of scope is conceptually justified. The objective of this chapter is to examine this claim.

II. CONSTITUTION IN AND BEYOND THE STATE

My subject is the extending usage of the term 'constitution', initially with respect to the European Union (EU) and then in the international arena, both as a guiding formulation for the sphere beyond the nation state and, more generally, as providing

[*] I am indebted to Mitch Cohen, *Wissenschaftskolleg zu Berlin*, for the translation and Anna Katharina Mangold for helpful comments.

the foundation for a new form of international law. The basic claim being made by advocates of constitution beyond the state is that above the traditional norms of international law, in particular beyond treaties under international law, there lies another layer of norms and principles, and that—this being the decisive point—these norms should bind states. States should be subject to duties that arise independent of, or against, their will.[1] The claim to be examined here goes further and suggests that these higher duties and norms add up to a whole, to a constitution (or at least add up to larger orders). This notion of the constitution beyond the state is propounded in two main variants. In the strong hypothesis, one speaks of international constitutionalism; in the weaker variant, of a (mere) constitutionalisation. The latter, weaker hypothesis avoids the apparent problem of the first: that there is no presentable and perceptible formal constitution on the international level, either as a whole or in relevant partial arrangements.

The traditional understanding of the constitution on the state level is unavoidably the starting point for further considerations. Those who want to apply the term to political units beyond the states must have a clear idea of this concept. Consider two representative analyses. In his systematic elucidation of the German Basic Law, Peter Badura begins with an abstract legal definition of 'constitution' that constitutionalists might use as their starting point: by constitution, Badura writes, 'one understands basic legal prescriptions summarized in a constitutional law ('a constitutional document') on the organization and exercise of state power, state tasks, and basic rights.' He then elaborates:

> The constitution is an order-creating and programmatic *act of foundation and shaping* that seeks to give the community a legal foundation in a concrete historical situation. The constitution traces back to a political decision by the political forces that determine *the instituting of the constitution*. ... The constitution has legal, but also political effects, because it is a symbol of state unity and commonality that influences legal consciousness and political life.[2]

Similarly complex is the definition by Dieter Grimm:

> The constitution in the modern sense is characterized by five components:
>
> (1) It is the epitome of legal norms, not a summary of philosophical foundations and not a description of actual power relations in a community.
> (2) The object of these legal norms is the institution and exercise of political rule or public power.
> (3) The constitution tolerates neither extra-constitutional powers nor extra-constitutional ways and means of rule.
> (4) Because rule is legitimate only when constituted and limited by constitutional law, constitutional law takes primacy over all other acts of

---

[1] See C. Tomuschat, 'Obligation arising for States without or against their Will' (1993-IV) 241 *RdC* (*Recueil des cours de l'Académie de Droit Internationale de la Haye*) 195–374.

[2] P. Badura, *Staatsrecht: Systematische Erläuterung des Grundgesetzes* (Munich: Beck, 3rd edn, 2003), 7 (emphasis in original).

rule. The latter are valid only when they remain within the framework of constitutional law.

(5) The norms of constitutional law are based in the people, because every other principle of legitimization of rule unhinges the remaining components and, in case of conflict, would prevail over the constitution.[3]

Such descriptions of the concept make it clear that 'constitution' is a complex phenomenon belonging to the spheres of both law and politics. The constitution certainly has normative content and makes normative claims. But also important is whether, and the degree to which, it is accepted among the people. And ultimately this recognition by the individual and the people gives the constitution its normative force.

The concept of the constitution is very attractive for the European and, to a degree also, for the international level mainly because this constitutional approach draws on the success story of constitutions. The success of national constitutions, especially after 1945, has been so great that hardly any state wants to eschew the honour of having a constitution, even if it is not a genuine constitution. Here we are speaking mainly of the smaller number of genuine, so-called Western constitutional states. For these states, it is true that there was and still is a success story of constitutions and in particular of constitutional jurisdiction. Constitutional jurisdiction is what first gave these constitutional texts the normative effectiveness they were striving for. Law enforced by this jurisdiction is law with a quality different from law without such jurisdiction; it is, so to speak, law in a different aggregate state. All constitutional states that have instituted a constitutional jurisdiction have made a leap to a higher level of normativity and legitimacy.

This high esteem for such constitutions is the starting point for the many proposals that are seeking to transport the idea of the constitution to the supranational and international levels. The hope is that of achieving similar successes to that obtained in the case in states. Here, a role is played by the expectation that the use of the proven 'honorary title' of constitution will ensure that a significant part of the achievements of national constitutions can be transferred to the newer political units. It is also hoped that, as a result of this transfer, a unified and binding concept of constitution can be adopted as the foundation of all three levels: national, European, international.

There is another quality of constitutions, emphasised mostly by jurists. With the establishment of constitutions, an internal hierarchy within the legal order is created. There now exist an easily identified group of fundamental legal norms; they are norms about norms, norms of a second and higher order. As fundamental norms, they stand above all others, above the vast number of norms contained in 'ordinary' law.[4] They take precedence over all other acts and legal norms. All of this is more

---

[3] D. Grimm, 'Gesellschaftlicher Konstitutionalismus: Eine Kompensation für den Bedeutungsschwund der Staatsverfassung?', in M. Herdegen (ed), *Festschrift für Roman Herzog* (Munich: Beck, 2009), 69–82. See also D. Grimm, 'Die Verfassung im Prozess der Entstaatlichung', in M. Brenner (ed), *Festschrift für Peter Badura* (Tübingen: Mohr Siebeck, 2004), 145–68, and Grimm in this volume.

[4] The term 'ordinary' law in this extreme form exists only in German law. The term may and must initially surprise, because it designates rather relativisingly precisely the laws

precisely described as the concept of the primacy of the constitution.[5] Once again, the establishment of constitutional jurisdiction is the immanent, logical conclusion of this concept or of this institutional formation of higher rank.

This concept of the hierarchical order of precedence is so attractive that, not surprisingly, it is employed also outside public law, and outside law in general. The theory of societal constitutionalism exhibits the attraction of this construction of primacy: of rules about rules.[6] This is also true of the economic theory of constitutional economics, which focuses on rules about rules: of meta-rules that govern the other rules.[7]

But it might be noted that although the traditional understanding is the starting point, it is not necessarily the authoritative standard for evaluating a broader understanding of the concept. This raises the basic methodological problem. It is assumed that the European and international level are units with special characteristics: units *sui generis* in relation to the state, so to speak. But actually there is little that can constructively be said about what is special about units *sui generis* and initially one can only measure these units with respect to their degree of distance from the characteristics of states. That is, the comparison must be with what the new units precisely are not: states. And as long as one does not have any convincing positive understanding of these special qualities, this is unavoidable.

III.   CONSTITUTIONAL LAW BEYOND THE STATE

Nothing in the broad inventory undertaken in 2007 under the title *Zur Zukunft der Völkerrechtswissenschaft in Deutschland* (The Future of International Law Jurisprudence in Germany) in the Max Planck Society's *Zeitschrift für ausländisches und öffentliches Recht*

---

passed by parliament. This relativisation of laws has internal consistency, however, namely because of the primacy and the comprehensive meaning of constitutional law in the German legal order. This formation of terminology once again reflects the earlier observation: the primacy of the constitution at the same time means the lower ranking of the laws. See R. Wahl, 'Der Vorrang der Verfassung' (1981) 20 *Der Staat* 485–516. See also id, *Verfassungsstaat, Europäisierung, Internationalisierung* (Frankfurt: Suhrkamp, 2003), 121–60.

[5] Wahl, 'Vorrang', above n 4; id, *Verfassungsstaat*, above n 4, 161–87; id, 'Der Vorrang der Verfassung und die Selbständigkeit des Gesetzesrechts' (1984) *NVwZ* 401–9.

[6] D. Sciulli, *Theory of Societal Constitutionalism* (Cambridge: Cambridge University Press, 1992); G. Teubner, 'Globale Zivilverfassungen: Alternativen zur staatszentrierten Verfassungstheorie' (2003) 63 *ZaöRV* 1–28; A. Fischer-Lescano and G. Teubner, *Regimekollisionen* (Frankfurt am Main: Suhrkamp, 2006), 43, 57.

[7] J. M. Buchanan, *Constitutional Economics* (Oxford: Blackwell, 1991); id, *The Economics and the Ethics of Constitutional Order* (Ann Arbor: University of Michigan Press, 4th edn, 1994); I. Pies (ed), *James Buchanans konstitutionelle Ökonomik* (Tübingen: Mohr, 1996); G. Grözinger and S. Panther (eds), *Konstitutionelle politische Ökonomie: sind unsere gesellschaftlichen Regelsysteme in Form und guter Verfassung?* (Marburg: Metropolis-Verlag, 1998); V. Vanberg and J. M. Buchanan, 'Constitutional Choice, Rational Ignorance and the Limits of Reason' (1991) 10 *Jahrbuch für Neue Politische Ökonomie* 61–78; V. Vanberg, 'Market and State: The Perspective of Constitutional Political Economy' (2005) 1 *Journal of Institutional Economics* 23–49. See also (since 1990) the journal *Constitutional Political Economy*.

und Völkerrecht is so often cited as the constitutionalisation of international law, albeit with numerous variants in wording.[8] In hardly any relevant pan-European or international context has the (primarily, if not exclusively German) literature felt drawn towards adopting the time-honoured concept of the constitution. The aforementioned intention to live from the high degree of esteem for this term in the context of the state is conspicuous—even if states are otherwise conceived as being in a process of erosion. At least with the 'demise' of the state, in the currently predicted phase of de-statification (*Entstaatlichung*), one wants to profit from one of its greatest achievements: the idea of the constitution.[9] Thus, in various contexts, terms like world constitutionalism,[10] international constitutionalism,[11] global constitutionalism,[12] international democratic constitutionalism,[13] multi-level constitutionalism,[14] European constitutionalism beyond the state,[15] and postnational constitutionalism[16] appear in the literature. An interesting variant is that of 'compensatory constitutionalism', expressing the hope that the promotion of constitutionalism on the European or international level will compensate for deficits and losses of constitutionalism on the state level.[17]

---

[8] *ZaöRV* 67 (2007) with articles by Benvenisti, Kadelbach, Keller, Marauhn, Nolte, Oeter, Paulus, Peters, de Wet, and Zimmermann, all with titles varying the given main theme. Recently, there have been three inaugural lectures regarding this topic: O. Dörr, ' "Privatisierung" des Völkerrechts' (2005) *Juristenzeitung (JZ)*, 905–16; M. Nettesheim, 'Das kommunitäre Völkerrecht' (2002) *JZ* 569–78; R. Uerpmann, 'Internationales Verfassungsrecht' (2001) *JZ* 565–73.

[9] Cf trademark law, where the behaviour of someone who seeks to exploit the fame of a trademark for himself is called 'acting parasitically on the major trademark'.

[10] R. St John Macdonald and D. M. Johnston (eds), *Towards World Constitutionalism: Issues in the Legal Ordering of the World Community* (Leiden: Martinus Nijhoff, 2005).

[11] J. Klabbers, A. Peters, and G. Ulfstein, *Constitutionalization of International Law* (Oxford: Oxford University Press, 2009).

[12] A. Peters, 'Global Constitutionalism in a Nutshell', in K. Dicke (ed), *Weltinnenrecht: Liber amicorum Jost Delbrück* (Berlin: Duncker & Humblot, 2005), 535–50.

[13] B.-O. Bryde, 'International Democratic Constitutionalism', in Macdonald and Johnston (eds), above n 10, 103–25.

[14] I. Pernice, 'The Global Dimension of Multilevel Constitutionalism: A Legal Response to the Challenges of Globalisation', in P.-M. Dupuy (ed), *Völkerrecht als Wertordnung: Festschrift für Christian Tomuschat* (Kehl: Engel, 2006), 973–1006.

[15] J. Weiler and M. Wind (eds), *European Constitutionalism beyond the State* (Cambridge: Cambridge University Press, 2003).

[16] N. Walker, 'Post-national Constitutionalism and the Problem of Translation', in Weiler and Wind, above n 15, 53.

[17] A. Peters, 'Compensatory Constitutionalism: The Function and Potential of Fundamental International Norms and Structures' (2006) 19 *Leiden Journal of International Law* 579–610; E. de Wet, 'The Emergence of International and Regional Value Systems as a Manifestation of the Emerging International Constitutional Order' (2006) 19 *Leiden Journal of International Law* 611–32. See also R. Wahl, 'Verfassungsdenken jenseits des Staates', in I. Appel and G. Hermes (eds), *Mensch—Staat—Umwelt* (Berlin: Duncker & Humblot, 2008), 135–54.

Constitutional thinking addressed here is often directed specifically at the UN Charter as the constitution of the international community; in this variant, the focus is on the constitutionalisation of the entire order of international law.[18] But the WTO also receives constitutional recognition as a partial order.[19] In addition, there is the evolutionary concept of constitutionalisation, in which a great deal of what is constitutional is expected from further development in the future, but which already places a label on the development.

The constitutionalist interpretation finds similar diversity and an even more frequent use in the German literature, which is generally considered the original source and primary habitat of this approach.[20] The German formulations speak of *überstaatliches Verfassungsrecht* (constitutional law beyond the state),[21] *internationales Verfassungsrecht* (international constitutional law),[22] *kommunitäres Völkerrecht* (communitarian international law),[23] constitutionalisation,[24] and *Der Staat der Staatengemeinschaft* (the state of the community of states).[25] The influence of the private-law-based, or system-theoretical, concept of the civil constitution has already been referred to.

[18] Recently M. Knauff, 'Konstitutionalisierung im inner- und überstaatlichen Recht: Konvergenz oder Divergenz?' (2008) 68 *ZaöRV* 453–90, with a systematisation of the forms of appearence.

[19] J. Trachtman, 'The Constitutions of the WTO' (2006) 17 *European Journal of International Law* 623–46. Otherwise J. L. Dunoff, 'Constitutional Conceits: The WTO's "Constitution" and the Discipline of International Law' (2006) 17 *European Journal of International Law* 647–75. Cf M. Hilf, 'Die Konstitutionalisierung der Welthandelsordnung: Struktur, Institutionen und Verfahren', in W. H. von Heinegg (ed), *Entschädigung nach bewaffneten Konflikten: Die Konstitutionalisierung der Welthandelsordnung* (Heidelberg: Müller, 2003), 257–82.

[20] The constitutionalist interpretation is considered to be a German concept, eg A. Paulus, 'Zur Zukunft der Völkerrechtswissenschaft in Deutschland: Zwischen Konstitutionalisierung und Fragmentierung des Völkerrechts' (2007) 67 *ZaöRV* 695–720, at 697, 699, 703, 718. Too few problems take British authors into consideration using the terms constitution and constitutionalism, probably because those terms and concepts are not part of the British law and its tradition.

[21] See S. Kadelbach and T. Kleinlein, 'Überstaatliches Verfassungsrecht: Zur Konstitutionalisierung im Völkerrecht' (2006) 44 *Archiv des Völkerrechts* (AVR) 235–66.

[22] Uerpmann, above n 8; critically, U. Haltern, 'Internationales Verfassungsrecht: Anmerkungen zu einer kopernikanischen Wende' (2003) 128 *Archiv des Öffentlichen Rechts* (AöR) 511–57.

[23] Nettesheim, above n 8.

[24] C. Walter, 'Die EMRK als Konstitutionalisierungsprozess' (1999) 59 *ZaöRV* 961–83; id, 'Constitutionalizing (Inter)national Governance' (2001) 44 *German Yearbook of International Law* 170–201; critically R. Wahl, 'Konstitutionalisierung: Leitbegriff oder Allerweltsbegriff?' in C.-E. Eberle (ed), *Der Wandel des Staates vor den Herausforderungen der Gegenwart: Festschrift für Winfried Brohm zum 70. Geburtstag* (Munich: Beck, 2002), 191–207.

[25] W. G. Vitzthum, *Der Staat der Staatengemeinschaft: Zur internationalen Verflechtung als Wirkungsbedingung moderner Staatlichkeit* (Paderborn: Schöningh, 2006).

Evidence of the use of constitutional concepts in the international arena can be found in the positive law of various international courts, in the architecture of the WTO, and in several, much-noted, spectacular problem constellations and cases.[26] Eight illustrations of these usages can be listed as follows.

1. At the top of the frequently mentioned examples stands *the limitation of states' immunity in cases of severe violations of human rights*. The leading case is that of the former Chilean President, *Pinochet*.[27] In this case, the English House of Lords eventually removed Pinochet's immunity, in proceedings that were not, overall, convincing. But policy considerations—the health issues that were pleaded—prevented the implementation of the penalty, and ultimately the process contained a mixture of rigorous decisions and political considerations. In contrast, the *Cour de Cassation* did not permit a suit against the Libyan head of state, Gaddafi, over the attack on a passenger plane.[28]

2. *Limitation of states' immunity in the case of states' foreign ministers*. The most conspicuous case is that of the Foreign Minister of the self-styled Democratic Republic of Congo, who is alleged to have been involved in severe violations of human rights. In accordance with the principle of international law operating in Belgium at the time, a Belgian investigating judge issued an arrest warrant against the Foreign Minister. In proceedings filed by the Democratic Republic of Congo, the International Court of Justice (ICJ) maintained the traditional immunity of Foreign Ministers. But this was a majority decision and a notable minority dissented.[29] In the literature, this immunity problem has rightly been interpreted as

[26] The major cases each time initiated a very extensive discussion whose references cannot be given here in total—D. Thürer, 'Modernes Völkerrecht: Ein System in Wandel und Wachstum: Gerechtigkeitsgedanke als Kraft der Veränderung?' (2000) 60 ZaöRV 557–604, at 560, considers 'eight scenarios' that he regards as a 'thematic thread' and as approaches to a paradigm for a newly emerging system of international legal order. For a more detailed survey of the cases and their problems, see Knauff, above n 18, and Dörr, above n 8.

[27] For an account of the complicated circumstances of the different decisions see Thürer, ibid, at 568 et seq. See also C. Maierhöfer, 'Weltrechtsprinzip und Immunität: Das Völkerstrafrecht vor Den Haager Richtern—Urteil des IGH Demokratische Republik Kongo Belgien' (2003) EuGRZ 545–54, at 545, nn 1–3; M. Ruffert, 'Pinochet Follow Up: The End of Sovereign Immunity?' (2001) 48 Netherlands International Law Review (NILR) 171–95; K. Ambos, 'Der Fall Pinochet und das anwendbare Recht' (1999) JZ 16–24; C. Tangermann, Die völkerrechtliche Immunität von Staatsoberhäuptern (Berlin: Duncker & Humblot, 2002).

[28] Cour de Cassation, decision of 13 March 2001, (2001) Revue géneralé de droit international public (GDIP) 473.

[29] Judgment of the ICJ of 14 January 2002 (Democratic Republic of the Congo v Belgium), excerpts in (2003) EuGRZ 563; Maierhöfer, above n 27; C. D. Classen, 'Rechtsschutz gegen fremde Hoheitsgewalt: Zu Immunität und transnationalem Verwaltungshandeln' (2005) 96 VerwArchiv 464–84; M. Goldmann, 'Arrest Warrant Case', in R. Wolfrum (ed), Max Planck Encyclopedia of Public International Law (Oxford: Oxford University Press, 2nd edn, 2009 et seq); S. Zeichen and J. Hebestreit, 'Kongo v. Belgien: Sind Außenminister vor Strafverfolgung wegen völkerstrafrechtlicher Verbrechen immun?' (2003) 41 Archiv des Völkerrechts (AVR) 182–200; O. Dörr, 'Staatliche Immunität auf dem Rückzug' (2003) 41 AVR 201–19.

a stage for the conflict between diverging conceptions of international law.[30] At issue is the understanding of international law either as the coordinating law of sovereign states or as the constitution of the 'international community of mankind'. The disagreement between majority and minority in the court was over differing views of the process of production of international law and differing views of international law as such. It is no surprise that the methodology of majority and minority were fundamentally different.[31]

3. A topic widely discussed recently is the immunity of states against civil suits for damages due to torture or other human rights violations.[32] Suits for damages from Greek citizens against the Federal Republic of Germany over Nazi crimes in the Greek community of Distomo have drawn much attention; the verdict against Germany handed down by the highest Greek courts was initially declared inadmissible in the implementation phase, whereupon the plaintiffs strove for the implementation of their demands in Italy.[33] Currently, the entire dispute is before the ICJ, which—with Italy's and Germany's agreement—will aim to clarify the underlying primary issue of immunity.[34]

4. A standard case on the reinterpretation of a Convention that previously applied solely to states in favour of third parties is the case of the German citizen, LaGrand.[35]

---

[30] Maierhöfer, above n 27, at 548, 549. The immunity of foreign ministers is not comprehensively regulated in treaties, and is therefore a question of customary law. The ICJ holds with state practice and explains that, even for the case of war crimes or crimes against humanity, in state practice there is no exception to the generally recognised immunity of foreign ministers. The dissenting judges' opinions took various forms.

[31] The fundamental international law decision to protect elementary human rights suffices—according to this opinion—to deduce new rules from it. For the dissenters, the concept of *jus cogens* and its asserted higher priority over immunity took central importance, while it played no role in the argumentation of the court. In the opinion of the—constitutionally thinking—minority, a direct connection should be established between the will and interest of single individuals—who thereby become something like 'world citizens'—and international law, bypassing the states, from whose consensus a norm of international law no longer need be derived. But no practicable process of legal recognition can be seen that could directly register the wills of all 6 billion people and the basic values they share despite all cultural differences and from which concrete norms could then be derived.

[32] W. Cremer, 'Entschädigungsklagen wegen schwerer Menschenrechtsverletzungen vor nationalen Zivilgerichtsbarkeit' (2003) 41 *AVR* 137–68; ECtHR in the decision *Al-Adsani v UK* ((2000) *EuGRZ* 403, with comment by Maierhöfer, 391).

[33] Case *Distomo, Corte suprema di Cassazione* (Judgment of 29 May 2008, No 14199), German translation: (2008) *NVwZ* 1100–1. See also IMI-decision (military interned/forced labourer) of the same Court (Order of 29 May 2008, No 14201) (2008) *NVwZ* 1101–2; also E. M. Frenzel and R. Wiedemann, 'Das Vertrauen in die Staatenimmunität und seine Herausforderung' (2008) *NVwZ* 1088–91.

[34] Frenzel and Wiedemann, above n 33; Cremer, above n 32; Dörr, above n 29.

[35] Judgment of the ICJ of 27 June 2001 (*LaGrand—Germany v United States of America*) (2001) *EuGRZ* 287, (2002) 91 *JZ* with comment by C. Hillgruber, 94; K. Oellers-Frahms, 'Die Entscheidung des IGH im Fall LaGrand: Eine Stärkung der internationalen Gerichtsbarkeit und der Rolle des Individuums im Völkerrecht' (2001) *EuGRZ* 265–72. For a comprehensive

This and several parallel cases concerned violations of Article 36 of the Consular Convention of 1963. The USA failed in several cases to report to a consulate of the state of an arrested (and then convicted and executed) foreigner, as stipulated in the Convention. In the LaGrand case, the Federal Republic of Germany obtained an interim decision from the ICJ, although this did not postpone the execution. At the core of the case is the—controversial[36]—reinterpretation of the Convention (which, as a consular convention, was originally intended to protect the states' interests in orderly diplomatic intercourse) into a treaty applicable to third parties and containing subjective rights for affected parties.[37]

5. The *Tadic* judgment, the first ruling of the International Criminal Tribunal for the Former Yugoslavia, sets minimum standards of humanity and justice in civil war.[38] Since what were addressed were crimes in a civil war, this judgment is one of the first instances in which at least some aspects of international law was applied in relation to internal events, and which therefore interfered with the internal affairs of states.[39]

6. An extreme example is so-called humanitarian intervention.[40] At the forefront of this many-layered topic stands the noble and recognised goal of helping people whose human rights are in danger of violation. But ultimately the means of pursuit is military action, which itself necessarily endangers and usually also destroys life. This specialised topic will not be further examined here. But the dilemma is clear: the noble values being pursued do not safeguard against very problematic, namely deadly, interventions and actions resulting from that pursuit.

7. We will mention only in general the innovations and improvements through the *international criminal jurisdiction* before and after the Rome Statute. Here we can note a development with some gradual steps of progress and with great political reservations.

---

account of the facts and the controversial arguments, see B. Grzeszick, 'Rechte des Einzelnen im Völkerrecht: Chancen und Gefahren völkerrechtlicher Entwicklungstrends am Beispiel der Individualrechte im allgemeinen Völkerrecht' (2005) 43 *AVR* 312–44, especially 316 et seq.

[36] See K. Oellers-Frahms, above n 35; B. Simma, 'Eine endlose Geschichte? Art. 36 der Wiener Konsularkonvention in Todesstrafenfällen vor dem IGH und amerikanischen Gerichten', in P.-M. Dupuy (ed), above n 14, 423–48; Hillgruber, above n 35; Grzeszick above n 35.

[37] *Case concerning Avena and Other Mexican Nationals (Mexico v United States of America)*, ICJ Reports 2004, 12 et seq (with comments).

[38] See <http://www.icty/org>, links: *The Cases, Completed Cases, Tadić*. Also J. Menzel, T. Pierling, and J. Hoffmann (eds), *Völkerrechtssprechung: Ausgewählte Entscheidungen zum Völkerrecht in Retrospective* (Tübingen: Mohr Siebeck, 2005), 787, with references at 791.

[39] Thürer, above n 26.

[40] Intervention for humanitarian reasons: Thürer, above n 26; Nettesheim, above n 8; Paulus, above n 20. On the NATO intervention in Yugoslavia, see Thürer, above n 26, at 574 (facts and grounds) and 579 et seq, there clearly stating that an intervention for humanitarian reasons—if at all—can only be justified by means of a new methodological interpretation of the UN-Charter. For the consideration that great innovations are often preceded by such a change of methodology, see below section IV. 8.

8. The *Listing Procedure* carried out by the UN or, more precisely, by a committee of the UN, has brought international law one of its current major cases, namely the proceedings of the cases *Yusuf* and *Kadi*. To combat terrorism, the UN ordered the freezing of all bank accounts of persons registered on a list. The proceedings concern the legality of the listing procedure, with the plaintiffs claiming that they have been wrongly placed on the list. With this instrument of counter-terrorism, the Security Council has adopted a type of legislation. The key question is whether there are legal limits to the Security Council's power to legislate and whether these limits lie solely in *ius cogens* or also in other legal prescriptions. At any rate, this question about the limits placed on the Security Council addresses the constitutional dimension in, and tests the strength of, international law.[41]

IV. CONSTITUTIONAL THOUGHT: AN OVERVIEW

In the following section, the basic ideas of constitutionalist theories will be synthesised, in ideal-typical form, from the rich and highly differentiated literature.[42] At the core of these theories lies the constitutionalisation hypothesis: namely, that international law should not be solely state-centred or consensus-determined.[43] The wills of individual states should not be the standard; rather, an independent layer of fundamental norms should exist above the states.

---

[41] Joined cases C-402/05 P and C-415/05 P *Kadi and Al Barakaat IF v Council of the EU and Commission of the EC* [2008] ECR I-6351, (2009) *Europarecht (EuR)* 80; (2008) *EuGRZ* 480. For commentary, see S. L.-T. Heun-Rehn, 'Die europäische Gemeinschaft und das Völkerrecht nach Kadi und Al Barakaat' (2008) *ELR* 327–38; H. Sauer, 'Rechtsschutz gegen völkerrechtsdeterminiertes Gemeinschaftsrecht?' (2008) *NJW* 3685–8; K. Schmalenbach, 'Bedingt kooperationsbereit: Der Kontrollanspruch des EuGH bei gezielten Sanktionen der Vereinten Nationen' (2009) *JZ* 35–43; J. A. Kämmerer, 'Das Urteil des Europäischen Gerichtshofs im Fall Kadi: Ein Triumph der Rechtsstaatlichkeit?' (2009) *EuR* 114–30; S. Remberg, 'Recht auf Verteidigung und effektiven Rechtsschutz gegen Vermögensbeschlagnahme wegen Terrorismusverdacht durch Ratsbeschluss' (2008) *ERL* 60–7; C. Ohler, 'Gemeinschaftsrechtlicher Rechtsschutz gegen personengerichtete Sanktionen des UN-Sicherheitsrats' (2008) *EuZW* 630–3; C. Tomuschat, 'Die Europäische Union und ihre völkerrechtliche Bindung' (2007) *EuGRZ* 1–12; S. Steinbarth, 'Individualrechtsschutz gegen Maßnahmen der EG zur Bekämpfung des internationalen Terrorismus' (2006) *ZEuS* 269–85; S. Hörmann, 'Völkerrecht bricht Rechtsgemeinschaft? Zu den rechtlichen Folgen einer Umsetzung von Resolutionen des UN-Sicherheitsrates durch die EG' (2006) 44 *Archiv des Völkerrechts (AVR)* 267–327.

[42] For references to the rich German literature, see: Dörr, above n 8; Nettesheim, above n 8; Kadelbach and Kleinlein, above n 21; Thürer, above n 26; Uerpmann, above n 8; Peters, above n 17; de Wet, above n 17. Critically taking different perspectives: A. von Bogdandy, 'Constitutionalism in International Law: Comment on a Proposal from Germany' (2006) 47 *Harvard International Law Journal* 223–42; Haltern, above n 22; C. Hillgruber, 'Dispositives Verfassungsrecht, zwingendes Völkerrecht: Verkehrte juristische Welt?' (2006) 54 *Jahrbuch des Öffentlichen Rechts (JöR)* 57–94.

[43] For a summary of the constitutionalisation hypothesis, see Paulus, above n 20, at 700.

From this basic conviction, constitutionalist developments assume the following internally consistent derivations.

1. If international law is not state-centred, then it requires a new reference point and a new subject. This new subject is the community of states or, more properly termed in the frame of the constitutionalists, the international community. The *international community* is not simply a new concept;[44] it is also the standard-setting concept, the lynchpin. The concept offers an answer not only to new problem situations of global reach, but also to the common interests of (most) states to combat the human rights violations of some states.

2. If the content of international law is no longer to depend on consensus (or be the result of contractual agreement), then it requires substantive anchoring. That is why the new international law is building on and evolves from general values and principles. Recourse to values is of such importance to the writing of constitutionalists that influential essays invariably adopt the corresponding thesis in their titles. Illustrative are: *Der Schutz der Menschenrechte als zentraler Inhalt des völkerrechtlichen Gemeinwohls* (The Protection of Human Rights as Central Content of General Welfare under International Law) and 'The Emergence of International and Regional Value Systems as a Manifestation of the Emerging International Constitutional Order'.[45] It is the highest values that lend some norms the character of *ius cogens*, or compelling law,[46] ie norms that remain binding even if individual states reject their validity.[47] A similarly important role is played by the recourse to common goods, ie global goods, as is found in internation law.

3. The concept of *ius cogens* is a cornerstone of the new thinking and the embodiment of constitutionalisation. *Ius cogens* has its own attraction as a category, although

---

[44] Nettesheim, above n 8, at 569–70, 571 et seq, with comprehensive references to other literature; A. Paulus, *Die internationale Gemeinschaft im Völkerrecht* (Munich: Beck, 2001); Bryde, above n 13, at 107: 'The core of a constitutionalised international law is the general acceptance of a common interest of mankind that transcends the sum of individual interests.'

[45] B. Fassbender, 'Der Schutz der Menschenrechte als zentraler Inhalt des völkerrechtlichen Gemeinwohls' (2003) *EuGRZ* 1–16; id, 'The Meaning of International Constitutional Law', in R. St John Macdonald and D. M. Johnston (eds), above n 10, 837–51, at 838; de Wet, above n 17, at 614; T. Rensmann, 'The Constitution as a Normative Order of Value: The Influence of International Human Rights Law on the Evolution of Modern Constitutionalism', in P.-M. Dupuy (ed), above n 14, 259–78; id, *Wertordnung und Verfassung: Das Grundgesetz im Kontext grenzüberschreitender Konstitutionalisierung* (Tübingen: Mohr Siebeck, 2007); Thürer above n 26.

[46] Regarding *ius cogens* see Stefan Kadelbach, *Zwingendes Völkerrecht* (Berlin: Duncker und Humblot, 1993); Kadelbach and Kleinlein, above n 21, at 235, 251 et seq; J. A. Frowein, 'Die Verpflichtungen erga omnes im Völkerrecht und ihre Durchsetzung', in R. Bernhardt (ed), *Völkerrecht als Rechtsordnung, internationale Gerichtsbarkeit, Menschenrechte: Festschrift für Hermann Mosler* (Berlin: Springer, 1983), 241–62; id, 'Jus cogens' (1997) 3 *Encyclopedia of Public Law* 65–9; C. Tomuschat and J.-M. Thouvenin (eds), *The Fundamental Rules of the International Legal Order: 'Jus Cogens' and Obligations 'Erga Omnes'* (Leiden: Nijhoff, 2006).

[47] The central problem of whether the imagined values are really universal or not is hardly mentioned and even less solved by argumentative means.

its area of application is small. It is impossible to overlook the great discrepancy between the theoretical esteem for *ius cogens* and its very low relevance in the practice of international law.[48] Nevertheless, conceptualisations of hierarchies of norms and the deduction from abstract values are very popular among constitutionalists.[49]

4. If international law is not to remain formal law, then it must become substantive law. Logically, a *materialisation* of international law is required.[50]

5. If international law is not to exhaust itself in legal positivism, then the new international law relies on *ethical foundations*. The idea of justice is characterised as the power of change.[51] Accordingly, it is said that international law must orientate itself more towards human values and the value and meaning of justice. In this sense, international law adopts principles of morals and integrates legal philosophy.[52]

6. In advanced versions, the state is grasped as a member and the *states as members of the international community*. The states are responsible for the realisation of worldwide general interests. They are declared organs of the international community and thereby take on a serving role in the realisation of superordinated purposes. The state is viewed as part of the community of states, and the community has primacy.

7. If the states are not the final purpose of the law and also not of international law, then it is consistent that, as in every other law, also in international law the *individual person* is understood as the final purpose. The world population is the legitimate reference point of international law and at the same time the rights of the individual do not form an exception, but become a normal component of international law. The 'individual in international law' becomes a privileged theme and an essential pillar of a constitutionally orientated international law. It is therefore stated with much pathos: all law serves the human being. International law, too, must serve the human being and must not be merely law among states. International

---

[48] For the related concept of obligations *erga omnes*, see B.-O. Bryde, 'Verpflichtungen Erga Omnes aus Menschenrechten', in W. Kälin (ed), *Aktuelle Probleme des Menschenrechtsschutzes* (Heidelberg: Müller, 1994), 165–90; Tomuschat and Thouvenin, above n 46; D. Schindler, 'Die erga-omnes-Wirkung des humanitären Völkerrechts', in U. Beyerlin (ed), *Recht zwischen Umbruch und Bewahrung: Festschrift für Rudolf Bernhardt* (Berlin: Springer, 1995), 199–212.

[49] Erika de Wet reports about the VICI-project of the Netherlands Organisation for Science Research (*NWO*): 'The Emerging International Constitutional Order: The Implications of Hierarchy in International Law for the Coherence and Legitimacy of International Decision-making' (2007) 67 ZaöRV 777–98.

[50] Explicitly Nettesheim, above n 8, at 571, with several relativisations of this demand.

[51] Thürer, above n 26.

[52] Ibid 581, regarding the acceptance of intervention for humanitarian reasons: 'Therefore one has to consider whether the accent lies on the text of the Charter or the spirit and meaning of the modern constitutional order. As with national constitutional law, the question is if and to what extent the constitutional law can be interpreted in an evolutionary and goal orientated manner, in the sense of an optimal realization of basic human values and whether the providers of the constitutional order can acquire implied powers.' It is questionable whether the Kosovo-case could be the starting point and catalyst of an advancement of international customary law (581–2).

law does not serve the states; the states serve international law. This proclaims an anthropocentric turn in international law.[53] At the same time, a harmony between national, European, and international law results on the basis of this unified individualistic orientation.

8. From the standpoint of scholarship, each great change in law begins with a change in method of interpretation, with the creation and prevalence of a new preconception. If state-centredness is abandoned, then the will of states can no longer be the sole standard for interpreting contracts. The objective method of interpretation necessarily moves into the foreground as something new, whereas international law was traditionally the domain of the subjective method.[54] This is easily explained. If the subjective method had the specific function of not obligating states, as masters of contracts, to more than what they agreed to consciously and explicitly in the contracts, then it suggests itself that a conception that builds a layer of principles and guidelines superseding the states must make itself independent of the will of the states by means of objective interpretation. The methodology is pivotal, and those who are able to make a new method prevail can claim to have gained decisive legal-political ground.

V.   CRITIQUE

If we move from the ideal-typical description of constitutionalist theories to critique, then at the outset there is considerable agreement on the nature of the changes taking place in the international field and its law, changes that are paralleled in the equally great 'transformative change' affecting states.[55] There can be no doubt about the persistent nature of the changes taking place in the international realm and affecting international law. The crucial question is whether this change is so great and so uniform that it can be characterised as amounting to a constitutional turn. In order to answer this, it is necessary to examine normative assumptions and political content of the constitutional claim.

---

[53]   For the relation between international law and the individual, see P. Häberle, 'Nationales Verfassungsrecht, regionale "Staatenverbünde" und das Völkerrecht als universales Menschenrecht: Konvergenzen und Divergenzen', in C. Gaitanides (ed), *Europa und seine Verfassung: Festschrift für Manfred Zuleeg* (Baden-Baden: Nomos, 2005), 80–91; P. Kunig, 'Das Völkerrecht und die Interessen der Bevölkerung', in P.-M. Dupuy (ed), above n 14, 377–88.

[54]   Thürer, above n 26; Nettesheim, above n 8; M. Herdegen, 'Das "konstruktive Völkerrecht" und seine Grenzen: Die Dynamik des Völkerrechts als Methodenfrage', in P.-M. Dupuy (ed), above n 14, 898–911.

[55]   The expression 'transformations of the state' is the central expression of the project in Bremen: see S. Leibried and M. Zürn (ed), *Transformation des Staates* (Frankfurt: Suhrkamp, 2006). It is fitting because it avoids the 'from—to'. If something undergoes a transformation the perpetuation of former decisions continues to resonate, and the process cannot be easily and pithily be put into a 'from—to' formula.

Normativism

What is immediately—and negatively—conspicuous is the purely normative approach of the advocates. It is, of course, not inaccurate to understand law as a demand for what ought to be. But what is disconcerting is that there should be no non-normative prerequisites or effectiveness prerequisites for this normativity, at any rate, none is discussed. The theory of international constitutionalism and of the values and value systems postulated by constitutionalism does not and cannot name the institutions and processes that could serve as paths to their realisation. The constitutionalist theories postulate a pure normativity and pure values; they thereby claim validity in, of all places, the international world, a field characterised by power relations and conflicts of interest.[56] But an overarching fundamental order of primacy, which is a particular interest of these theories, does not come for free, but only through the fulfilment of important prerequisites.

It might be noted, by way of comparison, that the primacy of state constitutional law could not and cannot be taken for granted or be implemented in reality simply by edict. The material primacy of the constitution develops with and through the institution of constitutional jurisdiction. The German constitutions since the beginning of the nineteenth century differ from today's fundamentally in that the former, without constitutional jurisdiction, were only semi-effective constitutions that were raised to the level achieved today only after 1949 with the victory of the Federal Constitutional Court. The values found today in the basic rights of Germany's constitutional document, the *Grundgesetz* or Basic Law, and in other constitutions were already formulated and present in the philosophical and political–theoretical literature of the eighteenth century. But that was far from giving them legal effectiveness, even after the promulgation of the first constitutions.

Only when the values postulated in the literature were first adopted in the texts of the constitutions (and concretised there), and much later gained institutional anchoring and a venue for realisation with the institution of constitutional jurisdiction, could the development of what today is the standard for a constitutional norm begin: namely, fundamental content, substantive primacy, and procedures for implementation. An order of primacy that actually stands the test of reality does not arise solely within a normative cocoon. More is needed, namely the overall constellation of a constitutional state and in the history of constitutionalism, the path to this was (with the exception of the United States) very long.

The politically emptied concept of the constitution

The transposition, within the literature, of the concept of the constitution from the states to the European and international levels usually suffers from a narrow, politically emptied, under-complex, and diluted version of the concept of the state

---

[56] Paulus, above n 20, at 703: 'Eine Völkerrechtswissenschaft, die sich auf die bloße Normativität zurückzieht, vergisst, dass jedes Sein-Sollen eben doch ein Mindestmaß an Verwirklichungsmöglichkeit impliziert, um Autorität zu beanspruchen' ('A science of public international law which restricts itself to mere normativity overlooks the fact that, in order to claim authority, every ought implies at least a minimal chance of its realisation').

constitution.[57] This concept says the constitution is the highest norm, it has primacy, it politically organises fundamentals, and it expresses the relationship between political rule and the citizens. But the concept does not address the question of why this highest norm possesses the power to shape political–social life, why the nation and the individual should recognise it, and why this recognition confers on it the possibility of being effective.

The question of the transferability of the concept of the constitution 'beyond the state' takes on its necessary depth and its full seriousness only when one begins with what took shape as a constitution in the history of the state. The challenge is not that of offering a (new) definition of constitution as the supreme component of the legal order. In the course of the last two centuries, constitutions were striven for not only by jurists for legal use; they were also the object of intense and passionate political strivings. Numerous political movements worked for the enactment of a constitution: it was struggled for, politically and frequently with revolutions. Every overcoming of a dictatorship is sealed with the enactment of a constitution: in Germany in 1949, in Spain, Portugal, and Greece and in all transition states after 1989. Those who fought for a constitution knew why they did so. These movements were borne by important segments of the nation—in short, constitutions were and are parts of political–social movements and real political forces stood and stand behind them.

These forces were effective and important not only during the process of establishing a constitution. Citizens continue to support the constitution with their recognition and acceptance; the citizens' expectations of freedom are orientated towards the constitution. It is this esteem that gives the constitution its real power, a power that the norms of the constitution need if they are to have the effect that was previously improbable, namely to fetter the strongest institutions of political power and to eliminate unconstitutional action.

The complex constitutional-state constellation

This outline makes it clear that 'constitution' in the state is not only the highest norm but that 'constitution' is also an overall constellation of legal effects and qualities, of political hopes, of acceptance from 'below', and of real forces in political life. In Germany, constitutional court rulings are to a great degree 'carried' (*getragen*) by the citizens; this is precisely what gives the court its weight. All in all, one can speak of a complex, multifaceted *constitutional-state constellation*. It consists of a combination of

- principles;
- the formulation of general values in constitutional-law norms, ie the transposition of state philosophy into law in general;

---

[57] Ultimately, the same is true for the influential opinion of Christian Walter about the *constitutional functions* which are bundled at the state and are unbundled beyond the state (C. Walter, 'Die Folgen der Globalisierung für die europäische Verfassungsdiskussion' (2000) *Deutsches Verwaltungsblatt* (DVBl) 1–13; id, above n 24).

- the formation of institutions, whose importance cannot be overestimated. This begins with the establishment of representative parliaments that maintain an internal connection between democracy and the principle of the rule of law and it finds its high point during the twentieth century with the worldwide spread of constitutional jurisdiction;
- a shift in mentality among the rulers from a power orientation to a legal orientation;
- an equally necessary shift in mentality among subjects to the mentality of citizens and possessors of basic rights; and
- the anchoring of the idea of the constitution among the players in the political sphere and also among individuals.

What is termed the constitutional-state constellation here is called 'law in context' in parts of the scholarly literature.[58] It expresses the conviction that the constitutional question does not only concern the legal quality of the norms of constitutional law; the field is much broader.

In light of these considerations, the general discussion whether the concept of the constitution can be detached from the state takes on a new accent.[59] As is well known, the constitutionalists vehemently advocate such a detachment. For such advocates, the basic problem seems solved if this tie is broken and a concept of constitution—in some ways changed—is applied to the two other levels. But behind this connection between constitution and state stands not only an understanding of a concept; the complex concept of 'constitution' refers to and is in reality carried by the aforementioned constitutional-state constellation. More—and something more important—is required if the concept of constitution is to work on the European and international level. The objective here is not to register a copyright or trademark for the term 'constitution'. But the transposition is plausible and adequate for the actual problem only if something substantively comparable to the aforementioned constitutional-state constellation is present on the two other levels. This remains a matter of dispute.

The essential point is to avoid a technocratic or diminished concept of the constitution, a rump concept. That is why the complexity of the traditional legal–political idea of the constitution in the state is underscored. The constitutionalist interpretation in international law bears the burden of proof that a similar constellation of legal and political components stands behind its concepts. This new constellation need not be exactly the constitutional-state constellation, but it does have to be a constellation that combines the normative and the political, values and institutions,

---

[58] Haltern, above n 22.

[59] From the comprehensive discussion shall here be cited only: E. de Wet, 'The International Constitutional Order' (2006) 55 *International and Comparative Law Quarterly* 51–76.
Traditionally the term 'constitution' was reserved for domestic constitutions. Most municipal constitutions today provide a legal framework for the political life of a community for an indefinite time. They present a complex of fundamental norms governing the organisation and performance of governmental function in a given state and the relationship between state authorities and citizens. This is a rather abstract definition.

and that is politically supported by some kind of 'community'. In regard to the latter, the normative construct of an international community probably does not suffice; rather, in some way or other, a real, perceptible, and acting connection must exist between persons.[60]

With respect to the overall constellation, it is evident that on the international level there has been

- great progress made in terms of principles, values, and concepts;
- much less progress in terms of political buttressing: the international order and international law do not reach people nearly as much as state law does; and
- minimal progress in institutionalisation.

A similar critique is levelled against the neglect of the political processes that finally buttress the acceptance of the constitution. In a state, the constitution is a layer of norms within a political unit in which the fundamental adherence to the norms results from the individual's relationship of belonging to this state as a citizen. This resource, too, is not available in this way on the international level. If it is characteristic of state and constitutional law that the political realm must be addressed, then this is even more true for international law. It is surprising that the constitutionalist interpretation of the understanding of 'international law' is narrowly limited to texts and values, constructions and theories, and this in a time when the study of history, for example, is undergoing a thorough cultural turn, in which it grasps rule and the exercise of rule comprehensively and in which it explicitly regards documents and texts as insufficient for the purpose of understanding the complex phenomena of political rule and allegiance. Substantially contributing to this narrowing are system-theoretical theories with their painful abstractions and avoidance of analysis of actual processes.

The constitutionalist viewpoint is holistic. Drawing on the concept of the constitution as the entire basic order of a political unit, it seeks to capture the rapidly developing international field and its international law in one great formula. This grand endeavour has failed and cannot currently succeed. An important reason for this is the high degree of differentiation among the individual sectors, regimes, or contractual orders of international law. To postulate grand formulas or mere value orders first and only then to begin a detailed analysis of all these areas, sectors, and partial orders is to take the third or fourth step before the first. There is good reason why the theme of fragmentation

---

[60] A. von Bogdandy, 'Konstitutionalisierung des europäischen öffentlichen Rechts in der europäischen Republik' (2005) *JZ* 529–40, n 9: 'Dass eine Konstitutionalisierung ohne einen entsprechenden politischen Willen zum Zusammenschluss nicht gelingt, zeigt die vorerst gescheiterte Konstitution eines globalen Völkerrechts.' ('Constitutionalisation cannot succeed without a corresponding political will for unification; this is demonstrated by the fact that for the present the constitution of a global public law has failed.')

has become a major theme.[61] It has also become a counter-concept to constitutionalism and to constitutionalisation, if only because the high degree of differentiation and the internal complexity of the international level that it reveals and takes as fundamental, is incompatible with the unified world and the holistic approach of constitutionalism.

VI. THE STATE OF THE ART

The concept of the constitution on the European level

On the European level, which from the beginning seemed predestined to take up the idea of the constitution, a major learning process has taken place. Even if the Lisbon Treaty should take effect, neither its wording, nor its substance, nor its symbols fulfil the hopes that were originally placed in the European constitutional treaty. The question arises: What did the political movement in favour of a European constitution originally intend?

The movement initially advanced suggestions from the jurisprudence, including the characterisations of the European Court of Justice.[62] But the aim of the constitutional treaty was also to accelerate the course of integration, by reforming the machinery of government on the European level after the accession of so many new states and generally advancing the political integration that was always also to be pursued along with the initial path of economic integration. The constitution discussion was an offer to enhance *political* integration by using the highly esteemed term of 'constitution', by revising the understated language of the earlier treaties,[63] and by equipping the Union with the symbols of a flag and an anthem. Thus far, the constitution project began properly. It did not relate solely to the legal sphere; rather, the intent was to strengthen the political basis, the political infrastructure of the EU, so to speak, and above all to increase the citizens' acceptance of, and attachment to, the EU.

The initiators of the European constitution project wanted a constitution for the individuals and the nations in Europe in the full sense of a combination of the legal and the political. The individuals were to identify more with the EU, feeling an attachment to it similar to the attachment they felt and still feel for their (nation) state. The problem, however, was that one can make offers for more attachment and identification, but the success of this depends on whether the citizens also want to take this qualitative step onto a new level of integration. At any rate, two nations, the French and the Dutch, apparently did not want to accept this offer. And thus the

---

[61] For further references, see A. L. Paulus, 'Subsidiarity, Fragmentation and Democracy: Towards the Demise of General International Law?', in T. Broude and Y. Shany (eds), *The Shifting Allocation of Authority in International Law* (Oxford: Oxford University Press, 2008), 193–213.

[62] Beginning with the Opinion delivered by Advocate-General Lagrange of 25 June 1964 concerning the ECJ, Case 6/64 *Costa v ENEL* [1964] ECR 1279, at 1289; Case 294/83 *Les Verts v European Parliament* [1986] ECR 1357, at 1365, para 23: 'charte constitutionelle de base qu'est le traité'.

[63] In the first decades, the Treaty establishing the European Community consciously avoided the terms 'constitution' and 'laws'.

fate of the constitutional treaty illustrates the point that the theoretical concepts of academicians and the slogans of politicians and EU elites do not suffice. The individuals themselves have to decide whether to accept the offer of increased integration.

Thus, political processes and political movements in favour of European integration are necessary,[64] but texts that academicians claim resemble the character of constitutions are not enough. In formulating the constitutional package, the politicians rightly assumed that the legal order of primacy and the legal design as a whole are insufficient and that symbols and words play important roles. But this insight is also useless so long as the nations of Europe, or some of them that are permitted to express themselves, have not boarded the train of increased integration.

Consequently, in a long process on a winding path that lasted almost ten years, the great—even decisive—political question of a European constitution was answered—in a negative fashion. A European constitution worthy of the name must also connect the legal and the political. The mere order of primacy, the creation of fundamental and overriding norms is not enough. A constitution cannot successfully be instituted while ignoring the people and the nations. An explicit constitution-formulating convention, which has occasionally been held in the history of the constitutional state, is not always necessary. But the emergence of a constitution involves more than the drafting of a mere legal document: there must be a secured site for the nations and the individuals, where these are recognised to be the bearers (*Träger*) of the constitutional process. If this does not exist, then the intrastate referendums on the treaty become referendums on Europe's path as a whole. Whether the concept of the constitution can be detached from the state is ultimately a secondary and superficial conflict. Of course it can—provided something is offered that is comparable to the concept of the constitution.

The constitutional concept at the international level

The constitutional project is even more problematic at the international level.[65] Whereas in the EU there is a certain acceptance of some form of European integration and a corresponding feeling of community and belonging,[66] in the international

---

[64] Here, the possibility of developing a stronger feeling of pan-European identity among the nations is in no way denied or assumed to be unlikely. But such a development must not be simply postulated, it must actually occur. This is a strategic point where actual events and normative claim are inseparably tied and mutually dependent, just as empirical and normative sciences depend on each other in this point.

[65] Wahl, above n 17, 135–54.

[66] In the text, the wish for integration and the feeling of belonging has been consciously relativised. Thinking and languages have to do justice to a problem that has been mostly neglected. In regard to integration or the feeling of belonging to the EU, the issue is not yes or no, but degrees. Since 1958, the respective members of the EC or EU have had a *limited* feeling of belonging (expression taken from Gertrude Lübbe-Wolff). The point is always the degree of feeling of belonging; in the prehistory of the constitutional contract, one strives for a higher degree of feeling of belonging.

sphere, all the characteristics associated with community and a political structure are absent. In a number of circumstances, 'international community' is a meaningful term which expresses the fact that, beyond the consensus of all states, in certain—albeit very few—problem situations there exists a value relation distinct from that created by state consent. But there is no international community in the strong sense of the term as an entity capable of acting or of legitimising action. And the notion of having democratically elected delegates representing such an international community, in some world forum, is entirely utopian.

From the outset, the use of the term 'constitution' in this context invokes a legal concept of constitution, a mere order of primacy of legal norms. The establishment of fundamental values and the hope that courts (initially national courts, then perhaps international ones) will implement these values directly in positive law are not unjustified. But all prerequisites for the strong variant of constitutionalism are lacking. Overwhelmingly, the opinion is voiced that the UN Charter is not the world's constitution; it is accepted that its work in its own sphere is important, but its responsibilities are far from covering all sectors of international politics. The attempt to extend the UN Charter and to define it as the core of a future substantive world constitution was problematic from the beginning and, at any rate, has failed.[67]

But the weak variant, the assertion of a progressing constitutionalisation, also meets doubts and misgivings. The constitutional idea in general international law, conceived as the one great peg (*Klammer*) on which to hang many individual arrangements and which could function as an order of primacy for treaties and customary law, has—to summarise almost ten years of discussion—not succeeded. The project failed because of its sweeping ambition in seeking to transpose itself as the juristic mark (*Kennzeichen*) of *ius cogens*, and promoting the validity of a series of other concepts (common goods, common interest, and the like[68]), independently of the current consensus of the states. The concept of the constitution was to serve as the means of transport, but this interest hardly extended beyond the constitution's claim to hierarchical superiority.

In general, what has not progressed during the last ten years is the meshing of individual components into a coherent concept that, with the name 'constitution', recalls similar syntheses and integration achievements in state constitutions. Instead, the difficulties of such an idea have clearly emerged. As for German and European voices in particular, they have often transposed the earlier, positively evaluated experience with the project of a European constitutional treaty to the international level. The European discussion was to serve as a door opener for the international discussion.[69] It is therefore not surprising that the constitutionalist interpretation was

---

[67] Paulus, above n 20, at 699; Fassbender, above n 45, 1–16, nn 5, 15.

[68] In the same way, the figure of the world order treaties must not only be generally described, but also formed in detail. In the German tradition, one says it must be doctrinally or dogmatically elaborated, which means a great deal of work.

[69] F. C. Mayer, 'European Law as a Door Opener for Public International Law', in J.-M. Thouvenin and C. Tomuschat (ed), *Droit international et diversite des cultures juridiques—International Law and Diversity of Legal Cultures* (Paris: Pedone, 2008), 345–59.

even less successful on the international level. As a consequence, we should eschew for the foreseeable future the comprehensive approach of international constitutionalism. And, for reasons of scientific clarity, we should also avoid usage of the term 'constitution'.[70] Further steps of progress in international law will take place on a more concrete level in individual sectors and in patient analyses, as is taking place in the project on Global Administrative Law. Only a problem-saturated and practically-oriented international law can once again take the path of abstraction—but in a much more reflective mode.

The concept of societal constitutionalism

The defence of the term 'constitution' is mounted in particular against the thesis of 'societal constitutionalism'.[71] Insightful observations and analyses, including much that is innovative and worth considering, are presented under this name. But the use of the word 'constitution' is not understandable. As the name suggests, the lynchpin of this approach is society or segments of society (societal constitutions). This revives and gives a new content to the old European concept of civil society, although now the plural, civil constitutions, is used.

The thesis assumes these civil constitutions exist independently of state boundaries and state politics and that, in accordance with their respective inner character, they act in a worldwide association. In the context of a systems theory that becomes ever more abstract, these regimes, being such civil constitutions, are based solely on societal factors. The character of a constitution should be acknowledged for these regimes because they have developed fundamental rules into a higher-ranking order. The order of primacy, the set of rules on rules, is interesting. But the constitution is emptied of everything political, everything that otherwise characterises constitutions. With great pathos, the theory addresses the individual person, but what it has in view is individuals solely as societal beings; every political connection to and every participation in a political unit is removed. The individual is conceived as a subjective individual who is supposed to have rights and duties. But nothing is said about the individual as a political being, as *citoyen*. What the American and French Revolutions launched—the combination of political freedom and the individual's political participation alongside the protections of the rule of law—has no place in these concepts.

---

[70] Let us recall once more the fate of the European constitutional treaty. Back then, in their double role as scientific observers and legal policy shapers, numerous scholars of Europe used powerful rhetoric to defend the concept and the constitution and saw major progress in transposing concepts and terms from their narrow nation-state application to the European level. In their often very powerful will to help shape politics, which always also endangers scholarship, they used the concept of the constitution to help bring citizens over hurdles to a deepened union. With the concept of the constitution, citizens were to advance to the next step of integration. The intentional and also instrumentalised use of the concept of the constitution was of no avail here, but was rather a component of the failure. It is not difficult to predict the same for the international level.

[71] See above n 6 and, critically, Grimm, 'Gesellschaftlicher Konstitutionalismus', above n 3.

Societal constitutionalism is the furthest away from the originally rich and comprehensive constellation of the constitution; of all conceptions it offers the least in the way of a comparable transposition of this overall constellation into present-day circumstances. The use of the terms 'societal constitutions' and 'regimes', in Sciulli's and Teubner's sense, is based on a great number of premises that cannot all be discussed here. But it is clear that the theory of societal constitutions has demanding and strong presuppositions. It presupposes the self-development of societal systems that apparently function mostly without addressing any form of public and sovereign tasks.

Beyond that, the theory is characterised by a number of absences: no politics takes place in it, there is no parliament as legislature, no politically accountable legislation, no public law, no constitutional law, no sovereign one-sided relationships. It is difficult to imagine that the pure civil society it imagines can be made a reality. The theory cannot entirely ignore political steering, but it is hard to judge what type, by means of laws or treaties under international law, is silently assumed. But this issue is not explicitly discussed.

The proponents of societal constitutionalism enjoy discovering the new so much that they have no attention left for already existing achievements. Overall, this literature lacks a basic acceptance of a figure of simultaneity, namely, that along with all the newness one sees or hopes to have in the future, much that is old retains great importance and may even be the indispensable prerequisite for the new. This is a fundamental objection. The decisive problems of the present and the future not only concern speculation on which completely new situation the current constellation will develop into; the decisive problems lie in the description of the *simultaneity* of different phases, different components, different principles—of the state, the EU, and international subjects, and of state, European, and international law. The overall constellation of all levels, all layers of law, and all public tasks that must be managed, must be kept in focus.

VII. CONCLUSION

The term 'constitution' is a demanding concept which can be understood only as an overall constellation of numerous components. The narrowing in the literature is based primarily in the narrowing and political emptying of the concept. The objective of this chapter has not been to place 'constitution' under trademark protection, nor to protect the term as an exclusive characteristic of state constitutions. To be defended are the comprehensive and complex components of the concept of the constitution: the diversity of its preconditions, its institutional formations, and the developed mechanisms of its realisation. 'Constitution' is also to be defended against the many who want to exploit the noble aura of the term without first achieving the necessary prerequisites. But so much of what is meant by 'international constitution', 'international constitutionalism', and 'constitutionalisation' is mere anticipation, distant hope, contourless 'emergence', and the invocation of evolution.

This, however, is not the last word. It may be true that the constitutionalist approach to international law has reached its zenith, and it might well have failed. Yet it cannot be ignored that the discussion has offered much insight into the need to use supranationally founded ideas in international law. To gather in the harvest is a worthwhile continuation of this discussion. Obligations arising for states without or against their will exist, be it *ius cogens* or obligations *erga omnes*. And the phenomena which fall under the heading of societal constitutionalism are important enough to be analysed further and in conjunction with the related sovereign or public law figures or elements. But important though these elements are, they do not provide the foundation for a totally new construction of international law. Rather, they are elements added to the existing and changing building of international law. If a constitutionalist approach beyond the state needs a new start, then, this has to be more modest and must engage with other fields of discussion, such as the frag-mentation of international law, the emergence of global administrative law, and the emergence of sectoral international law. International law has many manifestations and a considerable dynamic: it cannot be apprehended or newly conceived solely by deduction and abstraction.

PART V

GLOBAL ADMINISTRATIVE LAW: A VIABLE SUBSTITUTE?

❦ 12 ❦

Global Administrative Law and
the Constitutional Ambition

Nico Krisch[*]

I. INTRODUCTION

As the political and the state have become ever more incongruent and public power has moved beyond national governments into a plurality of international and transnational sites, we are struggling to find the analytical and normative instruments to come to terms with the resulting new order. Countless structuring proposals compete, leaving us with the sensation of a 'disorder of orders';[1] in some ways, we do indeed seem to operate in a 'twilight' in which our vision has become blurred and orientation difficult. This twilight signals the demise of the state-centric, 'Westphalian' order that frames modern constitutional and political theory. But it is less clear which of our substantive political commitments we may be able (or want) to usher into the new daylight.

Some of the commitments in question are closely associated with key elements of domestic legal and political orders, and it is on two such elements I will focus: consti-tutionalism and administrative law. Both have sparked efforts at translation to the postnational or global levels, and they have increasingly come to be seen as compet-ing approaches not only to the study, but also the construction, of the postnational space. I am unsure that 'competition' or talk of 'potential substitutes' (as the editors suggest) accurately describe the relationship of global constitutionalism and global administrative law; too different are the two projects in their scope and aims and too complementary could they eventually turn out to be. But there may indeed be good reason for pursuing one project rather than the other at this point: it is especially the *type* of project global administrative law represents—of a smaller scale, with a more modest reach—that might make it more suitable for academic study and political reform than constitutionalist approaches with their holistic vision.

[*] I am grateful to Euan MacDonald and Julia Black for comments on an earlier draft.

[1] N. Walker, 'Beyond Boundary Disputes and Basic Grids: Mapping the Global Disorder of Normative Orders' (2008) 6 *International Journal of Constitutional Law* 373–96.

The argument in this chapter proceeds in four stages. After sketching the challenge both global constitutionalism and global administrative law face in the precarious legitimacy of transnational and global governance (II), I will examine more closely the scope and aims of both projects. It is in their respective ambitions that the key difference between the two lies: constitutionalist visions set out to describe and develop a fully justified global order (III), while global administrative law approaches are more limited in scope, focusing on particular elements of global governance and confining themselves to the analysis and realisation of narrower political ideals, especially accountability (IV). Such a limited approach does, however, raise serious problems, both on the practical and the normative level. I focus here only on two sets of issues: the difficulty in separating 'administrative' from 'constitutional' issues (V) and the risk of legitimising illegitimate institutions, in part by elevating them to the level of law (VI). Although the resulting challenge for global administrative law is serious and will condition the further trajectory of the project, it should not distract from the significant advantages its more limited ambition entails.

II. THE PRECARIOUS LEGITIMACY OF GLOBAL GOVERNANCE

Both global constitutionalism and global administrative law are, in their different ways, attempts at tackling the perceived legitimacy deficit of global governance. With the relocation of public power to the global level, legitimacy standards for transnational institutions have come to approximate more closely those we apply to domestic governments, and seen in this light, most transnational institutions fail badly—be it the UN Security Council with its unrepresentative membership and secretive decision making, the World Bank with its unfairly weighted voting, or the Codex Alimentarius Commission with its skewed procedures for reaching decisions. None of them seems to satisfy democratic principles even remotely, legality appears as at most a weak factor in decision making, and rights play only a marginal role. Yet some argue that the full application of domestic standards of legitimacy is mistaken, or at best premature, as the problems raised by global institutions are of a different kind to those we face in domestic politics and that they can largely be addressed through the channels of domestic constitutional orders, thus obviating (or at least alleviating) the need to develop new global frameworks.[2] Before assessing the respective potential of global constitutionalism and global administrative law, we should therefore gain a clearer picture of the extent and form of the challenge global governance presents.

---

[2] A. Moravcsik, 'Is there a "Democratic Deficit" in World Politics? A Framework for Analysis' (2004) 39 *Government & Opposition* 336–63.

Domestic constitutionalism and its limits

The classical way of legitimising international institutions is based on the delegatory relationship with member states: the powers of these institutions derive from member states through their constitutive treaties; they are accountable to member states through the central representative body within the institution; and member states can control the ultimate effect of institutional decisions through domestic implementation. In this picture, the legitimacy concerns outlined above are of little weight, since whatever substantive problems international institutions raise will be dealt with through the channel of member states, and the central site for controlling transnational governance would be domestic constitutional settings.[3]

However, constructing the accountability of global governance around delegation and control—and thus addressing legitimacy issues through the prism of *domestic* constitutionalism—bears only limited promise. This is, first, because the initial delegation of powers is usually very thin: the founding treaties of international institutions generally contain only vague guidance as regards the scope of powers, especially informal powers,[4] and even this limited determination disappears when it comes to transnational government networks which typically operate without a formal basis altogether.[5] Moreover, delegation is entirely absent as regards outsiders (non-members) that may be affected by decisions,[6] or in the case of private regulators. The latter do not depend on any form of delegation but, even when they cooperate with governments, are typically self-appointed.[7] Because of the need for flexibility in those institutions and the difficulty of creating and speedily adapting treaty mandates, more extensive formal bases and greater specificity will usually be hard to achieve.

---

[3] In this vein, see, eg E. Schmidt-Aßmann, 'Die Herausforderung der Ver-wal-tungs-rechts-wissen-schaft durch die Internationalisierung der Ver-wal-tungs-be-zie-hun-gen' (2006) 45 *Der Staat* 315–38 (English: 'The Internationalization of Administrative Relations as a Challenge for Administrative Law Scholarship' (2008) 9 *German Law Journal* 2061–80).

[4] For example, the Organisation for Economic Co-operation and Development's (OECD) founding treaty defines as the organisation's main goal 'to promote policies … to achieve the highest sustainable economic growth and employment and a rising standard of living in Member countries'; and the OECD's organs are granted the power 'to take decisions … [and] make recommendations' 'to achieve its aims' (see Arts 1 and 5 OECD Convention). On the additional uncertainties surrounding the interpretation of powers of international institutions, see J. Klabbers, *An Introduction to International Institutional Law* (Cambridge: Cambridge University Press, 2002), 60–81.

[5] See A.-M. Slaughter, *A New World Order* (Princeton, NJ: Princeton University Press, 2004).

[6] The Basel Committee for Banking Supervision, for example, consists of only eleven members but its decisions are designed to apply far beyond this circle (see M. S. Barr and G. P. Miller, 'Global Administrative Law: The View from Basel' (2006) 17 *European Journal of International Law* 15–46, at 39–41).

[7] On the example of forestry regulation, see E. Meidinger, 'The Administrative Law of Global Private-Public Regulation: The Case of Forestry' (2006) 17 *European Journal of International Law* 47–87.

Moreover, the level of control each member state can exercise over an international institution will usually be very low. This is in part because of the problem of multiple, diverse principals: delegation structures are relatively unproblematic and may allow for meaningful degrees of control and accountability if there is only one principal (or few principals), as is typically the case in domestic settings where central governments or parliaments delegate power to lower levels or independent institutions. The situation becomes more problematic when the number of principals increases: each of them can then retain only a smaller fraction of control, and mechanisms for holding agents to account become more cumbersome.[8] Greater control would only flow from veto rights, but these would risk stalemate in any institution with a significant number of members.

A more promising avenue for domestic control might then be the implementation of international decisions. Whether binding or non-binding, most norms and decisions in global governance depend on domestic implementation for their actual effectiveness; global regulatory action is typically not followed by its ultimate addressees (state officials, individuals, companies) unless it becomes part of the domestic legal and regulatory framework. In the classical vision of international law, this opens up space for states' sovereign choices as to their domestic policies—even if such choices contradict international rules, they remain decisive in the domestic realm (even though they might entail responsibility on the international level). This in turn allows domestic constitutionalism to take centre stage, by determining when and how international norms can enter domestic law, and by defining the substantive limits and procedural conditions for the engagement with the international sphere.[9] For this to be an effective tool of national control, however, it has to operate in a relatively permissive environment: if non-implementation is to remain a real (rather than merely formal) option, it must not be overly costly. In classical international law, this was certainly the case, as non-compliance even with binding rules was rarely subject to meaningful sanctions. Yet today, enforcement has gained teeth in many areas of global governance. If refusing compliance with WTO rules exposes a country to trade sanctions that cost millions, sometimes hundreds of millions, of dollars, it presents a conceivable option for only very few actors.[10] Well beyond that, where international standards help solve coordination games in global markets,

---

[8] On international institutions, see A. P. Cortell and S. Peterson, 'Dutiful Agents, Rogue Actors, or Both? Staffing, Voting, Rules and Slack in the WHO and WTO', in D. G. Hawkins et al (eds), *Delegation and Agency in International Organizations* (Cambridge: Cambridge University Press, 2006), 255–80; D. A. Lake and M. D. McCubbins, 'The Logic of Delegation to International Organizations', in Hawkins et al, ibid, 341–68, at 361–7.

[9] This is certainly the ambition of some constitutional courts: see, eg *Bun-des-ver-fas-sungs-ge-richt*, Judgments of 12 October 1993, Maastricht, BVerfGE 89, 155; 14 October 2004, *Görgülü*, BVerfGE 111, 307. See also M. Kumm, 'Constitutional Democracy Encounters International Law: Terms of Engagement', in S. Choudhry, *The Migration of Constitutional Ideas* (Cambridge: Cambridge University Press, 2007), 256–93.

[10] See, eg the *EC-Beef Hormones* case in the WTO and the ensuing sanctions; M. Böckenförde, 'Hormone Ban in Dispute Again' (2008) 12 (25) *ASIL Insight* 18 December 2008.

opting out is often not a real option as it entails exclusion from those markets, or at least significant hurdles for access.[11] Non-compliance—even with non-binding instruments—thus often comes at a prohibitive cost, and the prospect of domestic constitutionalism retaining control through implementation is accordingly limited. This problem is exacerbated when global decision making involves domestic regulators directly: if they are implicated in the setting of global standards (as they typically are in government networks), their commitment to compliance will often be too strong to allow for much flexibility at the implementation stage.[12]

Thus neither the delegatory relationship nor domestic implementation can guarantee significant national control over global governance institutions beyond the stage of their creation. This significantly conditions the viability of the domestic constitutional route: except for particularly powerful states, or in contexts in which the costs of non-compliance are low, the prospect of domestic constitutionalism shaping global governance or controlling its impact will be limited.

Legitimacy, inclusiveness, effectiveness

If the domestic constitutional route thus offers little help in alleviating the legitimacy problems of global governance, it might still be asked whether those problems are really as grave as they at first sight appear. Rather than seeing global governance as a threat to democracy and self-government, it might be regarded as strengthening them: strengthening them, that is, by readjusting the boundaries of the polity in a more inclusive way and by re-establishing some of the effectiveness domestic democracies have lost in the process of globalisation.

This point is based on the lack of congruence of nation-state boundaries with the range of those affected by political decisions. In an interdependent world, political challenges as well as regulatory responses straddle national boundaries in any number of areas. Consequently, leaving ultimate responsibility to national polities effectively disenfranchises outsiders that are significantly affected by decisions.[13] Expanding the scope of the polity and moving political decisions up to transnational and international levels may then be seen as a response to the legitimacy deficits that stem from the under-inclusiveness of the state-based, 'Westphalian' order.

Creating structures of global governance can also be perceived as a gain rather than as a loss from the perspective of the national constituency. As domestic

---

[11] On the structure of coordination games in international standardisation, see S. D. Krasner, 'Global Communications and National Power: Life on the Pareto Frontier' (1991) 43 *World Politics* 336–66.

[12] See R. B. Stewart, 'The Global Regulatory Challenge to U.S. Administrative Law' (2005) 37 *NYU Journal of International Law and Politics* 695–762, at 699–712, also on steps to nevertheless strengthen domestic accountability processes. On the latter, see also A.-M. Slaughter, 'Disaggregated Sovereignty: Towards the Public Accountability of Global Government Networks' (2004) 39 *Government & Opposition* 159–90, at 171–4.

[13] See, eg D. Held, *Democracy and the Global Order* (Cambridge: Polity Press, 1995), ch 10; I. M. Young, *Inclusion and Democracy* (Oxford: Oxford University Press, 2000), ch 7.

governments have become unable to tackle central challenges—from environmental problems to tax evasion—alone, transnational regulatory institutions have become central to re-establishing the problem-solving capacity of public actors. Insofar as democracy depends on effective institutions, adjusting decision-making structures to the scope of the problems becomes itself a democratic demand.[14]

Although this may alleviate the legitimacy problems of global governance, it will not entirely remove them. For those arguments only carry weight if decision making beyond the state can indeed be seen as an exercise of democracy—if it can be understood as sufficiently linked to individual and collective self-government. The actual provision of public or collective goods will hardly ever serve to entirely remove questions of input legitimacy from view: even if everybody receives benefits from an institution, some typically gain more and some less; distributional conflict remains ubiquitous.[15] And even if it is true that decisions of a technical character trigger weaker demands for input legitimacy than those involving redistributive measures, domestic political practices still require them to be embedded in a democratically controlled framework that defines what counts as a public good and is, if necessary, able to adjust that determination.[16] Democracy may not be the only source of legitimacy for public power, but other sources are likely to serve as complements, not substitutes for it.[17]

However, even if we accept this point in principle, the degree of input legitimacy we require on the global level may still differ from that which we typically ask for domestically.[18] In the national framework, the tension between the provision of substantive goods and democratic procedures is usually limited, simply because it operates in the shadow of relatively strong, public, problem-solving capacity through state institutions.[19] On the global level, though, this tension is more pronounced, and if we demand a high level of procedural integrity, we may have to sacrifice substantive benefits to a much larger extent. This becomes evident

---

[14] eg Held, above n 13, ch 11.

[15] See, eg Krasner, above n 11.

[16] See F. Scharpf, 'Legitimationskonzepte jenseits des Nationalstaats', *MPIfG Working Paper* 04/6, ss 2 and 3 <http://www.mpifg.de/pu/workpap/wp04-6/wp04-6.html>; E. Schmidt-Assmann, *Das Allgemeine Verwaltungsrecht als Ordnungsidee* (Heidelberg: Springer, 2nd edn, 2004), 259–61.

[17] However, in a sociological rather than normative account, one may find those different sources (which may also be more variegated than the input/output dichotomy suggests) to compete: see J. Black, 'Constructing and Contesting Legitimacy and Accountability in Polycentric Regulatory Regimes' (2008) *Regulation & Governance* 137–64, 145–6.

[18] This may also hold for the type of input legitimacy: democratic governance may follow other than the electoral patterns characteristic of the domestic context. I cannot pursue this here: see T. Macdonald and K. Macdonald, 'Non-Electoral Accountability in Global Politics: Strengthening Democratic Control within the Global Garment Industry' (2006) 17 *European Journal of International Law* 89–119; J. Bohman, *Democracy across Borders* (Cambridge, Mass.: MIT Press, 2007).

[19] See Scharpf, above n 16, s 3.

in Jürgen Habermas's vision of global politics: because of his insistence on strong democracy, he generally restricts political integration to the regional level (where strong democracy may be possible) and conceives of global politics only in classical international (interregional) terms.[20] This may, however, lead to severe costs in the provision of global public goods and we may ask whether his approach (just as most modern political theory since the rise of the absolutist state) is not based too much on a preoccupation with *limiting* public power to invite translation to the postnational environment. If we take a more Hobbesian, or possibly also republican, perspective, we may place stronger emphasis on *unleashing* public power and will perhaps rebalance the weight of substantive outcomes and procedural integrity for the global level. Whether this should go as far as Fritz Scharpf's suggestion that Pareto-optimal solutions may be legitimised by output considerations alone[21] is doubtful—too contested will be the qualification as Pareto-optimal itself, and too strong the conflict over the distribution of gains even if all actors are (absolutely) better off. But one might still accept that the gains in the provision of public goods by (input-deficient) international institutions compared to an absence of such institutions (and the consequent retreat of public power to the national realm) may to some extent legitimise their operation.

III. THE CONSTITUTIONAL AMBITION

In spite of the caveats above, the general legitimacy problem in global governance remains: domestic constitutionalism does not usually provide an effective remedy, and the greater inclusiveness and effectiveness that may come with global decision making can help legitimise global governance only to a modest extent. Given the size of the challenge, it must thus appear tempting to undertake a large-scale remaking of the current order of global governance, one that would go beyond the current institutional structure and refound it in a manner more closely aligned with domestic political ideals. It is thus not surprising that over the last decade calls not only for a democratisation but also a full-scale 'constitutionalisation' of international affairs (and international law) have gained currency; constitutionalism today appears to many to be the yardstick against which the current order and proposals for its reform ought to be measured.

Visions of global constitutionalism

What precisely 'constitutionalism' in the global context means remains disputed; the debate has produced a great number of different 'constitutionalisms', ranging from emphases on human rights and judicial review in international institutions to broader calls for a legalisation of postnational politics and visions of a global order subject

---

[20] J. Habermas, *Die postnationale Konstellation* (Frankfurt am Main: Suhrkamp, 1998), ch 4; *Der gespaltene Westen* (Frankfurt am Main: Suhrkamp, 2004), ch 8.

[21] Scharpf, above n 16, s 4.

to an identifiable constitutional document.[22] Here I will focus on a particular set of constitutionalist visions, 'foundational' ones, that provide the closest link with key domestic traditions. Other proposals, especially those focusing on legalisation, rights, and review, evoke the domestic tradition of 'power-limiting' constitutionalism that has been increasingly overshadowed by foundational approaches in the twentieth century and does not generate a comparable normative appeal either—whether they are adequately categorised as 'constitutionalist' is thus subject to doubt.[23]

Foundational constitutionalism, on the other hand, connects to the constitutional tradition spurred by the American and French revolutions, a tradition that places particular emphasis on the idea of a constitution as 'founding' and comprehensively organising the public power existing in a polity. A constitution in that sense—typically but not necessarily contained in a written document—represents a tool not only to establish limits to public institutions but also to realise self-government by defining the extent and procedural rules for the exercise of (delegated) governmental powers. Outside that framework, public power can no longer be legitimately exercised; all such power has to be traceable to the original *pouvoir constituant* via the constitution.[24]

It is not difficult to see the appeal of this vision and why it would also be attractive on the postnational level. After all, it is a structure by which a polity can make a comprehensive claim to agency and wrestle its affairs back from the forces of chance, history, and power. And it is a structure in which central pillars of modern political thought—the rule of law, individual rights, and collective self-government—are brought together.[25] Unsurprisingly then, efforts to draw on it for the postnational level have become increasingly widespread. The most tangible political result has been the European draft constitutional treaty, which appeared as an opportunity to place the European Union on a new foundation and open up new legitimacy resources. On the global level, the United Nations Charter has been reinterpreted

---

[22] See only N. Walker, 'Taking Constitutionalism beyond the State' (2008) 56 *Political Studies* 519–43; B. Fassbender, ' "We the Peoples of the United Nations": Constituent Power and Constitutional Form in International Law', in M. Loughlin and N. Walker (eds), *The Paradox of Constitutionalism: Constituent Power and Constitutional Form* (Oxford: Oxford University Press, 2007), 269–90.

[23] See also Loughlin in this volume. The argument is developed in greater detail in N. Krisch, *Beyond Constitutionalism: The Pluralist Structure of Postnational Law* (Oxford: Oxford University Press, forthcoming 2010), ch 2. It should be noted that in the current debate there is no watertight distinction between the two strands; many approaches incorporate elements of both. I focus here on the ideal type of a foundational approach and those contributions to the literature that approximate it most closely. I am grateful to Euan MacDonald for urging me to clarify this point.

[24] See C. Möllers, 'Verfassunggebende Gewalt—Verfassung—Konstitutionalisierung', in A. von Bogdandy (ed), *Europäisches Verfassungsrecht* (Berlin: Springer, 2003), 1–57, at 3–18.

[25] Of course, foundational constitutionalism has never escaped critique, most notably for the limitations comprehensive constitutions impose on the realisation of the will of the people, and for the tendencies of juridification they engender. But it has proved attractive enough to become quasi-universal as a precondition for domestic governmental legitimacy.

as a constitutional document, towering above and framing other regimes of global governance as well as individual states.[26]

More broadly, such a tendency is visible in the many approaches that seek to give the current, largely unstructured, historically accidental, and power-driven order of global governance a rational, justifiable shape in which the powers of institutions and their relationships with one another are clearly delimited. A good example is David Held's quasi-federal vision of the global order.[27] Starting from the principle of 'equivalence' of decision makers and decision takers, Held envisages a political structure in which all those affected by a particular issue have a right to participate in decisions on it. Thus striving for inclusiveness while at the same time seeking to respect subsidiarity—locating decision making as close to the individual as possible—the institutions he seeks to construct at the different levels of the global polity are to be assigned powers on issues for which decision making at a lower level would be insufficient. Some issues, such as education or housing, would thus remain at the national or subnational level while others, like environmental problems with transboundary effect, would be dealt with on the regional or global level. To be sure, he acknowledges that the distribution of powers will—as in many national contexts—often be contested and complex to resolve, but in his view, a resolution in a public setting based on an overarching principle is preferable to leaving them 'to powerful geopolitical interests (dominant states) or market based organizations to resolve them alone'.[28]

The holistic ambition and its problems

In good constitutionalist fashion, such a principled construction of the global institutional order is thus regarded as reason's antidote to the mere forces of history. Connecting in this way to domestic, foundational constitutionalism means adopting a holistic ambition, an ambition to construct a comprehensive, justified political order, and therein lies its appeal but also the source of serious problems.

Many of these problems are connected to the fact that such a comprehensive reconstruction would not only require massive institutional change but also a transformation of the societal basis on which the global order rests.[29] To use an example already mentioned above, Jürgen Habermas—a protagonist of foundational constitutionalism in the European context—refrains from extending such a vision to the

---

[26] B. Fassbender, 'The United Nations Charter as Constitution of the International Community' (1998) 36 *Columbia Journal of Transnational Law* 529–619.

[27] Held, above n 13. For other examples, see, eg Young, above n 13; M. Kumm, 'The Legitimacy of International Law: A Constitutionalist Framework of Analysis' (2004) 15 *European Journal of International Law* 907–31.

[28] D. Held, 'Democratic Accountability and Political Effectiveness from a Cosmopolitan Perspective' (2004) 39 *Government & Opposition* 364–91, at 382.

[29] See also the discussion in E. MacDonald and E. Shamir-Borer, 'Meeting the Challenges of Global Governance: Administrative and Constitutional Approaches', Discussion Draft (2008), at <http://www.iilj.org/courses/documents/MacDonald.Shamir-Borer.92508.pdf>.

global level as it would stand in tension with the social fragmentation of the global polity: in his view the discursive conditions that ground democracy (ideally) in the nation state, and might do so in certain areas of strong regional integration, are largely absent in the global realm.[30]

Yet the problems of the holistic approach go farther in a polity that is, more than even the most multicultural domestic settings, characterised by strong—perhaps radical—social and cultural diversity. Already on the national plane, it has been questioned whether foundational constitutionalism is a fitting vision for diverse societies in which consensus is elusive even on the most basic, procedural level. In particular, the claim to found the political system on impartial rules that guide and circumscribe everyday political contestation has been critiqued as concealing the contested nature of fundamental issues and as legitimising the dominance of particular social positions (and the groups behind them).[31] The more diverse and contested the social space is, the less attractive seems the idea of freezing the political order in a seemingly neutral consensus, and the more appealing the recourse to either punctual, contractual settlements between groups or to institutional provisions that keep fundamental issues open to continuing contestation and revision.

This problem becomes particularly accentuated in the global context in which there is no agreement on the scope of the ultimately decisive polity, or on any form of hierarchy between different levels of the global polity—subnational, national, regional, or global. All those different levels are beset by legitimacy problems that hamper claims to supremacy: the global polity cannot institute any form of thick, democratic procedures of participation to ground its decisions, but regional, national, or subnational levels also face legitimacy deficits because of their under-inclusiveness, as on issues that significantly affect outsiders, their claim to decision making can always only be limited and provisional.[32] In such circumstances, the comprehensive determination of decision-making roles that holistic constitutionalist proposals invariably entail—typically in a quasi-federal form—will hardly be satisfactory; giving any level the final say on an issue of global reach will always appear as problematic.[33]

Finally, the holistic ambition also raises problems of a more pragmatic character. On the one hand, it will always seem somewhat unrealistic in a global political context so far removed from ideal models. But while this might not be problematic in itself—after all, much of modern political theory will have sounded

---

[30] J. Habermas, *Der gespaltene Westen* (Frankfurt am Main: Suhrkamp, 2004), 133–42.

[31] See, eg J. Tully, *Strange Multiplicity: Constitutionalism in an Age of Diversity* (Cambridge: Cambridge University Press, 1995); C. Mouffe, *The Democratic Paradox* (New York: Verso, 2000); R. Hirschl, *Towards Juristocracy: The Origins and Consequences of the New Constitutionalism* (Cambridge, Mass.: Harvard University Press, 2004).

[32] For a similar account in the European context, see M. Maduro, 'Europe and the Constitution: What if This is as Good as it Gets?' in J. H. H. Weiler and M. Wind (eds), *European Constitutionalism beyond the State* (Cambridge: Cambridge University Press, 2003), 74–102.

[33] See N. Krisch, 'The Pluralism of Global Administrative Law' (2006) 17 *European Journal of International Law* 247–78.

unrealistic or, utopian at its beginnings—it might caution us to distance the constitutionalist project from current reform proposals. For if the gap with reality is too big, attempts at entering discussions about reforms in the here and now will likely lead to a lowering of demands—to the pursuit of a much more limited 'constitutionalism' that, rather than redeeming the promise of the domestic ideal, will legitimise deficient structures. More problematically yet, the attempt at refounding global governance on a grand scale in current political circumstances might easily play into the hands of those actors currently dominating international affairs: in a setting as inegalitarian as that of global politics, efforts at providing a stable framework of rules and institutions—at 'constituting' international society—are bound to sanction structures that primarily benefit the powerful. The attempt by some to characterise the UN Charter as a constitution[34] can be seen as precisely that: using constitutional language here is much more likely to legitimise an institution that reinforces the distribution of power after the Second World War than to provide inroads for critique sufficient to redeem the promise of political self-government constitutionalism evokes.

IV. THE (LIMITED) AMBITION OF GLOBAL ADMINISTRATIVE LAW

The holistic ambition of foundational constitutionalism thus sits uneasily with the societal and political circumstances of contemporary global politics: less comprehensive approaches might fare better in this context. Among such approaches are the more circumscribed versions of constitutionalism mentioned above, aiming at a greater legalisation of international politics or a stronger enforcement of human rights against the institutions of global governance, much in the older, power-limiting tradition of domestic constitutionalism. While these fall short of the full promise of the constitutionalist tradition,[35] they certainly have a number of substantive virtues. I cannot analyse those in detail here, but will instead focus on a different project with a limited ambition, that of 'Global Administrative Law' (GAL), and explore to what extent that limited ambition is sustainable and attractive. As I mentioned in the introduction, GAL in this reading is not a direct rival to constitutionalist visions: with its more limited ambition and different aims, it operates on a somewhat distinct plane.

GAL starts from the insight that much of global governance can be understood in administrative terms, as global administration that operates in a 'global administrative space' in which the boundaries between the domestic and international spheres have largely broken down. What it is interested in are the 'mechanisms, principles, practices, and supporting social understandings that promote or otherwise affect the

---

[34] Fassbender, above n 26.

[35] See above text at n 23.

accountability of global administrative bodies',[36] and it has led to studies of a whole range of institutions and their existing or incipient forms of transparency, participation, and review.[37]

Just like the constitutionalist projects sketched above, GAL is concerned with the legitimacy of global governance, but it approaches it from a different angle. It focuses on questions of accountability and on the extent to which a global administrative body 'gives account and another [actor] has the power or authority to impose consequences as a result'.[38] Accountability is a broad concept, and in the understanding just cited includes both circumscribed mechanisms such as judicial review and broader forms of responsiveness through electoral processes or even peer reputation.[39] Yet because it denotes a particular relationship between actors, and a particular response to legitimacy claims of particular actors, the concept lends itself to a relatively specific use in the observation and analysis of institutional practices and can therefore to some extent avoid the all-encompassing normative connotations of notions such as 'legitimacy'.[40]

GAL seeks to explore and map existing and emerging accountability practices, and it does so in a framework borrowed from administrative law. Here again, like constitutionalist models, it draws on domestic concepts for the understanding and construction of global structures. However, in GAL this move does not imply the prescriptive assumption that the tools of domestic administrative law *ought* to be transferred into the institutions of global governance, eg by establishing judicial review mechanisms wherever individuals are directly affected or by instituting public participation whenever global administrative bodies are engaged in rule making. Instead, administrative law serves mainly as an inspiration and contrast: it serves as a framework for identifying converging and diverging developments in institutional practice, and it helps us sharpen our sensitivity to the problems and possibilities of establishing accountability mechanisms on the global level. Through reflection on the transferability of domestic concepts, the similarities and dissimilarities in both institutional structures and environmental conditions come into

---

[36] B. Kingsbury, N. Krisch, and R. B. Stewart, 'The Emergence of Global Administrative Law' (2005) 68 (3) *Law & Contemporary Problems* 15–61, at 17.

[37] See the symposium issues of (2005) 68 (3) *Law & Contemporary Problems*; (2005) (4) *NYU Journal of International Law and Politics*; (2006) 17 (1) *European Journal of International Law*; the Viterbo GAL seminar series with papers at <http://www.iilj.org/GAL/GALViterbo.asp>; and the *Working Paper Series* and further materials at <http://www.iilj.org/GAL>.

[38] Black, above n 17, 150.

[39] R. W. Grant and R. O. Keohane, 'Accountability and Abuses of Power in World Politics' (2005) 99 *American Political Science Review* 29–43; J. Ferejohn, 'Accountability in a Global Context', *IILJ Working Paper* 2007/5, at <http://iilj.org/publications/2007-5Ferejohn.asp>. But see also the call for greater specificity in R. B. Stewart, 'Accountability, Participation, and the Problem of Disregard in Global Regulatory Governance', Discussion Draft (2008) 5–37, at <http://iilj.org/courses/documents/2008Colloquium.Session4.Stewart.pdf>.

[40] Legitimacy can of course also be used in a sociological sense, but the debates I refer to in this chapter are typically concerned with its normative scope.

much clearer view.[41] B. S. Chimni's work on the Codex Alimentarius Commission is a case in point: by studying the costs and benefits of stakeholder participation in its regulatory functions, we gain a more precise idea of the limits of using certain administrative law tools and with it a better sense of the conditions under which such tools may further broader normative goals.[42] Using domestic administrative law as a background rather than as the basis for prescription also reflects the variations in administrative law structures from country to country. GAL scholarship has largely used the prism of US administrative law but has also drawn on other sources,[43] and the resulting comparative angle also allows a sharper understanding of the differences in background assumptions between administrative law systems.[44] Thus, turning to administrative law for inspiration is mainly an attempt to expand the intellectual and practical resources for thinking about global governance, for bringing out similarities and differences, rather than for particular, transferable prescriptions.[45]

Yet GAL's ambition is more limited than that of constitutionalist projects in a third—and probably even more consequential—way. Apart from its more analytical and systematising aspects, GAL has a strong normative component, but its normative ambition operates on a (relatively) small scale. It does not aim at a full account of the conditions under which global governance, or global administration, would be legitimate or justified but instead aims at elucidating the respective normative values and presuppositions of particular institutional alternatives.[46] It thus seeks to bracket some of the more intractable issues such as the question of how to ensure democracy on a global scale, and to work instead within a given institutional and social environment, accepting (for the time being) the constraints this environment imposes. For example, in their work on the Basel Committee on Banking Supervision Michael Barr and Geoffrey Miller inquire into the benefits of the recent steps towards stronger participation in the Committee's regulatory process and how it has empowered certain domestic actors, thereby moving it closer to domestic representative institutions and more generally to domestic ideas of inclusiveness in the process. Likewise, they highlight the continuing limits of effective participation for particular types of domestic groups as well as, more generally, for developing

---

[41]   See, eg R. B. Stewart, 'U.S. Administrative Law: A Model for Global Administrative Law?' (2005) 68 (3) *Law & Contemporary Problems* 63–108.

[42]   B. S. Chimni, 'Co-Option and Resistance: Two Faces of Global Administrative Law' (2005) 37 *NYU Journal of International Law and Politics* 799–827.

[43]   Apart from the symposia, above n 37, see especially the materials on the workshops in Buenos Aires, New Delhi, and Cape Town as well as the Viterbo seminar series, all at <http://www.iilj.org/GAL>. See also the symposium in (2008) 9 (11) *German Law Journal*, and C. Möllers, A. Vosskuhle, and C. Walter (eds), *Internationales Verwaltungsrecht* (Tübingen: Mohr Siebeck, 2007).

[44]   See, eg the comparison in Stewart, above n 39, 37–56; and the critical analysis in C. Harlow, 'Global Administrative Law: The Quest for Principles and Values' (2006) 17 *European Journal of International Law* 187–214.

[45]   For an example of an approach stressing differences, see Krisch, above n 33.

[46]   Kingsbury, Krisch, and Stewart, above n 36, 42–51.

countries.[47] They do not situate this analysis in a broader theory of global democracy or a full account of what would make an institution like the Basel Committee legitimate; instead they can be seen to operate on a narrower normative basis, assuming that the absence of certain forms of participation would be problematic for a host of different normative theories if they were to be worked out fully. Richard Stewart has explicitly adopted such an approach in his recent work, operating on the assumption of an existing 'working consensus'—rather than a comprehensive theory—on the undesirability of disregard for certain actors in decision making.[48] A similar approach is characteristic for studies that primarily deal with rights-based mechanisms: for example, Mark Pallis's account of UNHCR's accountability to the individuals affected by its refugee status determinations is not concerned with the broader conditions of UNHCR's legitimacy; it focuses only on the more specific, rights-based elaboration of a procedural minimum standard the violation of which would be problematic *whatever* broader theories of legitimacy require beyond it.[49]

With this relatively narrow normative focus, the GAL approach resembles the early steps of continental European administrative law systems in the nineteenth century, most of which developed in a normatively largely unsatisfactory—usually monarchical, often authoritarian—environment and limited itself to advances on specific, circumscribed normative fronts: protecting rights or ensuring legality in order to ensure at least a minimum degree of predictability and consistency.[50] This type of approach does not exclude broader democratic theorising; in fact, explorations of alternatives to election-centred democracy and their potential for realisation on the global level form part of the GAL project,[51] as do inquiries into the democratic limitations of the participatory agenda that underlies many institutional developments in global regulatory rule making.[52] But the project of developing a global administrative law does not depend on the result of those explorations. It is a project with a partial, not a comprehensive aspiration and seeks an independent existence both as an analytical project and as a normative one, albeit on narrower (and potentially less contested) grounds.

---

[47] Barr and Miller, above n 6.

[48] Stewart, above n 39, 11–13.

[49] M. Pallis, 'The Operation of UNHCR's Accountability Mechanisms' (2005) 37 *NYU Journal of International Law and Politics* 869–918.

[50] At a later stage, they also served to ensure executive compliance with parliamentary legislation. See, eg on Germany M. Stolleis, *Geschichte des öffentlichen Rechts in Deutschland* (Munich: Beck, 1992), ii. 240–3, 381–4. See also, on the independent value of legality D. Dyzenhaus, 'Accountability and the Concept of (Global) Administrative Law', *IILJ Working Paper* 2008/7 13–24, at <http://www.iilj.org/publications/2008-7Dyzenhaus.asp>.

[51] eg J. Cohen and C. F. Sabel, 'Global Democracy?' (2005) 37 *NYU Journal of International Law and Politics* 763–97; Macdonald and Macdonald, above n 18; Ferejohn, above n 39.

[52] eg Harlow, above n 44; M. Shapiro, ' "Deliberative", "Independent" Technocracy v. Democratic Politics: Will the Globe Echo the EU?' (2005) 68 (3) *Law & Contemporary Problems* 341–56.

V. THE LIMITATIONS OF THE LIMITED AMBITION

Just how limited the ambition of GAL can and should be must remain open to question. Bracketing broader normative and institutional (ie 'constitutional') questions creates significant problems: disentangling the two sets of issues will often prove impossible or undesirable, not least because it might conceal or distract from the most pressing concerns about practices of global governance.

Disentangling administrative from constitutional issues is usually already difficult on a practical level. In the early stages of the evolution of administrative law in Europe, the separate pursuit of administrative law often appeared artificial but it was largely inevitable: the monarchical, authoritarian constitutional structures in which it was embedded seemed too resistant to change.[53] Today, in domestic settings, administrative and constitutional law are typically closely connected in both practice and scholarship, even if the extent of this connection differs from country to country— in the USA, the two operate at a certain distance, while in Germany, for example, such distance seems to have largely disappeared.[54] In the global context, a separation appears easiest when it comes to rights-based mechanisms, such as judicial or quasi-judicial review or due process, as rights may provide a grounding for them that is independent from broader contextual or consequentialist considerations.[55] The problems are more obvious when it comes to questions of transparency and participation in rule making. For example, how to interpret and assess the participation of developing countries in the regulatory procedure of the Basel Committee largely depends on the composition of the Committee and broader issues of its control; if developing countries had an effective voice within the Committee (and in its creation and design), they might not need procedural participation in the same way to make their concerns heard.[56] Regulatory procedure and constitutional set-up are thus, to some extent, interchangeable forms of engagement, and looking at one without the other is impossible. The challenge of disentanglement becomes ever greater if one considers the impact of the broader institutional context. To take again the Basel Committee's example, the weight of the Committee's regulatory efforts largely depends on its linkages with other institutions, such as the Financial Stability Forum and the International Monetary Fund.[57] As Basel standards are reinforced and implemented in these other sites, the freedom of states to ignore them becomes ever more virtual, rendering procedural safeguards ever more important.

---

[53] See Stolleis, above n 50.

[54] On Germany, see Schmidt-Assmann, above n 16, 10–12.

[55] The discussion of UN sanctions in the European courts can be seen as reflecting such an approach; see ECJ, Joined cases C-402/05 P and C-415/05 P *Kadi and Al-Barakaat IF v Council of the EU and Commission of the EC* [2008] ECR I-6351.

[56] Cf Barr and Miller, above n 6.

[57] See M. de Bellis, 'Global Standards for Domestic Financial Regulations: Concourse, Competition and Mutual Reinforcement between Different Types of Global Administration' (2006) 6 (3) *Global Jurist Advances*, at <http://www.bepress.com/gj/advances/vol6/iss3/art6>.

The adequacy of such safeguards, though, cannot be assessed without taking into account the bigger picture of the overall regime complex, ie the different institutions involved, their authority, composition, procedures, and control mechanisms, and the formal and factual links between them. Disentangling the 'administrative' from the 'constitutional' then looks increasingly difficult.

Such disentanglement also raises significant normative problems. John Ferejohn has recently emphasised the imbalance between legal and political accountability mechanisms in global governance when compared with domestic administrative structures.[58] In domestic settings, tools such as judicial review, the requirement of giving reasons or public participation in rule making are embedded in a broader structure in which the public can exchange its rulers at will, largely arbitrarily—in fact, insofar as judicial review is meant to enforce parliamentary statutes, it acts as a 'transmission belt' for democracy's arbitrary choices.[59] In the global context, such political accountability is largely lacking, and this may not only be a problem in itself but may also alter our interpretation of the more widespread (and more easily established) legal accountability mechanisms. A notice-and-comment proce-dure without an electoral, parliamentary yardstick may more easily be skewed in favour of particular interests, and a judicial review mechanism that acts as a trans-mission belt for non-democratically created law also plays a role quite different from its domestic model, even if it succeeds in furthering legal certainty and ensuring a degree of consistency in decision making.[60] More broadly, the lack of a democratic, parliamentary 'anchor' shifts the load of including the public in decision making to administrative procedures alone and might thus overburden them.[61] And, as Carol Harlow has observed, the imbalanced growth of legal, judicial accountability mechanisms may lead to a 'juridification' of global governance, narrowing further the space for democratic political engagement.[62] This suggests a potential trade-off between democracy and the rule of law in the shaping of GAL. It may also indicate a certain liberal, perhaps even libertarian bias in the attempt at bracketing broader questions of order in global governance. Focusing on the accountability (and thus largely on constraints) of existing institutions may overemphasise the threat these institutions pose at the expense of more positive, liberal, or republican visions that see them as forms and fora for realising self-government or non-domination.

These difficulties also suggest a particular problem associated with the concept of accountability at the centre of the GAL project. In a common interpretation, accountability is understood to include solely ex-post checks to decision making,[63]

---

[58] Ferejohn, above n 39.

[59] On the role and limitations of the 'transmission belt' model in the US context, see R. B. Stewart, 'The Reformation of American Administrative Law' (1975) 88 *Harvard Law Review* 1667–813.

[60] On the independent value of the latter, see Dyzenhaus, above n 50.

[61] Kingsbury, Krisch, and Stewart, above n 36, 48–50.

[62] Harlow, above n 44, 211–14.

[63] Grant and Keohane, above n 39, 30.

but insofar as prior participation and later review fulfil similar functions, focusing on those ex-post checks may miss a significant part of the picture and may lead to distorted normative assessments. Yet if one broadens the understanding of the concept, as much of the GAL literature has done,[64] it becomes increasingly difficult to delineate its boundaries. Such a move does not necessarily affect analytical clarity: accountability continues to denote the particular relational dimension between a governance actor and those communities with legitimacy claims on it.[65] On a normative level, though, the situation is more difficult. Mechanisms of accountability, however defined, are part of a broader interplay of elements of control or influence which may be seen as standing in a zero-sum relationship: if one actor gains greater influence over decision making, another one loses some of hers.[66] In this picture, institutions of global governance do not have an accountability deficit; they may only be accountable to the wrong accountability holders.[67] Yet if we cannot assess the adequacy of any mechanism of accountability independently of all other forms of influence in an institution and of a broader normative theory of who ought to control the institution, the prospect of disentangling the 'administrative' from the 'constitutional' becomes ever dimmer.

VI. LEGITIMISING ADMINISTRATIVE STEERING?

If fully disentangling the 'administrative' from the 'constitutional' is thus not an attractive—or even feasible—option, the limited ambition of GAL can be maintained only by a deliberate narrowness of focus and provisionality of claims. Both analytically and normatively, GAL may then focus on global accountability mechanisms of an administrative-law style but retain awareness of the institutional context in which those mechanisms are embedded and the broader normative questions they raise. GAL inquiries might stop short of addressing those latter issues directly, or at least might not provide answers or prescriptions for them, but keeping them present will help situate the analysis and assessment of the practices it chooses to concentrate on. For example, when analysing rule-making processes within the Organisation for Economic Co-operation and Development (OECD), a GAL approach will need to explicate the context in which the institution as a whole is embedded—it may not develop an answer to what the place of the OECD in the global institutional architecture should ultimately be (and indeed whether it should have any) as this would require the form of comprehensive analysis it has chosen to refrain from, but awareness of the broader context will emphasise the relative nature of whatever claims it can make about narrower procedural issues. In the absence of a comprehensive

---

[64] See Kingsbury, Krisch, and Stewart, above n 36.

[65] See text above at n 17.

[66] See Black, above n 17, 153.

[67] R. O. Keohane, 'Global Governance and Democratic Accountability', in D. Held and M. Koenig-Archibugi (eds), *Taming Globalization: Frontiers of Governance* (Oxford: Polity, 2003), 130–59, at 145; Krisch, above n 33, 249–51.

theory, GAL may not be able to make ultimate claims about how the emergence of broader participation rights in OECD rule making can be compared to domestic administrative-law analogues or assessed normatively. But GAL can study the process leading up to it, the effects of it, and the politics around it, and it may also interpret and assess it in the light of alternative imaginations of the broader order. Any such effort will then be relative and provisional—it will depend on assumptions about elements of a broader theory, and these assumptions need to remain explicit. In this way, we can reconstruct the assertion that GAL seeks to 'bracket' some of the broader issues, such as a theory of global democracy,[68] as an expression of a particular kind of limited ambition: an ambition to come up with relative, provisional conclusions on the interpretation and assessment of a selected range of phenomena. In this sense, GAL is a self-consciously 'modest' project.

However, even if such a denotation is attractive, the connotations of the project may be more problematic, for it might suggest a degree of legitimacy of a structure that in fact is largely illegitimate. Despite all protestations to the contrary, critics might say, GAL with its use of terms such as law and administration evokes analogies to domestic institutions that are mostly misplaced, and with its focus on accountability it conceals and distracts from more fundamental problems—such as those of democracy—in the global realm.[69] This is, of course, a serious challenge. Even if one should take care not to overdraw the contrast with the domestic sphere where much administrative action today is also far removed from democratic practices, global governance is particularly problematic in this respect. Its links with domestic democracy are weak, its decentred processes of decision making resist the application of the classical instruments that connect administration with electoral or public deliberative processes, and anything resembling a public sphere is missing on the global level. In this situation, the pursuit of the partial, modest agenda of GAL might indeed seem blind to the true challenges, perhaps actively distracting from them, and a broader approach might seem called for. Yet such a broader approach would likely be beset by some of the same difficulties we have identified above in global constitutionalism's comprehensive ambition; in particular, the distance between current institutional and social conditions and any meaningful conception of democracy is likely to entail either an apologetic downgrading of democratic demands or the utopian insistence on high standards devoid of a chance of realisation. Then, again, a more circumscribed project may be more attractive, as long as its goals and limitations are kept explicit.

Yet there are other, potentially more consequential objections to GAL's approach to global governance. Because it invokes the vocabulary of law, it might—as Alexander Somek points out—create idealisations that 'distort our perception of administrative realities' and present as a practice of law what in fact is driven by administrative rationality.[70] In Somek's view, global governance is characterised by the absence of

---

[68] Kingsbury, Krisch, and Stewart, above n 36, 51.

[69] This risk is highlighted in S. Marks, 'Naming Global Administrative Law' (2005) 37 *NYU Journal of International Law and Politics* 995–1001.

[70] Somek in this volume.

legal relationships: actors are not engaged by rules in a merely external fashion but are made to internalise the project of global regulators and to share the teleology of the rules rather than just obey them. This observation is probably true, at least in part, for the public actors (international institutions, states, regulators) that take part in global governance; for a regulatory regime to work in the absence of enforcement capacities, it depends on a positive attitude of participants and subjects. This does not necessarily imply a loss of freedom as compared to the 'legal' relationship, as Somek implies: being engaged by the rules because one co-authors them, as happens in regulatory networks, may well be a gain in self-government.[71] Yet it might indeed signal the absence of 'law' and consequently call into question the appropriateness of naming 'global administrative *law*' what might perhaps better be called 'global administration'.

Such a conclusion would, however, rely on an overdrawn dichotomy between legal and administrative (or managerial) rationality: rather than merely opposed modes of action, the two are better seen as poles on a continuum. Domestic administration is not characterised by a legal relationship alone; administrative law is caught in an uneasy tension between those different rationalities already in the national context.[72] In global administration, the tension plays out somewhat differently, but the difference is merely gradual: we may situate global governance on a different point on the continuum, further towards administrative rationality, but this does not mean law is absent—it may simply be less extensive and consequential. In fact, GAL points precisely to the inroads into the managerial that law, rules, and normative expectations have made, mostly in procedural terms, through legality control, participation, and transparency. Take, for example, the World Bank Inspection Panel, which—despite all its shortcomings—institutionalises respect for (internal) rules even when they lead to a clash with expediency in a given case. And not only has the Panel had an effect on the operation of the World Bank itself, it has also helped create a broader expectation that development banks be subject to review mechanisms, leading to emulation in a number of other institutional contexts.[73] This does not displace administrative rationality in any of the banks concerned, but it conditions it to some extent—just as administrative law does in the domestic context.

However, it may still be asked—as David Dyzenhaus has recently done[74]—whether there is any particular role of 'law' as such in GAL, given that much of the practices it is concerned with have an ambiguous or clearly informal status. There is, of course,

---

[71] By contrast, those actors external to the rule-making process, forced to follow the rules because of the costs of non-compliance, may be said to be in a legal relationship (subject to rules they are expected merely to comply with) but are hardly any freer. Think only of states not members of the Basel Committee or the Financial Action Task Force but still subject to its regulation.

[72] See Dyzenhaus, above n 50, 13–16; Somek in this volume.

[73] See D. Bradlow, 'Private Complainants and International Organizations: A Comparative Study of the Independent Inspection Mechanisms in International Financial Institutions' (2005) 36 *Georgetown Journal of International Law* 403–94.

[74] Dyzenhaus, above n 50.

a significant amount of 'hard' law in the foundational documents of international institutions as well as in the domestic or regional law that affects global regulatory regimes; often we can indeed observe an oversupply of legal rules, with undecided hierarchies and a need for conflict resolution among them.[75] Moreover, many global rules turn into formal law once they are implemented by domestic (legislative or administrative) actors. Still, much of global regulatory governance takes the form of explicitly non-binding rules, and many of the procedural developments GAL describes are not the result of binding rules either. Yet they often share many characteristics of law and many of the elements of its particular internal morality.[76] For example, World Bank policies on issues such as resettlement or indigenous peoples are general, public, and relatively clear rules that are not easily changed and that the Bank's administrative action has to be congruent with; moreover, the Inspection Panel, among other avenues, offers a way to police that congruence. This may not be conclusive—the Panel's findings can eventually be set aside by the Bank. But ignoring them comes at a significant cost, and even if the Inspection Panel may initially have been set up, in part, to further administrative efficiency, the dynamic it has created means it can certainly no longer be simply reduced to such considerations.

As in other institutions, this supports Dyzenhaus's observation that rule *by* law often (though by no means always) fosters the rule *of* law.[77] This does not imply that all those rules and practices should be awarded the status of formal law, binding on its subjects and on a par with norms of international or constitutional law—this would indeed often contradict the understanding of the participants and may often not be desirable either.[78] But not all law needs to be the same; some rules might share certain but not all characteristics with others; and different legal orders may operate in different spheres and be only loosely coupled with one another. And it will certainly be fruitful, as Dyzenhaus urges us, to investigate further into the extent to which the rules and practices of GAL do indeed bear the characteristics of law and are thus set apart from mere administrative, managerial rationalities; this should also force us to address the question of which concept of law is adequate to conceptualising global normative practices. The tension between 'law' and 'administration' in global governance will not disappear, but rather than obscuring it, GAL—like its domestic counterpart—can be seen as making it explicit: as defining it as a challenge, as a subject of investigation, and thus drawing it out into the open.

---

[75] Krisch, above n 33.

[76] See the discussion in Dyzenhaus, above n 50, 21–4. See also B. Kingsbury, 'The Concept of Law in Global Administrative Law' (2009) 20 *European Journal of International Law* 23–57.

[77] Ibid 22.

[78] See also Kingsbury, Krisch, and Stewart, above n 36, 29–31; N. Krisch and B. Kingsbury, 'Introduction: Global Governance and Global Administrative Law in the International Legal Order' (2006) 17 *European Journal of International Law* 1–13, at 12. However, Benedict Kingsbury is more openly sympathetic to reconceptualising many of the practices as part of a new *ius gentium* (B. Kingsbury, 'Omnilateralism and Partial International Communities: Contributions of the Emerging Global Administrative Law' (2005) 104 *Journal of International Law and Diplomacy* 98–124, at 110–15).

VII. CONCLUSION

Many certainties have disappeared in the globalised world, among them the long-established separation between the domestic and international spheres in politics and law. The gaps left by that disappearance are wide, and the need to fill them is urgent: too fragile is the legitimacy of the global and transnational governance institutions that have assumed many of the functions domestic governments used to perform. As I have suggested in this article, though, the most obvious steps to fill the gap are highly problematic. Attempts at radically reshaping, indeed refounding, the global political structure by following a form of 'global constitutionalism' may exert a strong appeal in the current, very unsatisfactory situation, but they are unlikely to suit the extremely diverse, contested and rapidly changing character of global society. Moreover, seeking to establish a coherent, well-ordered structure of political institutions in the global realm today may not only exceed our abilities to understand the parameters in which it would have to operate, or predict how these parameters will develop in the future; it might also play into the hands of those actors that dominate current global politics and are thus likely to shape any new institutional order.

Instead of such large-scale, 'constitutionalist' endeavours we are thus better advised to pursue projects of a more limited ambition, and I have focused here on one of these—global administrative law. GAL has a narrower ambit than constitutionalist approaches, in that it focuses on accountability mechanisms in global regulatory governance; it is less prescriptive about the uses of domestic models; and it operates on a narrower normative basis, bracketing to some extent the question which fully worked-out, comprehensive theories can ultimately ground global and transnational institutions. But this more limited ambition creates serious problems, not least because questions of overall structure can hardly be disentangled—practically and normatively—from those of concrete accountability mechanisms. Moreover, by bracketing the broader questions GAL may be seen to distract from them, or even to legitimise illegitimate structures by elevating them to the level of 'law'. This can be avoided by being explicit about GAL's limited aims and only provisional claims, but it is a very fine line to walk.

To the more philosophically minded, limiting one's ambitions in this way may appear insufficient; they will insist on theorising on a larger scale, with comprehensive aims. This is intellectually understandable: bracketing central issues may simply appear as shying away from the most difficult questions. And even as a matter of institutional design, confining ourselves to partial, limited solutions may make us lose sight of the overall edifice, leading to an incoherent whole that we might eventually have to rebuild altogether—it might create a 'monstrous' structure, similar to the one Pufendorf deplored (and sought to overcome) in the Holy Roman Empire.[79] Yet just as remaking the Empire's institutions in a coherent fashion found its limits in the political and social conditions of early modernity, thinking about the design of global governance cannot succeed without consideration of the complex shape

---

[79] Severinus de Monzambano (Samuel von Pufendorf), *De statu imperii Germanici* (1667), ch VI, §9.

of global politics and society today, of our incomplete understanding of it and our limited ability to effect change. In the 'twilight' in which we find ourselves today proceeding in small steps, with limited ambition, may be the only sensible option. In the case of GAL, it may be one that allows us to sharpen our focus and begin to answer crucial questions of global governance without leaping to grand designs borrowed from dissimilar contexts and likely at odds with the fluid and diverse character of the postnational polity.

❧ 13 ❧

Administration without Sovereignty

Alexander Somek[*]

I. COUNTERFACTUAL SOCIAL FACTS

Legal statements involve sociological commitments. This may not be true of all
cases. It is obvious, nonetheless, that a summons to appear in court, for example,
presupposes the existence of addressees who are capable of understanding what
they have been ordered to do and also interested, potentially, in avoiding sanctions.
The social universe conjured up in a summons is not the world in which power is
diffused in networks or where the rationality of different social systems is bound to
remain incommensurable. The world taken for granted by legal statements exhibits
the ontological features of what is called, heedlessly perhaps, 'ordinary life'. It is
a world mostly inhabited by individual human beings. The communication in the
relation between the legislature and the legislated is not shrouded in mystery. The
subjects are capable of understanding their obligations. Conversely, those wielding
the powers conferred by the legal system are capable of controlling the behaviour of
norm addressees by threatening them with sanctions. Therefore, legal enactments
appear to be self-referentially concerned with the stipulation of being adhered to.
It is as though they reflected the belief that if it were not for law society would fall
apart—a belief imparted with the notorious truism *ubi societas, ibi ius.*

   The sociological presuppositions of law may strike one as either terribly naïve or
distressingly prosaic. It is almost preposterous to assume that the addressees actually do understand the law; and, of course, it is more than trite to remind everyone
of the inescapability of enforcement. But both presuppositions merely reveal law's
very own sociology of law. Distressingly enough, this sociology rests on a perplexing
composite of idealisation and insight. The law needs to be clear. On a factual level,
this sounds ludicrous. But dropping the expectation altogether would be cynical,
for otherwise expecting compliance would be nothing short of preposterous. From

[*] The question addressed in this chapter was the subject of a discussion in my seminar
on 'Rethinking Public International Law'. I would like to thank my students for patiently
following my exposition of the problem. Nico Krisch and John Reitz provided valuable
comments and challenges.

the perspective of the legal system it needs to be believed that the law is, despite its complexity, clear enough to quell doubts regarding the reasonableness of compliance. What there is becomes systematically assimilated to what there ought to be. In other words, the law idealises the social context of its operation and thereby invites misreading reality as a manifestation of the ideal.

However, law's sociology also works the other way around. Reality becomes a by-product of idealisation. The law signals that if it were not for its existence the social world would collapse.[1] When state authority disappears so-called failed states sink into chaos. No law, no order. It has to be that way, for this conforms to what we have come normatively to expect. It is a self-fulfilling prophecy. Hobbes's political philosophy provides us with a most instructive example of how idealisations influence the real. Hobbes believes us to make a cognitive assumption for a normative reason. That is, in order to be good curators of our own self-interest we had better believe others to pursue their own self-interest aggressively, at any rate, when push comes to shove. On a cognitive plane, it may not be the case that people pursue their self-interest, for it may often be profoundly unclear what this really means. Nonetheless, our own interest in survival counsels in favour of acting on the basis of a stereotype that involves the idealisation that people do in fact pursue their self-interest. To act on the irrefutable presumption that people pursue their self-interest presupposes that they are capable of doing so. Hence everyone pursues what he believes to be in his self-interest because of the belief that everyone else is doing so. Ought implies can. It has this power over us even when it is profoundly unclear if what you ought to do is also what you can do. The result is, again, the idealisation of social facts. Social facts are cast in the light of idealisations.

Hence, the context against which we render something intelligible *as* valid law is laden with idealisations. The law comes surrounded with a normative aura. The addressees understand the law (*yeah!*). They are self-interested and self-directing (*applause*).[2] None of these idealisations can be legislated or brought about legally. They are, logically, *prior to law*. They involve idealisations of our selves and of our mutual engagements. Their presence should not come as a surprise. Modern law is addressed to us as specimens of one and the same type of moral agent. This is a counterfactual presupposition. But it is not *merely* counterfactual. Everyone had better be capable of manifesting in some manner the universal conception of agency in practical life.

These idealisations are, of course, not innocent. The presupposition underlying private law according to which adult contracting parties are equally capable of procuring their own interests can be sustained only so long as a situation is not marked by serious inequalities of power and wealth. There is a degree, however, to which idealisations may legitimately conceal, for they may actually help to neutralise differences that ought not to matter from a legal point of view. Nevertheless, idealisations may

---

[1] This is, in a sense, equivalent to what Hart thought to be the minimal content of natural law (H. L. A. Hart, *The Concept of Law* (Oxford: Clarendon Press, 1961), 189–95).

[2] They are what Pierre Schlag would describe as 'legal subjects' (P. Schlag, 'The Problem of the Subject' (1991) 69 *Texas Law Review* 1627–743).

also reach a point at which their use appears to distort social realities. This is the case, as is well known, wherever agreements are deemed to be invalid owing to unequal bargaining power.

Legal statements are sociological. They are sociological in the sense that they take for granted the existence of conditions that are normatively presupposed by the law in order to render its own existence feasible and, not least, legitimate. For the purpose of the exposition that follows I would like to refer to these presuppositions as *counterfactual social facts*.[3] They are manifest in facts such as the intelligibility of authoritative enactments, the capability of agents to engage in planning their conduct and to adjust their plans in accordance with changing circumstances, the rough predictability of the operation of courts, the responsiveness of the system of government, and the democratic input into the political process. These are social facts that the legal system takes for granted in order to conceive of itself as reasonably fair and acceptable.

The few examples have also shown, however, that *systematically* the law has to be inclined either to assimilate the ideal to reality or to construe reality as the expression of an ideal. Owing to the presence of counterfactual social facts, therefore, the law has a built-in tendency towards ideological self-obfuscation.

II. COMPETING DESCRIPTIONS

Dieter Grimm's unwavering scepticism with regard to the premature celebrations of constitutionalism beyond the nation state[4] expresses precisely a concern about the obstructive influence of counterfactual social facts.[5] The promise that resides in the inherited concept of the constitution becomes drained of its normative force, where major elements of the original context of constitutional law, such as consolidated state authority, can no longer be taken for granted. What cannot be sustained in a transnational context, in particular, is the concept of the constitution as a comprehensive regulation of state power that facilitates collective self-determination. Using the attribute 'constitutional' in order to describe fragmentary transnational processes is likely to create serious distortions.

---

[3] I cannot, for the purpose of the discussion that follows elaborate in which respect my view of counterfactual social facts is both similar to and dissimilar from Lon Fuller's take on what constitutes the internal morality of law. There is a similarity for it highlights the fact that certain idealisations are part of the practice of law; the approach is fundamentally different, nonetheless, for it abstains from consolidating a number of idealisations into a 'procedural' version of natural law. Rather, the presence of counterfactual social facts is itself taken to be a social fact about raising and defending legal claims. See, by contrast, L. L. Fuller, *The Morality of Law* (New Haven, Conn.: Yale University Press, rev edn, 1964), 91–106.

[4] For one example among many others (with references to other examples), see A. Peters, 'Compensatory Constitutionalism: The Function and Potential of Fundamental International Norms and Structures' (2006) 19 *Leiden Journal of International Law* 579–610.

[5] See D. Grimm, 'The Constitution in the Process of Denationalization' (2005) 12 *Constellations* 447–63.

However, constitutionalism is not the only theoretical vocabulary that has been used in order to account for transnational structures. Indeed, over the last few years, the number of contenders has grown considerably. Above all, 'governance', in particular 'governance without government' and talk of new 'sites' of authority haven taken centre stage.[6] Sociological approaches that highlight the systemic effects underlying the behaviour of international actors, such as constructivism[7] and systems theory, compete for shedding light on a situation for which the long-serving counterfactual social facts, such as 'states' and the 'national interest' no longer appear to be of any avail. Whereas the social ontology of 'realistic' approaches to international affairs appears to enjoy considerable support by American legal scholars,[8] a highly tentative and fluid discourse on soft-law, 'hybridity', and governance has come around in Europe.[9]

What the use of these various vocabularies indicates is keen awareness that the inherited categories of public international law are no longer capable of capturing a new reality. In fact, owing to the idealising moment inherent in tacit references to counterfactual social facts the traditional legal sociology of international law tends to ascribe to state governments more power then they actually possess.[10]

None of these contending vocabularies, however, has as of yet attained the stature of a *lingua franca*. Yet, the attempt to account for global structures of governing in terms of 'global administrative law' is nonetheless remarkable.[11] It stands out, for it is based on the realisation that most of the more recent developments in transnational law have indeed enhanced its administrative dimension.[12] What is to be observed today, from the preparation of side agreements to the GATT all the way down to the regulation of foodstuffs in the European Union (EU), is an increase of transnational

---

[6] See, most prominently, J. N. Rosenau, *Along the Domestic-Foreign Frontier: Exploring Governance in a Turbulent World* (Cambridge: Cambridge University Press, 1997). 'Governance', generally, refers to processes of regulating and ordering issues of the public interest.

[7] See D. Bederman, 'Constructivism, Positivism, and Empiricism in International Law' (2001) 89 *Georgetown Law Journal* 469–97, at 477; P. A. Karber, ' "Constructivism" as a Method of International Law' (2000) 94 *Proceedings of the American Society of International Law* 189–92; J. Brunée and S. J. Toope, 'International Law and Constructivism: Elements of an Interactional Theory of International Law' (2000) 39 *Columbia Journal of Transnational Law* 19–73.

[8] J. L. Goldsmith and E. A. Posner, *The Limits of International Law* (New York: Oxford University Press, 2005).

[9] See G. de Burca and J. Scott (eds), *Law and New Governance in the EU and the US* (Oxford: Hart, 2006).

[10] This observation has been made, very aptly, by A.-M. Slaughter, *A New World Order* (Princeton, NJ: Princeton University Press, 2003).

[11] For a manifesto, see B. Kingsbury, N. Krisch, and R. B. Stewart, 'The Emergence of Global Administrative Law' (2005) 68 *Law and Contemporary Problems* 15–61.

[12] See J. H. H. Weiler, 'The Geology of International Law: Governance, Democracy and Legitimacy' (2004) 64 *Heidelberg Journal of International Law (ZaöRV)* 547–62.

regulatory cooperation and of joint efforts at implementation. The new world of international law is the world of loosely coupled but often highly interactive and effective national and international bureaucracies.

III. A REMARKABLE PARADIGM SHIFT

It should not go unnoticed that as the project unfolds the concept of administrative law is given a more American twist.[13] The focus lies, hence, not so much on individual administrative acts[14] but on the establishment of new regulatory authority.[15] The rights dimension hence receives less attention than the governance dimension, for the guarantees of transparency and participation are the regulators' modality of respecting the interests of stakeholders and affected groups.[16] Nevertheless, a whole range of phenomena enters the purview of global administrative law, ranging from administration by formal organisations, such as the World Health Organization, over collective action by more or less formalised transnational networks of national regulatory officials all the way down to private institutions with regulatory functions, such as the International Organization for Standardization.[17]

Intriguingly, the range of phenomena studied reveals a departure from a basic analogy. In the exemplary case, a legislature delegates regulatory authority to an agency, which, after giving notice, scheduling hearings, and providing reasons, adopts an implementing regulation. By analogy, in the paradigmatic international context a treaty typically takes the place of legislation and a general act adopted by an international organisation the place of the regulation. Hence, acts by the United Nations Security Council, which have increasingly come to exhibit a general nature,[18] would derive their authority from the delegation effected by all acceding signatory states of the UN Charter. If I understand the project correctly, it is the very point of global administrative law to emphasise that what used to be the paradigmatic make-up of the modern 'regulatory state' is merely a limiting case of how the administrative process becomes re-enacted on a global scale. Remarkably enough, the paradigm shift amounts to precisely this 'decentring' of the image of delegation

---

[13] For similar observations, see C. Harlow, 'Global Administrative Law: The Quest for Principles and Values' (2006) 17 *European Journal of International Law* 187–214, at 209.

[14] This is not always the case: the declaration of refugee status by the UNHCR is an individual administrative act.

[15] See Kingsbury et al, above n 11, at 16.

[16] On the pedigree of 'governance' from the pluralistic transformation of American administrative law into an instrument of participation and agreed upon rule making, see the highly perceptive comments by M. Shapiro, 'Administrative Law Unbounded: Reflections on Government and Governance' (2001) 8 *Indiana Journal of Global Legal Studies* 369–77, at 376.

[17] See Kingsbury et al, above n 11, at 20–3.

[18] See J. E. Alvarez, 'Hegemonic International Law Revisited' (2003) 97 *American Journal of International Law* 873–88.

of authority to rule-making and rule-applying bodies. Not only can regulation on the basis of delegation no longer be considered the paradigmatic core of administrative law, no other relation can claim to have taken its place. Individual acts by the Security Council are just as paradigmatic an instance of global administrative law as standard setting by the Codex Alimentarius Commission.

On a descriptive level, hence, global administrative law sweeps so broadly that one is inclined to take it to be a *re-description* of modern international law.[19] It actually provides a picture of the international law under the dominating influence of administrative rationality. The absence of a paradigm reveals the 'rhizomatic' quality of this situation.[20] There is neither system nor centre, merely family resemblances among different processes.

Against this background, it is all the more surprising that the normative thrust of global administrative law is relatively straightforward. Indeed, the purveyors of the idea are confident that from the mush of the decentred paradigm will emerge 'the mechanisms, principles, practices, and supporting social understandings that promote or otherwise affect the accountability of global administrative bodies, in particular by ensuring they meet adequate standards of transparency, participation, reasoned decision, and legality, by providing effective review of the rules and decisions they make'.[21]

Global administrative law links the description of variegated phenomena with the pursuit of a limited normative agenda, which is committed to core principles of the rule of law and values associated with 'good governance'.[22] Hence, global administrative law has set for itself quite pragmatic objectives, which are, incidentally, far more modest than the claims made by those advancing in one way or another the cause of constitutionalisation.[23]

The only problem that is posed by this project is whether or not even in this case the use of *legal* vocabulary involves a mismatch in the relation between counterfactual social facts and the conditions under which operates what is supposed to be law.

---

[19]   See N. Krisch and B. Kingsburg, 'Introduction: Global Governance and Global Administrative Law in the International Legal Order' (2006) 17 *European Journal of International Law* 1–13.

[20]   © Deleuze and Guattari (see G. Deleuze and F. Guattari, *A Thousand Plateaus*, trans B. Massumi (London: Continuum, 2004)).

[21]   Kingsbury et al, above n 11, at 17. See also ibid at 28.

[22]   For apt remarks as regards this more limited agenda, see S. Marks, 'Naming Global Administrative Law' (2005) 37 *International Law and Politics* 995–1001. Harlow, above n 13, at 198–203, goes to great pains to distinguish rule of law principles, such as legality and limited powers, from good governance values, such as transparency and participation. She sees the latter originating from World Bank and International Monetary Fund policies and denies them the stature of genuine administrative law principles. I can imagine that American scholars would have a different take on this.

[23]   For self-conscious modesty, see N. Krisch, 'Postnational Constitutionalism?' (manuscript, 2008).

In other words, the project may, in spite of its forward-looking orientation, give rise to idealisations whose use is likely to be unwarranted in the face of existing realities.

IV. GLOBALISATION'S *GUTE POLIZEY*

Lest I be misunderstood, I add that the problem is not whether administrative processes are by their very nature not susceptible to legal control. The rise of administrative law in the context of nineteenth-century European monarchies serves as a reminder that the task is not too arduous to be achieved. The question is whether in certain instances a *description* of social processes in traditional legal terms may not render them obscure owing to the law's intrinsic tendency to idealise the context of its operation. This danger is all the more virulent in settings that are marked by the prevalence of administrative rationality. In other words, when speaking of law we ought to take heed of the mutations that legal relationships undergo when they become absorbed by processes of administration.

Since its inception, administrative *action* has been teleological in its orientation and both comprehensive and particularising with regard to its scope.[24] Administrative rationality is *comprehensive*, for with the rise of the modern state administrative processes are self-reflexively concerned with strengthening the vitality and enhancing the presence of the state. The expenditure of energy in discrete processes of administration is therefore ultimately fine-tuned and calibrated in light of these final objectives. Every act of administration is always part of a larger ambition. At the same time, administrative rationality is also *particularising*. Foucault may well have been right in assuming that, from earlier Christian doctrines of good governing, it inherits an individualising 'pastoral' orientation.[25] The administrators are expected to manage the lives of citizens and to see to the flourishing of the population.[26] Whatever seems to be conducive to the life of the population or, as one would have put it in the nineteenth century, the nation or, nowadays, the health and safety of the global consumer, is in and of itself within the purview of the administration.[27]

It is in this connection that, owing to the subject at hand, the professed concern with the vitality of social life confers comprehensive competence.[28] Maybe one does not go wrong in assuming, again with an eye to Foucault, that administrative

---

[24] The following remarks are taking their cue from, without thereby slavishly following, M. Foucault, ' "Omnes et Singulatim": Toward a Critique of Political Reason', in *Power*, ed J. D. Faubion, trans R. Hurley (New York: New Press, 1994), 298–325.

[25] See ibid at 309.

[26] See ibid at 323.

[27] On the early cosmopolitan connotation of *Polizey*, which suggests administrative action that is geared toward creating polite citizenry that is conversant in wordly affairs, see H. Maier, *Die ältere deutsche Staats- und Verwaltungslehre (Polizeiwissenschaft): Ein Beitrag zur Geschichte der politischen Wissenschaft in Deutschland* (Neuwied: Hermann Luchterhand Verlag, 1966), 128–9.

[28] For the Christian origin of the idea of the sanctity of life (*pace* Agamben), see H. Arendt, *The Human Condition* (Chicago, Ill.: Chicago University Press, 1957), 313–14.

rationality is 'bio-political' in its orientation, for it is concerned with the preservation, the moral quality, the conveniences, and the pleasures of life.[29] Any particular measures that are taken by the administration nonetheless serve the comprehensive ultimate objective of reinforcing state power. Administrative rationality is a means 'to develop those elements constitutive of individuals' lives in such a way that their development also fosters the strength of the state'.[30]

The calibration of action with regard to attaining both the comprehensive and the particularising objectives would be severely hampered if it had to play by pre-established rules of law. The management of life-enhancing processes—be it the provision of wholesome food, the stipulation of sanitary public baths, or the correction of damaging customs, such as smoking, drinking, gluttony, or unprotected sex—needs to be, thus understood, indeed an activity that defies the discipline of law.[31] In other words, the administrators need to be in a position to adjust the investment of resources from one situation to the next in accordance with felt necessities at the time of action. No general rule can determine in advance the type of response that would be adequate to a particular situation. In fact, from within the perspective of managing the life of the population (or global prosperity) rules can merely establish some provisional standard. Denying existing rules their authority does in no manner undermine the rationality of administration; it does not, at any rate so long as the activity remains geared to both the comprehensive and the particularising objectives.[32]

What is more, it is not by accident that administration—the *gute Polizey*—is associated with sovereign power in the sense of a power that is essentially *legibus solutus*. In the administrative context this power works, though, not through the spectacular demonstrations of *omnipotentia terranea*, which puts itself on display in gruesome public executions, but through the omnipresence of measures of correction, learning, nurturing, fostering, facilitating, promoting, educating, training, optimisation, and advice. The macro- and micro-management of life can best flourish when it enjoys the backing of sovereign power. Under this condition, it is not hampered by jurisdictional constraints or held back by the demand to respect a rule or a right. The coupling with sovereignty explains why administrative power is so menacing. Administrations regulate, to be sure. But they resort to regulation only as an expedient in order to get things done. Even deregulation is a method of administrative goal attainment.[33] When there is promise that things might get

---

[29] See Foucault, above n 24, at 321. See also M. Foucault, *Society Must Be Defended: Lectures at the Collège de France 1975–1976*, trans D. Macey (New York: Picador 2003), 243.

[30] Foucault, above n 24, at 322 (a view that Foucault attributes to Justi).

[31] See Harlow, above n 13, at 191.

[32] See M. Oakeshott, *On Human Conduct* (Oxford: Oxford University Press, 1975), 116–17, who may in turn have drawn on Fuller's account of the contrast between adjudication and managing. See Fuller, above n 3, at 207–8; L. L. Fuller, *The Principles of Social Order*, ed K. Winston (Durham, NC: Duke University Press, 1981), 195.

[33] For an overview, see C. Crouch, *Post-Democracy* (London: Polity Press, 2004).

done more effectively through direct action, administrative rationality is the first to override its own pre-established constraint.

The eudemonism of life-enhancing administrative action encounters different conditions in the age of globalisation. This change does not affect its comprehensive and particularising momentum: what has altered is the entity whose life is the object of comprehensive concern. No longer does the state occupy this position, but rather, in Marxian parlance, the life process of society,[34] which has come to adopt as its final cause the want-generation and want-satisfaction of the global consumer. What one encounters in this context is administrative rationality that has been stripped of its backing by sovereignty. It therefore needs to negotiate and calibrate its relative authority in each case with an eye to the overall stabilisation of global economic processes. Such deferential fine-tuning with regard to other agents wielding administrative authority would not be necessary, constitutional constraints aside, under territorial rule. Territoriality is the consequence of the absence of substantive jurisdictional limitations. Occupying supreme authority over a territory is what distinguishes sovereignty from the functionally differentiated claims to supremacy that purportedly inhere in self-contained regimes.[35] The WTO may well have built into its operation the claim to have the final say over how to resolve 'trade and ...' questions, but it would have to expect resistance if it decided to ride roughshod over the findings of a human rights regime. It is the mark of sovereign power that it does not have to accommodate other powers. Sovereign power is capable of overcoming obstacles wherever they might arise, lest it is not what it purports to be.

I do not claim that my brief characterisation of administrative rationality is either original or complete.[36] I merely point out that where administrative rationality dominates it appears doubtful whether belief can be sustained in the presence of the law's counterfactual social facts. I would like to argue, instead, that the new situation for which there exists already a fair number of competing descriptors is best understood—in particular, from a historical point of view—when conceived of as *administration without sovereignty*. Neither talk about 'law beyond state', to which global administrative law in any case formulates a contribution,[37] nor some lofty-softy 'constitutionalism' is adequate to capture the essence of transnational governance processes. They are not, for they miss the most important point, that is, the demise of the traditional legal relationship.

---

[34] For an apt observation, see Arendt, above n 28, at 255.

[35] See A. Fischer-Lescano and G. Teubner, 'Regime-collisions: The Vain Search for Legal Unity in the Fragmentation of Global Law' (2004) 25 *Michigan Journal of International Law* 999–1046.

[36] For a similar description, see M. Loughlin, *The Idea of Public Law* (Oxford: Oxford University Press, 2003), 17–18.

[37] See S. Cassese, 'Administrative Law without the State? The Challenge of Global Regulation' (2005) 37 *New York University Journal of International Law and Politics* 663–94, at 673: 'The centrality of the state to the notion of public powers has become an optical illusion.'

V. THE LEGAL RELATIONSHIP

It is only with reluctance that I take up a topic that smacks of a stale debate. But it is unavoidable to come close to addressing the concept of law, even though this is precisely what I would still like to avoid.[38] I express uneasiness about having to do so for the simple reason that the topic has suffered enormous intellectual setbacks in recent debates over legal positivism. One debate is (still) concerned with examples of 'wicked law' whose encounter supposedly renders untenable the distinction between law as it is and law as it ought to be.[39] The other debate, if the existing scholarship even amounts to one, affects the purportedly conventional nature of standards used to identify valid law. The first debate is useless because it does not address the underlying problem of political resistance. The second debate is wrongheaded because it overlooks that, even though there are undeniably conventions for raising and contesting legal claims, these claims do not merely self-referentially point to conventions.[40] This is also the case for the concept of law. We refer to some matters as law conventionally while what we thereby intend aspires to more than mere conformity with more or less settled practice. Even if we may find, in some cases, an appeal to conventions sufficient, we do not rest content on conventional grounds.

The concept of law presupposes the concept of legality. From Enlightenment legal philosophy we inherited an understanding of legality according to which the relationship between the commander and an addressee is legal if the latter is not required to share the point of view of the former.[41] The addressee is free to obey with complete indifference towards the lawgiver's plans and objectives.[42] That the relationship between lawgivers and addressees and, indeed, any person entering into a legal relationship with another is characterised by legality is part of the law's counterfactual social facts. Legal subjects are expected to have such a detached attitude. A legal relationship presupposes the mutual ascription of counterfactual social facts with regard to how control is exercised by someone over another and what it takes to

---

[38] Scholars of global administrative law usually also avoid addressing this question, for this would get in the way of promoting the pragmatic objectives of increasing transparency, accountability, and possibly also democracy. For this observation, see D. Dyzenhaus, 'Accountability and the Concept of (Global) Administrative Law' <http://iilj.org/courses/documents/Dyzenhaus.TheConceptofGlobalAdministrativeLawFinal.pdf>. I would like to thank Nico Krisch for drawing my attention to this paper.

[39] For the latest outgrowth of this debate, see R. Alexy, *The Argument from Injustice: A Reply to Legal Positivism*, trans B. Litschweski Paulson and S. Paulson (Oxford: Oxford University Press, 2002).

[40] For a forceful critique, see R. Dworkin, *Justice in Robes* (Cambridge, Mass.: Harvard University Press, 2006), 140–86.

[41] Enlightenment legal philosophy was concerned with freedom from interference by others: see, eg J. G. Fichte, *Grundlage des Naturrechts nach Prinzipien der Wissenschaftslehre*, ed M. Zahn (Hamburg: Meiner, 1979), 118–19.

[42] See Fuller, above n 3, at 209.

be controlled by someone else. The use of coercion as a means of last resort signifies the existence of such a mutually detached, 'external' relationship.[43]

Traditional international law involves a legal relationship. The norm giver and the norm addressee are not, owing to their relationship, members of a common project or joint enterprise.[44] They may remain foreign to one another in the sense that the addressee is always free to point to limits of obligation without having to explain why what he has or has not done does not amount to disloyal, inconsiderate, or unproductive behaviour. The relationship is *external*, for it merely requires conduct to be norm oriented. Governing by law is not directed at some goal of optimisation, nor does it involve a learning process. It is about laying down, and doing, what is right and avoiding what is wrong. It is a separate matter whether determining what is right or wrong involves a reference to rules or a classification of the weight of different arguments,[45] but there would be no legal relationship if without further qualification all kinds of arguments were admitted to some process of optimisation.

Owing to its external character, the legal relationship, traditionally understood,[46] is also marked by *distance*. One party does not assist, counsel, train, support, or educate the other party into what it takes to secure compliance. Unless parties have decided to establish a common administration, working towards the retraining or transformation of partners would transcend a legal relationship. But even when parties agree to endure counselling or training, the terms of the agreement define the limit from which the distance can be perceived that governs the relation between partners. What matters, in the final event, is that the addressees undertake to engage in conduct that they have agreed to, or were ordered to, espouse. In other words, the addressee, even though liable to comply with a rule, neither becomes the rule giver's servant nor, worse still, his or her slave.[47]

The legal relationship, even when it creates a position of subordination does not give rise to comprehensive or unconditional subjection. This is the case because any power that is given to anyone is limited. The defenders of republican liberty—the liberty Skinner refers to as liberty before liberalism—understood perfectly well that domination can only be avoided when the jurisdiction of the superordinate power is limited.[48] The legal relationship cannot tolerate sovereignty. It involves

---

[43] See Immanuel Kant, *Metaphysik der Sitten, Werke in zwölf Bänden*, ed W. Weischedel (Frankfurt am Main: Suhrkamp Verlag, 1969), viii. 338–9.

[44] Evidently, this is a point I borrow from Oakeshott, above n 32, 128.

[45] The latter was integral to Dworkin's original project: see his *Taking Rights Seriously* (Cambridge, Mass.: Harvard University Press, 2nd edn, 1978).

[46] I add this historical marker, for I would like to leave open the question whether legality cannot be seen in a process of historical transformation. But see A. Somek, 'Legalität heute: Variationen über ein Thema von Max Weber' (2008) 47 *Der Staat* 428–65.

[47] On the following, see Q. Skinner, *Liberty before Liberalism* (Cambridge: Cambridge University Press, 1998).

[48] See also R. Bellamy, *Political Constitutionalism: A Republican Defence of the Constitutionality of Democracy* (Cambridge: Cambridge University Press, 2007), 159.

jurisdictional limits. This is not to say that the absence of sovereignty in and of itself corroborates the presence of a legal relationship. On the contrary, the void becomes all too easily filled with administration without sovereignty.

The significance of such jurisdictional limits can be seen by spinning even further the analogy between compliance with legal norms, on the one hand, and the execution of tasks, on the other. Since the addressee is not subjugated to the unconditional command of the lawgiver he or she remains in a position similar to that of a craftsperson or a contractor. They determine themselves how they go about fulfilling their promises and doing their work. They are not under permanent guidance or direction. The analogy appears to be particularly apt for the classical international legal relationship where the labour of compliance is entirely left to the obligated subject. In the case of non-self-executing treaties the obligated states are free to adopt the norms that accommodate their international obligation to their internal situation. But even being commanded to do something—Austin style—is different from suffering the type of subordination that is characteristic of service or apprenticeship (apprenticeship, in fact, describes accurately the situation of those who are being assisted into being capable of compliance).

Conceiving the negative of a legal relationship in terms of servitude and apprenticeship captures merely a segment. The non-legal relationship is not necessarily hierarchical. Tongue in cheek, I add that it may well be heterarchical. Teams of technicians committed to their expertise can become slaves of their ambition, in particular, when they mutually push their standards to new heights. More generally, competitive situations create subordination not merely under the shifting predilections of consumers but also to the conditions of actions that are the contingent result of uncoordinated efforts. It would be worth exploring in what respect market situations create domination that is the opposite of legality; it is, however, beyond the purview of this chapter.

Bluntly speaking, the legal relationship is a negation of administrative rationality, and administrative law the resulting unstable synthesis. Legalisation introduces a break into the overall teleological compass of administrative action and creates obstacles for particularistic interference. The synthesis is unstable, for administrative rationality is always inclined to make legal form subservient to its own ends. The legal constraints on administrative action can either consist of norms that it needs to comply with— these norms may be as nebulous as the notorious reason-giving requirements—or of the obligation to secure the consent or to avoid the veto of others. I concede that this is, if anything, an almost obscenely trivial characterisation of what may strike one as 'legal' about administrative law;[49] nevertheless, simply because of its very meagreness it is all the more apt for presenting the contrast that I would like to defend.

---

[49] I should like to emphasise that the tendency prevalent among students of the common law to see the rule of law triumph as soon as there is judicial review of administrative action (and the ensuing judicial elaboration of standards) strikes me also as not particularly ingenious. See Harlow, above n 13, at 191–2. Similarly, Dyzenhaus, above n 38, at 28, appears to be convinced that, indeed, a legal relationship obtains so long as the decision-making body offers a 'reasoned opinion' for its decisions. This must strike one as clearly insufficient, for any legal decision needs to explain the weight of reasons with an eye to the existence

VI. THE GLOBAL ADMINISTRATIVE RELATIONSHIP:
INTERNSHIP TO PARTNERSHIP

Why the world envisaged by global administrative law does not involve a legal relationship in the sense reconstructed above becomes clear, remarkably enough, already in the opening pages of Slaughter's *The New World Order*.[50] Even though the author presents in this work her own account of what transnational governing processes are all about, she describes quite perceptively what the various relationships between and among the actors engaged in administrative networks involve.

First, the influence exercised in those networks is based on the imparting and sharing of information. This means, by contrast to the legal relation, that norm-oriented behaviour is not part of the picture.[51] Rather, the point appears to be that the participants in networks are expected to rise from their present level of knowledge and skills to the next. Broadly understood, this involves some process of teaching, learning, and growth. What really matters are processes and not acts. As has been observed by Shapiro this means that 'dialogue itself evolved into governance'.[52]

Second, the basic image of the relationship is not that of distanced agreement and compliance but one of either unidirectional or multidirectional 'capacity-building'. Of course, building the capacity to comply is a better means of securing compliance than trust in the fidelity of the partner or the effectiveness of sanctions.

Third, it is understood, mutually and generally, that all action taken within networks contributes to a process of problem solving. This explains why an ostensible oxymoron such as 'regulation by information'[53] can pass muster. It explains also why the usual ersatz material for norms, such as 'best practice', 'benchmarking', or mutual learning and adjustment, have become the sweethearts of the advocates of transnational governing. Where 'problem solving' serves as the preferred descriptor of an activity, ideological conflict does not enter the picture. Problem solving is the antithesis of political struggle. It is the activity in which those engage who already share a certain view of the world and share a mutual understanding of the values that they adhere to.

Multi-level regulatory problem solving, such as the determination of permissible food ingredients, has as one of its points of reference WTO side agreements and the default standards set by the Codex Alimentarius Commission. But the WTO dispute

---

of a legal relationship (hence, for example, by drawing a line between principle and policy arguments).

[50] See A.-M. Slaughter, *The New World Order* (Princeton, NJ: Princeton University Press, 2004), at 4.

[51] It has been pointed out by Luhmann already that with the rise of world society cognitive expectations will play a more important role than the normative expectations characteristic of law (see N. Luhmann, 'Die Weltgesellschaft', in his *Soziologische Aufklärung: Aufsätze zur Theorie der Gesellschaft* (Opladen: Westdeutscher Verlag, 2nd edn, 1975), ii. 51–71, at 55).

[52] Shapiro, above n 16, at 372.

[53] Slaughter, above n 50, at 24.

settlement process is merely one of the relevant locales. National and regional institutions are also involved. In the context of such multi-level systems, decisions are increasingly understood to be provisional formulations of standpoints in a context where convergence is the hoped-for result. The counterfactual social facts characteristic of the legal system cannot be taken for granted here. The substantive standards applied suffer from a high degree of de-formalisation, which has been rightly decried by Koskenniemi.[54] One finds neither prescriptions nor proscriptions, merely certain factors that pull in different directions but nonetheless need to be taken into account for decision making in individual cases. There is no relation of indifference. It is understood that regulators positioned at different levels, such as the WTO and the EU, are part of a common enterprise and may well entertain different ideas for what it may take to arrive at the best result. Decisions in individual cases are treated as though they were contributions to an ongoing learning process which is to result in the final catholic consensus that Peirce believed to be the epiphany of truth.[55] The normative is no longer normative. It is transformed into something cognitive.

The emerging view of the social universe perceives the life process to depend on the capacity on the part of various actors to participate in problem-solving processes, which in turn involve expertise and widespread communication. It is a world of partnerships and apprenticeships. In fact, it is the world that one first personally encounters in 'internships'. It is also a world that requires a high degree of mutual accommodation and comity among units operating in different jurisdictional spheres. The mutual accommodation among cooperating units is concomitant with the lack of sovereignty. From it emerges the most remarkable feature of the modern governing relationships, namely that they are ultimately grounded in reflexive administrative processes. These processes take place in a setting that is marked by the absence of sovereignty,[56] which is manifested in two indeterminacies: the indeterminacy of jurisdiction, on the one hand, and the indeterminacy of sources on the other. Both give rise to a remarkable development. A style of reasoning that has its roots in the common law tradition comes to play havoc with reason and to enchant members of the discipline. Regardless of whether one considers the legality thereby abandoned or transformed, it is clear that the counterfactual social facts underpinning a traditional legal relationship can no longer be sustained.

---

[54] See M. Koskenniemi, 'The Fate of Public International Law: Between Technique and Politics' (2007) 70 *Modern Law Review* 1–30.

[55] See C. S. Peirce, 'Some Consequences of Four Incapacities', in *The Essential Peirce*, ed N. Houser and C. Kloesel (Bloomington: Indiana University Press, 1992), i. 28–55, at 54.

[56] The absence of traditional legality's counterfactual social facts—such as norm-oriented behaviour, a mutually detached relationship, or respect for jurisdictional limits—is *indirectly* confirmed by this absence of sovereignty. I do not want to claim that the existence of a legal relationship presupposes the existence of sovereign power; what I would like to suggest, however, is that it is easier to establish legal relationships within a homogeneous sphere of power.

VII. INDETERMINATE JURISDICTION

Global administrative law conceives of global problem solving as taking place in a pluralist universe where institutions located at different levels contend to resolve certain issues. The relevant institutions, such as a WTO dispute settlement panel or the United Nations Security Council, can be tied to constituencies whom they arguably represent or are, at any rate, answerable to.[57] According to Krisch's intriguing reconstruction, no potential constituency is disqualified from deciding on certain issues.[58] The national constituency lends a voice to the concerns of local communities. The international constituency represents the interests of states across borders. The cosmopolitan constituency, finally, stands for the perspective of 'a truly global public'.[59] But no constituency is qualified to exercise exclusive jurisdiction.[60] The national is not, for it is not sufficiently capable of taking into account the effect that its acts have on its neighbours. The international constituency suffers from a severe democratic legitimacy deficit, and the cosmopolitan is not associated with any community at all. A consociational solution does not seem to be of any avail either, for it would allow for too much veto power to obstruct the process.[61] The solution that Krisch recommends would apparently embrace concurrent jurisdiction without pre-emption. Decisions should be taken anywhere; however, any other constituency would retain a right to contestation before the decision-making institution or anywhere else:

> The resulting picture of global governance would then be one of a constant potential for mutual challenge: of decisions with limited authority that may be contested through diverse channels until some (perhaps provisional) closure might be achieved.[62]

This is a world that does not recognise the final legal word.[63] Krisch perceives correctly that the absence of a final legal solution is likely to have a moderating effect in a situation where all representatives of constituencies believe the long-term benefits of cooperation to exceed the short-term gains of ostensible defection. Sweet harmony of agreement is likely to pervade a world of 'smooth cooperation,

---

[57] Global administrative law is basically understood to address accountability problems. See Krisch and Kingsbury, above n 19, at 1, 4.

[58] On the following, see N. Krisch, 'The Pluralism of Global Administrative Law' (2006) 17 *European Journal of International Law* 247–78, at 253–5.

[59] See ibid at 255.

[60] See ibid at 269–70.

[61] See ibid at 264–6.

[62] Ibid at 266–7.

[63] In a similar vein, see G. Teubner, 'Altera Pars Audiatur: Law in the Collision of Discourses', in R. Rawlings (ed), *Law, Society, and Economy* (Oxford: Oxford University Press, 1997), 150–76.

compromise and mutual accommodation'.[64] But this is only a positive way of saying that what is to be encountered here is the pragmatic logic of administrative problem solving and not reasons that invoke a legal constraint. Instead of being put to work on substantive issues, administrative rationality is applied to dealing with the presence of others. The mutual influencing of different jurisdictions, the fluid and provisional pragmatic approximation,[65] and the mindful processing of disagreement are nothing short of *administrative rationality in action*.

The reason why the outcome of such processes of mutual self-observation is not a product of legality can be seen all the more clearly by examining the attempt that has been made to present such processes of mutual accommodation, adaptation, learning, and creative problem solving as emerging from the 'auto-constitutionalisation' of regimes. In the course of their highly original analysis of the fragmented nature of the world's legal system, Fischer-Lescano and Teubner see processes of autonomous societal constitutionalisation at work whenever and wherever reflexive processes of various social spheres become combined ('coupled') with reflexive processes of the legal system. The idea is intriguing. According to social systems theory, reflexive processes occur in social systems whenever the system's internal logic and operation becomes applied to itself.[66] This is the case, for example, when the scientific system, which is the wellspring of theories about the world, begins to develop theories about theories. The legal system switches into a reflexive mode when secondary rules come to address the creation and application of primary rules of obligation. Hence, science would avail itself of a constitution if theories about theories—ie philosophy of science—were to inform the adoption of legal standards for the admission of standards of truth. Arguably, science already *has* a constitution, thus understood, but it is an entirely negative constitution, for it prohibits the adoption of such secondary rules out of concern for the freedom to conduct research. Alternatively, the market economy can be said to apply its most elementary principle, the principle of allocative efficiency, to itself when it identifies failures in the actual operation of the market to attain efficient results. When this reflexive process is combined with secondary rules for the intervention into the economy, competition law ostensibly comes to play the role of the 'constitution of the economy'. The self-reflection of politics, that is, the application of partisan struggle to partisan struggle, becomes constitutionalised when it is used to define the rules of the political game. The procedural core of the constitution, and only the procedural core, is the political constitution of society. Higher law may be ubiquitous, but only to a limited extent does it affect the constitution of politics.

Even though such a use of the concept of the constitution may strike one as fundamentally at odds with Grimm's historical sensibilities,[67] it has certain purchase,

---

[64]   Krisch, above n 58, at 267.

[65]   See ibid at 263.

[66]   See N. Luhmann, 'Reflexive Mechanismen', in *Soziologische Aufklärung* (Opladen: Westdeutscher Verlag, 4th edn, 1974), i. 92–112.

[67]   See above n 5.

nonetheless, for it invites re-conceiving of all legal systems—domestic as well as transnational—in terms of patchworks of overlapping and potentially colliding constitutions of social sectors. However, in the cases that are of interest here, and these are the cases affecting global administrative law, these purportedly 'auto-constitutionalised' regimes experience the necessity 'to take into account', 'to learn from', and 'to defer by default' how their respective peer regimes have dealt with certain issues. The pragmatic ingenuity that comes into play in such processes confirms that *no* secondary rules are being followed. It is the administrative process with its dual orientation towards the whole and towards the particular that accounts for the decision making. Primary rules, that is, are not brought to life, put to work, and eliminated on the basis of secondary rule of procedure, but rather on the basis of intuitively arrived at provisional adjustments.

VIII.   THE EXALTATION OF THE COMMON LAW

I would like to anticipate, at this point, two potential objections. According to the first objection, I am guilty of bringing to bear on the subject matter a narrowly formalistic and positivistic concept of the legal relationship, which has long turned out to be indefensible even for legal systems of a municipal kind. By contrast, it is not at all implausible to assume that background moral and political principles, rather than neatly stated secondary rules, inform all legal problem solving.[68] Denying such principles a legal status is tantamount to committing a classical fallacy of legal positivism.

The second objection has it that even if the pedigree of processes of mutual adjustment might be in doubt, there would be no point in denying the product the quality of law.

I would reply to the first objection in two related ways. First, I readily concede that the concept of legality is not immune to historical transformation. I believe, indeed, that the legal relationship has been amended not only by the 'super-legal' dimension hinted at by the objection, but has also been tentatively transformed into a more experimental and provisional relation of mutual engagement.[69] It should not escape our attention, however, that in this latter and more 'creative' format, the legal relation becomes easily prey to administrative rationality.[70] The application of norms and coordination of conduct pursuant to norms is then rendered indistinguishable from management and flexible adjustment.[71] Secondly, how co-optation works can

---

[68] This objection would have its backing in Dworkin's keen analysis of legal reasoning (see Dworkin, above n 45).

[69] See W. H. Simon, 'Toyota Jurisprudence: Legal Theory and Rolling Rule Regimes', in G. de Búrca and J. Scott (eds), *Law and New Governance in the EU and the US* (Oxford: Hart, 2006), 37–64.

[70] See Somek, above n 46.

[71] It remains to be explored in the future whether this development needs to be viewed as a process that is as irreversible as was the 'emancipation of dissonance' in music.

be seen from a different angle. It is a truism that every act of law application also contains a law-creating element. A preferred strategy for explaining how it is that the creative element becomes part of application is pointing to the power of the law-applying official to do so. Accordingly, valid law is created on the basis of power-conferring norms. But this is not the only possible account of how a synthesis of existing law and some creative element is brought about in the adoption of legal acts. It can be argued that the synthesis in the relation of application and its creative element is made possible by 'good arguments', 'sound judgment', the (right) 'moral attitude', or convincing reasons. However, good arguments, sound judgment, and convincing reasons are person-relative entities. Someone needs to have the power to declare that he or she has been persuaded by them. Otherwise one would not arrive at law, but merely at some intermediate result of a discussion. Legal systems presuppose the systematic mediation of norms by other norms. The work cannot be done by moral intuition. If the work is done by moral intuition one does not get a full-fledged legal system, but some extension of community morality into the realm of the justification of coercion. What is called 'common law' may well have to be described in such terms. In any event, if the adoption of legal acts is not mediated by legally circumscribed powers but by considerations of administrative expediency then legality is turned into an appendix of the latter.

This is of relevance to the second objection. It is not possible to create law from a system of argumentation. One can make statements, arrive at conjectures and provisional outlooks, and arrange for some *modus vivendi*. This, in fact, appears to be the state that the international system has come to embrace.[72] But it is not unimportant to note that the rampant intuitionism gives rise to an exalted version of the common law, which is, strangely enough, celebrated under different headings, such as 'international constitutional law' or 'networks' of adjudicative expertise. An exalted common law has lost its moorings in positive law. In fact, it is common law in the state of its own negation, that is, in a state *before* the rule of *stare decisis* has made it into what was to become of it.[73] There are no limits to authority. Legal materials from various jurisdictions provide occasion for wide-ranging reflections from case to case. Nothing is fixed, everything is in flux. Common law in such an exalted state does not offer any resistance to administrative rationality. Therefore, it is particularly vulnerable to co-optation.

I conclude that the supposed management of 'regime collisions' or the jurisdictional open-endedness of global administrative law cannot reflect guidance by secondary rules. They are plainly and simply second-order administrative processes. This diagnosis is reconfirmed by looking at what these processes deem relevant to their success: concern for the stability of the overall project on the one hand (and therefore, 'default reference' to related regimes) and particularisation on the other. Particularisation, above all, underlies the praise of fluidity and experimentation that Krisch has for the global administrative process. As long as settlements are

---

[72] It is all the more remarkable that this is then called 'constitutionalisation'.

[73] The idea that the beginning of something presupposes its negation is a common theme of Jewish and German Romantic mysticism.

of no general relevance and do not establish a precedent, they do not prejudice a continuing process of mutual accommodation.

IX. INDETERMINATE SOURCES

The exalted state in which common law is thrown back onto its origin is a manifestation of the absence of sovereignty. The latter is an ultimate power-conferring norm that permits allocation of jurisdiction. A sovereign is one who decides over the limits of his or her own jurisdiction and, hence, indirectly the jurisdiction of others. When sovereignty disappears, all that one is left with is unauthorised administrative action. There are no jurisdictional bounds.

But the absence of sovereignty is also reflected in the manner in which proponents of global administrative law conceive of sources of law.[74] At the outset it is claimed that customary law, treaties, and general principles of law are to be considered sources of global administrative law. The proponents of this claim need to concede, however, that 'it is unlikely that these sources are sufficient to account for the origins and authority of the normative practice already existing in the field'. They would have us look, rather, at spontaneous law-making practices and express confidence that the norms governing global administrative practice might emerge from a *ius gentium*, that is, basically, the understandings of those who are familiar with basic administrative law principles from their home jurisdiction. Remarkably, the authors have no qualms about their submission that it is practice that ought to matter, whereas, at the same time, they confirm that 'uncertainty remains about the basis for determining such norms and their legal status'.[75] They candidly admit that disagreement about the sources is part of the law-making process:

> Moreover, under a *ius gentium* approach, disagreement is inevitable about whose practices to count and whose not to count for the emergence of a rule, and as to how much consistent practice might be necessary to generate a strong pull for cohesion.[76]

The authors express confidence that future research might be able to do the work. There is little reason to be confident, however, for the study of the emergence of customary international law has shown that the emergence of custom itself is a matter of conflicting principles.[77] Customary law is, if anything, a deficient form of law from a formal point of view. This deficiency, however, benefits those claiming to be masters of the artificial reason of the law.[78]

---

[74] See Kingsbury et al, above n 11, at 29.

[75] Ibid at 30.

[76] Ibid at 31.

[77] See M. Byers, *Custom, Power and the Power of Rules: International Relations and Customary International Law* (Cambridge: Cambridge University Press, 1999).

[78] See Thomas Hobbes, *A Dialogue between a Philosopher and a Student of the Common Laws of England*, ed J. Cropsey (Chicago, Ill.: University of Chicago Press, 1971).

X. CONCLUSION

There was a time when even the most steadfast defenders of the international legal system readily conceded that this system was still in a primitive state and actually aspired to see it transformed before it was to form the basis of a world order that rests on principles of legality.[79] The situation has changed. Since nobody appears to believe any longer in a change of the world order by political means, scholarship is increasingly taking comfort from the academic equivalent of practical change, namely the re-description of social realities. If the world cannot be changed you imagine it changed and pretend the work of your imagination to amount to the real.[80] It should not surprise us that this is happening in a cultural context where confidence boosting or communication strategies are believed to be key to altering one's life.

Re-descriptions often involve the use of idealisations. This is, in and of itself, not problematic, for idealisations are part of how the law itself perceives social realities in its own context of operation. Idealisations turn out to be problematic, however, when they purport to see a legal relationship where in fact such a relation is absent. The law's most elementary idealisation does not apply then.

The most ludicrous form of re-description is the application of constitutional vocabulary to international law. In this chapter, I have not addressed this phenomenon at all. Owing to its lower degree of exuberance, global administrative law promises to offer a more plausible account of existing international processes. I have tried to explain why the idealisations of global administrative law might actually distort our perception of administrative realities.

Beyond critically examining the claims of global administrative law, the analysis yields an important result. If it is true that domestic political and legal processes are increasingly under the substantive influence of global coordination processes then it seems that ultimately second-order administrative processes are increasingly taking the place of norms. Hence, it would not amount to a valid defence of the purported legality of global administrative 'law' if one were to say that formality and flexibility affect merely the relations among administrators in the multi-level system, whereas for private persons compliance with international standards is mediated through national administrative law. If it is true, as claimed by proponents of global administrative law, that the latter is increasingly under the sway of the former then informality also seeps into national systems. Moreover, with an exalted common law providing the overall 'legal' background mentality, the disintegration of legality transcends the boundaries of the administrative branch, narrowly understood, and spills over into the judiciary. Administrative processes seep into legal processes, altering their shape from the inside.

---

[79] See H. Kelsen, *Peace through Law* (Chapel Hill: University of North Carolina Press, 1944).

[80] Did I say Judith Butler? On the ideological distortion of public international law by its proponents, see S. Marks, *The Riddle of All Constitutions: International Law, Democracy, and the Critique of Ideology* (Oxford: Oxford University Press, 1999).

If this, in turn, is true, what we encounter, then, is a far cry from the demise of the state under conditions of globalisation. On the contrary, it is the eventual triumph of the state over law. What we perceive, however, is the face of the state that is often ignored, for it is not as spectacular as sovereignty. It is the state, understood as the agency busying itself with governing, that is, the state qua administration. The state, thus understood, is not identical with law, for it does not partake of the law's normativity.

Finally, the triumph of run-of-the-mill governing also marks ascendancy of the state over politics. The de-politicised state introduces the omnipresence of administrative problem solving. I conclude, that instead of ushering in law beyond the state, globalisation may well reinstitute the lawless state. Who would have expected that?

PART VI

THE EMERGENCE OF SOCIETAL CONSTITUTIONALISM

⤔ 14 ⤕

Beyond the Holistic Constitution?

Neil Walker

I. THE POLITICS OF CONSTITUTIONAL DEFINITION

The modern state, understood as the key unit within the global framework of authority, was for long the undisputed domicile of constitutionalism and the guarantor of its relevance. So what is to become of constitutionalism in the contemporary world, when the configuration of economic, political, and cultural forces that produced the state-centred global framework of authority is no longer so securely in place, and where other key sites of authority are emerging? This is an issue both for the old state setting and for the new non-state settings. On what terms, if at all, can constitutionalism remain viable in the old state setting, and on what terms, if at all, can constitutionalism be adapted to new settings?

The direct focus of the present chapter is on the latter set of questions, but in order to address these some conceptual ground clearing is required. In undertaking this initial survey, we encounter an exaggerated version of a familiar problem. As is common when dealing with social and political concepts that register both at the 'object' level of everyday use and at the 'observer' level of theoretical inquiry, the answers that many analysts seek or expect when addressing the prospects of constitutionalism seem often to be anticipated in their stipulation of the definitional preliminaries. However, just because so much uncertainty surrounds a conceptual leap of such audacious proportions as is contemplated in taking constitutionalism beyond the state, the absence of agreement over definitional preliminaries is uncommonly pronounced and conspicuous in the instant case. This fractured beginning, in turn, leads to an unusually high level of mutual disengagement and a general polarisation of theoretical positions. We are faced, in fact, with an irony of overproduction. On the one hand, in academic circles at least, the unsettling of old taken-for-granted certainties about the place of constitutionalism within the global scheme means that never has discussion of law and politics so frequently, so explicitly, and so self-consciously occurred within a constitutional register, and never has the constitutional idea been so insistently reasserted in its old state setting or so vigorously sponsored in new non-state settings. On the other hand, because the stakes are so high and the value of the currency so volatile, never has discussion of constitutionalism cultivated such little common ground.[1] There is scant cross-fertilisation from the different points of departure, and what exchange does take place often appears to be the dialogue of the deaf.

This is not intended as a partisan point. Those who want or expect constitutionalism to travel beyond its state domicile are as likely to load the conceptual dice in favour of their preferred conclusion as those who start from the prejudice that no such mobility is possible or desirable. What is more, each side tends to encourage the other in its conceptual myopia.

On the part of the advocates of post-state constitutionalism we encounter a series of conceptual starting points that are in danger of treating constitutionalism in superficial terms, as too easily detached from its statist moorings. This is most evident in the case of what are best described as *nominal* definitions of constitutionalism. Here, constitutionalism is deployed merely as an affirmative label for whatever concept, institution, or attitude of governance, wherever situated, that its sponsor endorses or considers pivotal to the regulatory regime in question, whether we are talking about human rights protection, anti-discrimination measures, or even just a commitment to 'the Rule of Law'. The purpose here is ideological: to give the feature(s) of governance to which one is committed or to which one attributes central significance the additional gravitas of affirmation in a powerful and familiar symbolic register, or to deny such affirmation to other approaches that lack the favoured feature(s) or even oppose the priority given to them. Implicit in this ideological agenda stands the conviction, or at least the unexamined premiss, that there is simply nothing that privileges the relationship between the state and constitutionalism, and so nothing of special value to be lost in the move beyond that relationship. The point of the nominalist position, in sum, is precisely *not to argue* the case for the mobility of the constitutional idea beyond the state but, by treating constitutionalism as a floating signifier, to elevate the case to the exalted position of the unarguably correct.[2]

A second deracinated version of constitutionalism concentrates on *formal* features. Unlike nominalism, here the state, as the undisputed source of the modern constitutional idea, retains some influence over the destination meaning, if much

---

[1] See, eg N. Walker, 'The Idea of Constitutional Pluralism' (2002) 65 *Modern Law Rev* 317–59.

[2] We must be careful not to be too critical of nominalist positions. First, often good arguments are made for this or that aspect of governance from within a nominalist position; it is just that these arguments are not enhanced by the use of constitutional language. Second, often nominalism shades into formalism or materialism (see text below), and indeed formal or material borrowing from the state tradition may be the inarticulate premiss underlying the nominalist position. Third, nominalism may connect to the vital 'placeholding' function of constitutionalism, discussed in section V below, in that through its insistence on a constitutional register it speaks not only to a desire to obtain ideological advantage for one's position, but also to an awareness of how much continues to be at stake in the very idea of a political framing of our social arrangements. For just one example of a writer who uses the language of transnational constitutionalism in this loose but provocative way, see C. Joerges, ' "Good Governance" in the European Internal Market: An Essay in Honour of Claus-Dieter Ehlermann', *EUI Working Papers*, RSC 2001/29.

attenuated. The formalist approach suggests that the very manner in which—the form through which—the political world may be understood and organised from a juridical perspective may borrow from or be inspired by the state constitutional template. This is most obviously the case with regard to the idea of a constitutive juridical instrument, whether or not specifically so-called 'Constitutional' (as in the case of the abortive EU constitutional text of 2004),[3] that is so familiar from state public law. In the context of non-state legal and institutional orders we may find instruments that are similarly formally constitutive in one or more of various senses, whether with reference to their norm-generative or foundational quality, their assertion of entrenched status, their precedence over other system norms, or their claim to provide an encompassing framework for and measure of the limits of the 'body politic' that they create or recognise.[4] And even where such generative, entrenched, trumping, embracing, and delimiting features of a legal and institutional order are independent of a self-styled documentary Constitution, or indeed of a single and unrivalled constitutive instrument of any sort, as we have seen in the case of the advocates of WTO constitutionalism,[5] or of the constitutionalisation of the international order,[6] or of the various 'civic' or 'societal' constitutions such as the *lex mercatoria* of the international economy or the *lex digitalis* of the Internet,[7] the mere emergence of some combination of these formal features may still be enough for the juridical initiative in question to be deemed constitutional in kind.

A third form of constitutionalism beyond the state concentrates not on formal matters but on the manifestation of a family resemblance between certain *material* features of state constitutionalism and the new transnational legal outgrowth. Aspects of transnational law are deemed to be constitutional not, or not only, because they appear on the commentator's approved list, as with nominalism, but because the mechanisms or concepts in question—from general structural formulae such as separation of powers and institutional balance to more specific principles such as

---

[3] Treaty Establishing a Constitution for Europe [2004] OJ C310.

[4] For a concise statement of the formalist position, see A. Stone Sweet, 'Constitutionalism, Legal Pluralism and International Regimes' (2009) 16/2 *Indiana Journal of Global Legal Studies* 621–45.

[5] See, eg D. Cass, *The Constitutionalization of the World Trade Organization* (Oxford: Oxford University Press, 2005); E.-U. Petermann, 'The WTO Constitution and Human Rights' (2000) 3 *Journal of International Economic Law* 19–25.

[6] See, eg E. de Wet, 'The International Constitutional Order' (2006) *International and Comparative Law Quarterly* 55–76; for an approach which, unusually, seeks to locate the constitutionalisation of the international order in documentary terms—in the form of the UN Charter, see B. Fassbender, 'The United Nations Charter as the Constitution of the International Community' (1998) 36 *Columbia Journal of International Law* 529–619.

[7] See, eg G. Teubner, 'Societal Constitutionalism: Alternatives to State-Centred Constitutional Theory?', in C. Joerges, I.-J. Sand, and G. Teubner (eds), *Transnational Governance and Constitutionalism* (Oxford: Hart, 2004), 3–28; G. Teubner and A. Fischer-Lescano, 'Regime-Collisions: The Vain Search for Legal Unity in the Fragmentation of Global Law' (2004) 25 *Michigan Journal of International Law* 999–1045.

subsidiarity or proportionality—were long ago nurtured in the state constitutional context and, indeed, have often been self-consciously received into transnational law from these state sources.[8] As is the case with formalism, however, the connection between the non-state version and the state original from the materialist perspective is tenuous. It is dependent upon analogy, and in some cases conscious imitation. How deep the analogy runs and what is lost—or gained—in translation from one context to another is rarely the subject of sustained analysis.[9]

If we now turn to those who would oppose the movement of constitutionalism beyond the state, again they range from the primitive to the more sophisticated. Most basically, and more common within everyday 'object' discourse than in academic 'observer' discourse, there is a position that holds that the category of constitution is necessarily restricted to the state. That position is the negative image of nominalism, and just as impervious to counter-suggestion. Whereas nominalism holds to or simply assumes the solipsistic idea that all meaning is constructed without extra-linguistic check or constraint, *essentialism* holds or more often simply assumes the opposite. It maintains that meaning is fixed and invariable in its correspondence with some extra-linguistic reality, and so it follows that it is simply *meaningless* to conceive of constitutionalism beyond the fixed and invariable limits of the state.

Beyond essentialism, there are at least two positions—or rather a continuum of possibilities framed by two positions—that treat the idea of the constitution as deeply embedded in the state. One position is *culturalist* in nature. It holds the idea of a constitution to be hollow, or at least deficient, in the absence of certain attributes, including the idea of a democratically self-constituting and self-constituted 'people' possessing comprehensive powers of self-determination and self-legislation. These attributes, it is claimed, are ultimately contingent upon certain prior or emergent socio-cultural facts concerning identity, solidarity, and allegiance, absent which any self-styled constitutional project is fated to be either a dead letter or a much more modest affair. Since only the modern state has known such a socio-cultural formation, and since even if the modern state is no longer so robust in these terms it still constitutes a standing impediment to the development of similar cultural formations at non-state sites, there can be no real prospect of a full constitutionalism beyond the state.[10]

A second position runs even deeper than the culturalist argument without succumbing to the semantic sting of state-centred essentialism. This approach we may call *epistemic* in that it focuses on the very idea of the modern state and of

---

[8] On the migration of particular constitutional concepts from national to transnational level, see N. Walker, 'The Migration of Constitutional Ideas and the Migration of *the* Constitutional Idea', in S. Choudhry (ed), *The Migration of Constitutional Ideas* (Cambridge: Cambridge University Press, 2006), 316–44.

[9] For one attempt, see N. Walker, 'Postnational Constitutionalism and the Problem of Translation', in J. Weiler and M. Wind (eds), *European Constitutionalism beyond the State* (Cambridge: Cambridge University Press, 2003), 27–54.

[10] See, eg D. Grimm, 'The Constitution in the Process of Denationalization' (2005) 12 *Constellations* 447–65.

the political imaginary associated with the idea of the modern state as embracing 'a scheme of intelligibility … a comprehensive way of seeing, understanding and acting in the world'[11] that is prior to and prerequisite to a full, modern articulation of the idea of constitution. The key insight here, and what distinguishes it from the culturalist position, is that the concept of the modern state, understood as a particular type of relationship between territory, ruling authority, and people, is not merely the expression and fruit of a prior cultural achievement—an accomplishment of national solidarity that supplies the 'battery of power'[12] necessary to run the constitutional machine effectively. More than that, it is a political way of knowing and way of being in the absence of whose emergence the very idea of a constitutional polity is simply unimaginable. In both cases—culturalist and epistemic—the message is strongly conveyed that the modern idea and practice of constitutionalism could not have developed except in the context and through the container of the state, and while this does not, as a matter of logical necessity, rule out the possibility of a similar constitutionalism emerging in a context and through a container other than the state, it certainly stacks the odds against such a development and places a heavy burden on the defenders of post-state constitutionalism to explain just how this is possible.

II. CONSTITUTIONALISM AND META-POLITICS

This brief examination of nominalist, formalist, and materialist positions on the one side of the issue and of essentialist, culturalist, and epistemic approaches on the other side of the issue underlines the difficulty in finding common cause in the debate about constitutionalism beyond the state. How, if at all, do we move beyond this divide? Such a possibility would seem to depend upon trying to ascertain what is *most* basically at stake—*more* basically than is revealed in the various debate-closing applications of constitutional language—in the various positions, and upon locating some overlapping ground at this more basic level. Clearly, the extreme positions of nominalism and essentialism are distinguished on the one hand by blindness to any argument that would give any special title to the state and on the other by blindness to any trace of constitutionalism beyond the state. The assumptions and arguments behind this opposition only begin to be made articulate in the other, more moderate positions. On the one hand, the formalists and the materialists suggest that something of value may be retained and adapted from the state tradition when we relocate to post-state contexts. In the case of formalism, the key to translation, so to speak, is abstraction, whereas in the case of substantivism, the key is disaggregation. In the former case, the very idea of a cohesive legal and institutional order is seen as the basis of certain constitutional virtues in new contexts as much as in old, whereas in the latter, it is implied that one can pick some features out of the state constitutional mix, such as a Charter of Rights or a system of inter-institutional checks and

[11] See M. Loughlin, 'In Defence of *Staatslehre*' (2009) 48 *Der Staat* 1–28.
[12] M. Canovan, *Nationhood and Political Theory* (Cheltenham: Edward Elgar, 1996), 80.

balances, and these features will remain of significant value despite being deprived of either the fuller legal framework or the deeper socio-cultural context of the state. The culturalist and epistemic arguments, on the other hand, see the same glass as half-empty rather than half-full. For them, the new is an inadequate pastiche of the old rather than a contextually appropriate adaptation. The post-state constitution is a machine that, in the culturalist critique, is deprived of the crude social energy to power itself sufficiently or, in the epistemic critique, lacks the intelligent background software necessary to understand and activate its own operating procedures.

In the final analysis, if we are to overcome this opposition we must look beyond the reductive commitments and self-vindicating judgments of even the more thoughtful of the state-centred and post-state positions. We must ask whether there is something more general at issue that is capable of being acknowledged within both mindsets, and which can therefore serve as a common point from which to investigate their differences. What we need in methodological terms, therefore, is a way of treating constitutionalism that is alert to this possibility: a split perspective capable of identifying common ground at one level while at another level continuing to acknowledge difference in terms of that common ground. Such a split perspective can be supplied by recasting the debate in functional terms: no longer as a one-dimensional contest over diverse and rival conceptions of the ends of constitutionalism understood as ends that either are or are not exclusively associated with the state, but as a debate over diverse and rival conceptions of the constitutional means necessary to ends that would themselves be capable of commanding general agreement across state-centred and post-state positions.

In order to be genuinely inclusive and not simply to impose an artificial consensus, any such definition of ends must proceed at a very high level of abstraction. At this rarified level, what implicitly unites the two mindsets is a sense, corroborated both by the etymology of the constitutional idea and by its range of applications prior to the age of the modern state, that constitutionalism serves a deep and abiding function in human affairs, namely the meta-political function of shaping the domain of politics broadly conceived—of literally 'constituting' the body politic.[13] More expansively, constitutionalism in this deepest meta-political sense may be understood *as referring to that species of practical reasoning which, in the name of some defensible locus of common interest, concerns itself with the organisation and regulation of those spheres of collective decision-making deemed relevant to the common interest in a manner that is adequately informed by the common interest.* Furthermore, if we are to avoid simply repeating the familiar definitional impasse at this more general level, our meta-political sense of the 'common interest' underpinning our collective decision-making capacities as understood in each of its three key registers—authoritative (in whose name?), jurisdictional (covering which collective decision-making capacities?), and purposive (to what end, and how?)—must, in addition, be acknowledged as possessing an open

---

[13] See, eg G. Maddox, 'A Note on the Meaning of "Constitution"' (1982) 76 *American Political Science Review* 805–9. See also N. Walker, 'Taking Constitutionalism beyond the State' (2008) 56 *Political Studies* 519–43.

and indeed a reflexive quality. We cannot, therefore, either stipulate in advance or treat as permanently resolved what are the appropriate sites for the pursuit of the common interest, or what are the appropriate terms of engagement between these sites, or what kinds of things fall within the remit of the common interest, or what is the proper relationship between individual and collective goods or preferences in the identification and pursuit of the common interest. All of these are matters themselves apt for decision in accordance with the common interest, understood as located at the very deepest level of political self-understanding and self-inquiry, and so as necessarily possessing a self-challenging and self-amending quality. Accordingly, if, as I suggest, we equate constitutionalism with the deepest sense of meta-political inquiry, we cannot simply decide a priori to equate the common interest with the national or state interest, and so corroborate an initial theoretical preference for state constitutionalism. Equally, we cannot simply assume that post-state sites are as appropriate as are states as authoritative sources of the common interest, as jurisdictional containers of the common interest, or as forums and institutional mechanisms for the specification of the common interest, and thus simply wish away the state legacy.

Instead, in order to advance the inquiry and find a point of contentious engagement between the two mindsets, we must turn to the second level of inquiry—to the question of adequacy of means. If the common interest conceived of as the ultimate end of the constitutional project sounds at a level of abstraction—and of perpetual contestability—that does not necessarily or even presumptively discriminate between state and post-state sites, is there something about the appropriateness of the means that nevertheless pulls in one direction rather than another? Is there something about the constitutional method available in and supported by the state context that is more adequate to the pursuit of the common interest than is any constitutional method available in and supported by post-state contexts?[14] To answer that question we must first ask what, if anything, is distinctive to the constitutional method that has been available in and supported by the state. Then we must inquire whether that method, or any constitutional method or combination of methods that is the instrumental equivalent of the state constitutional method, may also be available or be made available in the post-state context.

III. HOLISTIC CONSTITUTIONALISM

There is indeed a constitutional method distinctive to the modern state, and it is best understood as possessing a holistic quality. The holistic method is a method of constitutional articulation and engagement in which the authority and meaning of

---

[14] Note that this challenge, as well as querying the force of the formalist and materialist arguments in favour of post-state constitutionalism, also brings back in many of the concerns of the culturalist and epistemic critics of post-state constitutionalism. However, it does so in terms that, by more clearly specifying the distinction between (state) means and (constitutional) ends, are less at risk of reducing the connection between state and constitution to a tautology.

the various parts are understood and treated as dependent on the integrity of the whole.[15] This holistic feature is no isolated thread, but something that gives texture to the various different aspects of state constitutionalism.

To appreciate this, however, we must first say something more about the constitutional concept itself. In so doing, we are no longer concerned, as in the previous section, with constitutionalism in the abstract—as a theoretical concept for making sense of and evaluating the social world—but with constitutionalism in the concrete—as an 'object' already at use 'in' the social world and in the social world of the state in particular. Considered as such an object concept, state constitutionalism can be viewed both diachronically and synchronically. Diachronically, state constitutionalism in the modern age describes a particular high point of accumulation of various distinct layers of situated 'constitutional' practice that have operated separately or in different combinations in the past. These layers are juridical, politico-institutional, popular, and societal.[16] Synchronically, state constitutionalism operates in terms of its own particular formulation of these layers and of their relationship with one another. Constitutionalism in (state) practice behaves, in other words, as a 'cluster concept',[17] associated simultaneously with a number of different but themselves interrelated definitive criteria.

It is in each of its four layers—or, if you like, in different parts of the cluster— that we can observe constitutionalism operating holistically, offering a frame for the 'constitutive' representation[18] and regulation of each of the particular dimensions of social 'reality' with which it is concerned. What is more, in the constellation of connections made under the sign of modern state constitutionalism between each of these layers we can also discern a further 'frame of frames', or 'holism of holisms'. Let us look more closely at each of the holistic frames of state constitutionalism, and then in combination.

To begin with, the juridical frame refers to an idea of self-contained legal order, complete with rules of self-production, self-organisation, self-extension, self-interpretation, self-amendment, and self-discipline, all of which combine to affirm the autonomous existence and comprehensive authority of the legal order against other internal and external

[15] See more generally, N. Walker, 'Out of Time and Out of Place: Law's Fading Co-ordinates' (2010) 14 *Edinburgh Law Review* (forthcoming). For an insightful but rather different treatment of holism, treated not as the basic *organising method* of modern political life, as in the present case, but as a descriptor of the key *ontological unit* in the ordering of political society (and so considered as equivalent to a fundamentally *pre-modern* idea of indivisible community, and contrasted with modern individualism), see A. von Bogdandy and S. Dellavalle 'Universalism Renewed: Habermas' Theory of International Order in Light of Competing Paradigms' (2009) 10(1) *German Law Journal* 5–30.

[16] See Walker, above n 13; and with specific reference to the EU, N. Walker 'European Constitutionalism in the State Constitutional Tradition' (2006) 59 *Current Legal Problems* 51–89.

[17] W. E. Connolly, *The Terms of Political Discourse* (Oxford: Blackwell, 3rd edn, 1993), 14.

[18] On the ways in which acts of representation of a legal object are routinely (re)constitutive of that legal object, see, eg H. Lindahl, 'Sovereignty and Representation in the European Union', in N. Walker (ed), *Sovereignty in Transition* (Oxford: Hart, 2003), 87–114.

normative forces. The politico-institutional frame refers to a system of institutional specification and differentiation of the sphere of the public and the political. Whereas the idea of autonomous legal order long pre-dates modernity and the modern state, the idea of a secular, specialised, and institutionally defined and delimited political realm, free from deference to particular interests or to any idea of transcendental order, is a key emergent feature of modernity. It is marked by a double move away from pre-modern forms of authority, involving both the drawing of a general distinction between public and private spheres of influence domains and the integration of the public into a single and comprehensive political domain. What is more, the creation and sustenance of this singular political domain, and indeed the consolidation of the autonomous legal order, is dependent upon 'the structural coupling'[19] and mutual support of the two self-contained spheres of the legal and the political.

For its part, the popular frame refers to the dimension of 'we the people', and so to the idea of the specialised and integrated public institutional realm being underpinned not just by the autonomy of the political but also by its democratic self-constitution and self-authorship. The societal frame, finally, refers to the idea that the constitution pertains to a particular 'society' self-understood and self-identified as such. Here the framing work of the constitution is mostly symbolic rather than normative. The Constitution depends for its normative effectiveness as a design for a reasonably cooperative and commonly committed form of common living on the plausibility of the very idea of an integrated society—whether the emphasis is on the thin 'political society' of the state or the thicker 'cultural society' of the nation—that its very production and perseverance *as* a Constitution seeks to announce and promote.

If we look more closely at the points of interconnection between the various frames we can begin to appreciate how a broader 'holism of constitutional holisms' emerges under the template of the modern state. At the juridical and politico-institutional levels, the constitutional order (sometimes in conjunction with self-styled 'organic laws') typically place a mix of *structural* (politico-institutional level) and *substantive* (juridical level) requirements on public actors, which may be either specific functional institutions (eg industry-specific regulators) or generic government organs—Parliament, Executive, and Judiciary. The structural requirements are both internal and external. They are concerned with the internal governance system of the institution in question—decision-making procedures, representational rules, internal review and accountability rules, etc, as well as with the situation of the institution in question within a wider institutional complex—including the checks we associate with ideas of horizontal separation of powers, of federated vertical division of authorities, and of institutional balance more generally. The substantive requirements include, in positive and constitutive vein, jurisdiction or mandate rules which specify the public purposes of the institutions in question and the boundaries of these purposes, as well as, in negative vein, certain conduct-constraining rules that may take the form of general individual rights catalogues or other more detailed

---

[19] N. Luhmann, *Das Recht der Gesellschaft* (Frankfurt am Main: Suhrkamp, 1993); Eng. trans *Law as a Social System*, trans K. A. Ziegert (Oxford: Oxford University Press, 2008).

rules which are likewise concerned with trans-sectoral standards (eg freedom of information rules, anti-corruption rules).

A number of points may be made about the co-articulation of these different types of rules. First, there is the dependence of the substantive rules on the structural rules. The structural rules provide a general framework of orientation, coordination, and sanction that undergird the norm-specific guidelines contained in the substantive rules. Second, given their various boundary-setting and transversal qualities, the substantive rules associated with a particular constitutionally recognised function presuppose and are themselves supported and rendered more effective by their situation in a legal order that ranges more broadly than the particular functional specialism in question. That broader framework constrains and informs both by locating issues of the *vires* of particular institutions in a wider context of empowered institutions and by bringing general standards of the 'right' to bear in qualifying the pursuit of the particular 'good'. Third, the content of both the substantive and the structural rules is inscribed in a basic constitutional code that is relatively insulated from the particular institutions that are subject to these very substantive and structural rules. In particular, the combination of the autonomous rules of production of constitutional norms and their settled quality (perhaps entrenched in 'eternity' clauses or protected against simple majoritarian amendment rules, or at least subject to amendment provisions not within the gift of the affected institution itself), provides a form of protection against narrow forms of self-norming. Fourth, the constitutional code is not only insulated from particular interests but, more positively, it is receptive at points of origin, amendment, and continuing interpretation to notions of common interest informed, on the one hand, by the idea of the constitution as a form of popular self-authorisation over the totality of public affairs for a territory and, on the other, by the necessary discipline of ensuring widespread cooperation and compliance within the ambient society.

In summary, this combination of structural primacy, institution-transcending substantive rules, insulation of rules of constitutional norm production and maintenance from control by the institutions affected by these norms, and the openness of the same rules to broader forms of public influence and discipline provide the key ingredients of a holistic method of constitutionalism. The parts are supported by the whole both within and across the various different frames. Particular sector-specific rules and institutions alike depend for their meaning and authority on their location within broader regulatory and institutional orders, which broader orders are informed by a similarly wide-reaching and holistic conception of the singular public as both the source and the receptive environment of constitutional authority.

IV. CONSTITUTIONALISM BEYOND THE STATE

If we look beyond the state, what scope is there for the application of the holistic constitutional method? And where it is not available, how else, if at all, might constitutionalism's deep meta-political concern with the source, extent, and manner of pursuit of matters of common interest be met?

Clearly, some forms of post-state regimes or polities seem to fit quite well on the 'scale' of constitutionalism considered as a layered set of holistic frames. The recent debate about the adoption of a documentary Constitution for the European Union (EU), to take the best-known example, eventually crystallised as one about how an entity whose 'thin' credentials as a self-standing juridical and politico-institutional order are unarguable[20] might also be re-imagined and reconstructed in 'thick' terms as a popular and indeed 'political-societal' constitution—one with its own demo-cratically sensitive self-constituting authority and its 'own' transnational society as an object of reference.[21] The EU, in other words, clearly already possessed holistic constitutional qualities in certain layers, and the outstanding question concerned whether this could be extended across all the layers of modern constitutional prac-tice. Once the supporters of the project were no longer satisfied with the documen-tary constitutional process as an exercise in self-congratulatory consolidation of its thin (juridical and politico-institutional) credentials, or at least once they were no longer permitted by their opponents to treat the question so complacently, the thin versus thick question came more clearly into focus in the constitutional debate. That this ultimately led to the idea of a European Constitutional Treaty being voted down in the key French and Dutch referenda in 2005 neither undermines the relevance of the wide discussion nor, indeed, precludes its being revisited at some future point.[22]

In other cases such as the WTO or the UN, the debate over the nature and limits of constitutional holism is very much more confined to the thin legal and politico-institutional registers, with no pretence of and little ambition towards a popular constituent power or dedicated 'society' at the relevant sites.[23] Even here, there is no doubt about the applicability of a holistic method, even if to a truncated conception of constitutionalism. Indeed, it is precisely the well-established quality of a modest constitutional holism in these more limited regimes as much as in the hybrid regime of the EU that feeds much of the argument for post-state constitutionalism, with both formalist and materialist approaches trading in their different ways on the holis-tic qualities of the juridical and institutional layers.

Another type of case, however, stands more clearly detached from the tradition of state constitutionalism. Here we refer to the various other autonomy-assertive tran-snational societal actors exhibiting normative authority and institutional identity who increasingly claim or are deemed to possess constitutional standing,[24] whether in the field of internet (eg Internet Corporation for Assigned Names and Numbers) or transnational commercial regulation (eg *lex mercatoria*) or the regulation of sports (eg International Olympic Committee, World Anti-Doping Agency). In this context,

---

[20] See, eg J. H. H. Weiler, *The Constitution of Europe* (Cambridge: Cambridge University Press, 1999), ch 1.

[21] See, eg Walker, above n 16.

[22] See, eg N. Walker, 'Not the European Constitution' (2008) 15 *Maastricht Journal of European and Comparative Law* 115–21.

[23] See references at nn 5 and 6 above.

[24] See, eg Teubner, above n 7, and in this volume.

we find a much more comprehensive move away from the holistic method, and so an even starker confrontation of the question of whether and how the broader meta-political end of regulating our common affairs in accordance with considerations of the common interest can survive the erosion of the state-originated holistic consti-tutional method.

If we look first to the juridical and political-institutional layers, the idea of holistic self-containment fits ill with the combination of site-specific self-regulation and diverse external regulation we tend to find in these sectors. While there is typically a dense network of structural and substantive rules, we will not find the same holistic frame-work for their co-articulation. Internally, structural rules may be found in autono-mous enterprise or organisational laws. Externally, different legislative, executive, and judicial bodies at national, international, and supranational level will stand in various structural relationships with the actors. Substantively, again we will find the same complex mixture of self-regulation and uncoordinated external regulation, through for example, horizontal application of human rights rules and the general regimes of international standards bodies (eg Codex Alimentarius, International Organization for Standardization). What is lacking in either case is any idea of an integrated and comprehensive legal and institutional design external to the sector in question.

Equally, the idea of the holistic self-constitution of a popular 'subject' or of a societal 'object' does not translate easily to the domain of the new transnational societal actors. In either case—popular and societal—the wider and deeper embed-dedness associated with state constitutionalism is lost insofar as there is no sense of an integrated and generic 'public' context which stands beyond the special institu-tion in question but within which the special institution is fully incorporated. So there may be a significant degree of domain-specific self-authorship, but it neither is identical to nor delegated from any more integrated and generic public. Equally, there may be constituted a 'society' in the sense of a particular epistemic community and/or community of practice associated with the domain in question, but that too is neither identical to nor a subset of any integrated and generic 'public society'.[25]

It follows from this that none of the connecting elements—the 'holism of holisms'—of state constitutionalism can be guaranteed. In the first place, given the diversity of their pedigree (both as separate sets, and, even more so, when considered together), the relationship between the set of structural rules and the set of substantive rules lacks the coherence of the state model. So the structural rules cannot provide the func-tions of orientation, coordination, and constraint vis-à-vis the substantive rules in the

---

[25] We should, of course, bear in mind Teubner's qualification that the 'society' of the state constitutional imaginary was always in an important sense a partial vision (n 7 above). It was first and foremost a 'political society'—it was about the mutual self-constitution of law and politics and not necessarily concerned with other social sectors or subsystems (economics, culture, etc). But even if we allow this important point of social epistemology, we still have to take seriously the distinctively 'totalising' ambition contained in the claim of modern political society to constitute a generic and integrated public sphere, and also recognise the powerful historical synergy between this ambition and the development of a deeper 'cultural' nationalism.

'close fit' manner that characterises their relationship within the holistic state constitution. Secondly, there is no commonly bound general constitutional context to provide the transversal controls upon and wider jurisdictional context for sector-specific substantive rules. Because the transnational societal actor is not located within a wider complex of international societal actors, each subject to the same transversal rules and the same broader jurisdictional frame, the kinds of constraint and direction that a state constitution can provide by ensuring common negative standards and providing for the mutual coordination of different jurisdictional horizons cannot apply in the same way. Finally, the absence of any broader, singular, and autonomously-conceived transnational constitutional frame as an appropriate point of common reference both reflects and highlights the absence of any integrated and generic sense of the transnational public as the subject and object of any such regulatory field.[26]

V. BEYOND CONSTITUTIONAL HOLISM?

So the new transnational societal constitutionalism, such as it is, is clearly not simply a more thinly layered version of state constitutionalism, with the thicker popular and societal frame absent—as in the EU and in other less well-developed cases—but a constitutionalism that is reconfigured in each of its framing aspects. The idea of a holistic constitution is lacking in each of the four registers. What we have instead is a complex mix of discrete self-constitution and diffuse external constitution across all four registers—legal, politico-institutional, popular, and societal. [27]

To what extent, if at all, can we nevertheless conceive of this new non-holistic constitutional method as concerned with, and as effectively engaged in, the same

---

[26] On the effect of the decline of holistic constitutionalism on the overall global regulatory field, rather than on the pattern of regulation within particular sectors, see N. Walker 'Beyond Boundary Disputes and Basic Grids: Mapping the Global Disorder of Normative Orders' (2008) 6 *International Journal of Constitutional Law* 373–96.

[27] We should also distinguish non-holistic societal constitutionalism from the kind of postnational constitutionalism favoured by writers like Jim Tully. For him and others, the main focus of criticism remains the state form, not from the perspective of a functional differentiation which makes the holistic state constitution inadequate to the range and distribution of *collective practices* but rather from the perspective of a cultural differentiation (first nations, gendered identities, etc) which makes the holistic state constitution inadequate to the range and distribution of *collective identities*. His version of non-state constitutionalism, accordingly, is about the re-articulation of a much greater diversity of holistic identities than the state form allows rather than the transcendence of the very idea of holistic constitutionalism. However, as explained in the text below, and as Tully would endorse, any such generously and diversely populated constitutional landscape implies, distinct from the classic (inter)state version, the non-comprehensiveness of each holistic structure and the much greater zone of overlap between each holistic structure, and so the greater scope and need for (non-holistic) legal relations between these holistic structures. See, eg J. Tully, 'The Imperialism of Modern Constitutional Democracy', in M. Loughlin and N. Walker (eds), *The Paradox of Constitutionalism: Constituent Power and Constitutional Form* (Oxford: Oxford University Press, 2007), 315–38.

meta-political function as holistic state constitutionalism; namely, the reflexive consideration of the proper locus, jurisdiction, and content of the common interest in matters concerning the organisation and regulation of collective decision-making? On the face of it, absent the anchorage for a working conception of the common interest provided by the coincidence of at least some if not all of the four holistic frames under the same territorial coordinates, any prospect of a meaningful invest-ment in these meta-political questions of the common interest would seem distinctly unpromising. Yet, for at least three reasons, we should remain slow to dismiss the possibility of a non-holistic constitutionalism.

In the first place, there is the question of the viability of other possible constitutional worlds. What are the alternatives, and so what can and what should we compare the new non-holistic candidates for constitutional status with? The most telling compara-tor for current trends towards decisively non-holistic forms of constitutionalism is not, as often seems to be assumed by the advocates of state constitutionalism, the *past* of state constitutionalism, but the form and circumstances of its *present* incar-nation. The high-point of the holistic state constitutional method is long gone. In acknowledging this, we must also appreciate that much of what is new in transna-tional regulatory development, whether in the form of hybrid structures such as the EU or WTO or through the more radical forms of societal constitutionalism, is the result not of inadvertent drift or of so many grabs for power devoid of any public justification, but instead is in some part at least a response to the growing inade-quacy of the holistic state model in the face of the emergence of collective action and coordination problems that simply do not coincide with the political boundaries of the state. The new world even of the familiar and deeply embedded category of state constitutionalism, it follows, is not the same as the old. The new state constitu-tionalism may remain holistic in the sense that in each of the four framing registers it continues to emphasise the importance of the integrity of the whole and the interdependence of its parts, but this holism is qualified to the extent that it can no longer aspire to an all-embracing quality. Rather, state constitutionalism becomes an 'open' or 'relational' constitutionalism,[28] concerned to engage in accordance with a necessarily non-holistic logic with the very hybrid polities and non-holistic spheres of governance that have been the focus of our attention, and with which the norms, institutions, demoi, and societal 'objects' of the state constitutional order overlap. In short, by their emergence the non-holistic constitutional forms serve to indicate, and through their regulatory penetration they serve to reinforce the inadequacy of the very model of holistic state constitutionalism with which, ironically enough, they are often unfavourably compared. And to the extent that there remains a point of comparison between old and new constitutional constellations, it is a matter of more or less emphasis upon a now heavily qualified state constitutional holism rather than a stark either/or choice between holism and its opposite.

In the second place, there is the question of (meta-)political morality and prudence. Such important differences of emphasis as do remain between more or

---

[28] See, eg Walker, above n 9.

less holistic constellations, and the choices associated with these, are not necessarily beyond evaluation in terms that we find constitutionally meaningful. Rather, we remain capable of articulating at least some elements of the common language that would allow us to assess the relative merits and demerits of the holistic and non-holistic approaches to meta-politics, and to do so in such a way that suggests that the more holistic solution is not always the better or more 'constitutionally' appropriate.

Holistic constitutionalism, even in qualified form, can lay claim to many political virtues; to the formal equality and calculability dividends that may accrue to a legal order with a single all-embracing centre, to reliable juridical transmission of the (democratically formed) political will, to coordinated and mutually vigilant forms of institutional balance, to popular collective self-determination, and to a sense of societal solidarity necessary to make that collective self-determination effective. But such a model also demonstrates instability at either edge of its precarious accomplishment. On the one side, just because of its all-embracing reach and its exhaustion of the available mechanism of political influence and restraint, holistic constitutionalism is peculiarly prone to capture by powerful special interests and ideologies in any or all of its framing registers. On the other side, the same propensity to stretch across and absorb the entirety of the political sphere may mean that holistic constitutionalism attracts certain disabling tendencies, including a tendency towards inter-institutional stasis and gridlock and towards a thinly spread culture of common commitment. That is to say, comprehensive self-containment of the political sphere may always have been the major strength of holistic constitutionalism, but it also speaks to its irreducible vulnerability and ineradicable sources of danger.

This double-edged concern illustrates and so points us towards certain perennial preoccupations over the best mode of accommodation between certain contrasting but balancing virtues associated with the identification and pursuit of the common interest in constitutional arrangements—between attachment and detachment, the special and the general, the particular and the universal, the passionate and the constraining. Holism in the container of the state seeks ever more regulatory distance and abstraction (in substance, in structure, and in pedigree) and ever more investment in a broader scheme of political commitments as a guide to and means of avoiding concentration of power in particular institutions, all the while courting the opposite dangers of more expansive forms of political partiality or the dilution of the capacity for the effective mobilisation of political authority.

These moral and prudential concerns are not foreign to the new non-holistic constitutionalism. Rather, it is simply that its institutional logic is such that these concerns present themselves in inverse form. The problem for non-holistic constitutionalism is neither the corruption and capture nor the impotence of the regulatory whole, but precisely the same dangers of oversteering and understeering under the opposite condition of the *absence* of any such regulatory whole. And the key design puzzle in addressing these dangers of oversteering and understeering concerns the appropriate mode of articulation of the internal and external elements within the legal and politico-institutional structure (in the first two framing layers), bearing in mind the fundamental irreducibility of the 'constituency' and 'own society' of the relevant community of practice to some integrated and generic notion of the public (in the third and fourth framing layers). It is quite understandable, then, that so much of contemporary transnational 'constitutional' thinking is concerned to develop 'substantive' and 'structural' rules in a manner that seeks to compensate or substitute both for the myopically self-interested tendencies (oversteering) and for the absence of effective leverage over external factors of influence (understeering) that accompany the lack of embedding of narrow self-regulatory spheres in a wider, holistic constitutional framework. So, for example, we find an increasing emphasis on the language of universal human rights,[29] on the widespread franchising of general regulatory standards,[30] and on the promulgation and internalisation of codes of corporate responsibility[31] as ways of correcting for the sectoral self-interest of particular transnational societal actors, but also of encouraging or facilitating the greater mutual coherence of their regimes. On the structural side, too, we see a number of trends that have the same double purpose and effect of addressing the dangers of oversteering and understeering. This can be observed, for instance, in attempts to develop new forms of general discipline as well as to trace new ways of joining up connected regulatory concerns through initiatives such as the elaboration of general principles of Global Administrative Law,[32] the replication and refinement of New Modes of Governance,[33] and the 'rolling out' of local or sector-specific forms of democratic experimentation and problem solving.[34]

In all of this, admittedly, the similarities and continuities in the meta-political concern with the common interest in the organisation and regulation of collective decision making between past and present—and so between more or less holistic constitutional constellations—operate at a high level of abstraction, require careful translation, and certainly do not admit of any easy general conclusions. Still, there is something resiliently recognisable at stake between old and new understandings of these deep questions of regulation which may merit our continued use of constitutional language as an analytical and evaluative tool for both.

This brings us, finally, to a third consideration, namely the practical question of the use-value of constitutionalism. It is one thing to argue on the rarified level of theoretical observation that we can trace a connection between the old and the new,

[29] See, eg Petersmann, above n 5.

[30] See, eg H. Schepel, *The Constitution of Private Governance: Product Standards in the Regulation of Integrating Markets* (Oxford: Hart, 2005).

[31] See, eg D. J. McBarnet, 'Corporate Social Responsibility: Beyond Law, through Law, for Law. The New Corporate Accountability', in D. McBarnet, A. Voiculescu, and T. Campbell (eds), *The New Corporate Accountability: Corporate Social Responsibility and the Law* (Cambridge, Cambridge University Press, 2007), ch 1.

[32] See, eg B. Kingsbury, N. Krisch, and R. B. Stewart, 'The Emergence of Global Administrative Law' (2005) 68 (3) *Law & Contemporary Problems* 15–61; Krisch in this volume.

[33] See, eg G. de Burca and J. Scott (eds), *Law and New Governance in the EU and the US* (Oxford: Hart, 2006).

[34] See, eg C. F. Sabel and J. Zeitlin, 'Learning from Difference: The New Architecture of Experimentalist Governance in the EU' (2008) 14 *European Law Journal* 271–327.

and to remind ourselves that in terms of viable political possibilities the difference is no longer one of kind but of degree. If, however, below that rarified theoretical level, there is little actual use of constitutionalism as a common vernacular extending across the two contexts, and if what use there is has instead the divisive and mutually alienating consequences discussed in our opening section, then what is gained by retaining the constitutional idea for the emerging realm of transnational societal actors? This note of scepticism is deeply underscored, moreover, if we consider the key underlying reason for the scarcity of an inclusive use-language of constitutionalism in the post-state holistic regulatory context. This has to do with the lack of the additional, inclusively reflexive 'fifth layer' of constitutionalism within the non-holistic picture, namely the 'frame of frames' or 'holism or holisms'. Absent the coincidence of the other four frames, not only, as already noted, is it objectively the case that constitutionalism is deprived of the single anchorage of a convergence of sites and frames of common interest. At the intersubjective level, too, participants will lack the common 'we' perspective and point of commitment from which to address all questions of the common interest. Instead, we are bound to accept in a post-holistic context that questions of the common interest in collective decision making are simply not questions that, at the deepest level of political self-interrogation, we can envisage all interested constituencies affected addressing comprehensively *in* common.

Does this not, at last, provide the decisive argument against the value of retaining the language of constitutionalism in the non-holistic context? I would contend that it does not. The explicit adoption of constitutional language in non-holistic settings may remain largely restricted to theoretical and other elite discourse. But the trend, however hesitant and uneven, is towards wider use, and, as the example of the intermediate cases of the EU, WTO, etc show, there do exist recent precedents for largely theoretical discourses of post-state constitutionalism gradually to 'catch on' at deeper social and political levels. Much more important is what the resilience and resurgence of constitutional language, however patchy on the ground, might signify. Even—indeed especially—where, as compared to the holistic constitutional tradition, the central issues of non-holistic forms of regulation present themselves in such different ways and are offered a quite distinctive range of regulatory solutions, constitutional language retains a crucial longstop function as a kind of 'placeholder'[35] for certain abiding concerns we have. These concerns are, quite simply, that unless we can address the meta-political framing of politics in a manner that remains wedded to ideas of the common interest, however difficult this may be to conceive and however far we have travelled from our most familiar and perhaps most conducive framework for such a task, something of great and irreplaceable value will have been lost from our resources of common living.

---

[35] The reference is to Martti Koskenniemi, who has made a similar point about the contemporary fate of international law (see M. Koskenniemi, 'The Fate of Public International Law: Between Technique and Politics' (2007) 70 *Modern Law Review* 1–30, 30).

There is one final irony here. It is precisely because the language of constitutionalism, considered as a normative technology, finds it ever more complex and difficult to address the problems of communal living it poses in and for a post-state world, that it becomes all the more important to retain the language of constitutionalism, considered as a symbolic legacy, as an insistent reminder of what and how much is at stake. The day that constitutionalism's inability to provide stock answers to its abiding questions becomes a settled reason no longer even to ask these questions, is the day that constitutionalism, and the vital spirit of meta-political inquiry that it conveys, will indeed have entered the twilight zone.

The Morphogenesis of Constitutionalism

Riccardo Prandini

We are living through a new constitutional era, and we are overwhelmed by strange constitutional–constituent experiences. It is not a time of exceptional politics, as exists during the founding episodes of modern constitutions. It does not represent a demise of constitutionalism, since there is no such unique real thing to be demised. And it does not represent a transmutation because nothing is really mutating: there is only an emerging new form. We are facing a living and latent process of morphogenesis which reframes the very idea of constitution in a way which is more adequate to world society. This is a peculiar phase, which is taking place apparently without popular mobilisations and with difficulties in finding either the constituent powers or the real legal processes of constitutionalisation, and often without clear polities which are to be constituted.

In this chapter I argue that it is possible and necessary to talk about processes of constitutional morphogenesis. Morphogenesis is a socio-cultural cycle, whereby a given institutional and cultural structure (at T_0, here 'the modern constitution') gives rise—through cultural and structural interactions activated by societal actors—to new forms (morphogenesis) or which maintains the old ones (morphostasis). This process is contingent upon a plurality of variables, with nothing to be taken for granted.[1] My hypothesis is that at the centre of this process there are two connected problems: the recognition of a real polity, and its self-governance framed in a constitutional way.

I. FRAMING THE CONSTITUTIONAL FRAME

We need to identify the generative mechanisms that give rise to new and pluralistic forms of civil (non-state) constitution, that is, to discover their morphogenetic logic. This morphogenetic renewal comes from three main causes.

1. *Substantively*, nation states remain the most significant hosts to constitutional discourses, institutions, and structures. Only by starting from the state is it possible to elaborate a new discourse. We need both historical continuity *and* discontinuity.

---

[1] See M. Archer, *Realist Social Theory: The Morphogenetic Approach* (Cambridge: Cambridge University Press, 1995).

On the one hand, as the history of constitutionalism shows, there is nothing really *essential* in the relationship between constitutionalism and statehood. On the other hand, state constitutions have become, for different reasons, the real examples of what we mean in a modern sense by constitution.[2] Today, as a new morphogenetic cycle begins, the claims and the advocates of 'societal constitutionalism' often originate from contexts of constituted (non-state/non-modern) polities, which gradually try to elaborate a discourse concerning a new 'good working order'. Constitution, constitutionalism, and constitutionalisation should be conceived as processes in time, which can vary from a minimum level of institutionalisation to a maximum one.

2. *Sociologically*, we need to generalise *and* re-specify the modern constitutional frame. Generalising means separating and abstracting the core concepts of constitutionalism from historical contingencies, and in particular from the modern political system and the state apparatus. Re-specifying means that the generalised elements of constitution must be connected with different global social subsystems, with their specific operations, structures, media, codes, and programmes.

3. *Temporally*, generalisation and re-specification are conceptual operations concerned with the elaboration of a general theory of societal differentiation/ evolution. When a social system is pressed by internal and external stresses and strains it has to rearrange itself to cope with the new environmental—whether material, technological, human, cultural, or natural—situation. In this process of active and creative adaptation the system must upgrade its structures and processes by: generating new resources; differentiating new goals and sub-institutions; integrating them inside the new generalised system; and generalising its identity.[3]

For analytical purposes, I propose to freeze the morphogenetic process at a precise historical moment. As Norbert Elias has shown, during the sixteenth and seventeenth centuries the decentralised, plural, autonomous, localised, communal, and diverse socio-political powers of the medieval *Respublica Christiana* were slowly concentrated into a revolutionary institution: the national and absolutist state.[4] Public powers—the ability of making collectively binding decisions—were encaged in a new social subsystem and this gave rise to the modern idea of sovereignty, thickly connected with territoriality and nationality. After the transitional semantic of *Raison d'Etat*, *arcana imperii*, etc, and with the development of notions of public administration, rule of law, democracy, citizenship, and welfare, political power was reframed and limited, with the objective of guaranteeing the multiple processes of social internal differentiation against swamping tendencies. In this process of societal differentiation, constitutions and constitutional discourses were created to structurally couple the political (state) subsystem and the law of

---

[2] See H. Mohnhaupt and D. Grimm, *Zur Geschichte des Begriffs von der Antike bis zur Gegenwart* (Berlin: Duncker & Humblot, 2002).

[3] T. Parsons, *The System of Modern Societies* (Englewood Cliffs, NJ: Prentice-Hall, 1971); N. Luhmann, *Die Gesellschaft der Gesellschaft* (Frankfurt am Main: Suhrkamp, 1997).

[4] N. Elias, *Über den Prozeß der Zivilisation* (Frankfurt am Main: Suhrkamp, 1977).

(regional) society (see Fig. 15.1). Having abandoned the ancient solutions of *jus eminens* and *lois fondamentales*, the political subsystem had to solve the problem of arbitrariness of decision making and the legal system had to confront the issue of its foundation: the problem of the validity of law. Both subsystems became auto-referential, that is, they operated without any external foundation, whether of natural law, traditional legacies, customs, social stratification, or the will of God. As the fundamental juridical ordering of a (regional) polity, the constitution represented a new legal–political order, and performed the role of distinguishing auto-referentiality from etero-referentiality *within* the political system. With its functions of *constituting* the polity (inventing 'we the people' and transforming legally the *pouvoir constituent* into the nation), *defining* its goals and expectations (the so-called constitutional principle), *attributing*, *separating*, and *limiting* the power inside state institutions (no longer absolute and indivisible, but separable powers and ruled by law) and *regulating* procedures (distinguishing primary and secondary rules, and establishing procedural, jurisdictional, and accountability rules), the modern constitution represented a new frame for ordering territorially organised societies.[5]

As many scholars have emphasised, from a historical point of view constitutions emerge as a counterpart to the emergence of autonomous spheres of action typical for modern societies. As soon as expansionist tendencies arise within the political system, threatening to ruin the process of social differentiation itself, social conflicts emerge, as a consequence of which fundamental rights, as social counter-institutions, are institutionalised precisely where social differentiation was threatened by its own self-destructive tendencies. One effect of this structural coupling is to restrain both legal and political processes' abilities of mutual influence. The possibility of one system being swamped by the other is addressed, their respective autonomies

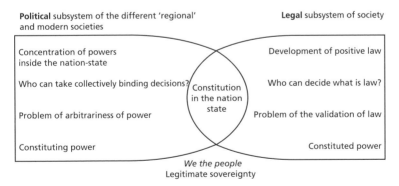

Figure 15.1

The modern structural coupling between the political and legal systems.

---

[5] Here I connect the substantive-historical argumentation of Neil Walker, with re-elaboration of the Parson's AGIL Scheme, as developed by Luhmann (see Walker in this volume; Parsons, Luhmann, above n 3).

enabled, and mutual irritation concentrated upon narrowly delimited and openly institutionalised paths of influence.[6]

While Luhmann and Teubner have underlined the 'control–integrative' function of the constitution, I believe that the conceptual horizon might be expanded. In fact, constitutions perform four main functions: they (1) *establish* a legitimacy principle for political power, (2) *regulate* the conditions for the real exercise of powers (ie they establish the basic legal norms which comprehensively regulate the social and political life of a polity and usually impose special impediments over unwarranted transformations), (3) *institute* the boundaries between the political system and the other subsystems (eg civil society), and (4) *determine* the ultimate goals of the polity. This modern territorial-state configuration framed the international world, and during the twentieth century exported the idea and the institutions of constitutionalism around the world. Constitutionalism became the most influential frame of reference for a legitimate regulatory framework of any national political community.

II. THE BOUNDLESS DEMANDS OF NORMATIVE EXPECTATIONS AND REGULATION

Why is a new morphogenetic cycle emerging?

The reasons for a new morphogenetic cycle are plural, and they originate from an extraordinary growth in the need to govern, regulate, regularise, and institutionalise the poly-contextuality of social relations.[7] It results from increasing demands of different governance regimes to coordinate communications and actions to achieve collective goals through collaboration. This boundless demand of 'good governance' is a strict corollary of growing systemic contingencies, and it gives rise to a plurality of forms of 'living law'. The state—conceived as the unitary representation of the political system in the territorially bounded society—and its law-making procedures no longer supply adequate responses to these tremendous demands. In a 'generalised anywhere'—the so-called 'atopic' society, a society without an institutional centre—new levels and structures of decision-making capacity and an unrestrainable expansion of positive and negative externalities drive new demands for governance as well as new kinds of regulatory institutions and normative instruments associated with its supply. Decisional powers and controlling powers grow together in an unplanned way, requiring enhanced structures of global governance and accountability similar to the previous constitutionalisation of the absolutist state.

---

[6] C. Joerges, I.-J. Sand, and G. Teubner (eds), *Transnational Governance and Constitutionalism* (Oxford: Hart, 2004).

[7] G. Teubner and A. Fischer-Lescano, *Regime-Kollisionen: Zur Fragmentierung des Weltrechts* (Frankfurt am Main: Suhrkamp, 2006).

National governments mostly conduct business as usual: the much announced death of the nation state is premature. At the same time, states are not well equipped to supply the normative ordering needed for the development and steering of a world society. Furthermore, it seems improbable that the world will soon switch into a global political community/polity, not even in the cosmopolitan way that Rawls and Habermas have suggested.[8]

In the last phase of the twentieth century, globalisation took off and most of the underpinning conditions of state sovereignty began to change. The modern system of international relations, based on the traditional idea of discrete-territorial political societies maintaining absolute internal sovereignty, is being transformed into a 'multi-level, concatenated network of diverse forces, resources, actors and interests' within a globalising world containing 'many forms of authority, many shades of legitimacy, diverse aspects of accountability and complex arrangements of partial or divisible sovereignty'.[9] This does not mean that states will lose all their powers: it could even enhance their influences in new spheres of action. The problem is that in the age of globalisation social evolution develops through the global extensions of the internal functional differentiation of modern societies beyond the nation states. This world society assumes peculiar forms of self-differentiation: not spatial/regional, but functional. It is differentiated in discrete subsystems: economic, legal, health, art, sport, scientific, etc. And, fuelled by the new media of communications and diffusion, most of these systems are becoming global.

For Luhmann, only the political and legal subsystems can be differentiated in a territorial-state form, because they need territorial boundaries. Within their borders, state politics and law can define and regulate relevant parts of the autonomy of all the other (national) subsystems. But the very existence of those boundaries indicates that the global diffusion of truth, pandemics, health risks, terrorism, education, finance, personal relationships, migration, news, information, or negative externalities cannot be controlled, regulated, or addressed by the state. At the same time, we must distinguish between three different observational operations: *function* as the observation of the whole system, *performance* as the observation from other subsystems, and *reflection* as self-observation. This is necessary in order to distinguish between, on the one hand, the (historical) concept of state as a particular form of reflection (ie auto-observation) on the national political system and, on the other hand, the function of a political system responsible for collective binding decisions. We must also draw a distinction between law as legislation and law as a pluralistic normative process inside the society. The conflation of these two different forms of observation produces only the hypertrophy of the *conscience d'état* and of the legislative-positive law.

[8] P. Niesen and B. Herborth (eds), *Anarchie der kommunikativen Freiheit* (Frankfurt am Main: Suhrkamp, 2007).

[9] J. Agnew, 'Sovereignty Regimes: Territoriality and State Authority in Contemporary World Politics' (2005) 92 *Annals of the Association of American Geographers* 437–61, at 439.

This means that we should speak of a variety of global governance regimes (or self-governance of lateral global subsystems) which are not embedded in the boundary of national territoriality, and that enact processes of collectively binding decision making outside the legislative procedures. In other words, there is no world government, nor global political parties, global elections, or global parliaments; there exists only governance regimes for the global economy (WTO), the world health system (WHO), labour interests (ILO), sport (IOC), etc. Most of these new institutions were created through treaties or agreements between nation states, but have developed autonomously and have bolstered their influence, legitimacy, and expertise by including non-state actors. Global governance does not evolve as a unitary political regime. In the words of Keohane and Nye, 'what we find is not world government, but the existence of regimes of norms, rules and institutions that govern a surprisingly large number of issues in world politics'.[10] We see the emergence of new regimes as specific forms of governance, that is, as 'norms, rules and procedures agreed to in order to regulate an issue-area'.[11]

The cognitive turn of decision-making processes in the knowledge society

According to Helmut Willke, the problem is 'governing the knowledge society', that is, a society that comprises a lateral global system.[12] His basic idea is that the preconditions for sound governance have changed and keep changing with the dynamics of the ongoing transformation from industrial societies to knowledge societies. In this morphogenetic process, the preconditions for decision making are shifting from normative to cognitive foundations. Knowledge is becoming the most important factor of production, surpassing the traditional factors of land, labour, and capital. The most important good today is expertise, that is, hyper-specialised knowledge needed to sustain and legitimate decision making. Politics is not enough! Parliaments are not competent! Politicians are not experts! So what follows?

This cognitive turn is linked to the erosion of the core principles of state government: authority, legitimacy, and accountability. Each of these political elements generalises itself, escapes the boundaries of nation states, and re-specifies itself in lateral global subsystems. In Willke's words:

> Global governance consists in large part in creating governance regimes for global contexts by establishing organizations (institutions), structures, processes and rule systems that have the capabilities to provide intelligent

[10] R. Keohane and J. Nye , 'Introduction', in D. Held and J. Donahue (eds), *Governance in a Globalizing World* (Washington, DC: Brookings Press, 2000), 1–27, at 16.

[11] E. Haas, 'Why Collaborate? Issue-linkage and International Regimes' (1980) 32 *World Politics* 357–405, at 380.

[12] H. Willke, *Smart Governance: Governing the Global Knowledge Society* (Frankfurt am Main: Campus, 2007).

decisions for highly complex and concatenated problems. Accordingly, a core element of global governance is to create and manage specific organizations as global institutions and cornerstones of global context: the WTO for the global economic system, the WHO for the global health system, the Basel Committee for the global financial system, the World Bank and the IFM for the global developmental context, etc. the crucial resource of all theses institutions is knowledge.[13]

It is important to define the differences between state and non-state political elements. These can be explained by reference to the principles of authority, legitimacy, and accountability. First, state authority is defined by formal rules of inclusion, participation, and representation into a territorial system. There are, however, at least four kinds of authority beyond nation-state arrangements: supranational, private, technical, and popular (global public opinion). The authority of expertise is quite different from state-based authority. Its rules derive from the standard set by knowledge, epistemic, scientific, and practical communities. This knowledge is no longer elaborated within the nation state and its political structures: it develops in private or quasi-public organisations and by the other actors in the area of rule making, arbitration, dispute settlement, standard setting, and organisation of societal sectors.

Second, for modern states the rules of formal legal legitimacy were popular participation, representation, the majority principle, and party competition. Nowadays, new forms of legitimacy are building on this legacy and are beginning to delineate derivatives of formal legitimacy. The most important are knowledge-based legitimacies. State structures of course seek to base their decisions on expert knowledge. But it is increasingly evident that territorial nation states are unable to cope with new global problems; they are unable to develop within their structures the specialised knowledge needed to solve transnational problems.[14]

Various forms of non-state governance, based on new forms of authority, accountability, and derivatives of legitimacy, are needed to complement the work of state institutions in complex and deterritorialised policy arenas in global society. It is sufficiently clear that there does not exist a global level of law-making, only pluralistic processes of juridification. Global law regimes are based on derivatives of legitimacy and diverse *foci* of authority, such as *lex mercatoria*, *lex constructionis*,

---

[13] Ibid 42.

[14] Ibid 48: 'A few of the global institutions, particularly WTO, WHO, WB, G-30, FSF or BIS and its Basel Committee, make exemplary use of existing expertise and in addition produce relevant knowledge with impressive speed and quality ... the familiar regulatory competition evolves into a pervasive matrix of cooperation and competition among national and transnational policy networks. National democratic political systems, in spite of their unique legitimacy, lose their status of autonomous players with unquestioned sovereignty. Instead they become mutually dependent parts of a complex supra-structure of multi-level political decision-making, ranging from the local to the global level.'

or *lex digitalis*.[15] These are 'living laws' based only on legitimacy acquired through expertise, reputation, fairness, and problem-solving capacity and which depend on mutual voluntary commitment, compliance, and consensus over deliberative fairness. These regimes—which included norms, rules, standards, regulations, and operating procedures such as audit and accounting regulations—are forms of self-organisation of functional arenas of the world society. They apparently lack the core elements of a full-fledged territorial society: the political system with its state sovereignty (the capacity of a public body to act as the final and indivisible seat of authority) and popular sovereignty (the people considered as subjects and objects of the law).

The collectivities—the people—addressed by global law are not defined within state boundaries, but only functionally and operationally. They are communities of choice, of practices and of interests, in which membership is not ascribed but achieved. Some global institutions have acquired reputations as intermediate appellate bodies, such as the International Court of Arbitration or the Appellate Body of the WTO, but they lack an executive branch for enforcement based on the legitimate monopoly of the use of force. Instead, they rely on powers of persuasion, deliberation, expertise, fair procedures, and impartiality. The relevance of these global regimes is so vast that we can now ask: 'what public task (and collective goods) will the democracies of this century be able to organize and implement on the basis of territories, and territorially limited collectives?'[16] Put another way: we are witnessing a new beginning in the morphogenetic cycle, and we can see retrospectively that the state monopoly of political governance is simply a relevant but historical incident of an ongoing process. And, as Anne-Marie Slaughter emphasises, we face for the first time a trilemma of social governance in the form of 'the need to exercise authority at the global level without centralized power but with government officials feeling a responsibility to multiple constituencies rather than to private pressure groups'.[17]

III. BEYOND THE GLOBAL PROCESS OF JURIDIFICATION

Inside the morphogenetic cycle

Fig. 15.2 shows the four-phased process of 'simple' juridification–normativisation. On the left side of the figure, where a new cycle begins opening the box of the established normative system, we find *pressures towards innovation*. This phase derives from the irritations (communications, actions, conflicts, claims, changes in institutions, etc) coming from both (1) internal (the different subsystems of society) and (2) external (individual consciences, bodies, human and ecological nature, etc) environments

---

[15] S. Sassen, *Territory, Authority, Rights: From Medieval to Global Assemblages* (Princeton, NJ: Princeton University Press, 2007).

[16] Willke, above n 12, 95–6.

[17] A.-M. Slaughter, *A New World Order* (Princeton, NJ: Princeton University Press, 2004), 257.

of the normative system. Irritations are new and unexpected normative claims coming from the outside of the normative subsystem of the global society. They are not yet normative events, since they first need to be transformed/translated as normative elements by some mechanism, that is, by the plural 'processes of juridification' developed by the society.

This translation takes place in the upper and central side of Fig. 15.2, where we find the 'processes of conditional opening' of the normative system. It opens itself to the innovations, but only translates them into its peculiar language. Here we find the mechanism of the *selection and recoding* of normative innovations. Law-making—and norm making—takes place outside the modern sources of national and international law: in agreements between global players, in private market regulation by multinational concerns, in internal regulations of international organisations, interorganisational negotiating systems, and through worldwide standardisation processes that come about partly in markets and partly in processes of negotiation among organisations. Regulations and norms are produced by new semi-public, quasi-private, or private actors which respond to the needs of a global society.[18] In the space between states and private entities, self-regulating authorities have multiplied, blurring the distinction between the public sphere of sovereignty and the private domain of particular interests. And legal norms are not only produced within conflict regulation processes by national and international official courts but also within non-political, social, dispute-settling bodies; international organisations; arbitration and mediation schemes; ethical committees; and treaty systems. The 'living laws' developing new jurisgenerative processes and the demands of governance regimes are socially selected and recoded where and when an urgent need of normative expectations and social arbitration emerges and where real competencies to reconstruct normativity develop.

On the right side of the figure, we can observe the third phase of the cycle. It is related to the 'closing' and the 'internal integration' of the previously 'irritated' and then selected normative expectations. In this phase selected innovations are accepted, retained in normative-legal documents, and socially institutionalised. The mechanisms for this institutionalisation concern the reconstruction of law and its methods, the creation of fictive hetero-references, overruling, dogmatic and doctrinal innovative interpretations, and the so-called 'democratic iterations'. These three phases of the new morphogenetic cycle are included inside what I call the sphere of 'living law', the endlessly normative social elaborations which try to respond to the huge and dramatic needs of 'juridification' across the world society.

In order to develop and maintain itself, this 'living law' needs to relate to a cultural pattern, a sort of identity scheme, which retains the function to record and interpret the whole morphogenetic cycle. It is the locus of 'latent pattern maintenance', where the latent meanings of the new laws are elaborated, becoming 'living' and (if necessary) positive laws. Here the normative system combines with the cultural symbolic environment (the 'ultimate reality' in the Weberian sense), that is, the

---

[18] See Sassen, above n 15.

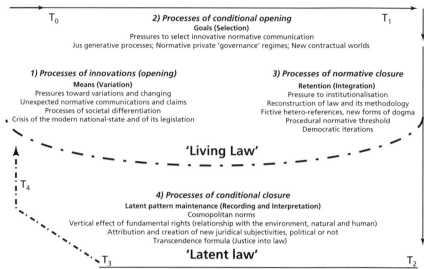

Figure 15.2

stored and maintained cultural symbols that represent the coherent memory of the social system. Not everything is acceptable in a particular (normative) world, so long as the system wants to maintain its internal coherence. Who (or what) decides on the maintenance of normative communications is properly hosted in this *locus* of cultural elaboration and interpretation.[19] It is here that the normative system, often through the production of conflicts, finds its ultimate transcendence and breaks its closure. The best example of this latent pattern of normativity is provided by the elaboration of new human or ecological rights. It is here that, as Seyla Benhabib argues, the emergence of international human rights regimes is intended to protect the individual in a global civil society and to articulate public standards of norm justifications.[20]

Constitutionalisation as a specific sub-process of the global normative morphogenesis

Constitutionalisation is not simply juridification or normative regulation: it is a very different social process. It is a specific and important part of the process of proliferation of diverse, overlapping, and interconnected legal orders at subnational, supranational, international, and private levels. Why is this problem of new constitutional morphogenesis emerging? The starting point (T_0) of the morphogenetic cycle concerns the constitution as the elaboration of a social–political

---

[19] L. Boltanski and L. Thévenot, *On Justification: Economies of Worth* (Princeton, NJ: Princeton University Press, 2006).

[20] S. Benhabib, *Another Cosmopolitanism* (Oxford: Oxford University Press, 2006).

vision and a frame of normative order in terms of which the state polity identified and regulated itself qua sovereign. Its function was not only to internally regulate the state, its relationships with the other social subsystems and with its environment (through individual rights), but also to define and constitute the polity itself. In the modern age, there is no politics without a constitutional frame and no constitutional law without a political form. The modern constitution is a contingent arrangement which is useful to define and design a specific polity (a collective selfhood, an imagined historical community) and to govern it, bypassing the paradoxes generated by the arbitrariness of power and the validity of law. It is a mechanism which enables the recognition, coordination, assimilation, and self-legitimacy of the legal–political system. If this is true, than we have to answer two fundamental questions. First, are states and their governments the basic units of contemporary political analysis, or must we abandon the idea that the sole centres of constitutional authorities are states? Second, what are the differences between a process of constitutionalisation and a mere process of self-regulation or juridification? I define the first question as the 'problem of the polity' and the second as 'the problem of self-governance'. The two problems are interconnected and represent the elements of what I call the 'relation of constitution' (Fig. 15.3).

To constitute means literally to give shape and form to something.[21] The logic of the 'relation of constitution' is: an X constitutes a Y at time T and only under certain conditions. Constitution does not mean identity of X and Y. If an X, for example

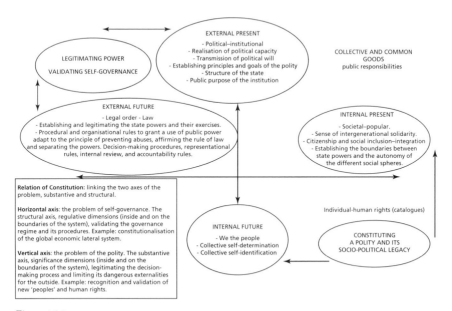

Figure 15.3

---

[21] L. Rudder Baker, *The Metaphysics of Everyday Life: An Essay in Practical Realism* (Cambridge: Cambridge University Press, 2007).

a group of individuals or of institutions, that in time *T*, within and under specific conditions, constitute a new polity *Y* and supply self-governance, then *X* and *Y* are not the same thing: *Y* is not a mere aggregation of *X*. If a *Y* is emerging, then new ontological powers, objects, and identities are generated. In particular, if we take into consideration a newly constituted polity, we face a new social object, usually inscripted in a normative document or in another form of 'recording'. To constitute a polity—not merely to institute it—means ordering the relations of its members through a self-governing normative order, and to recognise / validate it by way of a peculiar collective identity. The problem of the polity is connected to the issue of the arbitrariness of power (who can take legitimate collectively binding decisions?), and represents the substantive and vertical axis of the problem, linking the constitution of a 'we' with its goals. The problem of self-governance concerns the validity and recognition of law (and of the other normative regimes) and represents the structural and horizontal axis of the problem, linking the legal regulation of the polity with its internal integration.[22] The 'relation of constitution' couples these two axes, linking a specific way of self-governance (the fundamental law) to a recognised-validated polity (the sovereign people). If this does not happen, 'simple' juridification or mere self-governance occurs.

We might stop here, affirming with Neil Walker that in 'societal constitutionalism' the idea of a 'holistic constitution' is lacking in each of the four register-elements.[23] In a sense this is perfectly true, but only if we continue to take as our paradigmatic example a modern 'holistic' definition of the situation: (1) holistic legal order, (2) holistic political institution, (3) holistic societal reference, and (4) holistic popular we-ness. Those who affirm that if we remain inside the modern constitutional frame we can only encourage a proliferation of compensative devices for the four registers both substantively and structurally, are right. Specifically, on the substantive axis we see a franchising of universal human rights and standards of public behaviour and corporate responsibility, and on the structural axis we observe franchising of new modes of governance, the rolling out of democratic experimentalism, and the development of quasi-universal principles. But here we can differentiate two different meanings of societal constitutionalism: a 'defensive' one, where the objective is to protect the human beings—not constituted in a new global polity—from the newly emergent, non-state powers; and a 'pro-active' one, where the accountability, legitimacy, and regulation of the public exercise of power by transnational elites can be demanded by their own functional (and non-state) constituencies.

The vertical axis: generalising and re-specifying the polity

Who are this new 'we' that constitutionalise themselves? In order to answer this question we must again generalise and re-specify the concept of the polity for coping with the new cultures and identities which are emerging outside modern nation-state political sites.

---

[22] P. Donati, *Teoria relazionale della società* (Milan: Franc Angeli, 1991).

[23] Walker in this volume.

A new polity (not simply a group, or a lobby, or fluid collective movement) starts to constitutionalise itself when it begins to elaborate, in a reflexive way, two connected political issues. First, it seeks to define the we-ness, that is, the identity and the membership of the actors united in the new polity. 'We the people' is the relevant example only within a state democratic frame. At stake here is something more fundamental: the idea that a constitution pertains to a particular societal formation, self-understood, self-identified, and self-integrated as such. Here is the locus of the *pouvoir constituant* that might express itself not in a revolutionary way but, for example, through democratic iterations of specific functional/subsystemic constituencies. Second, it seeks to define the common goals, goods, and mission of the system, and seeks to select the key organs and representatives charged to announce, prescribe, and preserve that political character necessary to make collectively binding decisions. Here we find not a democratic procedure of representation, but expert groups legitimating through acknowledgement of their expertise and problem-solving capacity.

We see these two reflexive elaborations by observing the morphogenesis of a corporate agent into a corporate actor. By corporate agent I mean a group of people who objectively share a specific position in the society (from the point of view of particular 'goods', 'rights', 'status', etc). A corporate agent, always in the plural meaning, is not aware that it is sharing this position with other people (ie representatives): it is an agent *an sich*. A corporate actor, by contrast, is a group of people (or representatives) that not only objectively share something with others but are aware of sharing it: they are a collectivity *für sich*. In a specific sense, a corporate actor is constituted by the self-consciousness to belong to a 'we'. It is constituted by and of a group of individuals which come to think about themselves as a 'we', so that every member can act and reflect by reference to this membership: for example, a member of the WTO, WHO, Basel Committee, or Amnesty International. They belong to a collective identity that is a collective selfhood and not only a collective sameness. Sameness responds to 'What am I?' Selfhood to 'Who am I?'

The collective selfhood of a corporate actor is reflexive in a twofold sense. First, the members of a group consider themselves as a unity that intends to act collectively. Second, the act is undertaken for the sake of the collectivity. This collectivity is simultaneously the object and subject of an act, specifically a subject and the author of the laws. This new identity-constituted corporate actor has to elaborate and institutionalise its own goals and mission and the institutional authority to legitimate (inside the system) binding decisions. A polity is a structure with: the capacity to mobilise persons and resources for specific purposes, a peculiar degree of institutionalisation, specific goals, and a representation of collective identity.

It is useful to address the problem of polity by reference to the work of James Tully.[24] For Tully, the issue is whether or not modern constitutions can recognise the cultural diversity—the strange multiplicity—of their constituencies. In the

---

[24] J. Tully, *Strange Multiplicity: Constitutionalism in an Age of Diversity* (Cambridge: Cambridge University Press, 1995).

world society, there is a dramatic movement of intercultural voices, organised or not, represented or not, aiming to be constitutionally recognised: nationalist movements, supranational associations, intercultural voices, feminist movements, and indigenous people excluded by the present constitution. These politics of cultural recognition constitute the third phase of anti-imperialism promoted by peoples and cultures who have been excluded by the movements of decolonialisation and constitutional state building. The leitmotif of this new form of constitutional discourse is the aspiration of these 'agents' to self-rule (and so to become a corporate 'actor') in accordance with one's own customs and ways of life. Modern constitutionalism developed around two main forms of recognitions: the equality of independent, self-governing nation states and the equality of individual citizens. But today most of the new polities do not seek to build independent nation states in order to gain independence and self-government. They seek self-rule and recognition within, across, and beyond existing nation states through which they try to mediate two fundamental public goods: freedom and belonging.

The polities of these different and incomparable cultures are not nation states, and contemporary demands for cultural recognition are not of this inclusive type. The modern concepts of people, popular sovereignty, citizenship, unity, equality, and democracy, alongside the modern institutions of parliament, voting, courts, bureaucracy, police, and dissent, all presuppose the uniformity of a nation state with a centralised and unitary system of legal and political institutions. What the liberal, national, and communitarian constitutional modern traditions share is the idea of a culturally homogeneous and sovereign people establishing a constitution through a form of critical negotiation. By a self-conscious agreement, people give rise to a constitution that 'constitutes' the political association. The constitution lays down the fundamental laws which establish the form of government, the rights and duties of citizens, the representative and institutional relation between government and governed, and an amending formula. But today the process of constitutionalisation is more similar to the ancient constitutions, ie processes that do not need a positive and singular act of foundation, but an assemblage of laws, institutions, and customs, derived from certain fixed principles of reason, directed to certain fixed objects for the public good.

Facing the problem of multiplicity 'inside' a singular nation-state constitution, the argumentation of Tully is synthesised by the formula, *audi alteram partem*: that is, be able to understand the multiple narratives (not only national) through which citizens participate in and identify with their (political) associations. Constitutions are chains 'of continual intercultural negotiations and agreements in accordance with conventions of mutual recognition, continuity and consent'.[25] This new 'intercultural' constitutionalism is incompatible not only with the idea of exclusive integrity of the nation (it is compatible with it only if with 'nation' we mean the aspiration to belong to a group of people that governs itself by its own laws and ways) but also with individual freedom conceived in the modern liberal term (it is compatible if it respects the secure belief that what one has to say and do in politics and life is worthwhile)

[25] Ibid 184.

and also with the creation of undemocratic enclaves based on the modern idea of sovereignty, ie a single locus of political power that is absolute.

We have to abstract from the argument of Tully and reflect on the substantive / vertical axis of constitutionalisation. First, in a world society, processes of constitutionalisation will occur specifically when and where there will be a real demand for elaborating, articulating, and empowering areas of social autonomy, and sheltering them against the swamping tendencies of powerful social systems. We can foresee the prevalence of the control-integrative function of the constitution, with its corollary of the development of new human rights and cosmopolitan norms. But, as Tully has shown, there will be also a dramatic demand for self-rule and recognition by new and emerging (identity- or interest-based) polities in the global scale. Second, we will probably witness a sort of de facto process of constitutionalisation where the 'we' will originate indirectly from the need of governance. But with the cultural dialogue going global, we can also expect new and active constituent powers, represented by activists of an emergent global civil society or by the 'citizen' of new and unexpected societal subsystems. Finally, civil constitutions will probably not be produced by some sort of big bang, the spectacular revolutionary act of the constituent assembly, nor will these global regimes have a single original text embodied as a codification in a special constitutional document. On the contrary, civil constitutions will grow through evolutionary processes of long duration.

The horizontal axis: generalising and re-specifying the normative order

In this section I will try to answer the second question: the problem of 'self-governance'. What does it take for procedural norms, or a rule-guided practice of social cooperation, to be recognised as constitutional? Here we find the structural coupling between the juridical and the societal frames. In the first frame we are confronted with all the legal devices that shape a constitution: rule of self-production, self-organisation, self-extension, self-interpretation, self-amendment, self-enforcement, self-discipline, etc, including the rules that specify the terms of an order's internal stratification and those who posit its sovereignty over any external claim to priority. In the second we face the problem of defining the differences, boundaries, and powers between the political–institutional frame and the civil society, including the problem of flexible citizenship and membership.

It will be not predictable whether the new processes of civil constitutionalisation will be identical with the modern one, but the basic point remains the structural coupling between the law (of the different lateral subsystems) and their analytically political representations. Auto-constitutional regimes are defined by their duplication of reflexivity. Secondary rule making in law is combined with fundamental rationality principles in an autonomous social sphere. In different globalised subsystems we can find several emerging elements of a constitution: provisions on the establishment and exercise of decision making (organisational and procedural rules) on the one hand; the definition of individual freedoms, belonging, and societal autonomies (fundamental rights) on the other.

We can observe these emerging elements with the aid of the concept of societal contitutionalism elaborated by David Sciulli.[26] Sciulli is not concerned directly with the problems of democratic political form, the constitutional liberal concerns of separation of powers and human rights. His reflections represent a strong criticism of the idea that non-authoritarian social change is possible only by means of institutions and practices peculiar to Western democracy. Sciulli is searching for a 'social infrastructure'—a collegial form of organisation—capable of supporting a non-authoritarian social development. These collegial formations, that can be found everywhere and not only in Western societies, are not democratic in any formal way. So, the basic argument is that not every non-democratic collegial organisation is immediately authoritarian and that the best defence against authoritarianism is not only what we call constitutional liberal-democracy.

For Sciulli, a modern constitutional state may be relatively egalitarian and yet become everyday more manipulative. He sees a risky drift towards authoritarianism within the institutional setting of modern societies. It manifests itself in four thrusts: (1) fragmentation of logics of action, with the compartmentalisation of separate social spheres; (2) dominance of instrumental calculation across all the different domains; (3) comprehensive replacement of informal coordination with bureaucratic organisation; and (4) increasing confinement in the 'iron cage of servitude to the future', especially in social spheres. This drift has the nature of a dilemma because every conscious attempt to achieve control over the drift gets caught up in this logic. More freedom brings more authoritarian social control. More instrumental action leads to more substantive tendencies to control this action, but this in turn leads to more interpretative conflict. Market 'mock' competition is not able to ensure the balance between actors' subjective interests, as with the formal constitution. Every internal normative restraint (whether substantive, as in group competition, religious proscriptions, or division of powers; or procedural, as with elections and rational–legal enforcement) is impeded, because of its internality to the process of rationalisation itself.

To control this drift, the different actors of a complex society must develop and institutionalise a certain kind of norm, external to the logic of the drift itself, that is, a 'non-rational' normative restraint. Sciulli's seeks to find, within an existing civil society, the external procedural restraints on the inadvertent exercises of power. He locates them in a normative standard of 'reasoned social action' recognised even by competing actors: heterogeneous actors and competing groups are possibly integrated rather than demonstrably controlled within any complex social unit when the shared social duties, being sanctioned within it, can at least be recognised and understood by them in common. This normative threshold indicates the violation of the arbitrariness of power's exercise. It is, from Lon Fuller's perspective, a threshold of law's interpretability. Sciulli shows this empirically through the institutionalisation of various forms of professional conduct, centring on deliberative bodies, research

[26] D. Sciulli, *Theory of Societal Constitutionalism* (Cambridge: Cambridge University Press, 1992).

divisions of corporations, professional associations, universities, etc. These collegial formations are deliberative and professional bodies, wherein heterogeneous actors and competing groups maintain the threshold of interpretability of shared social duties. The sharing of these norms establishes a sort of new and specific polity.

In *Corporate Power in Civil Society*, Sciulli tries to develop an application of the societal constitutionalism to what he calls the American Corporate Judiciary (ACJ), in particular the State Courts of Delaware, California, and New York, which monitors how managers govern publicly traded corporations. For Sciulli the problem for those who remain within the constitutional liberal-social-democratic legacy is that their concepts fail to address manifestations of social authoritarianism, ie purposefully and inadvertently arbitrary exercises of collective power by powerful 'private' actors within civil society. They have difficulty in extending their concepts from the individual's relationship to the state to the individual's relationship to powerful organisations within civil society. They are only able to discuss arbitrary government and not other forms of arbitrary exercises of collective power.[27]

In this sense, the role of the ACJ is to define and limit how corporations may conduct themselves in civil society. In the market-driven culture, the problem of how managers govern the companies is left to competition and self-regulation. The limitations can be only economic, instrumental, and pecuniary in their sanctions. From this point of view there is no problem with the basic institutional design of a democratic society. The real problem is that the companies are the single most significant set of intermediary associations in American society and they have a huge impact not only on their members (or shareholders) but also on the lives of the stakeholders and of other citizens, what Sciulli call 'institutional externalities of corporate power'. Companies are embedded in society and their institutional settings are part of the society's structural design. The institutional design of a democratic society extends normative mediations of power from government to major intermediary associations in civil society. These associations (and other sites of professional practice, such as hospitals, universities, museums, governmental agencies) mediate the state's power and broaden individuals' loyalties beyond their families and primary groups. But the state cannot monopolise collective power in civil society. From the perspective of corporations, this means that they are able to exercise collective power in abusive ways. By monitoring corporate governance with an eye to institutional design, Delaware courts perform what Parsons called a pattern-maintenance (fiduciary) function for the entire society. So 'it is not an exaggeration to say that Delaware's Chancery Court and Supreme Court together function as the constitutional court of the United States for all intermediary associations, for all powerful private bodies in American civil society'.[28] Courts do not intervene in the productive functions of corporations, but only in the private governments of the corporations, deciding and evaluating their legitimacy, equality, and basic fairness.

---

[27] D. Sciulli, *Corporate Power in Civil Society: An Application of Societal Constitutionalism* (New York: New York University Press, 2001).

[28] Ibid 15.

The Delaware court remains concerned that certain changes in corporate governance can jeopardise a democratic society and undermine its own legitimacy as the country's constitutional court for intermediary associations. Sciulli emphasises that:

> Corporate law, like most law, is primarily about the rule-oriented structuring of social power, and it is specifically about the rules that structure the organization of economic power … the powers and restrictions of corporate law are formulated with a view toward achieving a set of rules for incorporated business that conduce to the public advantage. In the words of Professor Melvin Eisenberg, 'corporate law is constitutional law' in this fundamental sense.[29]

As constitutional law for powerful private persons, corporate law identifies the rights corporate officers exercise within structured situations in civil society and the duties corporate officers must bear when advancing either the corporate entity's collective interest or their own positional interests. But corporate law also identifies social norms and institutional arrangements to which corporate officers are expected to exhibit fidelity as they otherwise exercise their business judgement in 'private' domains. This reduces corporate officers' positional powers and freedom of contract in civil society and prevents one-sided exercises of collective power in structured situations.

This example shows very well that processes of constitutionalisation occur exactly when and where in the social sphere (not only in the political sphere) there emerges a social need to guarantee the chances of articulating, enhancing, and empowering areas of autonomy (social differentiation) for societal reflection and institutionalising them against swamping tendencies.[30] This is a clear example of defensive constitutionalism, without a real self-authorising polity, based on the spread of cosmopolitan norms. We can observe the same process in different functional subsystems. These processes confirm the idea that societal constitutionalism is for the moment powered by the attempts—on the horizontal axis of the 'relation of constitution'—to limit and to make accountable the anonymous matrix of social powers which threatens human rights. But if we want to conceptualise a fully fledged, new societal constitutionalism, it is also necessary to identify new democratic and constitutional experiments on the vertical axis, where non-predictable non-state polities will probably emerge.

---

[29] Ibid 25.

[30] G. Teubner, 'Societal Constitutionalism: Alternatives to State-Centred Constitutional Theory?', in Joerges, Sand, and Teubner, above n 6, 3–28.

⤫ 16 ⤬

Fragmented Foundations
Societal Constitutionalism beyond the Nation State

Gunther Teubner

I. THE NEW CONSTITUTIONAL QUESTION

Horizontal effects of constitutional rights

The question of the 'horizontal' effects of fundamental rights, ie the question whether they impose obligations not only on public bodies but also directly on 'private governments', acquires much more dramatic dimensions in the transnational sphere than it ever possessed in the nation-state context. The issue becomes particularly controversial where infringements of human rights by transnational corporations are alleged. I shall single out a few glaring cases: environmental pollution and inhuman treatment of local population groups, eg by Shell in Nigeria; the chemical catastrophe in Bhopal; disgraceful working conditions in 'sweatshops' in Asia and Latin America; the policy of excessive pricing of pharmaceuticals in the South African Aids drama; child labour attributed to IKEA and Nike; allegations against Adidas of having footballs produced by forced labour in China; the use of highly poisonous pesticides in banana plantations; 'disappearances' of unionised workers; environmental damage caused by big construction projects. The list could easily be extended. The scandalous events fill volumes.

What converts the legal question—the horizontal effects of fundamental rights—into a burning political issue is the ongoing privatisation of government. Legal doctrines of horizontal effects usually dodge the tricky question of whether private actors are directly bound by fundamental rights provisions. A host of doctrines, according to which fundamental rights only have 'indirect' effects in the private sphere, have been devised.[1] Simplifying grossly, there are two main constructions, albeit with numerous variants. Under the state action doctrine, private actors are in principle excluded from the binding effect of fundamental rights unless

---

[1] For a comparative view, see D. Friedman and D. Barak-Erez (eds), *Human Rights in Private Law* (Oxford: Hart, 2001); G. W. Anderson, 'Social Democracy and the Limits of Rights Constitutionalism' (2004) 17 *The Canadian Journal of Law & Jurisprudence* 31–59; P. Alston (ed), *Non-state Actors and Human Rights* (Oxford: Oxford University Press, 2005); A. Clapham, *Human Rights Obligations of Non-state Actors* (Oxford: Oxford University Press, 2006).

some element of state action can be identified in their behaviour. This might be the case either because state bodies are to some degree involved or because the private actor fulfils more or less broadly understood 'public' functions. Alternatively, under the doctrine of the structural effect of fundamental rights, those rights are to be respected across the whole legal system, including private law provisions enacted by the state. However, the limitation of the effect of fundamental rights to the legal system implies that private actors themselves are not subject to any fundamental rights obligations.

Globalisation makes this puzzle even more difficult to solve. In the transnational sphere, the question whether private actors are bound by fundamental rights is much more acute than in the context of the nation state. Here, the otherwise omni-present state and its national law are almost absent so that the state action doctrine and the theory of the structural effect of fundamental rights can be applied in only very few situations. At the same time, transnational private actors, especially trans-national corporations, intensively regulate whole areas of life through their own private governance regimes. Thus, the question whether they are directly bound by fundamental rights can no longer be evaded.

Societal constitutionalism

The more general legal theoretical question of the problem sketched out above is: how is constitutional theory to respond to the challenges arising from these two major trends of privatisation and globalisation? This is what today's 'constitutional question' ought to be. Today's constitutionalism moves beyond the nation state. It does so in a double sense: constitutionalism moves into the transnational context and into the private sector.[2] While the old constitutions of the nation states were simultaneously liberating the dynamics of democratic politics and disciplining repressive political power by law, the point today is to liberate and to discipline quite different social dynamics—and to do this on a global scale. Is constitutional theory able to generalise the ideas it developed for the nation state and to re-specify them for today's problems? In other words, can we make the tradition of nation-state constitutionalism fruitful and redesign it in order to cope with the phenomena of privatisation and globalisation?[3]

Contemporary constitutional theory is still state centred. This is a real *obstacle épistémologique*. It makes constitutional theory badly equipped to deal with private government on a transnational scale. The alternative to be developed is constitu-tionalism without the state. For constitutional theorists, this amounts to breaking a

---

[2] For the sociological theory of societal constitutionalism, see P. Selznick, *Law, Society and Industrial Justice* (New York: Russell Sage, 1969); D. Sciulli, *Theory of Societal Constitutionalism* (Cambridge: Cambridge University Press, 1992); Prandini in this volume.

[3] For a more detailed account, see G. Teubner, 'Societal Constitutionalism: Alternatives to State-Centred Constitutional theory?', in C. Joerges, I.-J. Sand, and G. Teubner (eds), *Constitutionalism and Transnational Governance* (Oxford: Hart, 2004), 3–28.

taboo.[4] For them, a constitution without a state is at best a utopia—a poor one, to be sure. But this formula is not an abstract normative demand for remote, uncertain futures. Instead, it is an assertion of a real trend that can be observed on a worldwide scale.

My thesis, in short, is that we are witnessing the emergence of a multiplicity of civil constitutions beyond the nation state. But the constitution of world society is not to be conceived exclusively within the representative institutions of international politics, and neither can it take place in a unitary global constitution overlaying all areas of society. It is emerging incrementally in the constitutionalisation of a multiplicity of autonomous subsystems of world society.[5]

II. FRAGMENTED GLOBALISATION

This emerging societal constitutionalism can be grasped only if one appreciates the polycentric form of globalisation. And one is able to arrive at such an understanding only if one gives up five widespread assumptions of social and legal theory in order to replace them with somewhat unusual ideas.[6] These five assumptions are considered in turn.

Rationality conflicts in a polycentric global society

A first assumption that must be given up is that globalisation of law is primarily a result of the internationalisation of the economy. The alternative to such an economy-led form of globalisation is 'polycentric globalisation'.[7] The primary

---

[4] D. Grimm, 'The Constitution in the Process of Denationalization' (2005) 12 *Constellations* 447–63.

[5] Authors who come close to this position are H. Brunkhorst, R. Prandini, U. K. Preuss, and N. Walker (in this volume); N. Walker, 'The Idea of Constitutional Pluralism' (2002) 65 *Modern Law Review* 317–59; C. Walter, 'Constitutionalizing (Inter)national Governance: Possibilities for and Limits to the Development of an International Constitutional Law' (2001) 44 *German Yearbook of International Law* 170–201, at 188 et seq; G. P. Calliess and P. Zumbansen, *Rough Consensus and Running Code: A Theory of Transnational Private Law*, Sonderforschungsbereich 597 (Bremen: Staatlichkeit im Wandel, 2007); K.-H. Ladeur and L. Viellechner, 'Die transnationale Expansion staatlicher Grundrechte: Zur Konstitutionalisierung globales Privatrechtsregimes' (2008) 46 *Archiv des Völkerrechts* 42–73; H. Schepel, *The Constitution of Private Governance: Product Standards in the Regulation of Integrating Markets* (Oxford: Hart Publishing, 2005); M. Amstutz, A. Abegg, and V. Karavas, *Soziales Vertragsrecht: Eine rechtsevolutorische Studie* (Basel: Helbing & Lichtenhahn, 2006).

[6] For a more elaborate discussion, see A. Fischer-Lescano and G. Teubner, 'Regime-Collisions: The Vain Search for Legal Unity in the Fragmentation of Global Law' (2004) 25 *Michigan Journal of International Law* 999–1045.

[7] D. Held, *Democracy and the Global Order: From the Modern State to Cosmopolitan Governance* (Cambridge: Polity Press, 1995), 62. See also J. W. Meyer et al, 'World Society and the Nation-State' (1997) 103 *American Journal of Sociology* 144–81; A. Schütz, 'The Twilight of the Global Polis: On Losing Paradigms, Environing Systems, and Observing World Society',

driver of this development is the functional differentiation of society. Each of several autonomous functional subsystems of society escapes its territorial confines and constitutes itself globally. This process is not confined to economic markets alone; it also encompasses science, culture, technology, health, the military, transport, tourism and sport, as well as, albeit in a somewhat retarded manner, politics, law, and welfare. Today, each of these subsystems operates autonomously at the global level.

What is of particular interest now is what might be called the external relations of these global villages. These relations are anything but harmonious. If anywhere, it is here that the notion of a 'clash of cultures' is appropriate. Through their own operative closure, global functional systems create a sphere for themselves in which they are free to intensify their own rationality without regard to other social systems or to their natural or human environment. In his pioneering analysis Karl Marx has shown the destructive potential of a globalised economic rationality. Max Weber went beyond that and deployed the concept of 'modern polytheism'. He identified the destructive potential within other areas of life and analysed the threatening rationality conflicts which arise. In the meantime, the human and ecological risks posed by highly specialised global systems, such as science and technology, have become apparent to a broader public.[8] Where countries of the southern hemisphere are considered, it is clear that real dangers are posed by the conflicts between economic, political, scientific, and technological rationality spheres that instigate the 'clash of rationalities'. According to Niklas Luhmann's central thesis, the underlying cause for these risks is to be found in the rationality maximisation engaged in by different global functional systems, which cloaks an enormous potential for the endangering of people, nature, and society.[9]

In this light, the alleged violations of human rights by transnational enterprises are not only conflicts between individual rights—between the property rights of the firms and the human rights of the people. Rather, they represent collisions of institutionalised rationalities. They are embodied in the different policies of transnational organisations. Such problems are caused by the fragmented and operationally closed functional systems of a global society, which, in their expansionist fervour, create the most pressing problems of global society.

in G. Teubner (ed), *Global Law without A State* (Aldershot: Dartmouth Gower, 1997), 257–93; B. de S. Santos, *Toward a New Legal Common Sense: Law, Globalization and Emancipation* (Evanston, Ill.: Northwestern University Press, 2003); K. Günther and S. Randeria, *Recht, Kultur und Gesellschaft im Prozeß der Globalisierung* (Bad Homburg: Reimers, 2001), at 28 et seq; N. Luhmann, 'Der Staat des politischen Systems: Geschichte und Stellung in der Weltgesellschaft', in U. Beck (ed), *Perspektiven der Weltgesellschaft* (Frankfurt: Suhrkamp, 1998), 345.

[8] See especially U. Beck, *Risk Society* (London: Sage, 1992).

[9] N. Luhmann, *Die Gesellschaft der Gesellschaft* (Frankfurt am Main: Suhrkamp, 1997), at 1088 et seq.

Transnational regulatory regimes

Secondly, we must give up the idea that legal systems only exist at the level of the nation state. Law has now established itself globally as a unitary functional system of the world society. Despite its unity at the global level, law must reckon with a multitude of internal contradictions. Thus, legal unity within global law is redirected away from normative consistency towards operative 'inter-legality'.[10]

A new internal differentiation of law has taken place. This new differentiation within law is the result of the drastic impact of social differentiation upon law. For centuries, law had followed the political logic of nation states and was manifest in the multitude of national legal orders. Each of them had its own territorial jurisdiction. In the last fifty years, however, in a rapidly accelerating expansion, transnational regulatory regimes, most prominent among them the World Trade Organization, established themselves as autonomous legal orders at the global level. In contrast to common assumptions, the emergence of global legal regimes does not entail the integration or convergence of legal orders. Rather, societal fragmentation impacts upon law in a manner such that political regulation of differentiated societal spheres requires the parcelling out of issue-specific policy arenas which juridify themselves.

Consequently, the traditional differentiation, in line with the political principle of territoriality, into relatively autonomous national legal orders is overlain by a principle of sectoral differentiation: the differentiation of global law into transnational legal regimes, which defines the external reach of their jurisdiction along issue-specific rather than territorial boundaries.

Transnational 'private' regimes

But this is still not sufficient to furnish us with a comprehensive understanding of legal globalisation. No light has yet been shed upon the equally rapid quantitative growth of non-statal 'private' legal regimes. Only these regimes give birth to 'global law without the State', which is primarily responsible for the multidimensionality of global legal pluralism.[11] A full understanding of this multidimensional legal pluralism can be obtained only if one gives up the third assumption in social and legal theory: that law derives its validity exclusively from processes of law-making initiated by the state, that law, to qualify as such, must either be derived from its well-known internal sources or from officially sanctioned international sources. Thus, we must extend our concept of law to encompass norms operating beyond the legal sources of the nation state and international law.

'Transnational communities', or autonomous fragments of society, such as the globalised economy, science, technology, the mass media, medicine, education, and transport, are developing a strong 'norm hunger', an enormous demand for regulatory

---

[10] B. de S. Santos, 'State Transformation, Legal Pluralism and Community Justice: An Introduction' (1992) 1 *Social and Legal Studies* 131–42; M. Amstutz, 'Vertragskollisionen: Fragmente für eine Lehre von der Vertragsverbindung', in M. Amstutz (ed), *Festschrift für Heinz Rey* (Zürich: Schulthess, 2003), 161–76.

[11] On the discussion of legal pluralism, see P. S. Berman, 'The Globalization of Jurisdiction' (2002) 151 *University of Pennsylvania Law Review* 311–545, at 325 et seq.

norms, which cannot be satisfied by national or international institutions. Instead, they satisfy their demand through a direct recourse to law. Increasingly, global private regimes are creating their own substantive law. They make use of their own sources of law, which lie outside the spheres of national law-making and international treaties.[12]

Today, the most prominent private legal regimes are the *lex mercatoria* of the international economy and the *lex digitalis* of the Internet.[13] To these, however, we must add numerous private or private–public instances of regulation and conflict resolution which create autonomous law with a claim to global validity.[14] These postnational formations are organised around principles of finance, recruitment, coordination, communication, and reproduction that are fundamentally postnational and not just multinational or international. Among them are multinational enterprises building their own internal legal order but also transnational regimes which regulate social issues worldwide. These private regimes clash frequently with the legal rules of nation states and other transnational regimes.

Constitutionalism in transnational regimes

The fragmentation of global society and its impact on law have ramifications for constitutional theory. At the global level, the locus of constitutionalisation is shifting away from the system of international relations to different social sectors, which are establishing civil constitutions of their own. According to the concept of constitutional pluralism, it is appropriate to speak of the 'constitution' of collective bodies outside the confines of the nation state when the following conditions, specified by Neil Walker, have been met:

   (i) the development of an explicit constitutional discourse and constitutional self-consciousness;
  (ii) a claim to foundational legal authority, or sovereignty, where sovereignty is not viewed as absolute;
 (iii) the delineation of a sphere of competences;
  (iv) the existence of an organ internal to the polity with interpretative autonomy as regards the meaning and the scope of the competences;
   (v) the existence of an institutional structure to govern the polity;
  (vi) rights and obligations of citizenship, understood in a broad sense;
 (vii) specification of the terms of representation of the citizens in the polity.[15]

---

[12] G. Teubner, 'Global Bukowina: Legal Pluralism in the World Society', in G. Teubner (ed), *Global Law without a State* (Aldershot: Dartmouth, 1997), 3–28.

[13] For the *lex mercatoria*, see A. Stone Sweet, 'The New Lex Mercatoria and Transnational Governance' (2006) 13 *Journal of European Public Policy* 627–46. On the *lex digitalis*, H. H. Perritt, 'Dispute Resolution in Cyberspace: Demand for New Forms of ADR' (2000) 15 *Ohio State Journal on Dispute Resolution* 675–703, at 691 et seq.

[14] Berman, above n 11, at 369 et seq.

[15] N. Walker, 'The EU and the WTO: Constitutionalism in a New Key', in G. de Burca and J. Scott (eds), *The EU and the WTO: Legal and Constitutional Issues* (Oxford: Hart, 2001), 31–57, at 33.

'Polity' in this context should not be understood in the narrow sense of institutionalised politics. The term also refers to non-political institutions of civil society, of the economy, of science, education, health, art, or sports—of all those social sites where constitutionalising takes place.[16] Thus, self-contained regimes fortify themselves as auto-constitutional regimes. The defining feature of self-contained regimes is not simply that they create highly specialised primary rules, ie substantive rules in special fields of law, but that they also produce their own procedural norms on law-making, law recognition, and legal sanctions: so-called secondary rules.[17] However, such reflexive norm building does not yet amount to constitutional norm building in the strict sense. Secondary rules become constitutional rules only when they develop closer parallels to the norms of political constitutions. Political constitutions do not simply contain higher legal norms. Instead, they establish a structural coupling between the reflexive mechanisms of law and those of politics.[18] Accordingly, the defining feature of auto-constitutional regimes is the existence of a linkage between legal reflexive processes and reflexive processes of other social spheres. Reflexive in this context means the application of specific processes to themselves, the norming of norms, the application of political principles to the political process itself, epistemology as the theorising of theories, etc.

Auto-constitutional regimes are defined by their duplication of reflexivity. Secondary rule making in law is combined with defining fundamental rationality principles in an autonomous social sphere. Societal constitutions establish a structural coupling between secondary rule making in law and reflexive mechanisms in the other social sector. A non-statal, non-political, civil society-led constitutionalisation thus occurs to the degree that reflexive social processes, which determine social rationalities through their self-application, are juridified in such a way that they are linked with reflexive legal processes. Understood in this way, it makes sense to speak of the existence of constitutional elements—in the strict sense of the term—within economic regimes, within the academic system, and within digital regimes of the Internet. Here, in such diverse contexts, we find typical elements of a constitution: provisions on the establishment and exercise of decision making (organisational and procedural rules) on the one hand and definitions of individual freedoms and societal autonomies (fundamental rights) on the other.[19]

---

[16] This is accentuated by Sciulli, above n 2; H. Brunkhorst, *Solidarity: From Civic Friendship to a Global Legal Community* (Cambridge, Mass.: MIT Press, 2005).

[17] B. Simma, 'Self-Contained Regimes' (1985) 16 *Netherlands Yearbook of International Law* 111–36; M. Koskenniemi, *Outline of the Chairman of the ILC Study Group on Fragmentation of International Law: The Function and Scope of the Lex Specialis Rule and the Question of 'Self-contained Regimes'* (2003), <http://www.un.org/law/ilc/sessions/55/fragmentation_outline.pdf>.

[18] N. Luhmann, 'Verfassung als evolutionäre Errungenschaft' (1990) 9 *Rechtshistorisches Journal* 176–220.

[19] A. Fischer-Lescano, 'Globalverfassung: Verfassung der Weltgesellschaft' (2002) 88 *Archiv für Rechts- und Sozialphilosophie* 349–78.

Importantly, societal constitution making intensifies conflicts between legal regimes, even conflicts between their fundamental rights concepts, since it fortifies the independence of the legal regime from other distinct legal regimes through reflexive mechanisms.

Collisions of regime constitutions

What does this mean for the idea of a unified world constitution? The ultimate assumption to give up is the hope for a unified global constitution, harboured, inter alia, by political philosophers like Jürgen Habermas: *Lasciate ogni speranza*. Any aspiration to the constitutional unity of global law is surely a chimera. The reason is that global society is a 'society without an apex or a centre'.[20] Following the decentring of politics, there is no authority in sight that is in a position to undertake the constitutionalisation of societal fragments.

After the collapse of legal hierarchies, the only realistic option is to develop heterarchical forms of law whose sole function is to create loose relations between the constitutional fragments. Collisions between the diverse regime constitutions might be coped with by a selective process of networking that normatively strengthens already existing factual networks between the regime constitutions: the linkage of regime constitutions with autonomous social sectors and, more importantly in this context, the linkage of regime constitutions with one another. Recent developments of network theory may hence become relevant for international constitutional law. This theory has identified the paradoxical logic of action in networks, the *unitas multiplex* of heterarchical configurations. As 'highly improbable contexts of reproduction of heterogeneous elements',[21] networks are counter-institutions of autonomous systems. Combining different logics of actions, they mediate between autonomous function systems, formal organisations, and, particularly relevant for our purposes, between autonomous regimes. Three guiding principles for the decentralised networking of legal regimes may be identified in the abstract:

  (i) Simple normative compatibility instead of hierarchical unity of law.
  (ii) Constitution making in transnational regimes and nation states through mutual irritation, observation, and reflexivity of these autonomous legal orders.
  (iii) Decentralised modes of coping with conflicts of regime constitutions as a legal method.[22]

---

[20] N. Luhmann, *Politcal Theory in the Welfare State* (Berlin: De Gruyter, 1990).

[21] D. Baecker, *Organisation und Gesellschaft* (Witten-Herdecke: Universität, 2002), at 14.

[22] For the European context, see C. Joerges, 'The Impact of European Integration on Private Law: Reductionist Perceptions, True Conflicts and a New Constitutional Perspective' (1997) 3 *European Law Journal* 378–406.

III. CONSTITUTIONAL RIGHTS IN TRANSNATIONAL PRIVATE REGIMES

Fundamental rights as limitations of the politics of the nation state

What are the consequences of societal constitutionalism for fundamental rights?[23] Apart from procedural rules on decision making, fundamental rights are the most important components of constitutions. In their specific modern sense, fundamental rights emerge with the autonomisation of a multiplicity of separate communicative worlds: of different 'matrices'. Historically first, and visible everywhere since Machiavelli, the matrix of politics becomes autonomous. It becomes detached from the strong moral-religious-economic ties of the old European society, and extends political power without any immanent restraints. With its operative closure and its structural autonomy the political system develops expansive, indeed downright imperialist tendencies. Centralised power for legitimate collective decisions has an inherent tendency to expand into society beyond any limit.[24] It liberates highly destructive force.

The political matrix's expansion marches in two divergent directions. First, it crosses the boundaries to other social sectors. Their response is to invoke their communicative autonomy against politics' intervention. This is the hour of birth of fundamental rights: fundamental rights demarcate from politics areas of autonomy attributed either to social institutions or to persons as social constructs.[25] In both cases, fundamental rights set boundaries to the totalising tendencies of the political matrix within society. Second, in its endeavours to control the human mind and body, politics expands with particular verve across the boundaries of society. Their protests are translated socially into political struggles of the oppressed against their oppressors, and finally end up, through historical compromises, in political guarantees of the self-limitation of politics vis-à-vis individuals. Unlike the aforementioned institutional and personal fundamental rights, these political guarantees are human rights in the strict sense.

Multiplication of expansive social systems

This model of fundamental rights, which is oriented towards politics and the state, works only as long as the state can be equated with society, or at least, be regarded as society's organisational form, and politics as its hierarchical coordination. However, insofar as other highly specialised communicative media—money, knowledge, law, medicine, technology—gain autonomy, this model loses its plausibility. At this point, the horizontal effects of fundamental and human rights become relevant.

---

[23] For a more detailed analysis, see: G. Teubner, 'The Anonymous Matrix: Human Rights Violations by "Private" Transnational Actors' (2006) 69 *Modern Law Review* 327–46.

[24] N. Luhmann, *Grundrechte als Institution: Ein Beitrag zur politischen Soziologie* (Berlin: Duncker & Humblot, 1965), 24.

[25] On the transformation of individual to institutional fundamental rights, see K.-H. Ladeur, *Kritik der Abwägung in der Grundrechtsdogmatik* (Tübingen: Mohr & Siebeck, 2004), at 77.

Fragmentation of society multiplies the boundary zones between autonomised communicative matrices and human beings. The new 'territories' each have boundaries of their own on their human environment. Here, new dangers arise for the integrity of body and mind and for the autonomy of institutional communicative spheres.

Thus, fundamental rights cannot be limited to the relation between state and individual. Specific endangerment of individual and institutional integrity by a communicative matrix arises not just from politics, but in principle from all social sectors that have expansive tendencies.[26] For the matrix of the economy, Marx clarified this particularly through such concepts as alienation, autonomy of capital, commodification of the world, exploitation of man by man. Today we see—most clearly in the writings of Foucault, Agamben, Legendre[27]—similar threats to individual and institutional integrity from the matrices of the natural sciences, psychology, the social sciences, technology, medicine, the press, radio, and television. The cruel experiments carried out on people by Dr Mengele in the concentration camps should not only be seen as an expression of a sadistic personality or as an enslavement of science through the totalitarian Nazi-policy. Recent research on the involvement of prestigious science institutions reveal that the experiments are also to be regarded as the product of the expansionistic tendencies of the natural sciences to seize every opportunity to accumulate knowledge unless they are restrained by external controls.[28]

By now, it should have become clear why it makes no sense to talk about the 'horizontal effect' of those fundamental rights which are enshrined in the political constitution. There is no transfer from the state guarantees of individual freedoms into 'horizontal' relations between private actors. Something else is needed instead. What is necessary is to develop new types of guarantees that limit the destructive potential of communication outside the sphere of institutionalised politics.

The anonymous matrix

If violations of fundamental rights stem from the totalising tendencies of partial rationalities, there is no longer any point in seeing the horizontal effect of fundamental rights as if the rights of private actors have to be weighed up against each other. The imagery of 'horizontality' unacceptably takes the sting out of the whole human-rights issue, as if the sole point of the protection of human rights were that individuals threaten other individuals.

---

[26] U. K. Preuss, 'The Guarantee of Rights: Horizontal Rights', in M. Troper (ed), *Traité International de Droit Constitutionnel, Tome III: Suprématie de la Constitution* (2009: forthcoming).

[27] M. Foucault, *Discipline and Punish: The Birth of the Prison* (London: Penguin Books, 1991); G. Agamben, *Homo Sacer: Sovereign Power and Bare Life* (Stanford, Calif.: Stanford Uiversity Press, 1998), at 15 et seq; P. Legendre, *Lecons VIII: Le crime du caporal Lortie. Traité sur le père* (Paris: Fayard, 1989).

[28] See H.-W. Schmuhl, *Grenzüberschreitungen: Das Kaiser-Wilhelm-Institut für Anthropologie, menschliche Erblehre und Eugenik 1927 bis 1945* (Göttingen: Wallstein, 2005).

Violation of the integrity of individuals by other individuals raises a completely different set of issues that arose long before the radical fragmentation of society in our day. It must systematically be separated from the fundamental rights question as such. In the European tradition, the conflict between individuals has been dealt with by attributing 'subjective rights' to persons. The theory of subjective rights in the Kantian tradition demarcates ideally the citizens' spheres of arbitrary freedom from each other in such a way that the law can take a generalisable form. This idea has been most clearly developed in classical law of tort, in which violations of subjective rights are central. But 'fundamental rights' as here proposed differ from 'subjective rights' in private law. They are not concerned with mutual endangerment of private individuals, ie intersubjective relations, but address concerns about the dangers to individual and institutional integrity that are created by anonymous communicative matrices.

Criminal law concepts of macro-criminality and criminal responsibility of formal organisations come closer to the issue.[29] They affect violations of norms that emanate not from human beings, but from impersonal social processes. But these concepts are still too narrow, because they are confined to the dangers stemming from 'collective actors' (states, political parties, business firms, groups of companies, associations) and miss the dangers stemming from the 'anonymous matrix', that is, from autonomised communicative processes (institutions, functional systems, networks) that are not personified as collectives. To treat the horizontal effect of fundamental rights in terms of subjective rights between individual persons would just end up being addressed in the law of tort with its focus on interpersonal relations. As a consequence, we would be forced to apply the concrete state-oriented fundamental rights wholesale to the most varied interpersonal relations, with disastrous consequences for elective freedoms in private life. Here lies the rational core of the excessive protests of private lawyers against the intrusion of fundamental rights into private law—though these complaints are in turn exaggerated and overlook the real issues.[30]

Both the 'old' political and the 'new' polycontextual human-rights questions should be understood with respect to people being threatened not by their fellows, but by anonymous communicative processes. These processes must in the first place be identified. Michel Foucault has seen them most clearly, radically depersonalising the phenomenon of power and identifying today's micro-power relations in society's capillaries in the discourses/practices of 'disciplines'.[31]

We can now summarise the outcome of our abstract considerations. The human-rights question in the strict sense must today be seen as endangerment of individual

---

[29] See, eg H. Jäger, *Makrokriminalität: Studien zur Kriminologie kollektiver Gewalt* (Frankfurt am Main: Suhrkamp, 1989).

[30] D. Medicus, 'Der Grundsatz der Verhältnismäßigkeit im Privatrecht' (1992) 192 *Archiv für die civilistische Praxis* 35–70; W. Zöllner, 'Regelungsspielräume im Schuldvertragsrecht: Bemerkungen zur Grundrechtsanwendung im Privatrecht und zu den sogenannten Ungleichgewichtslagen' (1996) 196 *Archiv für die civilistische Praxis* 1–36.

[31] Foucault, above n 27, at 135 et seq.

and institutional integrity by a multiplicity of anonymous and today globalised communicative processes. The fragmentation of world society into autonomous subsystems creates new boundaries between subsystem and human being and between the various subsystems. The expansive tendencies of the subsystems aim in both directions.[32] It now becomes clear how a new 'equation' has to replace the old 'equation' of the horizontal effect. The old one was based on a relation between two private actors—private perpetrator and private victim of the infringement. On one side of the new equation is no longer a private actor as the fundamental-rights violator, but the anonymous matrix of an autonomised communicative medium. On the other side is no longer simply the compact individual. Instead, the protection of the individual splits up into three main dimensions:

   (i) Institutional rights protecting the autonomy of social discourses—the autonomy of art, of science, of religion—against their subjugation by the totalising tendencies of the communicative matrix.

  (ii) Personal rights protecting the autonomy of communications, attributed not to institutions, but to the social artefacts called 'persons'.

 (iii) Human rights as negative bounds on societal communication, where the integrity of individuals' body and mind is endangered by a communicative matrix.

Justiciability?

How can the law describe these boundary conflicts when, after all, it has only the language of 'rights' of 'persons' available?[33] Can it, in this impoverished rights talk, in any way reconstruct the difference between interpersonal conflict and the conflict between the communicative matrix and the integrity of individuals? Here we reach the limits of legal doctrine, and the limits of court proceedings. In litigation, there must always be a plaintiff suing a defendant for infringing his rights. In this framework of mandatory binarisation as person-versus-person conflict, can fundamental rights ever be asserted against the structural violence of anonymous social processes?

    The only way this can happen is to use individual suits against private actors to thematise conflicts in which human rights of individuals are asserted against structural violence of the matrix. In more traditional terms, the institutional conflict that is really meant has to take place within individual forms of action. We are already familiar with something similar from existing institutional theories of fundamental rights, which recognise as their bearers not only persons, but also institutions.[34]

---

[32] In more detail, see A. Fischer-Lescano and G. Teubner, *Regime-Kollisionen: Zur Fragmentierung des globalen Rechts* (Frankfurt: Suhrkamp, 2006), ch 1.

[33] M. A. Glendon, 'Rights Talk: The Impoverishment of Political Discourse', in D. E. Eberly (ed), *The Essential Civil Society Reader* (Oxford: Rowman Littlefield, 2000), 305–16.

[34] For the impersonal concept of fundamental rights, see H. Ridder, *Die soziale Ordnung des Grundgesetzes* (Opladen: Westdeutscher Verlag, 1975); K.-H. Ladeur, 'Helmut Ridders Konzeption der Meinungs- und Pressefreiheit in der Demokratie' (1999) 32 *Kritische Justiz* 281–300.

Whoever enforces individual freedom of expression simultaneously protects the integrity of the political process.

Is this distinction justiciable? Can person-versus-person conflict be separated from communication-versus-individual conflict? Translated into the language of law, this becomes a problem of attribution. Whodunnit? Under what conditions can the concrete violation of integrity be attributed not to persons, but to collective actors, or to anonymous communication processes? If this attribution could be achieved, the genuine problematic of human rights would have been formulated even in the impoverished rights talk of the law.

In an extreme simplification, the 'horizontal' human-rights problematic can perhaps be described in more familiar legal categories as follows: the problem of human rights in private law arises only where the endangerment of body–mind integrity comes from social 'institutions' (and not just from individual actors). In principle, institutions include private formal organisations and private regulatory systems. The most important examples here would be business firms, private associations, hospitals, schools, and universities, as formal organisations on the one hand; and general terms of trade, private standardisation, and similar rule-setting mechanisms as private regulatory systems on the other. We must of course be clear that the term 'institution' represents only imperfectly the chains of communicative acts that endanger the integrity of mind and body, and does not completely grasp the expansive phenomenon that is really intended. This is the reason why we use the metaphor of the anonymous 'matrix' instead. But for lawyers, who are orientated towards rules and persons, 'institution' has the advantage of being defined as a bundle of norms and at the same time being able to be personified. The concept of the institution could accordingly re-specify fundamental rights in social sectors. The outcome would then be a formula of 'third-party effect' which could seem plausible also to a black-letter lawyer. It would regard horizontal effect no longer as balancing between the fundamental rights of individual bearers, but instead as the protection of human rights and rights of discourses vis-à-vis expansive social institutions.

Individual and institutional dimensions

Let us return to human rights violation by the transnational corporation. We can now see directions in which human rights might develop. It should be clear how inadequate it is in court proceedings to weigh up an individual's fundamental rights against the transnational corporation's individual rights. The matter is not one of 'corporate social responsibility', with a single corporate actor infringing the fundamental rights. A human right can become a reality only if the 'horizontal' effect of fundamental rights is reformulated from interpersonal conflicts to conflicts between a social system and its environment.

In the dimension of institutional rights, the conflict needs to be set in its social context, which requires us to observe that the conflict is due to a clash of incompatible logics of action. The critical conflict arises in the contradiction between norms of different social rationalities. The point is not, then, to impose controls on particular firms, but to develop abstract and general rules on incompatibilities between different social sectors, and to prepare the conflicting transnational regimes to respond to destructive conflicts between incompatible logics of action by building concerns of the other into the norms of their own rationality. Since there is no paramount court for the conflict, it can only be solved from the viewpoint of one of the conflicting regimes. But the competing logic of action, ie the normative principles of the one sector, has to be brought into the other's own context as a limitation.

Where the law ends

This sketch of legal ways to react to the conflict shows how inappropriate the optimism is that the human-rights problem can be solved using the resources of law. Can one discourse do justice to the other? This is a problem the dilemmas of which have been analysed by François Lyotard.[35] But it is at least a problem within society, one that Niklas Luhmann sought to respond to with the concept of justice as socially adequate complexity.[36] The situation is even more dramatic with human rights in the strict sense, located at the boundary between communication and the individual human being. All the groping attempts to juridify human rights cannot hide the fact that, in a strict sense, this is an impossible project. How can society ever 'do justice' to real people if people are not its parts but stand outside communication: if society cannot communicate with them but at most about them, indeed not even reach them but merely either irritate or destroy them? In the light of grossly inhuman social practices, the justice of human rights is a burning issue, but one which has no prospect of resolution. This has to be said in all rigour.

If a positive concept of justice in the relation between society and human being is definitively impossible, then what is left, if we are not to succumb to post-structuralist quietism, is only second best. In the law, we have to accept that the problem of the integrity of body and mind can only be experienced through the inadequate sensors of irritation, reconstruction, and re-entry. The deep dimension of conflicts between communication on the one hand and mind and body on the other can at best be surmised at by law. And the only signpost left is the legal prohibition, through which a self-limitation of communication seems possible. This programme of justice is ultimately doomed to fail, and cannot console itself with Jacques Derrida's words that it is 'to come, *à venir*'.[37] It has to face up to its being in principle impossible. The justice of human rights can, then, at best be formulated negatively. It is aimed at removing unjust situations, not creating just ones. It is only the counter-principle

---

[35] J.-F. Lyotard, *The Differend: Phrases in Dispute* (Manchester: Manchester University Press, 1987).

[36] N. Luhmann, *Rechtssystem und Rechtsdogmatik* (Stuttgart: Kohlhammer, 1974); N. Luhmann, 'Gerechtigkeit in den Rechtssystemen der modernen Gesellschaft', in N. Luhmann (ed), *Ausdifferenzierung des Rechts: Beiträge zur Rechtssoziologie und Rechtstheorie* (Frankfurt am Main: Suhrkamp, 1981), 374–418; N. Luhmann, *Law as a Social System* (Oxford: Oxford University Press, 2004), at 214 et seq.

[37] J. Derrida, 'Force of Law: The Mystical Foundation of Authority' (1990) 11 *Cardozo Law Review* 919–1046, at 969.

to communicative violations of body and soul, a protest against inhumanities of communication, without it ever being possible to say positively what the conditions of 'humanly just' communication might be.[38]

Nor do the emancipatory programmes of modernity à la Habermas help any further. No information comes from criteria of democratic involvement of individuals in social processes, since only persons take part, not bodies or minds. From this viewpoint one can only be amazed at the naivety of participatory romanticism. Democratic procedures are no test of a society's human rights justice. Equally uninformative are universalisation theories that proceed transcendentally via a priori characteristics or via a posteriori universalisation of expressed needs. What do such philosophical abstractions have to do with actual human individuals? The same applies to economic theories of individual preferences aggregated through market mechanisms.

Only the self-observation of mind–body—introspection, suffering, pain—can judge whether communication infringes human rights. If these self-observations, however distorted, gain entry to communication, then there is some chance of humanly just self-limitation of communication. The decisive thing is the 'moment': the simultaneity of consciousness and communication, the cry that expresses pain. Hence we observe the closeness of justice to spontaneous indignation, unrest, protest, and its remoteness from philosophical, political, and legal discourses.

[38] For an elaboration, see G. Teubner, 'Self-subversive Justice: Contingency or Transcendence Formula of Law?' (2009) 72 *Modern Law Review* 1–23.

Index